Population Geography

4th Edition

Problems, Concepts, and Prospects

Gary L. Peters
California State University
Long Beach

Robert P. Larkin
University of Colorado
Colorado Springs

KENDALL/HUNT PUBLISHING COMPANY
2460 Kerper Boulevard   P.O. Box 539   Dubuque, Iowa 52004-0539

To Carol, Jason, Erika, Joyce, Michael, and Christine

Contents

Preface

The scientific study of the human population is an interdisciplinary one involving demographers, geographers, sociologists, anthropologists, psychologists, political scientists, economists, biologists, physicians, and even philosophers. The dramatic growth of the human population in recent decades compels us to pay attention to the causes and consequences of population growth.

Our purpose in this book is to provide students with an introduction to the field of population geography, a task that requires drawing upon materials from many disciplines and integrating them into a text. We begin with a look at population growth because we feel that it sets the tone for generating an interest in the study of population. Following that, we look at demographic data, which are so essential to helping us understand population processes.

We then consider population distribution and composition, followed by discussions of major theories of population growth and change. The focus turns to the basic demographic processes of mortality, fertility, and migration, leading to a discussion of urbanization. The next two chapters deal with the relationship between population and the environment and with problems of population and food supply. A final chapter provides applications of population findings and presents three case studies.

Acknowledgments

It would be impossible to acknowledge individually each of the people from whom we have learned something about population although citations at the ends of chapters give credit to many of the major ones. Without the continued research and writing efforts of many people, this book could not have been written. We would also like to thank those instructors who continue to use this text and encourage you to keep sending us your comments.

A special word of thanks is due to the Population Reference Bureau, Inc. We have used many materials from their publications over the years, especially from the *Population Bulletin* and *Population Today*. They were also kind enough to allow us to reprint the *World Population Data Sheet* again, which is a great aid for both students and instructors. In addition, we would like to thank the Population Council, Inc., the Worldwatch Institute, and the United States Bureau of the Census.

Although this book has evolved over the years since its first publication in 1979, we would still like to thank Professor Paul Simkins for stimulating our initial interest in population geography during our student years at Penn State. Many of the ideas in this book probably can still be traced back to Paul, and we hope that he approves of the current edition. Of course, we alone remain responsible for whatever errors and shortcomings this book may have.

1992 World Population Data Sheet

Region or Country	Population Estimate mid-1992 (millions)	Birth Rate (per 1,000 pop.)	Death Rate (per 1,000 pop.)	Natural Increase (annual, %)	Population "Doubling Time" in Years (at current rate)	Population Projected to 2010 (millions)	Population Projected to 2025 (millions)	Infant Mortality Rate[a]	Total Fertility Rate[b]	% Population Under Age 15/65+	Life Expectancy at Birth Male/Female (years)	Urban Population (%)	Data Availability Code[c]	% Married Women Using Contraception (Total/Modern)	Government View of Fertility Level (H = too high, S = satisfactory, L = too low)	Per Capita GNP, 1990 (US$)
WORLD	5,420	26	9	1.7	41	7,114	8,545	68	3.3	33/ 6	63/67	43		55/47		$ 3,790
MORE DEVELOPED	1,224	14	9	0.5	148	1,333	1,392	18	1.9	21/12	71/78	73		72/47		17,900
LESS DEVELOPED	4,196	30	9	2.0	34	5,781	7,153	75	3.8	36/ 4	61/64	34		51/47		810
LESS DEVEL. (Excl. China)	3,031	33	10	2.3	30	4,361	5,562	84	4.4	39/ 4	58/61	37		43/36		1,000
AFRICA	654	43	14	3.0	23	1,085	1,540	99	6.1	45/ 3	52/55	30		-/-		630
NORTHERN AFRICA	147	35	8	2.6	27	216	274	72	4.8	42/ 4	59/62	43		32/28		1,070
Algeria	26.0	35	7	2.4	28	37.9	47.1	61	4.9	44/ 4	65/67	50	B	36/31	H	2,060
Egypt	55.7	32	7	2.4	28	81.3	103.1	73	4.4	41/ 4	58/61	45	B	38/35	H	600
Libya	4.5	37	7	3.0	23	7.1	9.3	64	5.2	50/ 2	65/70	76	B	-/-	S	–
Morocco	26.2	33	8	2.4	29	36.0	43.9	73	4.2	41/ 4	62/65	46	B	36/29	H	950
Sudan	26.5	45	14	3.1	22	42.2	57.3	87	6.5	46/ 2	52/53	20	B	9/ 6	S	–
Tunisia	8.4	27	6	2.1	33	11.3	13.4	44	3.4	38/ 5	65/66	53	B	50/40	H	1,420
Western Sahara	0.2	49	21	2.7	25	0.3	0.4	–	–	-/-	-/-	–	D	-/-	–	–
WESTERN AFRICA	182	47	17	3.0	23	312	449	111	6.7	46/ 3	48/50	23		7/ 3		410
Benin	5.0	49	19	3.1	23	8.9	12.8	88	7.1	46/ 3	45/49	39	C	9/ 1	S	360
Burkina Faso	9.6	50	17	3.3	21	17.0	26.0	121	7.2	48/ 4	51/52	18	C	-/-	H	330
Cape Verde	0.4	41	8	3.3	21	0.7	0.9	41	5.4	45/ 5	59/63	33	B	-/-	H	890
Côte d'Ivoire	13.0	50	14	3.6	19	25.5	39.3	92	7.4	48/ 3	52/55	43	C	3/ 1	S	730
Gambia	0.9	47	21	2.6	27	1.6	2.4	138	6.3	44/ 3	42/46	22	C	-/-	H	260
Ghana	16.0	44	13	3.2	22	26.9	35.4	86	6.4	45/ 3	52/56	32	B	13/ 5	H	390
Guinea	7.8	47	22	2.5	28	11.6	16.1	148	6.1	44/ 3	40/44	22	C	-/-	H	480
Guinea–Bissau	1.0	43	23	2.0	35	1.5	1.9	151	5.8	41/ 4	40/43	27	C	-/-	H	180
Liberia	2.8	47	15	3.2	22	5.5	8.3	144	6.8	46/ 4	53/56	44	B	6/ 6	H	–
Mali	8.5	52	22	3.0	23	14.2	21.7	113	7.3	47/ 4	43/46	22	B	5/ 1	H	270
Mauritania	2.1	46	18	2.8	25	3.5	5.0	122	6.5	44/ 3	46/49	41	B	1/ 0	S	500
Niger	8.3	52	20	3.2	22	15.1	24.3	124	7.1	49/ 3	43/46	15	B	-/-	H	310
Nigeria	90.1	46	16	3.0	23	152.2	216.2	114	6.5	45/ 2	48/49	16	B	6/ 4	H	370

Region or Country	Population Estimate mid-1992 (millions)	Birth Rate (per 1,000 pop.)	Death Rate (per 1,000 pop.)	Natural Increase (annual, %)	Population "Doubling Time" in Years (at current rate)	Population Projected to 2010 (millions)	Population Projected to 2025 (millions)	Infant Mortality Rate[a]	Total Fertility Rate[b]	% Population Under Age 15/65+	Life Expectancy at Birth Male/Female (years)	Urban Population (%)	Data Availability Code[c]	% Married Women Using Contraception (Total/Modern)	Government View of Fertility Level (H = too high, S = satisfactory, L = too low)	Per Capita GNP, 1990 (US$)
Senegal	7.9	45	17	2.8	25	13.1	17.4	84	6.3	46/ 3	47/49	37	B	11/ 2	H	710
Sierra Leone	4.4	48	23	2.6	27	7.3	10.2	147	6.5	44/ 3	41/44	30	C	–/–	H	240
Togo	3.8	50	13	3.7	19	7.1	11.3	99	7.2	49/ 2	53/57	24	B	34/ 3	H	410
EASTERN AFRICA	**206**	**47**	**15**	**3.2**	**22**	**359**	**528**	**110**	**7.0**	**47/ 3**	**50/53**	**19**		**–/–**		**230**
Burundi	5.8	47	15	3.2	21	10.1	14.9	111	7.0	46/ 3	50/54	5	C	9/ 1	H	210
Comoros	0.5	48	12	3.5	20	0.9	1.4	89	7.1	48/ 3	54/58	26	C	–/–	H	480
Djibouti	0.4	46	17	2.9	24	0.7	1.1	117	6.6	45/ 3	46/49	79	D	–/–	S	–
Ethiopia	54.3	47	20	2.8	25	94.0	140.2	139	7.5	46/ 3	46/48	12	C	4/ 3	H	120
Kenya	26.2	45	9	3.7	19	44.8	62.3	62	6.7	49/ 2	59/63	22	B	27/18	H	370
Madagascar	11.9	45	13	3.2	22	21.3	31.7	115	6.6	47/ 3	53/56	23	C	–/–	H	230
Malawi	8.7	53	18	3.5	20	14.9	23.1	137	7.7	48/ 3	48/50	15	B	7/ 1	H	200
Mauritius	1.1	21	7	1.5	48	1.3	1.4	20.4	2.2	30/ 5	65/72	41	A	75/46	S	2,250
Mozambique	16.6	45	18	2.7	26	26.6	35.6	136	6.3	44/ 3	46/49	23	C	–/–	S	80
Reunion	0.6	24	6	1.8	38	0.8	0.9	13	2.3	33/ 5	67/75	62	B	–/–	–	–
Rwanda	7.7	51	16	3.4	20	14.4	23.2	117	8.0	48/ 3	48/51	7	C	10/ 1	H	310
Seychelles	0.1	24	8	1.6	44	0.1	0.1	13.0	2.6	35/ 6	65/74	52	A	–/–	H	4,670
Somalia	8.3	49	19	2.9	24	13.9	17.8	127	6.6	46/ 3	44/48	24	C	–/–	S	150
Tanzania	27.4	50	15	3.5	20	50.2	77.9	105	7.1	48/ 3	49/54	21	C	–/–	H	120
Uganda	17.5	52	15	3.7	19	32.5	49.6	96	7.4	49/ 2	50/52	10	B	5/ 3	H	220
Zambia	8.4	51	13	3.8	18	15.5	24.2	76	7.2	49/ 2	51/54	49	B	–/–	H	420
Zimbabwe	10.3	41	10	3.1	22	17.0	22.6	61	5.6	45/ 3	58/61	26	B	43/36	H	640
MIDDLE AFRICA	**72**	**45**	**15**	**3.0**	**23**	**122**	**182**	**97**	**6.1**	**44/ 3**	**49/53**	**38**		**–/–**		**460**
Angola	8.9	47	19	2.8	25	14.9	21.6	132	6.4	45/ 3	42/46	26	D	–/–	H	–
Cameroon	12.7	44	12	3.2	22	23.1	36.3	85	6.4	46/ 3	54/59	42	C	16/ 4	H	940
Central African Republic	3.2	44	18	2.6	27	4.9	6.9	141	5.6	42/ 3	45/48	43	D	–/–	H	390
Chad	5.2	44	19	2.5	28	7.7	10.3	127	5.8	43/ 4	45/47	30	D	–/–	S	190
Congo	2.4	43	14	2.9	24	3.9	5.5	114	5.8	45/ 3	52/55	41	C	–/–	L	1,010
Equatorial Guinea	0.4	43	16	2.6	26	0.6	0.8	112	5.5	43/ 4	48/52	28	C	–/–	L	330
Gabon	1.1	41	16	2.5	28	1.4	1.8	99	5.2	33/ 6	51/54	43	D	–/–	L	3,220
Sao Tome and Principe	0.1	35	10	2.5	28	0.2	0.3	71.9	5.4	42/ 5	64/67	38	A	–/–	S	380
Zaire	37.9	46	14	3.1	22	65.6	98.2	83	6.1	43/ 4	50/54	40	C	–/–	H	230

Region or Country	Population Estimate mid-1992 (millions)	Birth Rate (per 1,000 pop.)	Death Rate (per 1,000 pop.)	Natural Increase (annual, %)	Population "Doubling Time" in Years (at current rate)	Population Projected to 2010 (millions)	Population Projected to 2025 (millions)	Infant Mortality Rate[a]	Total Fertility Rate[b]	% Population Under Age 15/65+	Life Expectancy at Birth Male/Female (years)	Urban Population (%)	Data Availability Code[c]	% Married Women Using Contraception (Total/Modern)	Government View of Fertility Level (H = too high, S = satisfactory, L = too low)	Per Capita GNP, 1990 (US$)
SOUTHERN AFRICA	47	35	8	2.7	26	76	106	57	4.6	40/ 4	60/66	52		45/43		2,390
Botswana	1.4	40	9	3.1	23	2.4	3.3	45	4.8	45/ 3	55/62	24	B	33/32	H	2,040
Lesotho	1.9	41	12	2.9	24	3.1	4.4	95	5.8	43/ 4	53/62	19	B	5/ 2	H	470
Namibia	1.5	43	11	3.1	22	2.9	4.1	102	5.9	46/ 3	59/61	27	D	26/26	–	–
South Africa	41.7	34	8	2.6	26	66.0	92.0	52	4.5	40/ 4	61/67	56	B	48/46	H	2,520
Swaziland	0.8	44	12	3.2	22	1.5	2.2	101	6.2	46/ 3	51/59	23	B	20/17	H	820
ASIA	3,207	26	9	1.8	39	4,207	4,998	68	3.2	33/ 5	63/66	31		56/52		1,680
ASIA (Excl. China)	2,042	30	10	2.0	34	2,787	3,407	81	3.9	36/ 4	60/63	34		47/41		2,520
WESTERN ASIA	139	36	8	2.8	24	226	313	63	4.7	41/ 4	64/68	62		–/–		–
Bahrain	0.5	27	3	2.4	29	0.8	1.0	20	3.9	35/ 2	70/74	81	C	–/–	S	–
Cyprus	0.7	19	9	1.1	66	0.8	0.9	11	2.4	26/10	74/78	62	B	–/–	L	8,040
Gaza	0.7	55	9	4.6	15	1.3	1.9	45	–	–/–	–/–	–	C	–/–	–	–
Iraq	18.2	45	8	3.7	19	34.1	51.9	67	7.0	45/ 3	66/68	73	C	–/–	L	–
Israel	5.2	21	6	1.5	45	6.9	8.0	8.7	2.9	31/ 9	75/78	91	A	–/–	L	10,970
Jordan	3.6	39	5	3.4	20	6.4	9.2	39	5.6	48/ 3	69/73	70	B	35/27	H	1,240
Kuwait	1.4	32	2	3.0	23	3.2	4.6	16	4.4	45/ 1	72/76	–	–	–/–	S	–
Lebanon	3.4	28	7	2.1	33	4.9	6.1	46	3.7	40/ 5	66/70	84	D	–/–	S	–
Oman	1.6	42	7	3.5	20	3.0	4.9	44	6.7	47/ 3	64/68	11	D	–/–	S	–
Qatar	0.5	27	2	2.5	28	0.7	0.9	26	4.5	28/ 1	69/74	90	C	–/–	S	15,860
Saudi Arabia	16.1	42	7	3.5	20	31.1	47.1	65	7.1	45/ 3	63/66	77	D	–/–	S	–
Syria	13.7	45	7	3.8	18	25.6	38.7	48	7.1	49/ 4	64/66	50	C	–/–	S	990
Turkey	59.2	29	7	2.2	32	81.2	98.1	59	3.6	35/ 4	64/69	59	B	63/31	H	1,630
United Arab Emirates	2.5	31	3	2.8	25	4.9	6.6	25	4.9	35/ 1	69/73	78	C	–/–	S	19,860
West Bank	1.6	44	8	3.6	19	2.4	3.0	40	–	–/–	–/–	–	C	–/–	–	–
Yemen	10.4	51	17	3.5	20	19.0	29.9	124	7.5	49/ 3	48/51	25	C	–/–	H	–
SOUTHERN ASIA	1,231	33	11	2.2	31	1,725	2,151	95	4.3	38/ 4	58/58	26		43/37		440
Afghanistan	16.9	48	22	2.6	27	34.5	48.5	172	6.9	46/ 4	41/42	18	D	–/–	H	–
Bangladesh	111.4	37	13	2.4	29	165.1	211.6	120	4.9	44/ 3	54/53	14	B	31/24	H	200
Bhutan	0.7	39	19	2.0	35	1.0	1.4	142	5.9	39/ 4	46/49	13	D	–/–	S	190
India	882.6	30	10	2.0	34	1,172.1	1,383.1	91	3.9	36/ 4	58/59	26	B	49/43	H	350
Iran	59.7	41	8	3.3	21	105.0	159.2	43	6.1	46/ 3	63/66	54	C	–/22	H	2,450

Region or Country	Population Estimate mid-1992 (millions)	Birth Rate (per 1,000 pop.)	Death Rate (per 1,000 pop.)	Natural Increase (annual, %)	Population "Doubling Time" in Years (at current rate)	Population Projected to 2010 (millions)	Population Projected to 2025 (millions)	Infant Mortality Rate[a]	Total Fertility Rate[b]	% Population Under Age 15/65+	Life Expectancy at Birth Male/Female (years)	Urban Population (%)	Data Availability Code[c]	% Married Women Using Contraception (Total/Modern)	Government View of Fertility Level (H = too high, S = satisfactory, L = too low)	Per Capita GNP, 1990 (US$)
Maldives	0.2	41	6	3.4	20	0.4	0.6	34	5.8	47/ 3	62/59	28	B	–/–	S	440
Nepal	19.9	42	17	2.5	28	30.2	40.8	112	6.1	42/ 3	50/50	8	B	14/14	H	170
Pakistan	121.7	44	13	3.1	23	195.1	281.4	109	6.1	44/ 4	56/57	28	B	12/ 9	H	380
Sri Lanka	17.6	21	6	1.5	46	21.4	24.0	19.4	2.4	35/ 4	68/73	22	A	62/40	H	470
SOUTHEAST ASIA	**451**	**28**	**8**	**1.9**	**36**	**592**	**696**	**61**	**3.4**	**37/ 4**	**60/64**	**29**		**46/43**		**–**
Brunei	0.3	28	3	2.5	28	0.4	0.5	9	3.5	36/ 3	69/72	59	B	–/–	S	–
Cambodia	9.1	38	16	2.2	32	10.5	13.4	127	4.5	36/ 3	47/50	13	D	–/–	L	–
Indonesia	184.5	26	8	1.7	40	238.8	278.2	70	3.0	37/ 4	58/63	31	B	50/47	H	560
Laos	4.4	46	17	2.9	24	7.2	9.8	112	6.8	44/ 4	48/51	16	C	–/–	S	200
Malaysia	18.7	30	5	2.5	27	27.1	34.9	29	3.6	37/ 4	69/73	35	B	51/30	S	2,340
Myanmar (Burma)	42.5	30	11	1.9	36	57.7	69.9	72	3.9	37/ 4	56/60	24	C	5/ 0	S	–
Philippines	63.7	32	7	2.4	28	85.5	100.8	54	4.1	39/ 4	63/66	43	B	36/22	H	730
Singapore	2.8	19	5	1.4	51	3.2	3.3	6.7	1.8	23/ 6	72/77	100	A	74/73	L	12,310
Thailand	56.3	20	6	1.4	48	69.2	76.4	39	2.4	34/ 4	64/69	18	B	66/64	H	1,420
Viet Nam	69.2	30	8	2.2	31	92.4	108.2	45	4.0	39/ 5	62/66	20	B	53/38	H	–
EAST ASIA	**1,386**	**19**	**7**	**1.2**	**57**	**1,664**	**1,839**	**32**	**2.1**	**27/ 6**	**69/73**	**34**		**71/69**		**2,910**
China	1,165.8	20	7	1.3	53	1,420.3	1,590.8	34	2.2	28/ 6	68/71	26	B	71/70	H	370
Hong Kong	5.7	12	5	0.7	99	6.3	6.2	6.7	1.2	21/ 9	75/80	–	A	81/75	–	11,540
Japan	124.4	10	7	0.3	217	129.4	124.1	4.6	1.5	18/13	76/82	77	A	64/60	L	25,430
Korea, North	22.2	24	6	1.9	37	28.5	32.1	31	2.5	29/ 4	66/72	64	D	–/–	S	–
Korea, South	44.3	16	6	1.1	65	51.7	54.8	15	1.6	26/ 5	67/75	74	B	77/70	S	5,400
Macao	0.5	17	3	1.3	52	0.6	0.6	10	1.5	25/ 6	77/81	97	B	–/–	–	–
Mongolia	2.3	36	8	2.8	25	3.5	4.6	64	4.6	44/ 4	62/67	42	C	–/–	H	–
Taiwan	20.8	16	5	1.1	62	24.0	25.4	6.2	1.7	27/ 6	71/76	71	A	78/62	S	–
NORTH AMERICA	**283**	**16**	**8**	**0.8**	**89**	**328**	**363**	**9**	**2.0**	**21/12**	**72/79**	**75**		**74/69**		**21,580**
Canada	27.4	15	7	0.8	89	32.1	35.0	7.1	1.8	21/11	73/80	78	A	73/69	S	20,450
United States	255.6	16	9	0.8	89	295.5	327.5	9.0	2.0	22/13	72/79	75	A	74/69	S	21,700
LATIN AMERICA	**453**	**28**	**7**	**2.1**	**34**	**609**	**729**	**54**	**3.4**	**36/ 5**	**64/70**	**70**		**57/48**		**2,170**
CENTRAL AMERICA	**118**	**31**	**6**	**2.5**	**28**	**166**	**204**	**50**	**4.1**	**40/ 4**	**65/71**	**64**		**49/42**		**2,170**
Belize	0.2	37	5	3.1	22	0.3	0.4	32	4.5	45/ 6	67/72	52	B	47/42	S	1,970
Costa Rica	3.2	27	4	2.4	29	4.5	5.6	15.3	3.3	36/ 5	75/79	45	A	70/58	H	1,910

Region or Country	Population Estimate mid-1992 (millions)	Birth Rate (per 1,000 pop.)	Death Rate (per 1,000 pop.)	Natural Increase (annual, %)	Population "Doubling Time" in Years (at current rate)	Population Projected to 2010 (millions)	Population Projected to 2025 (millions)	Infant Mortality Rate[a]	Total Fertility Rate[b]	% Population Under Age 15/65+	Life Expectancy at Birth Male/Female (years)	Urban Population (%)	Data Availability Code[c]	% Married Women Using Contraception (Total/Modern)	Government View of Fertility Level (H = too high, S = satisfactory, L = too low)	Per Capita GNP, 1990 (US$)
El Salvador	5.6	36	8	2.9	24	7.8	9.6	55	4.6	44/ 4	61/68	48	C	47/44	H	1,100
Guatemala	9.7	39	7	3.1	22	15.8	21.6	61	5.2	45/ 3	60/65	39	B	23/19	H	900
Honduras	5.5	40	8	3.2	22	8.7	11.5	69	5.6	46/ 3	62/66	44	B	41/33	H	590
Mexico	87.7	29	6	2.3	30	119.5	143.3	47	3.8	38/ 4	66/72	71	B	53/45	H	2,490
Nicaragua	4.1	38	8	3.1	23	6.4	8.2	61	5.0	47/ 4	59/65	57	C	27/23	H	–
Panama	2.4	24	5	1.9	37	3.2	3.7	21	2.9	35/ 5	71/75	53	B	58/54	S	1,830
CARIBBEAN	**35**	**26**	**8**	**1.8**	**38**	**43**	**49**	**54**	**3.1**	**33/ 7**	**67/71**	**58**		**51/48**		**–**
Antigua and Barbuda	0.1	14	6	0.8	84	0.1	0.1	24.4	1.7	27/ 6	70/74	58	A	53/51	S	4,600
Bahamas	0.3	19	5	1.5	47	0.3	0.4	26.3	2.2	30/ 5	69/76	75	A	–/–	S	11,510
Barbados	0.3	16	9	0.7	102	0.3	0.3	9.0	1.8	25/11	70/76	32	A	55/53	S	6,540
Cuba	10.8	18	6	1.1	62	12.3	12.9	11.1	1.9	23/ 9	74/78	73	A	70/67	S	–
Dominica	0.1	20	7	1.2	55	0.1	0.1	18.4	2.5	33/ 7	73/79	–	A	50/48	H	1,940
Dominican Republic	7.5	30	7	2.3	30	9.9	11.4	61	3.6	39/ 3	66/69	58	B	50/47	H	820
Grenada	0.1	33	8	2.5	28	0.1	0.1	15.9	4.9	43/ 6	69/74	–	A	31/27	H	2,120
Guadeloupe	0.4	20	6	1.4	50	0.4	0.4	9.9	2.4	27/ 8	71/78	48	A	44/31	–	–
Haiti	6.4	45	16	2.9	24	9.4	12.3	106	6.0	45/ 4	53/56	29	B	10/10	H	370
Jamaica	2.5	25	5	2.0	35	3.1	3.6	17	2.6	34/ 8	71/75	51	B	55/51	H	1,510
Martinique	0.4	18	6	1.2	59	0.4	0.5	9	2.0	22/ 9	74/81	82	B	51/38	–	–
Netherlands Antilles	0.2	19	6	1.2	55	0.2	0.2	6.3	2.1	26/ 7	72/76	53	A	–/–	–	–
Puerto Rico	3.7	19	7	1.2	59	3.9	4.2	14.3	2.2	29/10	70/78	72	A	70/62	–	6,470
St. Kitts-Nevis	0.04	23	11	1.2	60	0.05	0.1	22.2	2.5	32/ 9	63/69	45	A	41/37	H	3,330
Saint Lucia	0.2	23	6	1.7	40	0.2	0.3	20.8	3.3	44/ 6	69/74	46	A	47/46	H	1,900
St. Vincent and the Grenadines	0.1	23	6	1.6	43	0.1	0.2	21.7	2.6	38/ 5	70/73	21	A	58/55	H	1,610
Trinidad and Tobago	1.3	21	7	1.4	50	1.5	1.7	10.2	2.5	34/ 5	67/73	64	A	53/44	H	3,470
SOUTH AMERICA	**300**	**26**	**7**	**1.9**	**36**	**399**	**476**	**56**	**3.2**	**35/ 5**	**64/70**	**74**		**62/50**		**2,180**
Argentina	33.1	21	8	1.2	56	40.2	45.5	25.7	2.7	30/ 9	66/73	86	A	–/–	S	2,370
Bolivia	7.8	36	10	2.7	26	11.3	14.2	89	4.9	41/ 4	58/64	51	C	30/12	H	620
Brazil	150.8	26	7	1.9	37	200.2	237.2	69	3.1	35/ 5	62/68	74	B	66/57	S	2,680
Chile	13.6	23	6	1.8	39	17.2	19.8	17.1	2.7	31/ 6	71/76	85	A	–/–	S	1,940
Colombia	34.3	26	6	2.0	35	45.6	54.2	37	2.9	36/ 4	68/73	68	B	66/55	S	1,240
Ecuador	10.0	31	7	2.4	29	14.5	17.9	57	3.8	41/ 4	65/69	55	B	53/41	H	960
Guyana	0.8	25	7	1.8	39	1.0	1.2	52	2.6	33/ 4	61/67	35	B	31/28	S	370

Region or Country	Population Estimate mid-1992 (millions)	Birth Rate (per 1,000 pop.)	Death Rate (per 1,000 pop.)	Natural Increase (annual, %)	Population "Doubling Time" in Years (at current rate)	Population Projected to 2010 (millions)	Population Projected to 2025 (millions)	Infant Mortality Rate[a]	Total Fertility Rate[b]	% Population Under Age 15/65+	Life Expectancy at Birth Male/Female (years)	Urban Population (%)	Data Availability Code[c]	% Married Women Using Contraception (Total/Modern)	Government View of Fertility Level (H = too high, S = satisfactory, L = too low)	Per Capita GNP, 1990 (US$)
Paraguay	4.5	34	7	2.7	25	6.9	9.2	34	4.7	40/ 4	65/69	43	B	48/35	S	1,110
Peru	22.5	31	9	2.2	32	31.0	37.4	76	4.0	39/ 4	60/63	70	B	46/23	H	1,160
Suriname	0.4	26	6	2.0	34	0.6	0.7	31	2.8	34/ 4	67/72	48	B	–/–	S	3,050
Uruguay	3.1	18	10	0.8	83	3.5	3.7	20.4	2.4	26/12	68/75	89	A	–/–	L	2,560
Venezuela	18.9	30	5	2.5	27	27.3	34.6	24.2	3.6	38/ 4	67/73	84	A	–/–	S	2,560
EUROPE	**511**	**12**	**10**	**0.2**	**338**	**523**	**516**	**11**	**1.6**	**20/14**	**71/78**	**75**		**72/47**		**12,990**
NORTHERN EUROPE	**93**	**14**	**11**	**0.3**	**242**	**96**	**97**	**9**	**1.9**	**19/15**	**72/79**	**83**		**72/66**		**17,930**
Denmark	5.2	13	12	0.1	753	5.1	4.8	7.5	1.7	17/16	72/78	85	A	63/60	S	22,090
Estonia	1.6	14	12	0.2	365	1.7	1.8	25	2.0	22/11	66/75	71	B	–/26	–	–
Finland	5.0	13	10	0.3	224	5.0	4.8	5.8	1.8	19/13	71/79	62	A	80/77	S	26,070
Iceland	0.3	19	7	1.2	58	0.3	0.3	5.9	2.3	26/11	75/80	90	A	–/–	S	21,150
Ireland	3.5	15	9	0.6	122	3.4	3.3	8.0	2.2	27/11	71/77	56	A	60/–	S	9,550
Latvia	2.7	14	13	0.1	630	2.9	3.0	19	2.0	21/12	65/75	71	B	–/19	–	–
Lithuania	3.7	15	11	0.4	158	4.1	4.4	18	2.0	23/11	67/76	69	B	–/12	–	–
Norway	4.3	14	11	0.4	193	4.5	4.7	6.9	1.9	19/16	73/80	71	A	71/65	S	23,120
Sweden	8.7	14	11	0.3	210	8.9	9.0	6.0	2.1	18/18	75/80	83	A	78/71	S	23,860
United Kingdom	57.8	14	11	0.3	257	59.9	61.0	7.9	1.8	19/16	73/79	90	A	72/71	S	16,070
WESTERN EUROPE	**178**	**12**	**10**	**0.2**	**398**	**179**	**174**	**7**	**1.6**	**18/14**	**73/79**	**82**		**–/–**		**–**
Austria	7.9	12	11	0.1	495	8.2	8.2	7.4	1.5	17/15	73/79	55	A	71/56	S	19,240
Belgium	10.0	13	11	0.2	347	9.7	9.3	7.9	1.6	18/15	72/79	95	A	81/63	S	15,440
France	56.9	13	9	0.4	169	58.8	58.6	7.3	1.8	20/14	73/81	73	A	81/67	L	19,480
Germany	80.6	11	11	−0.1	(–)	78.2	73.7	7.5	1.4	16/15	72/78	90	A	–/–	L	–
Liechtenstein	0.03	13	7	0.6	110	0.03	0.03	2.7	1.4	20/10	66/73	–	A	–/–	L	–
Luxembourg	0.4	13	10	0.3	239	0.4	0.4	7.4	1.6	17/13	71/78	78	A	–/–	L	28,770
Netherlands	15.2	13	9	0.5	147	16.6	16.7	6.8	1.6	18/13	74/80	89	A	76/72	S	17,330
Switzerland	6.9	13	10	0.3	231	6.9	6.9	6.8	1.6	16/15	74/81	60	A	71/65	L	32,790
EASTERN EUROPE	**96**	**13**	**11**	**0.2**	**369**	**101**	**103**	**17**	**1.9**	**23/11**	**67/75**	**63**		**69/23**		**2,080**
Bulgaria	8.9	12	12	−0.0	(–)	8.8	8.6	14.8	1.7	20/13	68/75	68	A	76/ 8	L	2,210
Czechoslovakia	15.7	14	12	0.2	347	16.8	17.2	11.3	2.0	23/12	68/75	76	A	66/25	S	3,140

Region or Country	Population Estimate mid-1992 (millions)	Birth Rate (per 1,000 pop.)	Death Rate (per 1,000 pop.)	Natural Increase (annual, %)	Population "Doubling Time" in Years (at current rate)	Population Projected to 2010 (millions)	Population Projected to 2025 (millions)	Infant Mortality Rate[a]	Total Fertility Rate[b]	% Population Under Age 15/65+	Life Expectancy at Birth Male/Female (years)	Urban Population (%)	Data Availability Code[c]	% Married Women Using Contraception (Total/Modern)	Government View of Fertility Level (H = too high, S = satisfactory, L = too low)	Per Capita GNP, 1990 (US$)
Hungary	10.3	12	14	−0.2	(−)	10.5	10.4	15.4	1.8	20/14	65/74	63	A	73/62	L	2,780
Poland	38.4	14	11	0.4	187	41.3	42.7	15.9	2.0	25/10	67/76	61	A	75/26	S	1,700
Romania	23.2	12	11	0.1	578	24.0	24.4	25.7	1.6	23/11	67/73	54	B	58/ 5	L	1,640
SOUTHERN EUROPE	**144**	**11**	**9**	**0.2**	**344**	**146**	**141**	**12**	**1.5**	**20/13**	**72/79**	**68**		**70/34**		**12,860**
Albania	3.3	25	6	1.9	36	3.9	4.5	30.8	3.0	33/ 5	70/76	36	A	–/–	S	–
Bosnia-Hercegovina[e]	4.2	14	6	0.8	90	4.4	4.3	15.2	1.7	28/ 6	69/75	36	A	–/–	–	–
Croatia[e]	4.6	12	11	0.1	1,386	4.8	4.8	10.0	1.7	21/12	68/76	51	A	–/–	–	–
Greece	10.3	10	9	0.1	990	10.4	10.0	10.0	1.5	19/14	73/78	58	A	–/–	L	6,000
Italy	58.0	10	9	0.1	1,386	56.4	51.9	8.6	1.3	17/14	73/80	72	A	78/32	L	16,850
Macedonia[e]	1.9	17	7	1.0	70	2.2	2.3	35.3	2.1	29/ 7	70/74	54	A	–/–	–	–
Malta	0.4	15	8	0.7	92	0.4	0.4	11.3	2.0	23/11	74/78	85	A	–/–	S	6,630
Portugal	10.5	11	10	0.1	533	10.8	10.5	11.0	1.4	21/13	71/78	30	A	66/33	S	4,890
San Marino	0.02	12	7	0.5	144	0.03	0.03	*3.8*	1.3	17/13	73/79	91	A	–/–	–	–
Slovenia[e]	1.9	13	10	0.3	267	2.1	2.2	8.9	1.6	23/11	69/77	49	A	–/–	–	–
Spain	38.6	10	9	0.2	433	40.1	39.3	7.6	1.3	20/13	73/80	91	A	59/38	S	10,920
Yugoslavia[f]	10.0	15	9	0.5	131	10.8	11.0	24.4	2.1	24/ 9	69/74	47	A	–/–		–
FORMER USSR[d]	**284**	**17**	**10**	**0.7**	**104**	**328**	**362**	**39**	**2.2**	**26/ 9**	**65/74**	**66**		**–/19**		**–**
Armenia	3.5	24	7	1.8	40	4.5	5.0	35	2.9	30/ 5	69/75	68	B	–/12	–	–
Azerbaijan	7.1	26	6	2.0	36	9.5	11.4	45	2.7	33/ 5	67/74	53	B	–/–	–	–
Belarus	10.3	14	11	0.3	217	11.1	11.5	20	1.9	23/10	67/76	67	B	–/13	S	–
Georgia	5.5	17	9	0.9	80	6.1	6.5	33	2.2	25/ 9	68/76	56	B	–/ 8	–	–
Kazakhstan	16.9	22	8	1.4	50	21.9	26.8	44	2.7	32/ 6	64/73	58	B	–/22	–	–
Kyrgyzstan	4.5	29	7	2.2	31	6.6	8.7	35	3.7	37/ 5	64/72	38	B	–/25	–	–
Moldova	4.4	18	10	0.8	88	5.2	5.8	35	2.3	28/ 8	66/72	48	B	–/15	–	–
Russia	149.3	14	11	0.2	301	162.3	170.7	30	1.9	23/10	64/75	74	B	–/22	–	–
Tajikistan	5.5	38	6	3.2	22	9.1	12.2	73	5.0	43/ 4	67/72	31	B	–/15	–	–
Turkmenistan	3.9	34	7	2.7	26	5.5	6.8	93	4.2	41/ 4	62/68	45	B	–/12	–	–
Ukraine	52.1	13	12	0.1	1,155	53.3	52.9	22	1.9	22/12	66/75	68	B	–/15	S	–
Uzbekistan	21.3	33	6	2.7	25	32.8	43.1	64	4.0	41/ 4	66/72	40	B	–/19	–	–

Region or Country	Population Estimate mid-1992 (millions)	Birth Rate (per 1,000 pop.)	Death Rate (per 1,000 pop.)	Natural Increase (annual, %)	Population "Doubling Time" in Years (at current rate)	Population Projected to 2010 (millions)	Population Projected to 2025 (millions)	Infant Mortality Rate[a]	Total Fertility Rate[b]	% Population Under Age 15/65+	Life Expectancy at Birth Male/Female (years)	Urban Population (%)	Data Availability Code[c]	% Married Women Using Contraception (Total/Modern)	Government View of Fertility Level (H = too high, S = satisfactory, L = too low)	Per Capita GNP, 1990 (US$)
OCEANIA	**28**	**20**	**8**	**1.2**	**57**	**35**	**39**	**33**	**2.6**	**26/ 9**	**69/75**	**71**		**63/68**		**13,190**
Australia	17.8	15	7	0.8	83	21.5	23.9	8.0	1.9	22/11	73/80	85	A	76/72	S	17,080
Federated States of Micronesia	0.1	29	7	2.3	31	0.1	0.1	41	4.2	–/–	–/–	–	C	–/–	–	–
Fiji	0.8	27	7	2.0	35	0.9	1.1	20	3.1	38/ 3	62/60	39	B	41/35	H	1,770
French Polynesia	0.2	28	5	2.3	31	0.3	0.4	16	3.4	37/ 3	66/71	58	B	–/–	–	–
Marshall Islands	0.1	48	9	3.9	18	0.1	0.2	54	7.1	51/ 3	61/64	–	C	–/–	–	–
New Caledonia	0.2	24	6	1.8	39	0.2	0.3	18	2.8	33/ 5	69/76	59	B	–/–	–	–
New Zealand	3.4	18	8	1.0	71	3.8	4.0	7.6	2.1	23/11	72/78	84	A	70/62	S	12,680
Papua–New Guinea	3.9	34	11	2.3	31	5.7	7.3	99	5.4	40/ 3	53/55	13	B	5/–	H	860
Solomon Islands	0.4	41	5	3.6	20	0.6	0.8	32	6.3	47/ 3	60/61	9	B	–/23	H	580
Vanuatu	0.2	36	5	3.1	22	0.3	0.4	32	5.4	45/ 3	67/72	18	B	13/–	S	1,060
Western Samoa	0.2	34	7	2.8	25	0.3	0.4	43	4.7	40/ 4	64/69	21	B	–/19	H	730

(–)indicates data unavailable or inapplicable

[a] Infant deaths per 1,000 live births

[b] Average number of children born to a woman during her lifetime

[c] A=complete data . . . D=little or no data

[d] Estonia, Latvia, and Lithuania are shown under Northern Europe

[e] Former republics of Yugoslavia

[f] On April 27, 1992, Serbia and Montenegro formed a new state, the Federal Republic of Yugoslavia

ACKNOWLEDGEMENTS

The authors gratefully acknowledge the assistance and cooperation of staff members of the Center for International Research of the U.S. Bureau of the Census, the Population Division and the Statistical Office of the United Nations (UN), and the World Bank in the preparation of this year's *Data Sheet*. At PRB, Zuali Malsawma made valuable contributions in the data collection process and Jackie Guenther and Aichin Jones assisted in production.

NOTES

The *Data Sheet* lists all geopolitical entities with populations of 150,000 or more and all members of the UN. These include sovereign states, dependencies, overseas departments, and some territories whose status or boundaries may be undetermined or in dispute. **More developed countries,** following the UN classification, comprise all of Europe and North America, plus Australia, Japan, New Zealand, and the former USSR. All other regions and countries are classified as **less developed.** As a result of recent political developments, the republics of the former USSR and of Yugoslavia are shown separately. The names of the former Soviet republics considered to lie wholly or partly in Europe are shown in italics. Within the former USSR, Russia lies on both the Asian and European continents, as does Turkey.

World and Regional Totals: Regional population totals are independently rounded and include small countries or areas not shown. Regional and world rates and percentages are weighted averages of countries for which data are available; regional averages are shown when data or estimates are available for at least two-thirds of the region's population.

World Population Data Sheets from earlier years should **not be used as a time series.** Fluctuations in values from year to year often reflect revisions based on new data or estimates rather than actual changes in levels. Since data often refer to different years and are of greatly varying reliability, caution should be exercised both in the ranking of countries and in the relationship among variables. Additional information on likely trends and time series data can be obtained from PRB, and are available in UN, World Bank, and U.S. Census Bureau publications.

SOURCES

The rates and figures are primarily compiled from the following sources: official yearbooks and statistical bulletins of countries; UN *Demographic Yearbook, 1990* (forthcoming) and *Population and Vital Statistics Report, Data Available as of 1 January 1992* of the UN Statistical Office; *World Population Prospects as Assessed in 1990* of the UN Population Division; data files of the Center for International Research, U.S. Bureau of the Census; data from the publications of the Council of Europe and the European Communities; and long-term population projections of the World Bank. Other sources include recent demographic surveys, special studies and direct communication with demographers and statistical bureaus in the U.S. and abroad. Specific data sources may be obtained by contacting the authors of the *Data Sheet*.

For countries with complete registration of births and deaths, rates are those most recently reported. For developed countries, nearly all vital rates refer to 1990 or for a 12 month period ending at some point in 1991. For less developed countries, the reference date is usually for some point in the late 1980s or early 1990s. The complete registration of vital statistics (births and deaths) is indicated by an infant mortality rate shown to one decimal place.

DEFINITIONS

Mid-1992 Population: Estimates are based on a recent census or on official national data or on UN, U.S. Census Bureau, or World Bank projections. The effects of refugee movements, large numbers of foreign workers, and population shifts due to contemporary political events are taken into account to the extent possible.

Birth and Death Rate: These rates are often referred to as "crude rates" since they do not take a population's age structure into account. Thus, crude death rates in more developed countries, with a relatively large proportion of older persons, are often higher than those in less developed countries.

Rate of Natural Increase (RNI): Birth rate minus the death rate, implying the annual rate of population growth without regard for migration. Expressed as a percentage.

Population "Doubling Time": The number of years until the population will double assuming a *constant* rate of natural increase (RNI). Based upon the *unrounded* RNI, this column provides an indication of potential growth associated with a given RNI. It is not intended to forecast the actual doubling of any population.

Population in 2010 and 2025: Population projections are based on reasonable assumptions on the future course of fertility, mortality, and migration. Projections are based on official country projections, or on series issued by the UN, the U.S. Bureau of the Census, World Bank, or PRB projections.

Infant Mortality Rate: The annual number of deaths of infants under age one year per 1,000 live births. Rates shown with decimals are completely registered national statistics, while those without are estimates from sources cited above. Rates shown in italics are based upon less than 50 annual infant deaths and, as a result, are subject to considerable yearly variability.

Total Fertility Rate (TFR): The average number of children a woman will have assuming that current age-specific birth rates will remain constant throughout her childbearing years (usually considered to be ages 15–49).

Population Under Age 15/Age 65+: The percentage of the total population in those age groups, often considered the "dependent ages."

Life Expectancy at Birth: The average number of years a newborn infant can be expected to live under *current* mortality levels.

Urban Population: Percentage of the total population living in areas termed urban by that country or estimated in a source listed above.

Data Availability: Availability of data is graded from "A" to "D." An "A" indicates a country with both complete vital statistics (birth and death data) and a published national-level census within 15 years or a continuous population register. Countries rated "B" have one of those two sources plus either a usable census more than 15 years old or a national survey or sample registration system within 10 years, or both. "C" indicates that at least one census, survey, or sample registration system is available. "D" indicates that little or no reliable demographic information is available and that estimates are based on fragmentary data or demographic models. There is considerable variation in the quality of data even within the same category.

Contraceptive Use: The percentage of currently married or "in-union" women of reproductive age (15–49) who use any form of contraception. "Modern" methods include clinic and supply methods such as the pill, condom, IUD, and sterilization. Data are the most recent available from sources such as the Demographic and Health Survey program or official country estimates.

Government View of Current Fertility Level: This population policy indicator presents the officially stated position of country governments on the level of the national birth rate. Most indicators are from the UN Population Division, *Global Population Policy Database, 1989,* supplemented by recent reports from individual countries.

Per Capita GNP: Gross National Product includes the value of all domestic and foreign output. Estimates are from the *World Bank Atlas, 1991.* Per capita GNP for Nigeria was adjusted by PRB to reflect the new, lower 1991 census count in that country.

Introduction

By the end of 1992 the earth's population was pressing against the 5.5 billion mark. Without much doubt it will grow to more than 6.0 billion by the year 2000, a number that can not help but further strain this planet's ability to provide support for its many people. In the 1990s we are going to add more than 250,000 people to the planet every day, including holidays; and geographers must help communicate the causes and consequences of such growth to as wide an audience as we can.

It is not surprising to find that more and more attention is being focused on population issues. From scholarly journals to the popular press, a burgeoning literature on population dynamics and population problems confronts us. Business has discovered the importance of demographics as well, as is apparent in such publications as *American Demographics*. Our view of population, the geographic perspective, requires a brief look at the intellectual development of population studies as a geographic concern.

Because of the interdisciplinary nature of population studies, it is not always easy to distinguish population geography from other disciplinary contributions. However, we feel that we should briefly consider the ways in which some major population geographers have defined their area of study. Population geography is a relatively young subdiscipline of geography although geographers have long been concerned with population characteristics as a part of broader regional studies.

Even though the roots of the subdiscipline developed somewhat earlier, most experts would agree that Glenn Trewartha (1953) wrote the first definitive statement on population geography. In that article he noted that population geography had been, and continued to be, a neglected aspect of geography. Furthermore, he argued that population was a pivotal element in geography and that its continued neglect would seriously affect the development of geography.

Many geographers would probably still agree with Trewartha (1953, 87) that "the geographer's goal in any or all analyses of population is an understanding of the regional differences in the earth's covering of people. Just as area differentiation is the theme of geography in general, so it is of population geography in particular." The response to Trewartha's plea for increased attention to population geography was neither rapid nor overwhelming, at least not at first.

In the year following the publication of Trewartha's presidential address, James (1954, 107) wrote that "the fundamental problem of population geography is the search for a systematic method of outlining enumeration areas that are meaningful in terms of the question being asked." James (1954, 107) went on to note that "in the field of population geography the need is to find a way to generalize the distribution of people without obscuring the relationships of man to the other phenomena with which he is areally associated." James argued that demographic studies could benefit from the geographic perspective, especially from the regional concept and regional method. He also provided a useful review of population studies by American geographers, suggested numerous new research directions, and even offered a discussion of training requirements for population geographers.

After an embryonic decade or so, two books on population geography appeared in 1966, one by Wilbur Zelinsky (1966) and the other by Jacqueline Beaujeu-Garnier (1966). Zelinsky (1966, 2) commented at the time that a "rich harvest of facts and ideas has not yet been reaped by the population geographer because this is still the period of germination in the history of his discipline." Furthermore, he offered the following definition (Zelinsky, 1966, 5):

> Population geography can be defined accurately as the science that deals with the ways in which the geographic character of places is formed by, and in turn reacts upon, a set of population phenomena that vary within it through both space and time as they follow their own behavioral laws, interacting one with another and with numerous nondemographic phenomena.

Perceptively noting the burden that this definition placed on the reader, he offered a shorter version (Zelinsky, 1966, 5) in which he stated that "the population geographer studies the spatial aspects of population in the context of the aggregate nature of places." Zelinsky (1966) maintained that population geography was concerned with three "distinct and ascending levels of discourse": (1) simple description of the location of population numbers and characteristics, (2) explanation of the spatial configurations of these numbers and characteristics, and (3) the geographic analysis of population phenomena. Like Trewartha and James, Zelinsky emphasized areal differences in populations.

Beaujeu-Garnier's concept of population geography was perhaps best expressed in the following statement (1966, 3):

> If the demographer measures and analyzes the demographic facts, if the historian traces their evolution, if the sociologist seeks their causes and repercussions by the observation of human society, it is the business of the geographer to describe the facts in their present environmental context, studying also their causes, their original characteristics, and possible consequences.

According to Beaujeu-Garnier, the geographical study of population had three facets: (1) the distribution of people over the globe, (2) the evolution of human societies, and (3) the degrees of success the societies have achieved.

In his major work on the topic, Trewartha (1969, 1–2) stated that "the geography of population (or population geography) is concerned chiefly with one aspect of population study—its spatial distribution and arrangements." As he had in 1953, Trewartha (1969, 2) again emphasized the importance of population geography within the broader discipline of geography, noting that "population serves as the point of reference from which all other geographic elements are observed, and from which they all, singly and collectively, derive significance and meaning."

In the following year, Demko, Rose, and Schnell (1970, 4) offered yet another definition, conditioned by changes in methodology that were affecting most fields of geography by that time:

> Population geography is, therefore, that branch of the discipline which treats the spatial variations in demographic and nondemographic qualities of human populations, and the economic and social consequences stemming from the interaction associated with a particular set of conditions existing in a given areal unit.

Their emphasis was somewhat broader than those of previous definitions.

Clarke (1972, 2) said that population geography was "concerned with demonstrating how spatial variations in the distribution, composition, migrations, and growth of populations are related to spatial variations in the nature of places." Courgeau (1976, 261) stated that:

> Demography and population geography are concerned with the same topic: the study of human populations. Basically, they are quantitative disciplines that mainly use statistical data, but they also employ qualitative approaches. The main difference between the two sciences is the fact that the demographer places his emphasis on time whereas the geographer places his emphasis on space.

At least to some degree this distinction is true. However, demographers are often concerned with population distribution, the aspect emphasized so far in the definitions of geography.

Clarke (1984) noted the success that population geography had experienced as a subdiscipline, especially since the 1970s, and pointed out that since Trewartha's seminal paper in 1953 nearly 10 percent of all published geographical papers had dealt with some aspect of population. He also noted the diversity of studies under the population geography topic, along with a look at population and political changes, as well as data and advances in quantitative methods. However, he ended up noting that, despite many of the methodological advances of the 1970s and early 1980s, "The search for general methods and laws has often obscured the complexities of reality" (Clarke, 1984, 9).

Definitions of demography also vary. According to Bogue (1969, 1), "demography is the empirical, statistical, and mathematical study of populations." He suggested that demography focused on three factors: (1) changes in population size, (2) the composition of the population, and (3) the distribution of population in space.

Peterson (1975) defined demography as "the systematic analysis of population phenomena. . . ." However, he differentiated between formal demography and population studies, and argued that demography was concerned with the gathering, collating, statistical analysis, and technical presentation of data, whereas population studies were concerned with population characteristics and trends in their social setting. Along this latter line, Thomlinson (1976, 4) stated that "population study involves the number and variety of people in an area and the changes in this number and variety."

Since 1980 several new texts have appeared in both demography and population geography. Among them are Murdock and Ellis (1991), Overbeek (1982), Weeks (1992), and Weller and Bouvier (1981) in demography, along with Schnell and Monmonier (1983), Woods (1982), and Hornby and Jones (1980) in population geography. Though they are collections of readings, rather than texts, Pacione (1986), Woods and Rees (1986), and Menard and Moen (1987) provide considerable material of interest to both demographers and population geographers. The array of new texts in recent years affirms the growing interest in population issues in the social sciences, issues that will become more prominent as we move through the 1990s.

Obviously geographers and demographers share many common and overlapping interests in their respective studies of population. However, population geographers tend to place more emphasis on the spatial patterns of population characteristics and processes, whereas demographers, though often interested in population distributions, seldom make spatial patterns their central interest.

Focus on the spatial dimensions of demography and demographic techniques have been central in much of the recent literature of population geography. Findlay (1991, 64) noted that, "The 1980s may well be recorded by historians of population geography as the decade in which the subdiscipline became strongly demographic and moved in the direction of being redefined as spatial demography." This trend, exemplified by such works as Woods and Reese (1986) and Congdon and Batey (1989), was especially pronounced in the United Kingdom.

Findlay and Graham (1991) also looked at the nature of recent studies in population geography, first noting the emphasis on the spatial perspective, then criticizing population geographers for their neglect of postmodernist debates that took place in geography in the 1980s. "That these issues were not taken up and discussed in population geography in the 1980s," Findlay and Graham (1991, 156) argued, "meant that population geographers were failing to participate in the mainstream methodological debates within geography, but clung instead to the surer, but dated terrain of the 1960s and 1970s." Perhaps even more clearly, Findlay and Graham (1991, 158) commented that "A narrow definition of population geography as spatial demography is quite simply inadequate to face the challenge of what others expect geographers to contribute to the understanding of population."

Clearly, in population geography, as in most other pursuits in academia, we need to be more involved in solving key problems in society. With respect to geography and the work being done by geographers, Brunn (1992, 2), from his perspective as editor of the prestigious *Annals of the Association of American Geographers,* lamented recently: "I am sometimes concerned that, unlike other disciplines, we are apparently unwilling to tackle global problems on a global scale . . . we are not prepared to look at global and macroregional problems, processes, and models. . . . The time is propitious for us to get some idea of what we are doing and how we might proceed as a sound and worthy discipline into the next millennium."

Given their roots in geography, population geographers should not lose track of how the subdiscipline fits into, and interacts with, other branches of geography. Whether looking at international flows of refugees or crosstown movements within metropolitan areas, whether considering the relationships between people and global warming or the supply and demand for food in the Sahel, we should be able to find some solid geographic foundations upon which to build. In that process, people, and their relationships to places and environments at all scales, must remain central. As Stoddart (1987, 331) noted, for geographers, "The task is to identify geographical problems, issues of man and environment within regions—problems not of geomorphology or history or economics or sociology, but geographical problems: and to use our skills to work to alleviate them, perhaps to solve them." Perhaps the summary by White, et al. (1989, 282) provides as clear a picture as any of where we should be going:

> Geographers might disagree about the most significant topics within population geography, the most appropriate research questions, and certainly the most appropriate research methodologies. However, it is clear that despite these honest differences, population-geography research has grown rapidly since 1953, and shows no signs of slowing. Undoubtedly, population geography is pivotal to an understanding of the cultural landscape.

To the extent that geographers continue to be concerned with the earth as a home for humans, we need to focus more attention on the global and national interactions between growing populations and earth's capacity to support them. The world's population has more than doubled since the end of World War II and will probably double again before it stabilizes. As Senator Albert Gore (1992, 295) pointed out:

> Human civilization is now so complex and diverse, so sprawling and massive, that it is difficult to see how we can respond in a coordinated, collective way to the global environmental crisis. But circumstances are forcing just such a response; if we cannot embrace the preservation of the earth as our new organizing principle, the very survival of our civilization will be in doubt.

Before ending this introduction, it is useful to mention some of the periodicals in which population articles appear, so that both instructors and students can seek out more detailed and current studies with which to enrich the basic introduction to population geography that this text provides. First, however, anyone interested in population issues needs to know about *Population Index,* a quarterly publication that indexes population literature from a vast number of both American and foreign sources. The student's search for population information should start there.

A number of journals are dedicated exclusively to population articles. Among the major ones in English are *Demography, Population Studies, International Migration Review, American Demographics, Population and Development Review, Population Bulletin, Population Research and Policy Review,* and *Family Planning Perspectives.* The Population Reference Bureau, located in Washington, D.C., publishes not only *Population Bulletin* but also a number of other studies of population, as well as numerous materials of interest especially to those who teach population. Also located in Washington, D.C., is the Worldwatch Institute, which publishes an annual *State of the World* along with a variety of occasional publications that are of considerable interest. Additional articles on population topics appear frequently in the following geographic periodicals: *The Geographical Review, Annals of the Association of American Geographers, The Professional Geographer, The Canadian Geographer, Transactions of the Institute of British Geographers,* and *Area.*

Aside from the above demographic and geographic publications, population articles of interest also appear occasionally in *Science, Scientific American, Nature, Urban Affairs Quarterly, International Journal of Health Science, American Economic Review, International Journal of Comparative Sociology, Research on Aging, Journal of the American Medical Association, American Behavioral Scientist, The Gerontologist, Social Forces, Foreign Affairs, American Sociological Review, Sociology and Social Research, Annals of the American Academy of Political and Social Science, Economic Development and Cultural Change, Rural Sociology, Social Science Quarterly,* and the *New England Journal of Medicine.*

Though the periodicals mentioned above are primarily scholarly, numerous population articles appear in more popular arenas as well, including *Time, Newsweek, U. S. News and World Report, The Economist,* and *Forbes,* along with newspapers such as the *Los Angeles Times, The New York Times, The Washington Post, The Christian Science Monitor,* and *The Wall Street Journal.* Almost anywhere that students turn today, they are likely to come across something concerning population, so they must keep their eyes open and become informed, critical consumers of demographic information.

REFERENCES

Beaujeu-Garnier, Jacqueline. (1966) *Geography of Population.* New York: St. Martin's Press.

Bogue, Donald J. (1969) *Principles of Demography.* New York: John Wiley and Sons, Inc.

Brunn, Stanley. (1992) "Are We Missing Our 'Forests' and our 'Trees'? It's Time for a Census," *Annals of the Association of American Geographers* 82:1–2.

Clarke, John I. (1972) *Population Geography.* 2d ed. Oxford: Pergamon Press.

Clarke, John I., ed. (1984) *Geography and Population: Approaches and Applications.* Oxford: Pergamon Press.

Congdon, P. and Batey, P., eds. (1989) *Advances in Regional Demography.* London: Belhaven Press.

Courgeau, D. (1976) "Quantitative, Demographic, and Geographic Approaches to Internal Migration," *Environment and Planning* A 8:261–269.

Demko, George J., Rose, Harold M., and Schnell, George A., eds. (1970) *Population Geography: A Reader.* New York: McGraw-Hill Book Company.

Findlay, Allan M. (1991) "Population Geography," *Progress in Human Geography* 15:64–72.

Findlay, Allan M. and Graham, Elspeth. (1991) "The Challenge Facing Population Geography," *Progress in Human Geography* 15:149–162.

Gore, Senator Albert. (1992) *Earth in the Balance: Ecology and the Human Spirit.* Boston: Houghton Mifflin Company.

Hornby, William F. and Jones, Melvyn. (1980) *An Introduction to Population Geography.* Cambridge: Cambridge University Press.

Murdock, Steve H. and Ellis, David R. *Applied Demography: An Introduction to Basic Concepts, Methods, and Data.* Boulder, Colo: Westview Press.

James, Preston E. (1954) "The Geographic Study of Population," in Preston E. James and Clarence F. Jones, eds. *American Geography: Inventory and Prospect.* Syracuse, N.Y.: Association of American Geographers, pp. 106–122.

Menard, Scott W. and Moen, Elizabeth W. (1987). *Perspectives on Population: An Introduction to Concepts and Issues.* New York: Oxford University Press.

Overbeek, Johannes. (1982) *Population: An Introduction.* New York: Harcourt Brace Jovanovich, Inc.

Pacione, M., ed. (1986) *Population Geography: Progress and Prospect.* London: Croom Helm.

Petersen, William. (1975) *Population.* 3d ed. New York: Macmillan Publishing Company, Inc.

Schnell, George A. and Monmonier, Mark Stephen. *The Study of Population: Elements, Patterns, Processes.* Columbus, Ohio: Charles E. Merrill Publishing Company.

Stoddart, D. R. (1987) "To Claim the High Ground: Geography for the End of the Century," *Transactions of the Institute of British Geographers* 12:327–336.

Thomlinson, Ralph. (1976) *Population Dynamics: Causes and Consequences of World Demographic Change.* 2d ed. New York: Random House, Inc.

Trewartha, Glenn T. (1953) "A Case for Population Geography," *Annals of the Association of American Geographers* 43:71–97.

Trewartha, Glenn T. (1969) *A Geography of Population: World Patterns.* New York: John Wiley and Sons, Inc.

Weeks, John R. (1992) *Population: An Introduction to Concepts and Issues.* 5th ed. Belmont, Calif.: Wadsworth Publishing Company.

Weller, Robert H. and Bouvier, Leon F. (1981) *Population: Demography and Policy.* New York: St. Martin's Press.

White, Stephen E., et al. (1989) "Population Geography," in Gaile, Gary L. and Willmott, Cort J., eds. *Geography in America.* Columbus, Ohio: Merrill Publishing Co., pp. 258–289.

Woods, Robert. (1979) *Population Analysis in Geography.* London and New York: Longman.

Woods, Robert. (1982) *Theoretical Population Geography.* London and New York: Longman.

Woods, Robert and Rees, P., eds. (1986) *Population Structure and Models: Developments in Spatial Demography.* London: Allen and Unwin.

Zelinsky, Wilbur. (1966) *A Prologue to Population Geography.* Englewood Cliffs, N.J.: Prentice Hall, Inc.

Chapter 1

Population Growth and Change

In this chapter our aim is first to place the present world population into a broader historical perspective and then to consider current and future population trends. Only after we have seen where we have been, and how we got where we are, can we begin to consider our future. The roughly 5.5 billion people who currently share the planet face the prospect of being joined by at least another 5 billion before population growth can be curbed, unless dramatic or catastrophic changes occur that reduce humanity's numbers.

▓ MEASURING POPULATION GROWTH AND CHANGE

To understand the ways in which population processes operate to shape or alter the size or composition of a region's population, one must know the various measures of population growth and change. This section presents such measures as a basic demographic equation, rate of natural increase, rate of population growth, doubling time of populations, and a few cautionary notes about using these measures.

The Basic Demographic Equation

A fundamental characteristic of any population is its size. There are only four ways to alter the size of an area's population: birth, death, and in/out migration. For example, the population may be increased either by a birth within the area or by the migration into the area of a person from another location. Similarly, the population may be decreased either by the death of someone within the area or by the migration of a current resident to another area outside.

These basic demographic processes may be combined to produce the following equation:

$$FP = SP + B - D + I - O,$$

where FP = final population, some time interval beyond SP,
    SP = starting population,
      B = births during the interval,
      D = deaths during the interval,
       I = in-migration during the interval, and
      O = out-migration during the interval.

This is sometimes referred to as the "basic demographic equation."

The Rate of Natural Increase

For any given population, the rate of natural increase (RNI) equals the crude birth rate (CBR) minus the crude death rate (CDR). Thus

$$RNI = CBR - CDR.$$

The crude birth rate is the number of births per 1000 population in a one year period, or

$$CBR = (B/P) \times 1000,$$

where B = number of births in one year and
    P = mid-year population.

In 1992 the crude birth rate for the world was about 26 per thousand, and for the United States it was approximately 16 per thousand. The crude birth rate is influenced to some degree by the age and sex structure of a population.

The crude death rate is the number of deaths per 1000 population in a one year period, or

$$CDR = (D/P) \times 1000,$$

where D = number of deaths in one year and
    P = mid-year population.

In 1992 the crude death rate for the world and for the United States was about 9 per 1000 population. The crude death rate is affected far more strongly by the age and sex structure of the population than is the crude birth rate, so comparisons among countries need to be done with considerable care. This fact should be clearly evident when one considers that the crude death rate for the world and for the United States are the same.

Because the crude birth and death rates are both expressed per 1000 population, the rate of natural increase also is expressed in units per 1000 population. The units measuring natural increase are expressed by births minus deaths. As the crude birth rate for the world was 26 and the crude death rate was 9, the world's rate of natural increase for 1992 was equal to 26 minus 9, or 17 per 1000 population. Similarly, for the United States the rates were 16 and 9, respectively, and the rate of natural increase in the United States in 1992 was 16 minus 9, or 7 per 1000.

Note that the rate of natural increase is not necessarily the same as the rate of population growth. This is because the effect of migration is not included in the former measure. For the world, the rate of natural increase equals the rate of population growth because migration to and from the earth is currently nonexistent (the sojourns of astronauts do not yet qualify as migrations!). For the United States, however, the rate of natural increase is well below the actual rate of population growth because of a sizable annual net immigration.

The Rate of Population Growth

The rate of population growth is a measure of the average annual rate of increase for a population. Barring migration, it is possible to convert the rate of natural increase to the rate of population growth by simply converting the rate per 1000 to an annual percentage rate. For the world, the rate of natural increase was 17 per 1000, which is equivalent to an annual rate of population growth of 1.7 percent.

Keep in mind, however, that most of the time migration must be considered, so the rate of population growth usually differs from the rate of natural increase. To some extent the relative effects of natural increase and migration are inversely related to the size of the area under consideration. Whereas at the world scale migration plays no part at all in population growth, at the local scale migration may even be more important than natural increase in determining the overall rate of population growth.

In the United States example, the rate of natural increase amounts to an annual growth rate of 0.7 percent. Actually, the 1992 rate of population growth for the United States was closer to 1.0 percent. The difference between these two rates results from a net immigration in 1992. In other words, nearly 70 percent of the growth in the United States population in 1992 was due to natural increase and about 30 percent was due to immigration.

Doubling Time

The doubling time of a population is the number of years required for a population to double in size, assuming that the population continues to grow at a given annual rate. This growth is analogous to the growth of money in a bank savings account. In both cases the "interest" is compounded. Without going into detail, it is possible to approximate the doubling time for a population by dividing the annual rate of population growth into the number 70, which is derived from a compound growth formula. Thus, for world population, growing at 1.7 percent annually according to previous figures, the time required to double the present population is about 41 years. This assumes, of course, that the 1.7 percent growth rate holds true over the entire period. For the United States population, growing at 1.0 percent annually, the doubling time is close to 70 years.

However, this measure of population growth should not be used blindly, or the researcher will arrive at some very unrealistic figures. For example, in 1992 Saudi Arabia's population was growing at 3.5 percent a year. If this rate of growth continued, then Saudi Arabia's 1992 population of 16.1 million would reach 32.2 million in 2012, 64.4 million in 2032, and an astounding 518.4 million by 2092, which is now less than a century away. Growth at the same rate for only one more century would leave Saudi Arabia with a population of 16.6 billion, a number similar in magnitude to three times the current population of the entire world.

Both the power and absurdity of exponential growth are easily seen in this and similar examples. Keep in mind that these measures have limitations, as discussed below.

Some Warnings to Remember

The study of population is based largely on the collection and analysis of demographic data. These data vary considerably in reliability, so it is necessary to proceed somewhat cautiously and to develop a healthy skepticism about population information and its interpretation. In an informative article, Bouvier (1976, 8–9) suggested the following warnings that all researchers should heed:

- ▨ Warning 1: Do not use growth rates to indicate changes in birth rates.
- ▨ Warning 2: Do not use natural increase to indicate population growth except in those areas where migration is nonexistent.
- ▨ Warning 3: Do not confuse numerical growth or decline with rates of population growth or decline.
- ▨ Warning 4: Do not take population figures as gospel truth, especially if they come from areas with less than adequate data-gathering facilities.

Each of the these warnings should be considered carefully. Errors in demographic thinking often are caused by a failure to consider one or more of these caveats.

▨ WORLD POPULATION GROWTH

This section is concerned with the growth of the human population from prehistoric times to the present. Once we reach the twentieth century, the focus shifts from total world population to regional patterns of growth—mainly to the current division of the world into developing and developed regions—and to the differences in population among these regions. We generally use the terms *developing* and *developed* regions with reference to levels of economic development although occasionally developing countries also are referred to as *underdeveloped*.

Brief Overview of World Population Growth

To understand the current world population situation, as well as future prospects for the world's ever-increasing numbers, it is necessary to see how the population reached its current level—a world of more than 5.5 billion people growing at an average annual rate of about 1.7 percent. Each year around 91 million to 93 million people are added to what many of us already regard as an overcrowded planet; this represents an increase greater than the population of Mexico, which had about 85.7 million people in 1991. Every three years more people are added to the world's population than currently live in the entire United States and Canada combined.

This rate of growth can not continue indefinitely. As Berelson and Freedman (1974, 3) earlier noted, "The rate of growth that currently characterizes the human population as a whole is a temporary deviation from the annual growth rates that prevailed during most of man's history and must prevail again in the future." This recent period of rapid population growth is unique in demographic history both in terms of the rate of growth and in the absolute size of the world's population.

For most of human demographic history population growth was exceedingly slow. The annual rate of increase probably did not reach 0.1 percent (a doubling time of about 700 years) until sometime in the seventeenth century, after which it began to accelerate. This acceleration was gradual at first, but it became more noticeable after 1750.

What we now know about historical populations is mainly conjectural. Clever demographic detectives, using whatever clues they have been able to find, have pieced together the story of the human population's slow but inexorable expansion both in numbers and in occupied territories. Our knowledge of historical population sizes and growth rates remains speculative because censuses and other collections of population data were nearly nonexistent before the middle of the eighteenth century. Earlier censuses had been taken in a few places, but their data were questionable at best. Even today reliable statistics do not exist for perhaps half of the world's population.

Estimates of populations in prehistoric times vary considerably and are generally made on the basis of assumptions about the distribution of the human population and the *carrying capacity* of the land, that is, its capacity to sustain a given human population at a given level of technology. Deevey (1960) estimated that the world's population around one million years ago was about 125,000. According to his estimates, this population grew very slowly to approximately 3.34 million some 25,000 years ago and to 5.32 million around 10,000 years ago. By A.D. 1, Deevey and others estimate, the world's population was in the neighborhood of 250 million to 300 million. At that time the average annual rate of increase was probably on the order of 0.05 percent. At that growth rate it would take about 1,400 years for a population to double, compared to a doubling time of about 41 years for today's population.

The world's population did not reach its first billion until sometime around 1800. By then the annual rate of growth had increased tenfold to roughly 0.5 percent. Though all of human history had been required to reach this first billion, only 130 years were required to add the next billion. Thus, by 1930 there were 2 billion residents on our planet. In only 45 years this 2 billion doubled to the 1975 population of 4 billion, and

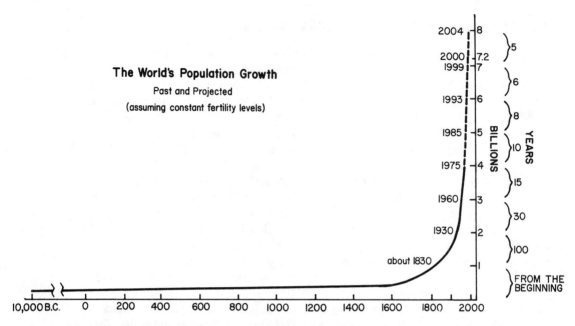

The World's Population Growth
Past and Projected
(assuming constant fertility levels)

▪ **FIGURE 1-1** Arithmetic Growth of World Population from 10,000 B.C. SOURCE: Modified from the Development Coordination Committee. (1975) *Development Issues.* (Washington, D.C.: Department of State), p. 71.

by 1987 the world's population had grown to 5.0 billion. Population projections suggest that between 1990 and the year 2000 we will add close to another 1.0 billion.

As a species we have certainly demonstrated our capacity for reproduction, but it is time for us to restrain ourselves before we destroy our own ecological niche. As Ornstein and Ehrlich (1989, 45) note:

> Increasing numbers is a "goal" of all organisms. But never before has there been an "outbreak" of a single species on such a global scale. Unfortunately it is not yet clear how enduring our unprecedented triumph will be, because it has created an unprecedented paradox: our triumphs can destroy us. As people strive to increase their dominance even further, they are now changing the earth into a planet that is inhospitable to civilization.

Figure 1–1 provides a graphic illustration of human population history. The slow growth that characterized so much of humanity's early history gives way, at first gradually then much more rapidly, to increased rates of population growth. These changes in growth rates involved alterations of both birth rates and death rates, with an emphasis on declining death rates. Such alterations, in turn, were linked to sweeping changes in the socioeconomic fabric of societies.

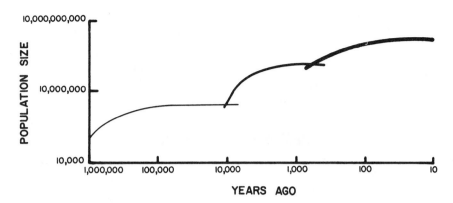

Figure 1–2 shows past population growth on a logarithmic rather than an arithmetic graph, allowing us to focus more on changes in the rates of increase. The contrast with Figure 1–1 is striking and suggestive. Rather than depicting a single period of population growth, the graph shows three periods of relatively rapid demographic increase, each one followed by a slowing of growth rates. Deevey (1960) argued that each period of accelerated population growth was a response to a revolution in which the earth's carrying capacity was dramatically increased. The earliest of the three revolutions was the toolmaking or cultural revolution; the second was the agricultural revolution; and the third was the scientific-industrial revolution, which continues today.

The implications of Figures 1–1 and 1–2 for future population growth differ dramatically. Figure 1–1 implies a continuing rapid increase in the size of the world's population. In contrast, Figure 1–2 suggests that the world probably will experience a decline of growth rates as the world population adjusts to the current technological levels and their concomitant limitations on population expansion. Barring another major revolution that once again would expand the earth's carrying capacity, Deevey's interpretation of population history implies a slowing of world population growth, one that we are already beginning to see. The world's growth rate seems to have peaked sometime in the late 1960s at around 2.1 percent from which it has dropped slightly to a level of about 1.7 percent in 1992. Though the direction of change is encouraging, we need to keep in mind that it represents only a change in doubling time from about 33 years to 41 years.

Three Major Periods of Population Growth

As we have already noted, Deevey (1960) suggested that population growth has occurred unevenly over time, mainly in conjunction with three major revolutions in human history—the cultural, the agricultural, and the scientific-industrial revolutions.

These three revolutions serve as the basis for subdividing our discussion of population growth into three discrete periods. This is appropriate because each of the revolutions must have opened up new possibilities for population growth, primarily because each one extended the earth's carrying capacity. However, the availability of population *facts* decreases rapidly as we move back in time, hence the following discussion must be approached with a degree of caution.

Cultural Revolution and Population Growth

The cultural, or toolmaking, revolution occurred in prehistoric time. What knowledge we have of events in that era must be drawn primarily from the archaeological record. Searching for the origin and evolution of the human population continues to occupy the time and energy of many researchers, particularly anthropologists. Periodically, new finds of the skeletal remains of early hominids push back the frontiers of our knowledge to yet earlier times. The current geographical search for early people has established an African origin. Skeletal remains uncovered in Africa suggest an age of 2.8 million to 3.8 million years for *Australopithicus afarensis,* as exemplified by "Lucy" (Johanson and Edey, 1981); 1.6 million to 2.2 million years for *Homo habilis;* and 1.4 million to 1.7 million years for *Homo erectus.*

A larger brain size is one of the primary features that distinguishes each one of these groups from the next. However, as Ornstein and Ehrlich (1989, 37–38) have suggested, ". . . although the human brain appears to have enlarged rapidly (in geological time) in response to the pressures of culture, it does not seem likely that the brain crossed any real physical threshold that suddenly permitted new kinds of cultural activities."

According to Wenke (1990), two scenarios currently highlight the debate about the continued search for human origins. One of these scenarios suggests that *Homo* ancestors, most likely *Homo erectus,* migrated out of Africa some 1.5 million years ago, followed by gradual diversification among scattered groups and, at the same time, a gradual evolution toward *Homo sapiens* among all the groups because of common genetic inheritances and similar adaptive pressures. The result of this first scenario, as Wenke (1990, 137) described it, was "that . . . all [groups] converged at about 30,000 years ago as one species, *Homo sapiens sapiens.*"

The other scenario begins in the same way, with the migration of *Homo* ancestors out of Africa some 1.5 million years ago. This scenario suggests, however, that after the initial migration considerably more divergence developed among groups as they spread out and adapted to different environments. Following the second scenario, according to Wenke (1990, 137), the final result is that "perhaps 140,000 years ago, *Homo sapiens* evolved in one place (probably Africa), and spread across the world, displacing most groups, driving some into extinction, and absorbing a small fraction of the others through intermarriage."

In recent years the latter scenario has received considerable support not from archaeological but from genetic evidence. Cann, Stoneking, and Wilson (1987) argued that the maternal lineage of all humans could be traced back to a single African woman who was alive perhaps 200,000 years ago, a woman now referred to by many as "Mitochondrial Eve." Their data were based on studies of mitochondrial DNA (deoxyribonucleic acid), which are inherited only from the maternal line. These DNA then form the basis for a "molecular clock," which in turn can be used to develop a branching tree. As Stringer (1990, 99) has noted, "One attempts to make a molecular clock by comparing genetic differences among various species or varieties within species and expressing their relatedness in a tree . . . then calibrates (or 'dates') the tree by comparing it with another group that diverged from the tree at a known date." Studies since 1987 have tended to confirm the African origin of "Mitochondrial Eve" and have given rise to considerable speculation about what that means for the Neanderthals (Stringer, 1990).

More recently, Barinaga (1992, 686), citing increasing questions that have been raised about the DNA methodology, noted that "the root of the human tree has been thrown open to question once again." Current criticism is focused primarily on how the mitochondrial DNA have been analyzed and whether or not these data can identify a geographic origin for our species. Excellent summaries of the two opposing views of human evolution over the past 200,000 years can be found in works by Wilson and Cann (1992) and Thorne and Wolpoff (1992).

Although these debates undoubtedly will continue, perhaps it is more important at this point for us to consider Wenke's (1990, 186) summary comment that "we should also take note of the fact that even though we are physically very much like our ancestors of 12,000 years ago, we are enormously different culturally . . . in a cultural sense we are not at all the same species as the human hunter-gatherers of the late Pleistocene . . . to live a life for which evolution has shaped us—we should probably eat a varied diet, live closely in a small group, and walk a lot."

As fascinating as such studies of early *Homo* and their ancestors may be, little is known of the population numbers involved, though they were undoubtedly small. As Deevey (1960, 5–6) commented, "For most of the million-year period the number of hominids, including man, was about what would be expected of any large Pleistocene mammal—scarcer than horses, say, but commoner than elephants." Not only were the numbers small, but the rate of growth in these numbers must have been exceedingly slow as well. For instance, the growth rate of *Homo sapiens sapiens* prior to the agricultural revolution was very small. Hunting, fishing, and foraging provided an existence though undoubtedly a precarious one. Life was most likely "nasty, brutish, and short."

Population densities on the eve of the agricultural revolution also were low, and populations were vulnerable to environmental changes such as climatic fluctuations. Estimates of population size are subject to wide margins of error and must be accepted with reservation; however, the order of magnitude seems reasonable. According to Deevey (1960), the world's population 10,000 years ago was 5.32 million, though others have suggested that it might have been twice that number. Even if we accept 10 million, the figure still represents a small base from which humanity has grown rapidly in a fairly short time.

Agricultural Revolution

An exact date for the beginning of the agricultural revolution is impossible to set, but it is likely that incipient cultivation and domestication developed sometime around 10,000 B.C. in the Near East. The rimland around the Fertile Crescent was one of the first sites of the early agricultural efforts that would gradually develop into a major revolution. As agricultural practices evolved and diffused, populations experienced tremendous changes; people switched from the wandering and tenuous life of hunting and gathering to the more sedentary and secure life of farming and raising livestock. These changes were gradual, as Cipolla (1974, 22) noted:

> It can be stated . . . with a fair degree of certainty, that the foundations of settled life in the Old World were first laid in South-West Asia between the ninth and the seventh millenium B.C. This seemingly took place where prototypes of the earliest domesticated animals and plants existed in a wild state and where the concentration on particular species as sources of food was stimulated by the ecological changes that marked the transition to Neothermal climate.

Between perhaps 7000 B.C. and 5000 B.C. there was some possible domestication of plants in Mesoamerica. Following 5000 B.C., a slow but consistent domestication continued there.

The introduction of farming allowed greater population densities to exist and probably produced the first food surpluses people had ever known. In turn, this freed some people from the arduous task of providing food, giving them leisure time to pursue other activities. A multitude of inventions and innovations followed, including the development of village settlements, irrigation, metallurgy, and long-distance trade. These inventions and innovations increased people's capacity to satisfy their needs from the environment and further multiplied the carrying capacity of the land. Trade, and the convergence of trade routes, certainly affected population distribution and the rise of early cities as well.

The demographic response to agricultural and related changes was an acceleration in the rate of population growth. As the agricultural revolution diffused to various parts of the earth's inhabited surface, its impact on population growth became more significant. However, as Deevey's interpretation suggested, once the impact of this revolutionary increase in the earth's carrying capacity had become sufficiently widespread, the rate of population growth slowed again. As a result, the population stabilized at a new, higher plateau.

By the beginning of the Christian Era, the earth's population was about 250 million to 300 million. Although this population continued to grow, its numerical progress was slow, with a varied regional distribution of growth. Cyclical changes within the overall pattern of growth were typical. The rate of population expansion was kept in check by available food supplies (often interrupted by famines), by wars, and by epidemics of various diseases.

Throughout history, famines have largely occurred in local regions only. Their impact on the death rate depends both on the severity of the famine and on the links

TABLE 1–1 ■ Population Losses from Major Famines

Location	Dates	Estimated Deaths[a] (millions)
India	1837	0.8
Ireland	1845	0.75
India	1863	1.0
India	1876–1878	5.0
East China	1877–1879	9.0
China	1902	1.0
China	1928–1929	3.0
USSR	1932–1934	4.0

[a]Famines before the nineteenth century are poorly documented, and estimates of the number of deaths vary widely.

SOURCE: Peter Haggett, *Geography: A Modern Synthesis,* Second Edition (New York: Harper and Row, Publishers, 1976), p. 153. Used by permission.

TABLE 1–2 ■ Population Losses from Major Conflicts

Conflict	Dates	Estimated Deaths (millions)
World War II	1939–1945	7.3
World War I	1914–1918	7.2
Taiping Rebellion	1851–1864	6.3
Spanish Civil War	1936–1939	6.3
1st Chinese Communist War	1927–1936	6.1
La Plata War	1865–1870	6.0
Indian Communal Riots	1946–1948	5.9
U.S. Civil War	1861–1865	5.8
Russian Revolution	1918–1920	5.7
Crimean War	1853–1856	5.4
Franco-Prussian War	1870–1871	5.4
Mexican Revolution	1910–1920	5.4

SOURCE: Peter Haggett, *Geography: A Modern Synthesis,* Second Edition (New York: Harper and Row, Publishers, 1976), p. 157. Used by permission.

between the famine-stricken area and other locations. Nonetheless, as Table 1–1 illustrates, famines on occasion have been devastating. When transportation linkages improve, the effects of local crop failures can be modified.

Wars have directly affected population growth rates at various times, as Table 1–2 clearly shows, but their impact is not always easy to assess. The simple counting of battlefield deaths alone generally underestimates the demographic impact of most wars, because these conflicts also disrupt food supplies and help to spread numerous diseases. Of war and pestilence, Zinsser (1967, 113) commented, ". . . typhus, with its brothers and sisters—plague, cholera, typhoid, dysentery—has decided more campaigns than Caesar, Hannibal, Napoleon, and all the inspector generals of history."

Epidemics often have a devastating impact on regional populations. Extreme examples include the Justinian Plague of A.D. 541–544 and the Black Death of A.D. 1346–1348. The latter may have decreased the European population by 25 percent, and local death tolls reached as high as 50 percent. Recovery of the European population after this decimation was slow, further hampered by the One Hundred Years War. By the sixteenth century, however, Europe had regained her lost population and was beginning a gradual acceleration in the rate of population growth although localized episodes of famine, war, and epidemics still occurred. The rapid growth and distribution of AIDS (discussed in Chapter 5) has convinced everyone who might have thought otherwise that major epidemics are still with us.

Industrial Revolution

The Industrial Revolution originated in England in the latter half of the eighteenth century although its roots may be found in earlier times. From England it spread rapidly into the countries of Western Europe and to the United States. By the beginning of the twentieth century it had reached Russia and Northern Italy. Japan was the first Asian country to embrace this revolution. As countries industrialized, industry replaced agriculture as the major economic sector of the nation. The Industrial Revolution continues today although so far it has diffused only partially to the developing countries. New inventions and innovations continue to pour forth almost daily from industrialized nations.

By about 1750 in England and Wales population growth accelerated, a trend that other countries quickly experienced as they began to industrialize. Before this time, crude birth rates and crude death rates both tended to be high. In average years births may have exceeded deaths, while in bad years the reverse was likely to be true. Death rates undoubtedly fluctuated more widely than did birth rates. High birth rates were deemed necessary to overcome the prevailing high death rates although a variety of social constraints kept birth rates generally lower than they might have been in most countries.

Even though the cultural and agricultural revolutions increased people's capacity to wrest a living from the earth, not until the scientific-industrial revolution did they begin to gain control over death rates for the first time. This control was the result of many changes that probably did no more than eliminate the high peaks in the cyclical fluctuations of death rates. Better agricultural practices and improved distribution systems cut down on the localized effects of famines. Early on, better sanitary practices and facilities decreased the deaths from a variety of preventable diseases. During the nineteenth century, major medical advances accelerated the downward trend in death rates.

The innovations associated with each revolution were not restricted to the areas where they arose but spread outward, as illustrated by the diffusion of the Neolithic farming cultures of Europe. In 6000 B.C. farming in Europe was primarily limited to a few sites near the Aegean Sea. During the next 1000 years it spread northward into the Danubian Basin and by 4000 B.C. to the North European Plain. An even more rapid diffusion of the industrial-scientific revolution has occurred. These innovations were carried by Europeans as they colonized new areas; in the current century there are few places that have not been touched by industrialization to some degree.

The speed and direction of diffusion was governed by such factors as distance, obstacles, nature of the environmental base, and receptivity of various social structures. One critical point to note is that the spread of new innovations was uneven, resulting in different demographics even within the same region. Whenever such innovations were introduced into a society, they had a traumatic effect that required the development of new forms of social organization, new patterns of leadership, and acquisition of new skills. Rapid population growth often accompanied these changing socioeconomic conditions.

One further point to be emphasized about Deevey's interpretation of world population growth has to do with the nature of the population growth curve for each revolution. After each rapid spurt in population growth, the growth rates declined somewhat—population numbers reached a plateau and further gains were slow. Although each revolution removed, at least partially, some pre-existing constraint upon population growth, it also may have set into motion forces that eventually brought growth under control. Obviously, identifying and understanding these forces is an urgent concern in our present circumstance.

In response to the Industrial Revolution, the world's population entered a period of rapid and sustained population growth. During the nineteenth century this growth was concentrated in the developed countries. By the middle of the twentieth century, however, population growth had subsided in the developed countries and was accelerating in the developing countries.

Human Population Today

Today's population situation is unique in the world's history. Not only is the current rate of increase still near the highest ever recorded but also the base population (5.5 billion) is the largest the world has known. The historical record shows that the acceleration of world population growth started with the European countries and the lands Europeans settled overseas. However, the areas that are growing the fastest today are Africa, Asia, and Latin America, the so-called developing countries, where more than three fourths of humankind dwell. Death rates in these countries have been falling during the last 25 years, whereas the birth rates have remained twice as high as those in the developed nations.

Between 1950 and 1987 the world's population grew from around 2.5 billion to over 5.0 billion, an increase of over 2.5 billion people in less than 40 years. During that time population growth had been unequally distributed geographically, with more than 85 percent of that growth occurring in the developing countries. In most of the developed countries today, fertility hovers near or below replacement level, so that an even higher percentage of population growth in coming decades will occur in the developing countries, those least able to absorb additional people.

Still another comparison between the developed and developing countries may be made regarding the age structure of their populations. A country that has a rapidly growing population has a large proportion of its residents in the younger age groups. In the rapidly growing areas of the world—Africa, Asia, and Latin America—high proportions of these populations are under 15 years of age, whereas in North America, Europe, and Oceania there are significantly lower proportions of young people. A population with a large percentage of older people will have different needs and requirements than a population with a great many younger people.

▒ POPULATION PROJECTIONS

So far we have viewed the present population situation mainly from the perspective of the past, but what does the future hold in store for the world's population? One answer to that question, based on a set of assumptions about the dynamics of a population over a given time period, is the population projection. Young (1968, ix) cautioned us long ago, however, to remember that:

> . . . the projection of a future population from a present growth rate is a hazardous undertaking at best. These rates contain many variables and are sensitive to small changes in these variables. Furthermore, since population growth is cumulative, very slight changes in present rates can make enormous differences when projected 100, 200, or more years into the future.

Demographers generally are careful to differentiate between projections and predictions. A *projection* for the size of a population at some future date is based on a set of *assumptions* about the demographic processes that will affect population growth over the time period. The simplest assumption is that the future rate of population growth will be the same as that of today.

For most situations, however, this is an unrealistic assumption. Typically, a projection is broken down into separate projections for the birth rate, death rate, and migration. These figures then may be combined into a single projection for the future population. What this figure shows is that, *if* the assumptions on which the projection is based hold true for births, deaths, and migration, *then* the projection will be accurate. However, demographers should not be held responsible if the assumptions are not fulfilled. Often a projection may alter people's reproductive behavior and set into motion events that ensure that the projection will be off the mark. Usually more than one projection is made and quite often a series of projections is made, using different assumptions about future birth, death, and migration rates.

Population Projections: A Brief Overview

First, we should distinguish among the following three commonly encountered terms: projection, forecast, and prediction. A population projection is made on the basis of the population at a given date and on assumptions made about births, deaths, and migration between that date and some future date. As Gibson (1977, 7) noted, "Population projections are 'correct' by definition (except for computational errors) because they indicate the population that would result if the base data (starting) population is correct and if the underlying assumptions about future change should turn out to be correct." The usefulness of projections, then, depends on what assumptions have been made and how well those assumptions accord with actual events.

Because it is difficult to decide what assumptions should be made about future birth, death, and migration rates, demographers generally make a series of projections based on different sets of assumptions. For example, the most recent Census Bureau projections for the United States include the following three different series: lowest, middle, and highest projections. For example, fertility assumptions for the three series are for ultimate lifetime births per woman of 1.5, 1.8, and 2.2, respectively. Life expectancy at birth in the year 2080 is assumed to be 77.9, 81.2, and 88.0 years, respectively. Annual immigration is assumed to be 300,000, 600,000 (reduced to 500,000 in 1998), and 800,000 persons, respectively.

Demographers prefer to avoid the term *prediction* altogether because it suggests that only one projection has been made and that there is a high degree of certainty it will occur. Past projections have often fallen so far from their marks that today most demographers, at best, venture to choose one of a series of projections as a forecast, usually only for short periods into the future, and then only reluctantly.

Two broad classes of population projections exist: mathematical and component. *Mathematical methods* are easier to understand and to apply. However, *component methods* are preferred for most projections, especially for those beyond the short term, usually five years or less. Mathematical methods employ some mathematical formula to a base population using an assumed rate of growth over the projection interval. In contrast, component models allow separate projections for births, deaths, and migration then combine the "components" into an overall population projection. These latter projections, of course, also can be done mathematically, and the terminology sometimes confuses people. For demographers and population geographers there is no escape from mathematics.

Different models exist within each class of projections, giving demographers a wide range of projection models to call upon. The model that should be used, of course, depends upon several factors, such as the size of the area for which projections are being made, the assumptions that can or should be made, the types of data that are available, and the length of the projection interval. With respect to scale, for example, national projections require different considerations than do projections for local areas.

For instance, understanding and projecting migration trends may be more critical for local area projections than is projecting the rate of births and deaths; on the other hand, projecting immigration at the national level may be much easier than projecting births, mainly because immigration is controlled, at least to some extent, by the national government. Also, data for local areas are not always available in sufficient detail for employing component models, thus making mathematical models more attractive, especially for short-term projections.

Population Projections: World and Major Regions

Despite the difficulties of developing population projections, they are deemed essential and useful for many reasons. For example, they can stimulate our thinking about the consequences of population trends. We need to keep in mind, however, what one perceptive United Nations study stated:

> The affairs of men are often subject to swings of the pendulum, erratic fluctuations, sometimes even dramatic upsets. That unsystematic variations will also occur in the future, particularly the long-range future, can be fairly taken for granted. But since these are intrinsically unforeseeable, only fairly smooth and systematic changes can be projected. In actual fact these may, at the most, constitute a long-term average trend around which there will occur unpredictable ups and downs. The calculated smooth changes should reflect those factors in the situation which are likely to prevail in the long run. (United Nations, 1974, 48).

Among the basic assumptions that the United Nations made in developing its population projections were the following: (1) at least a minimal degree of social order and control will be maintained; (2) efforts at maintaining or improving the quality of life will continue and will not be totally frustrated; and (3) although regional vital rates will move differently in terms of time, eventually everywhere mortality and fertility will fall slightly below the lowest levels now observed.

The United Nations population projections are shown in Table 1–3. The potential for population growth is considerably higher in the developing areas of the world than in the developed regions, as has been suggested already. Seven series are used, reaching world population totals in 2150 that range from a low of 4.299 billion to a high of 694.213 billion. By 2150 even the difference between the medium-low projection and the medium-high projection reaches more than 15 billion. After discussing these projections, Haub (1992, 7) concluded that, "Our knowledge of future world population is murky indeed . . . the coming reality will likely be a mix of many demographic futures, all summing to some unknown world total." What we can count on with some certainty, however, is that the United Nations' projections bracket the likely range of demographic futures, whatever that may be worth.

TABLE 1–3 ■ United Nations Long-Range Population Projections

	1990						
Year	Medium	High	Medium–High	Medium–Low	Low	"Instant Replacement"	Constant Fertility
1990	5,292	5,327	5,327	5,262	5,262	5,292	5,311
2000	6,261	6,420	6,420	6,093	6,093	5,792	6,463
2025	8,504	9,444	9,444	7,591	7,591	7,069	10,978
2050	10,019	12,506	15,328	7,817	7,813	7,697	21,161
2100	11,186	19,156	17,592	6,415	6,009	8,087	109,405
2150	11,543	28,025	20,772	5,633	4,299	8,351	694,213
Ultimate TFR	2.06	2.50	2.17	1.96	1.70	NA	NA

SOURCE: United Nations. (1991) *Long-Range World Population Projections: Two Centuries of Population Growth, 1950–2150.* (New York: United Nations).

TABLE 1–4 ■ Principal Fertility, Mortality, and Net Immigration Assumptions

Subject	1986	Ultimate level		
		Low assumption	Middle assumption	High assumption
Lifetime births per 1,000 women	1,825	1,500	1,800	2,200
Life expectancy at birth	75.0	77.9	81.2	88.0
Yearly net immigration (thous.)	662	300	500	800

SOURCE: United States Bureau of the Census. *Projections of the Population of the United States, by Age, Sex, and Race: 1988–2080.* Current Population Reports, Series P-25, No. 1018 (Washington, D.C.: U.S. Government Printing Office), p. 1.

Population Projections: The United States

The most recent population projections for the United States have been published by the Bureau of the Census (1989). These projections are crucial because they serve as the basis for many other projections, including projected demand for housing, for educational facilities, for healthcare institutions, and for a myriad of other needs. Only three of the projection series are considered here, each beginning with the estimated population as of July 1, 1986. The assumptions for each of the three series were mentioned previously and are summarized in Table 1–4.

TABLE 1–5 ▪ Population Projections for the United States

Year	Series		
	Lowest	Middle	Highest
1990	248,656	250,410	251,897
1995	255,239	260,138	265,151
2000	259,576	268,266	278,228
2005	262,363	275,604	291,710
2010	264,193	282,575	305,882
2020	264,536	294,364	335,022
2030	258,113	300,629	362,327
2040	245,694	301,807	388,123
2050	230,158	299,849	413,580
2080	184,614	292,235	501,483

SOURCE: United States Bureau of the Census. *Projections of the Population of the United States, by Age, Sex, and Race: 1988–2080.* Current Population Reports, Series P-25, No. 1018 (Washington, D.C.: U.S. Government Printing Office), p. 3.

The three projections diverge immediately, as is apparent in Table 1–5, although the total differences are small in 1990, at which time the lowest series was closest to the actual 1990 Census count of 248,709,873. This fact is deceptive, however, because the census figure probably represents an undercount of at least 5,000,000 people. By 1995 there is a difference of 9,912,000 between the lowest and highest series projections. In the year 2000 the difference increases to 18,652,000, a number about equal to the combined 1990 populations of Texas and Utah. Most incredible, however, is the difference of 316,869,000 by the year 2080. Because this represents an interval of less than 100 years into the future, the figure should be given careful consideration, especially in discussions of immigration policy and family planning programs in the United States.

Note that in the lowest series projection the population reaches a maximum in 2020 and begins a subsequent decline, whereas the medium series does not peak until 2040, and the highest series is still rising in 2080. If these differences are considered in the light of their impact on employment, housing, education, and other needs, then they are extremely important. Nevertheless, keep in mind that under any of these growth-rate scenarios, the population increase is slow when compared to population growth rates in the developing countries.

Lest students be lulled into thinking that the future course of fertility in the United States is no longer fraught with difficulties, they should consider arguments such as those that were made some time ago in two articles that appeared in *American Demographics.* Although the article by Easterlin, Wachter, and Wachter (1979) argued that the birth rate in the United States was likely to fluctuate over the next three to four decades, Westoff (1979) suggested that a low fertility rate was here to stay. Both views were supported with careful reasoning by authoritative demographers. What then should we assume about the future course of fertility in the United States? Between 1975 and 1990 the crude birth rate in the United States increased from 14.6 to 16.7, somewhat supporting the idea that we should continue to expect at least some fluctuation in crude rates, especially given the changing demographics of the population in the United States.

In addition to fertility assumptions, immigration assumptions need to be studied more closely. In 1988 legislation was passed in the Senate to increase the legal immigration limit to allow at least 590,000 new immigrants a year into the United States; this legislation eventually led to passage of the 1990 Immigration Act. Note that this figure exceeds the immigration numbers assumed by the medium series projections. No additional allowance is made for illegal immigration, though in all likelihood it will continue.

Bouvier (1992) argued that the Census Bureau assumptions, especially those about immigration, were on the conservative side and suggested for his own projections an annual immigration figure of 950,000. He projected populations of 279,000,000 by 2000 and 333,000,000 in 2020, comparable to the Census Bureau's highest series.

Similarly, Ahlburg and Vaupel (1990) criticized the Census Bureau for its conservatism in recent projections. They questioned Census Bureau assumptions for fertility, mortality, and immigration. They assumed for their own projections an annual immigration figure of 1,000,000 for their low immigration figure, slightly more than the figure used by Bouvier (1992), and twice that for their high figure. They make four different "combined scenarios," the lowest of which projects a United States population of 329,000,000 in 2020, whereas the highest projects a figure of 385,000,000 in 2020. Their lowest projection, then, is only slightly lower than the Census Bureau's highest projection. As Ahlburg and Vaupel (1990, 649) concluded, "Population projection is not a bloodless technical task, but a politically charged craft . . . it should not be left to a single agency. . . . A livelier competition of alternative assumptions and innovative methods not only would further the development of demographic analysis but also would serve the public interest." We agree.

In summary, selecting an appropriate growth rate for projecting a population requires the consideration of numerous variables. We must look not only at past trends and current patterns but also try to look at ways in which these trends may be altered in the future. Our projections can be no better than the assumptions upon which they are based. In addition, studying projections forces us to confront different scenarios about the consequences of different growth patterns and the possibility of designing policies to affect those patterns.

TABLE 1–6 ▨ Population Projections for Mexico to 2015, with Both Constant and Declining Fertility

Year	Population (in 1,000's)		Birth Rate (per 1,000)		Growth Rate (per 1,000)	
	High Fertility	Declining Fertility	High Fertility	Declining Fertility	High Fertility	Declining Fertility
1970	51,249	51,249	43.9	43.9	36.7	36.7
1975	61,758	61,758	43.3	43.3	37.8	37.8
1980	74,784	73,474	43.2	40.0	38.4	34.7
1985	90,651	86,166	43.5	37.4	38.7	31.9
1990	110,082	99,791	43.7	35.1	39.0	29.4
1995	133,868	113,896	43.9	32.1	39.2	26.4
2000	162,928	127,723	43.9	28.5	39.4	22.8
2005	198,404	140,410	44.0	24.7	39.5	18.9
2010	241,716	154,553	44.0	24.7	39.5	18.9
2015	294,535	169,745	44.0	24.7	39.5	18.8

SOURCE: John Isbister, "Birth Control, Income Redistribution, and the Rate of Saving: The Case of Mexico," *Demography,* 10, No. 1 (February, 1973), p. 91. Used by permission.

Population Projections: Mexico

Mexico is a developing country with an annual population growth rate of 2.3 percent in 1992, a growth rate that would double the population every 30 years if allowed to continue. Two decades ago Isbister (1973) made a series of population projections for Mexico for 1970–2015. Isbister's projections appear in Table 1–6 along with the assumed birth rates and resultant growth rates. It is still instructive today to look at these projections, partly to see how they have fared over the years and partly to see what problems have arisen that were not apparent when Isbister made his original projections.

Two factors are immediately apparent. First, under any conditions the growth of Mexico over the 45-year period was going to be monumental, along with the task of providing basic necessities and services for a rapidly increasing population. Second, there is considerable difference between the high fertility projection and the declining fertility projection. By the year 2000 this difference amounts to 32,205,000. Only 15 years later, because of the power of exponential growth, the difference is a staggering 124,790,000, a number somewhat larger than the 1992 population of Japan, the world's seventh most populous nation.

These projections serve to illustrate the magnitude of population growth in various places. To understand the likelihood of such growth occurring, as well as the major implications of such growth, we must understand the determinants of the population processes—births, deaths, and migration.

Mexico serves as an excellent example of the difficulties faced by those who attempt to develop useful population projections. During the 1970s Mexico's demographic picture changed dramatically. In the first part of that decade Mexico grew at an annual rate of around 3.5 percent although by 1992 that growth rate had dropped to 2.3 percent. The dramatic demographic turnabout resulted from unexpected government decisions. As Nagel (1978, 3–4) noted, "An apparently abrupt about-face came in April 1972 with the announcement of a government-sponsored national family planning program formalized by a new General Population law and [with the] creation of the National Population Council in 1974." With the government's changed attitude toward population problems, the stage was set for a sustained change in the fertility dynamics of the Mexican population. Thus, the earlier projections are turning out to be far too pessimistic.

In 1992 Mexico's population was 87.7 million, which was only slightly above Isbister's 1985 projection of 86 million under his declining fertility option. The Population Reference Bureau has projected a population of about 113 million for Mexico in the year 2000, a figure well below Isbister's 127.7 million under his declining fertility option.

Small Area Population Projections

Although national population projections are of considerable importance, they are not the only ones of interest. Political units, from states to counties and cities, need to know something about their demographic futures, as do local school districts, highway planners, and urban and regional planning departments. In addition, private corporations are interested in the changing demographics of local areas to better gauge local and regional changes in demand, in marketing strategies, and even in consumer tastes and preferences. Thus, the need for small area, that is, subnational, population projections exists and is growing.

At the same time, as one might expect, small area population projections are more difficult to make because local variations in fertility, mortality, and migration may be much wider than those at the national scale. Especially difficult to project are migration rates for local areas, because changes in the area's socioeconomic characteristics may quickly alter current migration patterns. For example, no one looking at the changes that occurred in the Asian population in Long Beach, California, during the 1970s would have projected that the city and neighboring Lakewood would have a population of more than 20,000 Cambodians by the early 1990s. At best, small area projections are a tricky business, and changing migration patterns are the major reason why this is the case.

Although the United States Bureau of the Census does develop state projections, shown in Table 1–7, the assumptions that must be made are difficult to choose. The different series result primarily from different assumptions about migration patterns. However, the Bureau wisely chooses not to do population projections for areas smaller than states, leaving that task to state and local agencies and to private firms such as Donnelley Marketing Information Systems. Detailed information on developing local area projections can be found in Irwin (1977).

TABLE 1–7 ◼ Projections of the Resident Population of Regions, Divisions, and States, by Series: 1990, 2000, and 2010

(Numbers in thousands. As of July 1. Series A, B, C, and D reflect different interstate migration assumptions. See text for explanations)

Region, division, and State	1990 Series A	Series B	Series C	Series D	2000 Series A	Series B	Series C	Series D	2010 Series A	Series B	Series C	Series D
United States	249,891	249,891	249,891	249,891	267,748	267,748	267,748	267,748	282,056	282,056	282,056	282,056
Northeast	50,850	50,707	50,814	51,179	52,419	51,005	51,662	53,583	53,801	50,763	51,961	55,028
New England	13,131	13,073	13,123	13,105	14,002	13,486	13,788	13,647	14,788	13,674	14,210	13,892
Middle Atlantic	37,719	37,634	37,690	38,074	38,417	37,519	37,874	39,936	39,013	37,089	37,751	41,136
Midwest	60,288	60,205	60,296	60,723	60,528	61,342	61,815	64,231	59,696	61,997	62,744	66,824
East North Central	42,390	42,285	42,413	42,711	42,557	42,779	43,499	45,176	41,982	42,916	44,142	46,922
West North Central	17,898	17,920	17,884	18,012	17,971	18,563	18,316	19,055	17,714	19,081	18,602	19,902
South	86,517	86,644	86,489	85,998	95,575	95,382	94,483	91,750	103,529	102,577	101,008	96,318
South Atlantic	43,918	43,427	43,805	42,941	51,930	47,770	49,843	44,966	59,828	51,233	54,725	46,201
East South Central	15,567	15,577	15,583	15,548	16,242	16,603	16,636	16,419	16,616	17,447	17,504	17,063
West South Central	27,033	27,640	27,101	27,509	27,402	31,009	28,004	30,365	27,085	33,898	28,778	33,054
West	52,237	52,336	52,292	51,990	59,226	60,019	59,788	58,186	65,030	66,719	66,344	63,886
Mountain	13,673	13,808	13,704	13,635	15,207	15,922	15,326	15,048	16,383	17,670	16,650	16,396
Pacific	38,563	38,527	38,589	38,355	44,019	44,097	44,462	43,138	48,647	49,049	49,694	47,490
New England:												
Maine	1,236	1,226	1,234	1,217	1,344	1,313	1,359	1,262	1,430	1,369	1,453	1,284
New Hampshire	1,140	1,120	1,143	1,098	1,410	1,255	1,373	1,148	1,650	1,336	1,525	1,169
Vermont	571	565	569	565	619	594	619	593	658	609	654	607
Massachusetts	5,921	5,896	5,903	5,953	6,159	5,909	5,959	6,190	6,431	5,879	5,985	6,280
Rhode Island	998	997	1,003	1,004	1,048	1,010	1,046	1,049	1,105	1,016	1,078	1,074
Connecticut	3,266	3,268	3,271	3,268	3,422	3,405	3,432	3,405	3,514	3,464	3,515	3,478
Middle Atlantic:												
New York	17,868	17,847	17,846	18,184	17,966	17,548	17,563	19,412	18,129	17,204	17,259	20,328
New Jersey	7,808	7,800	7,820	7,818	8,382	8,119	8,238	8,229	8,846	8,249	8,455	8,477
Pennsylvania	12,043	11,987	12,024	12,072	12,069	11,852	12,073	12,295	12,038	11,636	12,037	12,331
East North Central:												
Ohio	10,907	10,869	10,909	10,973	10,930	10,869	11,096	11,436	10,803	10,795	11,183	11,720
Indiana	5,617	5,589	5,613	5,626	5,696	5,697	5,831	5,910	5,655	5,747	5,973	6,093
Illinois	11,682	11,671	11,676	11,829	11,722	11,856	11,887	12,765	11,571	11,949	12,000	13,519
Michigan	9,292	9,264	9,328	9,364	9,365	9,331	9,692	9,879	9,301	9,323	9,941	10,209
Wisconsin	4,892	4,892	4,886	4,919	4,844	5,027	4,993	5,185	4,652	5,102	5,045	5,381
West North Central:												
Minnesota	4,377	4,360	4,371	4,378	4,566	4,568	4,615	4,672	4,632	4,706	4,773	4,895
Iowa	2,814	2,833	2,808	2,870	2,549	2,808	2,671	3,013	2,251	2,783	2,555	3,123

Missouri	5,207	5,195	5,212	5,200	5,473	5,425	5,495	5,434	5,665	5,619	5,708	5,604
North Dakota	658	673	657	678	596	698	615	728	531	721	588	776
South Dakota	716	718	715	724	715	746	723	775	704	777	732	827
Nebraska	1,604	1,614	1,601	1,627	1,539	1,660	1,583	1,730	1,443	1,701	1,563	1,819
Kansas	2,522	2,526	2,521	2,535	2,534	2,658	2,613	2,703	2,488	2,775	2,683	2,858
South Atlantic:												
Delaware	682	669	679	669	802	706	760	704	933	736	826	720
Maryland	4,774	4,706	4,760	4,684	5,608	5,073	5,370	4,936	6,446	5,338	5,836	5,073
District of Columbia	603	607	605	625	595	588	586	660	625	599	601	681
Virginia	6,229	6,153	6,214	6,107	7,275	6,741	7,066	6,482	8,222	7,167	7,700	6,704
West Virginia	1,842	1,879	1,847	1,892	1,651	1,882	1,717	1,958	1,482	1,877	1,622	1,996
North Carolina	6,688	6,623	6,670	6,555	7,717	7,226	7,492	6,803	8,735	7,730	8,193	6,913
South Carolina	3,560	3,549	3,558	3,523	3,962	3,894	3,956	3,743	4,304	4,176	4,292	3,899
Georgia	6,598	6,521	6,594	6,444	8,005	7,329	7,733	6,882	9,378	7,990	8,671	7,201
Florida	12,942	12,720	12,878	12,442	16,315	14,330	15,162	12,798	19,702	15,620	16,984	13,013
East South Central:												
Kentucky	3,745	3,760	3,745	3,775	3,689	3,887	3,813	3,978	3,562	3,978	3,861	4,119
Tennessee	5,009	4,986	5,012	4,949	5,424	5,386	5,533	5,156	5,727	5,711	5,961	5,270
Alabama	4,165	4,170	4,174	4,156	4,358	4,474	4,498	4,383	4,469	4,732	4,777	4,553
Mississippi	2,649	2,662	2,652	2,668	2,772	2,856	2,791	2,902	2,858	3,026	2,905	3,121
West South Central:												
Arkansas	2,421	2,433	2,427	2,422	2,509	2,615	2,562	2,544	2,559	2,784	2,670	2,648
Louisiana	4,368	4,491	4,379	4,501	4,141	4,868	4,258	4,927	3,876	5,206	4,183	5,324
Oklahoma	3,190	3,303	3,193	3,283	2,924	3,624	3,042	3,481	2,660	3,936	2,980	3,668
Texas	17,053	17,414	17,103	17,303	17,828	19,903	18,142	19,413	17,990	21,972	18,946	21,414
Mountain:												
Montana	797	820	796	815	744	897	766	858	692	969	752	899
Idaho	1,013	1,039	1,012	1,029	1,008	1,202	1,056	1,156	985	1,339	1,097	1,286
Wyoming	468	501	468	493	409	582	430	550	366	640	413	608
Colorado	3,331	3,410	3,350	3,370	3,424	3,861	3,548	3,649	3,385	4,202	3,694	3,863
New Mexico	1,539	1,561	1,545	1,539	1,735	1,818	1,727	1,701	1,922	2,036	1,881	1,863
Arizona	3,666	3,611	3,673	3,548	4,633	4,149	4,457	3,809	5,537	4,610	5,086	4,030
Utah	1,729	1,761	1,736	1,766	1,845	2,082	1,929	2,166	1,879	2,360	2,085	2,622
Nevada	1,130	1,105	1,122	1,075	1,409	1,331	1,414	1,159	1,618	1,515	1,641	1,224
Pacific:												
Washington	4,797	4,802	4,796	4,728	5,191	5,535	5,477	5,076	5,369	6,187	6,060	5,363
Oregon	2,822	2,843	2,822	2,809	2,903	3,206	3,086	2,986	2,922	3,548	3,335	3,135
California	29,287	29,199	29,313	29,168	33,963	33,328	33,981	33,218	38,096	36,968	38,112	36,935
Alaska	525	549	525	539	599	655	550	614	669	730	578	688
Hawaii	1,133	1,134	1,132	1,111	1,362	1,373	1,368	1,244	1,590	1,615	1,608	1,369

SOURCE: United States Bureau of the Census. *Projections of the Population of States by Age, Sex, and Race: 1989–2010.* Current Population Reports, Series P-25, No. 1053 (Washington, D.C.: U.S. Government Printing Office), p. 13.

Culture, Population Growth, and Planning

The United Nations designated 1974 as World Population Year and in August of that year convened the World Population Conference in Bucharest, Romania. The purpose of the conference was to focus world attention on the problems associated with population growth. The conference was the largest international population meeting ever held and had representatives from 136 governments around the world.

Although most governments recognized the existence of population problems in their own countries, as well as throughout the world, there was considerable disagreement and debate about the reasons for the problems and the solutions that should be implemented. A number of countries participating in the conference felt that the reason for high birth rates was the lack of social and economic development; they believed the emphasis should not be on population control and family planning programs but rather on development. One of the frequently heard slogans at Bucharest was "Take care of the people, and the population will take care of itself." However, a number of other countries, including the Western European nations, the United States, and Canada, felt that reductions in population growth rates would make a substantial contribution to economic development and that many countries first needed a decrease in their population growth to induce development.

A more lucid explanation of this relationship between population, family planning, and development was expressed by Nortman and Hoffstater (1975, 3):

> Whatever the stance on the political stage, the most ardent family planning advocates recognize that contraception "alone" will not produce housing, schools, or steel mills; and among the staunchest supporters of the "new economic order," many appreciate the demographic value of legitimated and government-subsidized family planning services.

At least three positions on the population problem can be isolated. One position is that population growth is a crisis issue so grave that catastrophe is near unless dramatic actions are taken to reduce growth. A second position is held by those who feel that although population growth will intensify and multiply other social problems, making the population problem important, it is not the overriding issue. A third position is held by those who feel that population is not a problem, or even a false problem, with the real issue being development or redistribution of income and power. In summary, the very nature of the population problem and the consequences of population growth are under closer scrutiny and examination today than at any time in the past.

Laissez-Faire Point of View

The general argument stated by those in favor of some form of population control is that individual fertility decisions do not produce what is socially optimal, or even desirable, in an area, hence such decisions cannot be left to individual families. As a result, parents intending to have children may end up transferring a significant part of the cost and responsibility for those children on to other people. These parents are therefore likely to have "too many" children.

On the other hand, some people favor a laissez-faire solution. They feel that fertility is a question of individual choice because it is the individual who bears the cost and receives the benefits of his or her own actions. In general the laissez-faire argument regarding population control is essentially the same as the laissez-faire argument in economics. According to this theory, under proper functioning of the free market, without controls, the prices (monetary and nonmonetary) that people pay for things reflect the real cost of production; and the prices they receive reflect the real value of what they produce. Thus, when an individual makes an economic decision, he or she bears all the costs and receives all the benefits. If the costs are less than the benefits, a positive decision is made; if the costs are greater than the benefits, a negative decision is made.

Laissez-faire population exponents feel that those best able to determine the costs and benefits of having children are those who are contemplating being parents. They are the ones who must assume the financial and social responsibility for each child, and they are the ones who will benefit from that child. There are some, however, who believe that the costs and benefits for the family are not the same as the costs and benefits derived by the society for each additional child. For the individual family, the ideal number of children may be five or six, whereas the ideal family size for their society may be only two.

Question of Cultural Genocide

Somewhat akin to the laissez-faire population exponents are those who feel that population control is a device proposed by more economically developed countries to control the less economically developed countries. Because the former group of countries are primarily the white, wealthier nations and the latter group are the nonwhite, poorer nations, many believe that population control is a form of "genocide."

"Genocide" is a controversial concept with many emotional overtones. The United Nations Genocide Convention defined genocide as any of the following acts committed with intent to destroy, in whole, or in part, a national, ethnic, racial, or religious group:

(A) killing members of the group;
(B) causing serious bodily or mental harm to members of the group;
(C) deliberately inflicting on the group conditions to bring about its physical destruction in whole or in part;
(D) imposing measures intended to *prevent birth* within the group;
(E) forcibly transferring children of the group to another group.

This definition was adopted unanimously by the General Assembly of the United Nations. According to the definition, mass sterilization of a compulsory nature would be considered genocide. Item (D) of the definition, "imposing measures intended to prevent birth within the group," is either directly or indirectly related to the family planning programs espoused by the United States and other developed countries. The important question thus becomes: Do family planning programs, as espoused by predominantly white, wealthy nations represent conscious, deliberate efforts to curtail nonwhite fertility, or do they reflect a genuine concern for the well-being and health of the rest of the world? In his analysis of population control, Darden concluded that, in his opinion,

> . . . the poor and nonwhite should oppose any program which involves institutional limitation of population growth. Why? Because there is no guarantee that relative poverty would decline if the poor and nonwhites accepted such a fertility program. There might be fewer poor people in absolute numbers, but the gap between rich and poor would either widen or remain constant. . . . In brief, institutionalized, coercive limitation of population growth is a policy aimed directly or indirectly at the poor and nonwhite and is therefore unacceptable as a solution to the problems of hunger, and other social ills in the United States and the world (Darden, 1975, 51).

Ethics of Population Control

As previously mentioned, there are those who believe that any form of coercive population control is unethical. However, a significant number of people feel that to solve the population problem and to limit population growth, it will be necessary to induce people to restrict the size of their families. They feel that the hazards of excessive population growth pose such critical dangers to the future of the species, the eco-system, individual liberty and welfare, and the structure of social life that nations must reexamine and ultimately revise the traditional value assigned to unlimited procreation and to the increase in population size.

In his work, Callahan (1971, 2) outlined some general ethical guidelines for governmental action and presented them in a "rank order of preferences" from the most preferable to the least preferable. They are listed here and deserve careful consideration.

According to Callahan, the government has an obligation to do everything in its power to protect, enhance, and implement freedom of choice in family planning. This means the first requirement is to establish effective voluntary family planning programs.

If it turns out that the voluntary family planning programs do not curb excessive population growth, the government has the right to go "beyond family planning." Callahan feels, however, that before governments take this second step they must justify the introduction of these new programs by showing that voluntary methods have been tried adequately and fairly. Callahan believes that the voluntary programs have not yet failed because they have not been applied in any massive, systematic way.

When the government has to choose among possible programs that go "beyond family planning," it has an obligation to try first those programs which, comparatively, are the least coercive. In other words, positive incentive programs and manipulation of social structures should be used before employing "negative" incentive programs and involuntary fertility controls. According to Callahan, if it appears that some degree of coercion is required, then the government should choose the policy or program that:

- entails the least amount of coercion,
- limits the coercion to the fewest possible cases,
- is not problem specific,
- allows the most room for dissent of conscience,
- limits the coercion to the narrowest possible range of human rights,
- least threatens human dignity,
- least establishes precedents for other forms of coercion,
- is most quickly reversible if conditions change.

In summary, the ethical considerations associated with population control are quite complex. Population policies, although they must take into account the interests and needs of particular regions and population groups, should have as their ultimate aim the best interests of the entire human species.

REFERENCES

Ahlburg, Dennis A. and Vaupel, James W. (1990) "Alternative Projections of the U. S. Population," *Demography* 27:639–652.

Barinaga, Marcia. (1992) " 'African Eve' Backers Beat a Retreat," *Science* 255:686–687.

Berelson, Bernard and Freedman, Ronald, eds. (1974) *The Human Population.* San Francisco: W. H. Freeman and Co., pp. 3–11.

Bouvier, Leon F. (1976) "On Population Growth," *Intercom* 4:8–9.

Bouvier, Leon F. (1992) *Peaceful Invasions: Immigration and Changing America.* Lanham, MD: University Press of America, Inc.

Callahan, Daniel. (1971) *Ethics and Population Limitation.* New York: Population Council.

Cann, R. L., Stoneking, M., and Wilson, A. C. (1987) "Mitochondrial DNA and Human Evolution," *Nature* 325:31–36.

Cipolla, C. M. (1974) *The Economic History of World Population.* Baltimore: Penguin Books.

Darden, Joe T. (1975) "Population Control or a Redistribution of Wealth: A Dilemma of Class and Race," *Antipode* 7:50–52.

Deevey, Edward S. (1960) "The Human Population," *Scientific American* 203:3–9.

Demeny, Paul. (1974) "The Populations of the Underdeveloped Countries," in *Scientific American*, eds. *The Human Population.* San Francisco: W. H. Freeman and Co., pp. 105–115.

Easterlin, Richard, Wachter, Michael, and Wachter, Susan. (1979) "The Coming Upswing in Fertility," *American Demographics* 1:12–15.

Gibson, Campbell. (1977) "Population Projections for the United States," *Intercom* 5:7–9.

Haub, Carl. (1987) "Understanding Population Projections," *Population Bulletin* 42(4):1–41.

Haub, Carl. (1992) "New UN Projections Show Uncertainty of Future World," *Population Today* 20(2):6–7.

Irwin, Richard. (1977) *Guide for Local Area Population Projections.* United States Bureau of the Census Technical Paper No. 39. Washington, D.C.: United States Government Printing Office.

Isbister, John. (1973) "Birth Control, Income Redistribution, and the Rate of Saving: The Case of Mexico," *Demography* 10: 85–98.

Johanson, D. C. and Edey, M. A. (1981) *Lucy: The Beginnings of Humankind.* New York: Simon and Schuster.

Nagel, John S. (1978) "Mexico's Population Policy Turnaround," *Population Bulletin* 33(5): 1–39.

Nortman, Dorothy; assisted by Hofstatter, Ellen. (1975) "Population and Family Planning Programs: A Factbook," *Reports on Population/Family Planning.* No. 2., 7th ed. New York: The Population Council.

Ornstein, Robert and Ehrlich, Paul. (1989) *New World, New Mind.* New York: Doubleday.

Peters, Gary L. (1980) "Population Projections: An Exercise for Population Geography," *Journal of Geography* 79:269–270.

Spencer, Gregory. (1980) "Measuring the Accuracy of U.S. Population Projections," *Intercom* 8(5):8–9.

Stringer, Christopher B. (1990) "The Emergence of Modern Humans," *Scientific American* 263(6):98–104.

Thorne, Alan G. and Wolpoff, Milford H. (1992) "The Multiregional Evolution of Humans," *Scientific American* 266(4):76–83.

United Nations. (1974) Department of Economic and Social Affairs. Population Studies No. 56. *Concise Report on the World Population Situation in 1970–1975 and Its Long-Range Implications.* New York: The United Nations.

United Nations. (1991) *Long-Range World Population Projections: Two Centuries of Population Growth, 1950–2150.* New York: United Nations.

United States Bureau of the Census. (1989) *Projections of the Population of the United States, by Age, Sex, and Race: 1988 to 2080.* Current Population Reports, Series P-25, No. 1018. Washington, D. C.: United States Government Printing Office.

United States Bureau of the Census. (1990) *Projections of the Population of States by Age, Sex, and Race: 1989 to 2010.* Current Population Reports, Series P-25, No. 1053. Washington, D.C.: United States Government Printing Office.

Wenke, Robert J. (1990) *Patterns in Prehistory.* Third Edition. Oxford: Oxford University Press.

Westoff, Charles E. (1979) "The Decline of Fertility," *American Demographics* 1(2):16–19.

Wilson, Allan C. and Cann, Rebecca L. (1992) "The Recent African Genesis of Humans," *Scientific American* 266(4):68–73.

Woods, Robert (1979) *Population Analysis in Geography.* London: Longman.

Young, Louise B., ed. (1968) *Population in Perspective.* New York: Oxford University Press.

Zinsser, Hans. (1967) *Rats, Lice, and History.* New York: Bantam Books, Inc.

Chapter 2
Population Data

As readers undoubtedly have surmised by now, population studies require an abundance and variety of data. Because populations and their associated characteristics are constantly changing, it is necessary to maintain current statistics. This dynamic nature of populations requires researchers and others to look at a full range of historic data and not only at information covering a short period of time.

Thus, because of the large masses of statistical information required and the need for historical data, the population analyst usually obtains information from reports by government agencies or other large organizations. In most cases the individual scholar has neither the money nor the time to gather the required information.

Three broad types of uses for demographic data can be distinguished: (1) planning, policy guidelines, and projections ranging from five years to the long term; (2) monitoring current demographic trends and applied programs; and (3) scientific study, at either the micro or macro level, of interrelationships between demographic phenomena and socioeconomic developments (Seltzer, 1973, 5). Each of these uses has specific requirements in terms of accuracy, timeliness, topical and geographical detail, and user confidence. The interrelationships of these variables for each data use are outlined in Table 2–1. The information in the table suggests that the greatest difficulties are encountered in monitoring current trends and programs; that the data used for longer range planning purposes is the easiest to acquire and has the least stringent specifications; and that the information needed for scientific inquiry is immediate.

CONCEPTUAL DIFFICULTIES

At first glance many of the basic demographic measurement concepts seem to be concrete and unambiguous. The concepts of "age," "death," and "live birth" seem to be straightforward and easy to define. The collection of accurate and reliable demographic data also involves some other concepts such as "city," "place of residence,"

TABLE 2–1 ■ Relevance of Specified Criteria for Assessing the Adequacy of Demographic Estimates, by Type of Data Use

(For a fuller description of the specified criteria, see Seltzer (1972). The terms "high," "medium," "low," and "varies" reflect somewhat speculative judgments.)

Type of Use[a]	Accuracy	Timeliness	Detail		User Confidence	Index of Total Burden[b]
			Topical	Geographical		
Planning and projections	Medium	Medium	Low	Medium	Varies	8–10
Monitoring current trends	High	High	Medium	High	Varies	12–14
Scientific study	High	Low	High	Low	High	11

[a]The assessments and the use types are an extension of distinctions developed by Tukey (1960). In terms of his dichotomy, "planning and projections" and "monitoring current trends" fall largely under the domain of decision theory, while "scientific study" would call for conclusion theory.

[b]Sum of scores where high = 3, medium = 2, low = 1, and varies = 1–3.

SOURCE: Reprinted with the permission of the Population Council from *Demographic Data Collection: A Summary of Experience,* by William Seltzer (New York: The Population Council, 1973), p. 6.

and "household," which might appear to be relatively ambiguous. However, under close scrutiny, even the seemingly unambiguous terms (age, death, live birth) are difficult to conceptualize.

Age Data

Information on the age structure of a population is essential to many areas of population analysis. Ryder (1964, 449) noted that age is the central variable in the demographic model. It identifies birth cohort membership. In addition, it serves as a measure of the interval of time spent within the population and, thus, of exposure to the risks of encountering events that may force one to leave the population. More generally, age is a surrogate for experiences that may cause changed behavior of various kinds. Age as the passage of personal time is, in short, the link between the history of the individual and the history of the population.

Shryock and Siegel (1971, 201) commented on the value of age data:

Age is the most important variable in the study of mortality, fertility, nuptiality, and certain other areas of demographic analysis. Tabulations on age are essential in the computation of basic measures relating to the factors of population change, in the analysis of the factors of labor supply, and in the study of the problem of economic dependency. The importance of census data on age in studies of population growth is even greater when adequate vital statistics from a registration system are not available.

Gathering data relative to the age structure of a population would appear to be a relatively simple process. The United Nations (1969, 18) defined age as the number of "completed solar years since birth." This type of information can be obtained by asking respondents either their ages as of their last birthdays or their dates of birth. Unfortunately, according to Seltzer (1973, 9), "these questions cannot be answered by populations that take no note of birthdays, and they will produce biased results when asked of those using a calendar other than the 'Western' solar calendar."

Even though the "Western" method of determining age seems logical and straightforward to those who live in countries where it is used, other traditions for determining age prevail in other areas of the world. If these traditions are not accounted for in the data-gathering process, then substantial error and confusion can occur. For example, one of the most common non-Western methods of determining age is that used by the Chinese, who consider a person to be one year old at birth. Thereafter, a person ages by one year each New Year's Day. However, as noted by Hock (1967, 861), "some of the Chinese respondents . . . reckon their ages according to the Chinese system, some according to the Western system, and . . . others might compute their ages according to Japanese reckoning, by adding one year to their age on the occasion of the Western New Year instead of the Chinese New Year." Similar results have been found in a study of South Korea. Thus, the answer to a seemingly simple question, "How old are you?", can have several interpretations.

Total Population

Another seemingly simple question deals with the total population of a place. However, after careful scrutiny even this concept has its problems. For example, does one assign people to the place that they customarily inhabit regardless of where they happen to be residing on the census day (*de jure*) or does one count them wherever they are physically present at census time regardless of their home place (*de facto*)? Different countries make different choices.

In Great Britain the *de facto* census is favored. This method has the advantage of showing exactly where everyone was at a given moment (census day). Its obvious disadvantage is that certain population figures may be increased or decreased because of tourists, traveling salespersons, or other transients. The United States, on the other hand, has traditionally conducted a *de jure* census: people are tabulated according to their permanent places of residence. The *de jure* method provides information that is not affected by temporary or seasonal movements of people; however, it has two principal shortcomings: (1) it involves costly, time-consuming work to transfer people from their places of interview to their places of usual residence and (2) it is sometimes difficult to be certain where a person's "usual" or "legal residence" is located. For the 1970 Census of the United States the "usual place of residence" was defined as follows:

> In accordance with census practice dating back to 1790, each person enumerated
> in the 1970 census was counted as an inhabitant of his usual place of residence,
> which is generally construed to mean the place where he lives and sleeps most of

the time. This place is not necessarily the same as his legal residence, voting residence, or domicile. In the vast majority of cases, however, the use of these different bases of classification would produce substantially the same statistics, although there may be appreciable differences for a few areas. (United States Bureau of the Census, 1971, IV-V).

No change in this definition was made for either the 1980 or 1990 census.

Definition of Urban

Even more troublesome than defining the total population is defining the term "urban." Almost every country has its own definition; this variety of definitions can make comparative studies of urbanization extremely difficult. Also, within some countries the definition has changed over time. Most urban definitions fall into one of the following four categories: size, administrative function, legal identity, and site characteristics.

In 1990 the United States Bureau of the Census defined as "urban" all territory, population, and housing units in urbanized areas and in places with populations of 2,500 or above outside urbanized areas. More specifically, the definition of "urban" included the following: (1) places with populations of 2,500 or more that have been incorporated as cities, not including the rural portions of extended cities; (2) census-designated places of 2,500 or more; and (3) other territory, incorporated or not, that is included in urbanized areas.

Other countries also use the size criterion, but with different sizes. In Denmark urban places are those with populations of at least 250, whereas in India urban places are those with populations of at least 5,000. Size definitions of urban places are often inadequate because the size of a minor civil division, such as a county, may be used in place of the size of an urban place. Exact definitions are necessary before comparative studies can be made.

Some countries prefer to use administrative units as designations of urban places, as is common in parts of Latin America. In Peru, for example, urban places are defined as "capitals of all departmentos and distritos plus all towns larger than the average size of these administrative centers not possessing rural characteristics." The major problem with this kind of definition is that places with no administration functions will be considered rural, regardless of their population size. Another possible criterion for defining urban places is legal identity; that is, towns with legal identity are classified as urban and all others are classified as rural. This definition traces its origin back to the chartered cities of the Middle Ages.

Finally, site characteristics may be used to define an urban place. A place may be considered urban if it has certain urban characteristics, such as piped-in water supplies, numbered streets, and lighting. Occasionally both site characteristics and the previously mentioned criteria are applied, and the resulting definition of an urban place can be quite complex.

The United States definition of urban has changed over time. In early censuses there was no distinction between rural and urban. A distinction was first made in the *Statistical Atlas of the United States* (1874), where urban was defined as towns with a population greater than 8,000. The United States Census of 1900 lowered the size limit to 2,500. Massive suburbanization, resulting in an increased number of people living in urban conditions but not within incorporated limits, rendered older definitions inadequate. In 1950 a density criterion for fringe areas was adopted, and an 11.5 percent increase in urban population was registered.

Subsequent to the 1980 Census, new definitions of larger urban regions were introduced to replace the previously used Standard Metropolitan Statistical Area. These new areas were defined by the Office of Management and Budget with support from the Bureau of the Census in 1983. The new types of metropolitan areas are as follows: Metropolitan Statistical Area (MSA), Consolidated Metropolitan Statistical Area (CMSA), and Primary Metropolitan Statistical Area (PMSA). These definitions remained in place for the 1990 census.

The MSA is a county or group of counties that has either a city of 50,000 or more people, using legal city boundaries as a definition of the city, or an urbanized area of 50,000 or more people with a combined metropolitan population of at least 100,000. MSAs are further categorized by size into four levels, A, B, C, and D. Whereas level A MSAs have at least one million people, those in level D have less than 100,000. The PMSA is a county or group of counties in which either local opinion supports separate recognition for a county or group of counties that demonstrate relative independence within the metropolitan complex or it had previously been recognized as a metropolitan area before the beginning of 1980 *and* local opinion supports its continued recognition as such. A county or group of counties may be recognized as a CMSA if it is a level A MSA *and* it includes a PMSA within it.

In addition the Census Bureau recognizes the Urbanized Area (UA), which is defined by population density. Each Urbanized Area includes a central city and the closely settled urban fringe around it. Together these areas must have at least 50,000 people and a population density that generally exceeds 1,000 people per square mile.

Several other problems occur when we attempt to define an urban place. One has to do with the process of annexation. For example, the 1950 population of the town of California, Pennsylvania, was 2,831 and the 1960 population was 5,978. Looking closely at this change, we see that most of the growth was due to annexation of surrounding areas. Tracing population changes over time often is difficult because of changes due to annexation.

Another problem is reclassification of areas from rural to urban on the basis of population size. For instance, if a place had a population of 2,499 in 1970 and grew to 2,500 in 1980, the net gain of one person would mean that all 2,500 persons were subtracted from the rural population and added to the urban population. It has been estimated that one third of the "gain" in urban population in El Salvador between 1950 and 1960, for example, was due to reclassification.

Migration and Areal Subdivisions

Conceptual problems concerning migration have always been an issue. As Petersen (1975, 41) noted, "We know whether someone has been born or has died, but who shall say whether a person has migrated?" Everyone agrees that when we go to the neighborhood grocery store we have not migrated. Likewise, there is agreement that when we leave our home in one country and establish residence in another we have migrated. However, between these two extremes problems arise. How far does one have to move in order to be considered a migrant? How long must one stay at the new location? The questions of how far and how long, as well as other considerations, play an important role in the definition of migration.

The area subdivisions used for collecting and mapping population data present further problems. As Zelinsky (1966, 22) pointed out, "Urban residence and function have generally spilled far beyond the political bounds of the metropolis; and if urban growth is rapid, no amount of technical alacrity can keep census divisions abreast of the actual urban-rural frontier." In summary, the collection and analysis of demographic data is wrought with conceptual problems, primarily problems of definition. Unless these discrepancies are addressed, gross inaccuracies can occur in demographic data.

▓ TYPES OF RECORDS

Information for demographic analysis generally comes from three sources: (1) census enumerations, (2) vital registrations, and (3) sample surveys. These sources are the most comprehensive records available and are generally provided by national governments. A variety of fragmentary demographic data exist and may occasionally serve useful purposes, but such data are usually collected for selected small populations. Examples include the following: school censuses, church records, records of births and deaths recorded by hospitals, city directories, auto title transfers, and marriage licenses. They are often readily available, and their use should not be overlooked; however, they generally are inadequate substitutes for the data available from the major sources of demographic information.

A census is a total count of the population of a specified area, generally a nation, and "a sort of social photograph of certain conditions of a population at a given moment which are expressible in numbers" (Wilcox, 1940, 195). Besides enumerating the population, most censuses collect other data, such as age, sex, place of residence, place of birth, income, occupation, education, and religion. The quantity of information collected is mainly a function of the amount of money available for financing the census. A census is a major, costly undertaking requiring considerable expertise and planning for it to be successful. Thus, censuses usually are conducted by national governments. The 1980 Census of the United States cost over $1.0 billion, nearly $5 per person enumerated, while the 1990 Census cost about $2.6 billion, or over $10 per person enumerated.

Vital registrations are also major sources of demographic data. Vital statistics are recorded and compiled at or near their time of occurrence and usually include such events as deaths, fetal deaths, births, marriages, divorces, and at times disease and illness. Unlike the census, which is a static, cross-sectional view of a population at a specific moment of time, a registration system is a dynamic recording of events that can change rapidly.

The major responsibility for reporting vital events to civil registration authorities, depending upon the country, is given to a local registrar, parents or relatives, or to physicians, midwives, undertakers, religious officials; persons with special duties relative to births and deaths. Seltzer (1973, 35) suggested that "ideally, a national birth and death registration system obtains a report of each event shortly after it occurs, and statistical summaries of these reports, in conjunction with externally derived population estimates, can be used to compute vital rates." If the vital registration system is functioning effectively, it is capable of producing precise mortality and fertility estimates.

In some nations, like the Netherlands, Finland, Belgium, and the Scandinavian countries, the vital registration system is so complete that a local registration bureau keeps a card for each individual. Major demographic events such as marriages, divorces, and changes in residence are noted on the card and this information can be available quite readily.

Because of the time and expense involved in a census, sample surveys are often used instead. Their advantages in terms of quality and cost are now well recognized. A major concern, however, is to ensure that they are a truly representative sample of the population. Many sample surveys dealing with demographic issues are conducted by census bureaus and other governmental and private agencies; sampling is also used within vital registration systems.

▓ CENSUS ENUMERATIONS

By authority of the Constitution of the United States the population of the United States must be enumerated every ten years. In other countries the time span between censuses may be as short as five years, or censuses may occur at infrequent intervals depending upon economic and political circumstances. The United Nations (1954, 1) regards a census as "the simultaneous recording of demographic data by the government, at a particular time, pertaining to all the persons who live in a particular territory." A census also should have the following characteristics:

- ▓ It should be of the population of a strictly defined territory.
- ▓ It should include everyone.
- ▓ It should be a personal enumeration.
- ▓ It should be conducted at one time, preferably on one day.
- ▓ It should be conducted at regular intervals.

Brief History of Census Enumerations

The thought of counting an area's population occurred to people even in ancient times. Perhaps the oldest account of census taking is that of the Incas, who organized their society according to a decimal system. Although this method was not a census in any modern sense, it was at least a variation on the general theme. Enumerations of various kinds were made in early times in Sumeria, Babylonia, and Egypt. A rather large, though fragmented, amount of data were recorded in ancient China, and a census of sorts was taken in Rome during the sixth century B.C.

Examples of early census counts can be found in the Old Testament. Some passages illustrate both the purpose of the counts and the reasons people resisted them. Many early population counts were for such purposes as conscription into the military service and the labor force, or for taxation. The word census comes from the Latin word, *censere,* which means "to value" or "to tax." Thus, it comes as no surprise to find that early attempts at enumeration were regarded with considerable suspicion and resentment. Two different Biblical accounts are given of a census of Israel that was to be taken by David. The accounts differ both in the reasons for the census and the results. However, they agree that after David took the census he became remorseful, felt he had sinned by enumerating the population of Israel, and was finally punished for his deed. According to Carr-Saunders (1936, 14), when the notion of taking a census was first proposed in England in the 1750s:

> the dire results of the census which David forced Joab to make were quoted by those who opposed the measure, and it was prophesized that some "public misfortune" or an "epidemical distemper" would follow if an enumeration were attempted.

The result was a long delay in the first census of England.

Modern Censuses

The beginning of modern census taking occurred in Scandinavia. Sweden began taking regular population counts in 1749, and Norway and Denmark began in 1769. The first United States census was taken in 1790; the United States was also the first country to legislate a continuing, time-specific census. Beginning dates for other early modern censuses are given in Table 2–2. Thus, the practice of regular census taking began in Western Europe around the middle of the eighteenth century and became widespread in Western Europe before the middle of the nineteenth century. During that time, enumeration efforts became somewhat more sophisticated.

It is not enough to know that a country has taken a census. We also need to know whether censuses are taken at regular intervals; in many countries, they are not. For example, China took a census in 1953 but did not conduct another one until 1982. Many improvements still need to be made in census taking and in gathering demographic knowledge, despite the fact that only about 2 percent of the world's population

TABLE 2–2 ▩ Beginning Dates for Early Censuses

United States	1790
England and Wales	1801
Belgium	1829
France	1835
Egypt	1897
Russia	1897

TABLE 2–3 ▩ Number of Countries Taking Censuses, 1955–1974

Region	Number of Countries and Territories	Taking at Least One Census in	
		1960 Round (1955–1964)	1970 Round (1965–1974)
North Africa/Middle East	24	16	18
Sub-Saharan Africa	51	29	47
North America	36	34	36
South America	15	13	14
Asia	31	25	23
Europe	40	38	36
Oceania	27	23	26
Totals	224	178	200

SOURCE: Reprinted with the permission of the Population Council from "World population: status report 1974," by Bernard Berelson, *Reports on Population/Family Planning,* no. 15 (January, 1974): 34.

live in countries that have never taken censuses. Between 1965 and 1974 nearly 90 percent of the world's countries took censuses. In Table 2–3 it can be seen that the greatest recent gains in census taking have been made in sub-Saharan Africa.

Census of the United States

The United States Bureau of the Census is the record keeper for the nation. The major output of the Bureau's data-collection activities are its statistical reports, which not only provide a record of the number of people in the United States but also document changes in characteristics of the people, manufacturing establishments, farms, retail stores, and a host of other business enterprises from which Americans derive their living. The Census Bureau publishes more statistics, encompasses a larger range of topics, and serves a greater variety of statistical needs than any other federal agency. According to U. S. law the Census Bureau is responsible for taking a variety of censuses, outlined in Table 2–4.

TABLE 2–4 ▨ Types of Censuses in the United States

Census	Periodicity	Recent Censuses
Population	10 years	1960, 1970, 1980, 1990
Housing	10 years	1960, 1970, 1980, 1990
Agriculture	5 years	1974, 1979, 1984, 1989
Business	5 years	1977, 1982, 1987, 1992
Construction industries	5 years	1977, 1982, 1987, 1992
Governments	5 years	1977, 1982, 1987, 1992
Manufactures	5 years	1977, 1982, 1987, 1992
Mineral industries	5 years	1977, 1982, 1987, 1992
Transportation	5 years	1977, 1982, 1987, 1992

SOURCE: United States Bureau of the Census.

From the beginning, however, the primary task of the Census Bureau has been to provide the federal government with an accurate count of the United States population. The count is to be conducted on the first day of April in every year that ends with a zero. The Bureau of the Census is required to notify the President by December of that year as to how many people he presided over eight months earlier.

The first census of the United States was strictly a head count and included only five questions, one of which was dropped in 1870—it asked the head of each household how many slaves he owned. It was conducted by 650 U. S. marshals and their deputies, and the results were issued in a single volume, fifty-six pages long. The entire operation cost $44,000, or approximately $0.011 or 1.1 cents per person. However, the censuses have changed considerably since 1790. The volume of output has increased from a single short volume to some 15,000 separate publications. Despite the fact that efficient, high-speed computers are now being used, it seemed unlikely that the total output of the 1980 census would be available for examination until after the 1990 census. The estimated cost of the 1990 census was $2.6 billion.

Although the United States was one of the first nations to establish a modern census, it lagged far behind in establishing a permanent bureaucracy to continue the task. Originally the State Department had the chore, but in 1830 it was transferred to the Department of the Interior. A full-time bureau was not established until 1902, when Congress decided to put the Census Bureau in the Department of Commerce and Labor. Later, when this department was split into two separate departments in 1913, the Census Bureau went into the Commerce Department, where it remains today.

Many changes in the type and number of census questions have been made since 1790. The largest number of questions ever asked was seventy in the 1970 census, although four fifths of the people enumerated did not have to respond to more than twenty. In 1980 and 1990 the number of questions declined slightly. Questions have been eliminated in the past because the information was no longer valid, for example, the number of slaves, or because the question was confusing. For instance, in 1960 enumerators were asked to rate the condition of the homes that they visited as either good, dilapidated, or deteriorating. This question was subsequently dropped because of the lack of agreement on the meaning of terms like "dilapidated." Whatever problems and shortcomings the Census Bureau might have, however, we will continue to take a decennial census. As Anderson (1988, 240) concluded in her excellent history of census-taking in the United States:

> The census remains both an apportionment tool and a baseline measure for American social science. These dual functions have provided the impetus for technical innovation in the past and will continue to do so in the future. . . . Americans will undoubtedly continue to conceive of social issues in terms of census categories and to redistribute the benefits and burdens among the people—"according to their respective numbers."

The 1990 Census of Population and Housing.   Official planning for the 1990 census began on October 1, 1983. Before each census a series of test censuses or "dress rehearsals" are carried out in a variety of settings. In preparation for the 1990 census, such dress rehearsals were conducted in Jersey City, New Jersey, and Tampa, Florida, in 1985; several areas of Los Angeles in 1986; rural North Dakota in 1987; and St. Louis, Missouri, in 1988.

The heart of the census, of course, is the questionnaire that must by law be filled out by all households in the United States. Actually there were two questionnaires for the 1990 Census, a "short" form that included six questions about population and six questions about housing and a "long" form, or "sample" form, that included the twelve questions on the "short" form plus additional questions. Thus, all households provide answers to the basic twelve questions and sample households (about 17 percent of all households or approximately 40,000,000 people in 1990) answered the additional questions. The questions on each form are shown in Table 2–5, and the actual "short" form is shown in Table 2–6.

Census Geography, 1990.   Results of the 1990 census are tabulated and published for a variety of different geographic areas. These areas fall into two categories: "statistical areas" and "political and administrative areas." The former are defined by the Census Bureau; examples include metropolitan statistical areas, urbanized areas, census tracts, block groups, and blocks. Boundaries for the latter are generally established by law; examples include states, cities, and congressional districts. Basic features

TABLE 2–5 ▦ 1990 CENSUS CONTENT

100-PERCENT COMPONENT

Population
Household relationship
Sex
Race
Age
Marital status
Hispanic origin

Housing
Number of units in structure
Number of rooms in unit
Tenure—owned or rented
Value of home or monthly rent
Congregate housing (meals included in
   rent)
Vacancy characteristics

SAMPLE COMPONENT

Population
Social characteristics:
Education—enrollment and attainment
Place of birth, citizenship, and year of
   entry to U.S.
Ancestry
Language spoken at home
Migration (residence in 1985)
Disability
Fertility
Veteran status

Housing
Year moved into residence
Number of bedrooms
Plumbing and kitchen facilities
Telephone in unit
Vehicles available
Heating fuel
Source of water and method of sewage
   disposal
Year structure built
Condominium status
Farm residence
Shelter costs, including utilities

Economic characteristics:
Labor force
Occupation, industry, and class of worker
Place of work and journey to work
Work experience in 1989
Income in 1989
Year last worked

NOTE: Questions dealing with the subjects
   covered in the 100-percent
   component will be asked of all
   persons and housing units. Those
   covered by the sample component
   will be asked of a portion or
   sample of the population and
   housing units.

SOURCE: United States Bureau of the Census. (1990) *Census '90 Basics*. CPH-I–8 (Washington, D.C.: U.S. Government Printing Office).

of census geography are shown in Figure 2–1, and the basic units are described in Table 2–7. Figure 2–2 shows the basic relationships that exist among different small census areas, and Figure 2–3 shows a portion of the detail of a census tract.

   TIGER and the 1990 Census.   TIGER is an acronym for the Census Bureau's Topologically Integrated Geographic Encoding and Referencing system, which was developed during the 1980s. Though conceptually its origin is earlier, work on

TABLE 2–6 ▪ 1990 Census Questionnaire (100 percent component)

Page 1

The 1990 census must count every person at his or her "usual residence." This means the place where the person lives and sleeps most of the time.

1a. List on the numbered lines below the name of each person living here on Sunday, April 1, including all persons staying here who have no other home. If EVERYONE at this address is staying here temporarily and usually lives somewhere else, follow the instructions given in question 1b below.

Include

- Everyone who usually lives here such as family members, housemates and roommates, foster children, roomers, boarders, and live-in employees
- Persons who are temporarily away on a business trip, on vacation, or in a general hospital
- College students who stay here while attending college
- Persons in the Armed Forces who live here
- Newborn babies still in the hospital
- Children in boarding schools below the college level
- Persons who stay here most of the week while working even if they have a home somewhere else
- Persons with no other home who are staying here on April 1

Do NOT include

- Persons who usually live somewhere else

- Persons who are away in an institution such as a prison, mental hospital, or a nursing home
- College students who live somewhere else while attending college
- Persons in the Armed Forces who live somewhere else

- Persons who stay somewhere else most of the week while working

Print last name, first name, and middle initial for each person. Begin on line 1 with the household member (or one of the household members) in whose name this house or apartment is owned, being bought, or rented. If there is no such person, start on line 1 with any adult household member.

	LAST	FIRST	INITIAL		LAST	FIRST	INITIAL
1				7			
2				8			
3				9			
4				10			
5				11			
6				12			

1b. If EVERYONE is staying here only temporarily and usually lives somewhere else, list the name of each person on the numbered lines above, fill this ———▶ ○ circle and print their usual address below. DO NOT PRINT THE ADDRESS LISTED ON THE FRONT COVER.

House number	Street or road/Rural route and box number	Apartment number
City	State	ZIP Code
County or foreign country	Names of nearest intersecting streets or roads	

NOW PLEASE OPEN THE FLAP TO PAGE 2 AND ANSWER ALL QUESTIONS FOR THE FIRST 7 PEOPLE LISTED. USE A BLACK LEAD PENCIL ONLY.

TABLE 2–6 ■ (Cont.)

Page 2 | *PLEASE ALSO ANSWER HOUSING QUESTIONS ON PAGE 3* ⟶

	PERSON 1	PERSON 2
Please fill one column ⟶ for each person listed in Question 1a on page 1.	Last name	Last name
	First name Middle initial	First name Middle init

2. How is this person related to PERSON 1?

Fill ONE circle for each person.

If **Other relative** of person in column 1, fill circle and print exact relationship, such as mother-in-law, grandparent, son-in-law, niece, cousin, and so on.

PERSON 1: START in this column with the household member (or one of the members) in whose name the home is owned, being bought, or rented.

If there is no such person, start in this column with any adult household member. ■

PERSON 2:
If a RELATIVE of Person 1:
○ Husband/wife   ○ Brother/sister
○ Natural-born   ○ Father/mother
 or adopted   ○ Grandchild
 son/daughter   ○ Other relative ⟍
○ Stepson/   ⌐ ⌐ ⌐ ⌐ ⌐
 stepdaughter

If NOT RELATED to Person 1:
○ Roomer, boarder, ○ Unmarried
 or foster child   partner
○ Housemate,   ■ ○ Other
 roommate   nonrelative

3. Sex
Fill ONE circle for each person.

PERSON 1: ○ Male   ○ Female
PERSON 2: ○ Male   ○ Female

4. Race

Fill ONE circle for the race that the person considers himself/herself to be.

If **Indian (Amer.)**, print the name of the enrolled or principal tribe. ⟶

If **Other Asian or Pacific Islander (API)**, print one group, for example: Hmong, Fijian, Laotian, Thai, Tongan, Pakistani, Cambodian, and so on. ⟶

If **Other race**, print race. ⟶

PERSON 1:
○ White
○ Black or Negro
○ Indian (Amer.) (Print the name of the enrolled or principal tribe.) ⟍
⌐ ⌐ ⌐ ⌐ ⌐
○ Eskimo
○ Aleut
Asian or Pacific Islander (API)
○ Chinese   ○ Japanese
○ Filipino   ○ Asian Indian
○ Hawaiian ■ ○ Samoan
○ Korean   ○ Guamanian
○ Vietnamese   ○ Other API ⟍
○ Other race (Print race) ⟍

PERSON 2:
○ White
○ Black or Negro
○ Indian (Amer.) (Print the name of the enrolled or principal tribe.) ⟍
⌐ ⌐ ⌐ ⌐ ⌐
○ Eskimo
○ Aleut
Asian or Pacific Islander (API)
○ Chinese   ○ Japanese
○ Filipino   ○ Asian Indian
○ Hawaiian ■ ○ Samoan
○ Korean   ○ Guamanian
○ Vietnamese   ○ Other API ⟍
○ Other race (Print race) ⟍

5. Age and year of birth

a. Print each person's age at last birthday. Fill in the matching circle below each box.

b. Print each person's year of birth and fill the matching circle below each box.

PERSON 1:
a. Age
b. Year of birth 1
0●0○ 0○   1● 8○ 0○ 0○
1○1○ 1○   9○ 1○ 1○
2○ 2○   2○ 2○
3○ 3○   3○ 3○
4○ 4○   ■ 4○ 4○
5○ 5○   5○ 5○
6○ 6○   6○ 6○
7○ 7○   7○ 7○
8○ 8○   8○ 8○
9○ 9○   9○ 9○

PERSON 2:
a. Age
b. Year of birth 1
0●0○ 0○   1● 8○ 0○ 0○
1○1○ 1○   9○ 1○ 1○
2○ 2○   2○ 2○
3○ 3○   3○ 3○
4○ 4○   ■ 4○ 4○
5○ 5○   5○ 5○
6○ 6○   6○ 6○
7○ 7○   7○ 7○
8○ 8○   8○ 8○
9○ 9○   9○ 9○

6. Marital status
Fill ONE circle for each person.

PERSON 1:
○ Now married   ○ Separated
○ Widowed   ○ Never married
○ Divorced

PERSON 2:
○ Now married   ○ Separated
○ Widowed   ○ Never married
○ Divorced

7. Is this person of Spanish/Hispanic origin?

Fill ONE circle for each person.

If **Yes, other Spanish/Hispanic**, print one group. ⟶

PERSON 1:
○ No (not Spanish/Hispanic)
○ Yes, Mexican, Mexican-Am., Chicano
○ Yes, Puerto Rican ■
○ Yes, Cuban
○ Yes, other Spanish/Hispanic
 (Print one group, for example: Argentinean, Colombian, Dominican, Nicaraguan, Salvadoran, Spaniard, and so on.) ⟍
⌐ ⌐ ⌐ ⌐ ⌐

PERSON 2:
○ No (not Spanish/Hispanic)
○ Yes, Mexican, Mexican-Am., Chicano
○ Yes, Puerto Rican
○ Yes, Cuban
○ Yes, other Spanish/Hispanic
 (Print one group, for example: Argentinean, Colombian, Dominican, Nicaraguan, Salvadoran, Spaniard, and so on.) ⟍
⌐ ⌐ ⌐ ⌐ ⌐

FOR CENSUS USE ⟶

PERSON 1: ○   ○   □
PERSON 2: ○   ○

TABLE 2–6 ▓ (Cont.)

PERSON 2

Last name

First name   Middle initial

If a RELATIVE of Person 1:
- ○ Husband/wife
- ○ Natural-born or adopted son/daughter
- ○ Stepson/ stepdaughter
- ○ Brother/sister
- ○ Father/mother
- ○ Grandchild
- ○ Other relative ⟍

If NOT RELATED to Person 1:
- ○ Roomer, boarder, or foster child
- ○ Housemate, roommate ▓
- ○ Unmarried partner
- ○ Other nonrelative

○ Male   ○ Female

- ○ White
- ○ Black or Negro
- ○ Indian (Amer.) (Print the name of the enrolled or principal tribe.) ⟍

- ○ Eskimo
- ○ Aleut

Asian or Pacific Islander (API)
- ○ Chinese
- ○ Filipino ▓
- ○ Hawaiian
- ○ Korean
- ○ Vietnamese
- ○ Japanese
- ○ Asian Indian
- ○ Samoan
- ○ Guamanian
- ○ Other API ⟍

○ Other race (Print race) ⟋

a. Age	b. Year of birth
	1
0 ○ 0 ○ 0 ○	1 ● 8 ○ 0 ○ 0 ○
1 ○ 1 ○ 1 ○	9 ○ 1 ○ 1 ○
2 ○	2 ○ 2 ○
3 ○ 3 ○	3 ○ 3 ○
4 ○ 4 ○	4 ○ 4 ○
5 ○ 5 ○	5 ○ 5 ○
6 ○ 6 ○	6 ○ 6 ○
7 ○ 7 ○	7 ○ 7 ○
8 ○ 8 ○	8 ○ 8 ○
9 ○ 9 ○	9 ○ 9 ○

- ○ Now married
- ○ Widowed
- ○ Divorced
- ○ Separated
- ○ Never married

- ○ No (not Spanish/Hispanic)
- ○ Yes, Mexican, Mexican-Am., Chicano
- ○ Yes, Puerto Rican
- ○ Yes, Cuban ▓
- ○ Yes, other Spanish/Hispanic (Print one group, for example: Argentinean, Colombian, Dominican, Nicaraguan, Salvadoran, Spaniard, and so on.) ⟍

○

○

NOW PLEASE ANSWER QUESTIONS H1a–H7b FOR YOUR HOUSEHOLD

H1a. Did you leave anyone out of your list of persons for Question 1a on page 1 because you were not sure if the person should be listed – for example, someone temporarily away on a business trip or vacation, a newborn baby still in the hospital, or a person who stays here once in a while and has no other home?

- ○ Yes, please print the name(s) and reason(s). ⟍
- ○ No

b. Did you include anyone in your list of persons for Question 1a on page 1 even though you were not sure that the person should be listed – for example, a visitor who is staying here temporarily or a person who usually lives somewhere else?

- ○ Yes, please print the name(s) and reason(s). ⟍
- ○ No

H2. **Which best describes this building?** Include all apartments, flats, etc., even if vacant.
- ○ A mobile home or trailer ▓
- ○ A one-family house detached from any other house
- ○ A one-family house attached to one or more houses
- ○ A building with 2 apartments
- ○ A building with 3 or 4 apartments
- ○ A building with 5 to 10 apartments
- ○ A building with 10 to 19 apartments
- ○ A building with 20 to 49 apartments
- ○ A building with 50 or more apartments
- ○ Other

H3. **How many rooms do you have in this house or apartment?** Do NOT count bathrooms, porches, balconies, foyers, halls, or half-rooms.
- ○ 1 room ▓
- ○ 2 rooms
- ○ 3 rooms
- ○ 4 rooms
- ○ 5 rooms
- ○ 6 rooms
- ○ 7 rooms
- ○ 8 rooms
- ○ 9 or more rooms

H4. Is this house or apartment –
- ○ Owned by you or someone in this household with a mortgage or loan?
- ○ Owned by you or someone in this household free and clear (without a mortgage)?
- ○ Rented for cash rent?
- ○ Occupied without payment of cash rent?

If this is a ONE-FAMILY HOUSE –

H5a. Is this house on ten or more acres?
- ○ Yes   ○ No

b. Is there a business (such as a store or barber shop) or a medical office on this property?
- ○ Yes   ○ No

Answer only if you or someone in this household OWNS OR IS BUYING this house or apartment –

H6. What is the value of this property; that is, how much do you think this house and lot or condominium unit would sell for if it were for sale?
- ○ Less than $10,000
- ○ $10,000 to $14,999
- ○ $15,000 to $19,999
- ○ $20,000 to $24,999
- ○ $25,000 to $29,999
- ○ $30,000 to $34,999
- ○ $35,000 to $39,999
- ○ $40,000 to $44,999
- ○ $45,000 to $49,999
- ○ $50,000 to $54,999
- ○ $55,000 to $59,999
- ○ $60,000 to $64,999
- ○ $65,000 to $69,999
- ○ $70,000 to $74,999
- ○ $75,000 to $79,999
- ○ $80,000 to $89,999
- ○ $90,000 to $99,999
- ○ $100,000 to $124,999
- ○ $125,000 to $149,999
- ○ $150,000 to $174,999
- ○ $175,000 to $199,999
- ○ $200,000 to $249,999
- ○ $250,000 to $299,999
- ○ $300,000 to $399,999
- ○ $400,000 to $499,999
- ○ $500,000 or more

Answer only if you PAY RENT for this house or apartment –

H7a. What is the monthly rent?
- ○ Less than $80
- ○ $80 to $99
- ○ $100 to $124
- ○ $125 to $149
- ○ $150 to $174
- ○ $175 to $199
- ○ $200 to $224
- ○ $225 to $249
- ○ $250 to $274
- ○ $275 to $299
- ○ $300 to $324
- ○ $325 to $349
- ○ $350 to $374
- ○ $375 to $399
- ○ $400 to $424
- ○ $425 to $449
- ○ $450 to $474
- ○ $475 to $499
- ○ $500 to $524
- ○ $525 to $549
- ○ $550 to $599
- ○ $600 to $649
- ○ $650 to $699
- ○ $700 to $749
- ○ $750 to $999
- ○ $1,000 or more

b. Does the monthly rent include any meals?
- ○ Yes   ○ No

FOR CENSUS USE

A. Total persons	B. Type of unit	D. Months vacant	G. DO ID

A. Total persons

B. Type of unit
Occupied   Vacant
- ○ First form
- ○ Cont'n
- ○ Regular
- ○ Usual home elsewhere

C1. Vacancy status
- ○ For rent
- ○ For sale only
- ○ Rented or sold, not occupied
- ○ For seas/ rec/occ
- ○ Usual home elsewhere
- ○ Other vacant

C2. Is this unit boarded up?
- ○ Yes   ○ No

D. Months vacant
- ○ Less than 1
- ○ 1 up to 2
- ○ 2 up to 6
- ○ 6 up to 12
- ○ 12 up to 24
- ○ 24 or more

E. Complete after
- ○ LR ○ TC ○ QA   JIC 1
- ○ P/F ○ RE ○ I/T ○
- ○ MV ○ ED ○ EN
- ○ P0 ○ P3 ○ P6   JIC 2
- ○ P1 ○ P4 ○ IA ○
- ○ P2 ○ P5 ○ SM ○

F. Cov.
- ○ 1b ○ 1a ○ 7 ○ H1

(Total persons column:)
0 0
1 1
2 2
3
4
5
6
7
8
9

(G. DO / ID grid:)
0 0 0 0 0 0 0 0 0 0
1 1 1 1 1 1 1 1 1 1
2 2 2 2 2 2 2 2 2 2
3 3 3 3 3 3 3 3 3 3
4 4 4 4 4 4 4 4 4 4
5 5 5 5 5 5 5 5 5 5
6 6 6 6 6 6 6 6 6 6
7 7 7 7 7 7 7 7 7 7
8 8 8 8 8 8 8 8 8 8
9 9 9 9 9 9 9 9 9 9

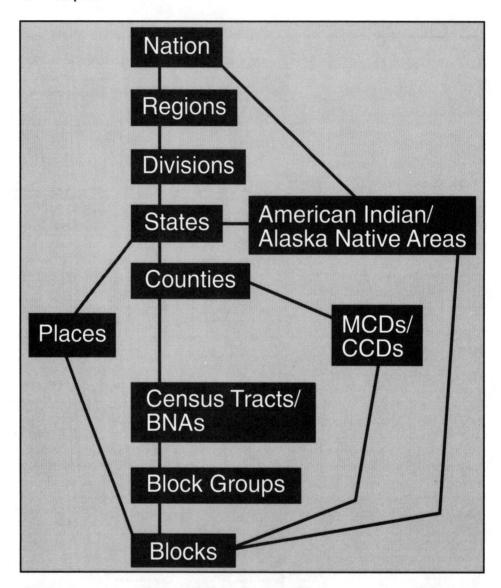

▨ **FIGURE 2–1** Basic 1990 Census Geographic Hierarchy. SOURCE: United States Bureau of the Census.

TABLE 2–7 ■ 1990 Census Geography

American Indian Reservations/Alaska Native Village Statistical Areas—The reservations and their boundaries were identified by the Federal Bureau of Indian Affairs and State governments. Boundaries for Alaska Native village statistical areas were established by the Census Bureau in cooperation with Alaska Native Regional Corporations and State participants.

Block Groups (BGs)—A collection of census blocks within a census tract or block numbering area (BNA), sharing the same first digit in their three-digit identifying numbers.

Blocks—Generally bounded by streets, political boundaries and other visible features, a block is the smallest geographic unit for which the Census Bureau tabulates data.

Census Tracts/Block Numbering Areas (BNAs)—**Census tracts** are small, locally delineated statistical areas within selected counties, generally having stable boundaries and, when first established by local committees, designed to have relatively homogeneous demographic characteristics. Block numbering areas are areas delineated by State officials or the Census Bureau for the purpose of grouping and numbering blocks in counties without census tracts.

Counties and Statistically Equivalent Areas—The primary divisions of most States, Puerto Rico, and the outlying areas: counties for 48 States; parishes for Louisiana; boroughs and census areas for Alaska; independent cities in Maryland, Missouri, Nevada, and Virginia; Yellowstone National Park in Montana; municipios in Puerto Rico; other entities in the outlying areas.

Metropolitan Areas (MAs)—An MA contains either a place with at least 50,000 inhabitants or an urbanized area and a total population of at least 100,000 (75,000 in New England). Contiguous counties (cities and towns in New England) are included if they have close social and economic links with the area's population nucleus.

Minor Civil Divisions (MCDs)/Census County Divisions (CCDs)—**Minor civil divisions** generally are legally defined county subdivisions such as towns and townships. In 21 States where MCDs do not exist or are not adequate for reporting subcounty statistics, the Census Bureau, in cooperation with State and local officials, delineates county subdivisions known as **census county divisions.**

Places—**Incorporated places** are concentrations of population, such as cities, that have legally prescribed boundaries, powers and functions. Densely settled population centers without legally defined corporate limits or corporate powers are defined by the Census Bureau in cooperation with State officials and local data users and are called **census designated places (CDPs).**

States and Statistically Equivalent Areas—The 50 States; in addition, the Census Bureau treats the District of Columbia, Puerto Rico, and the outlying areas (the Virgin Islands of the United States, Guam, American Samoa, the Northern Mariana Islands, and Palau) as State equivalents for statistical presentation.

Urbanized Areas (UAs)—A UA consists of one or more places and surrounding densely settled territory with a combined population of 50,000 or more inhabitants.

Voting Districts—**Voting districts** are defined by State and local governments for the purpose of conducting elections. They include election districts, precincts, legislative districts, and wards.

SOURCE: United States Bureau of the Census. (1991) *Census Geography— Concepts and Products.* CFF No. 8. (Washington, D.C.: U.S. Bureau of the Census), March, pp. 2–5.

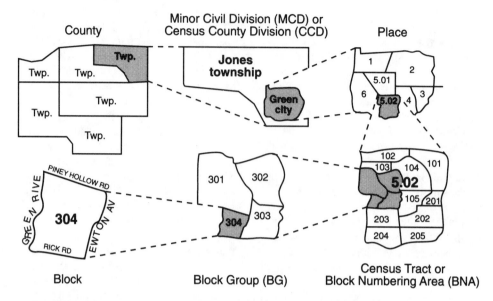

▓ **FIGURE 2–2** Geographic Relationships. SOURCE: United States Bureau of the Census. *Census Geography—Concepts and Products.* CFF No. 8 (Rev.). Washington, D.C.: United States Bureau of the Census, March, 1991, p. 2.

TIGER officially began in 1983 as the Census Bureau attempted to automate the mapping and other geographic activities that were required to support its censuses and surveys.

In preparation for the use of TIGER in conjunction with the 1990 census the Census Bureau consulted extensively with Geographic Information Systems (GIS) experts in both the private sector and the United States Geological Survey. The goal was to establish an integrated geographic data base for the entire nation. Computer tape files containing rivers, lakes, roads, railroads, and other water and transportation features from the United States Geological Survey were merged into its own Geographic Base File/Dual Independent Map Encoding (GBF/DIME) files by the Census Bureau to form the current TIGER system. TIGER has greatly accelerated map production by the Census Bureau and is now in a form that makes it far easier to manipulate, change, and update the data base. Figure 2–4 provides some idea of the possible uses for the TIGER system.

Products from the 1990 Census. Data from the 1990 census will be made available in several different ways, from traditional printed reports and computer tapes to microfiche, CD-ROM, and even an online service known as CENDATA. Table 2–8 shows the printed reports and their dates of availability while Table 2–9 shows the Summary Tape Files (STFs) and notes those that also will be available on CD-ROM.

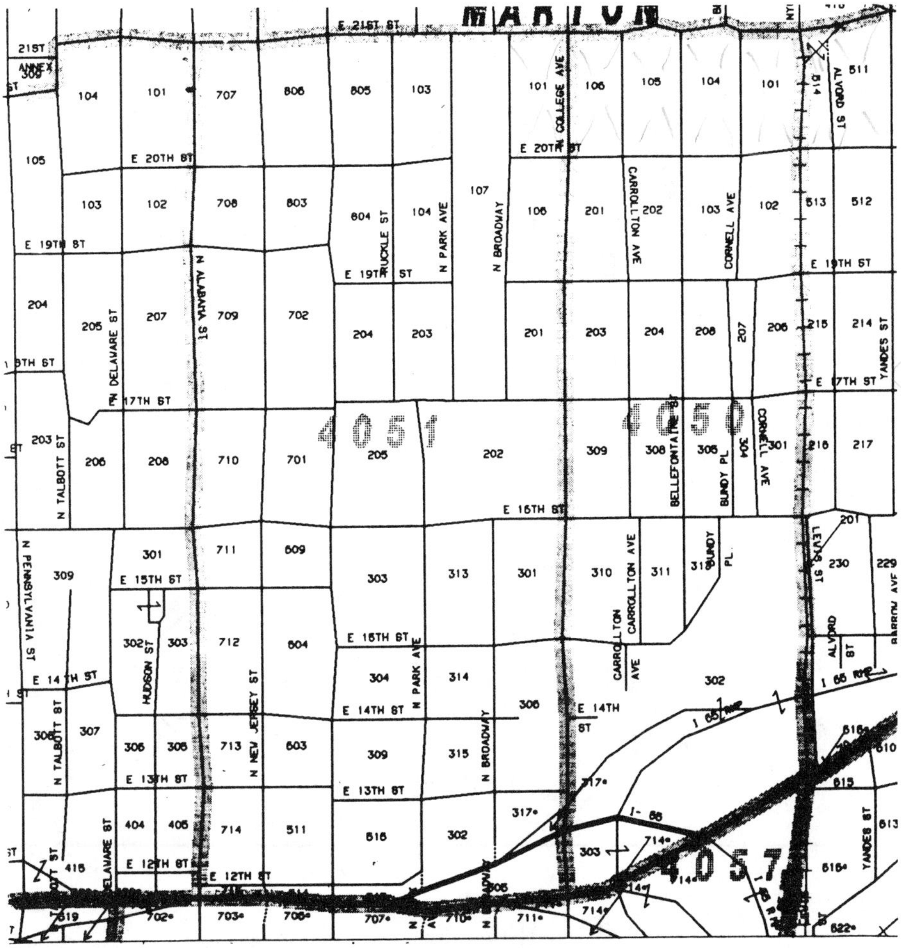

Excerpt from a map showing census tracts 4050 and 4051 and their blocks in Indianapolis. (This map has been reduced.)

■ **FIGURE 2–3** Census Tracts and Blocks Map. SOURCE: United States Bureau of the Census. (1990) *Census '90 Basics* CHP-I-8, (Washington, D.C.: U.S. Government Printing Office), p. 5.

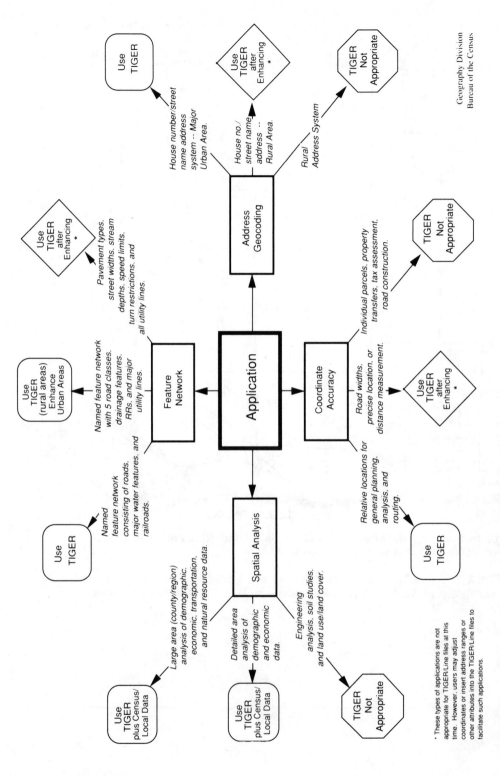

■ **FIGURE 2–4** Decision Tree for Potential TIGER/Line File Users. SOURCE: United States Bureau of the Census. (1990) *TIGER: The Coast-to-Coast Digital Map Data Base.* (Washington D.C.: U.S. Government Printing Office), p. 6.

* These types of applications are not appropriate for TIGER/Line files at this time. However, users may adjust coordinates or insert address ranges or other attributes into the TIGER/Line files to facilitate such applications.

Geography Division
Bureau of the Census

TABLE 2–8 ▦ 1990 Census of Population and Housing Printed Reports

Series	Title	Unit of issue/projected release date	Description	Geographic areas
POPULATION AND HOUSING 100-percent data				
1990 CPH-1	**Summary Population and Housing Characteristics**	A report for the U.S./1992; each State and DC/1991–1992*	Population and housing unit counts, and summary statistics on age, sex, race, Hispanic origin, household relationship, units in structure, value and rent, number of rooms, tenure, and vacancy characteristics	Local governmental units (i.e., counties, incorporated places, and towns and townships) and American Indian and Alaska Native areas
1990 CPH-2	**Population and Housing Unit Counts**	A report for the U.S./1992; each State and DC/1991–1992*	Total population and housing unit counts for 1990 and previous censuses	States, counties, minor civil divisions (MCDs)/census county divisions (CCDs), places, and summary geographic areas (for example, urban and rural, metropolitan and nonmetropolitan residence)
1990 CPH-3	**Population and Housing Characteristics for Census Tracts and Block Numbering Areas**	A report for each MSA and each State/ 1992–1993*	Statistics on 100-percent and sample population and housing subjects	In MSAs: census tracts/BNAs, places of 10,000 or more inhabitants, and counties. In the remainder of each State: census tracts/BNAs, places of 10,000 or more, and counties
1990 CPH-4	**Population and Housing Characteristics for Congressional Districts of the 103rd Congress**	A report for each State and DC/1993	Statistics on 100-percent and sample population and housing subjects	Congressional districts (CDs) and within CDs, counties, places of 10,000 or more inhabitants, MCDs of 10,000 or more in selected States, and American Indian and Alaska Native areas
Sample data				
1990 CPH-5	**Summary Social, Economic, and Housing Characteristics**	A report for the U.S./1993; each State and DC/1992*	Statistics on 100-percent and sample population and housing subjects	Local governmental units (i.e., counties, incorporated places, and towns and townships in selected States) and American Indian and Alaska Native areas

*Reports for Puerto Rico and the Virgin Islands of the United States are included.

TABLE 2–8 (Cont.) ■ 1990 Census of Population and Housing Printed Reports

Series	Title	Unit of issue/projected release date	Description	Geographic areas
1990 CP-1	**General Population Characteristics**	A report for the U.S./1992; each State and DC/1992*	Detailed statistics on age, sex, race, Hispanic origin, marital status, and household relationship characteristics	States, counties, places of 1,000 or more inhabitants, MCDs of 1,000 or more in selected States, State parts of American Indian and Alaska Native areas, and summary geographic areas such as urban and rural
1990 CP-1-1A	**General Population Characteristics for American Indian and Alaska Native Areas**	A single report/1992	Detailed statistics on age, sex, race, Hispanic origin, marital status, and household relationship characteristics	American Indian and Alaska Native areas, i.e., American Indian reservations, trust lands, tribal jurisdiction statistical areas in Oklahoma, Alaska Native village statistical areas and Alaska Native regional corporations
1990 CP-1-1B	**General Population Characteristics for Metropolitan Statistical Areas**	A single report/1992	Detailed statistics on age, sex, race, Hispanic origin, marital status, and household relationship characteristics	Individual MSAs and their component areas. For MSAs split by State boundaries, summaries are provided both for the parts and for the whole MSA
1990 CP-1-1C	**General Population Characteristics for Urbanized Areas**	A single report/1992	Detailed statistics on age, sex, race, Hispanic origin, marital status, and household relationship characteristics	Individual UAs and their component areas. For UAs split by State boundaries, summaries are provided both for the parts and for the whole UA
Sample data				
1990 CP-2	**Social and Economic Characteristics**	A report for the U.S., each State and DC/1993*	Statistics on 100-percent and sample population subjects	States (including summaries such as urban and rural), counties, places of 2,500 or more inhabitants, MCDs of 2,500 or more in selected States, and the State portion of American Indian and Alaska Native areas

*Reports for Puerto Rico and the Virgin Islands of the United States are included.

Series	Title	Unit of issue/projected release date	Description	Geographic areas
		POPULATION—Cont. **Sample data—Cont.**		
1990 CP-2-1A	**Social and Economic Characteristics for American Indian and Alaska Native Areas**	A single report/1993	Statistics on 100-percent and sample population subjects	American Indian and Alaska Native areas, as for CP-1-1A
1990 CP-2-1B	**Social and Economic Characteristics for Metropolitan Statistical Areas**	A single report/1993	Statistics on 100-percent and sample population subjects	Individual MSAs and their component areas, as for CP-1-1B
1990 CP-2-1C	**Social and Economic Characteristics for Urbanized Areas**	A single report/1993	Statistics on 100-percent and sample population subjects	Individual UAs and their component areas, as for CP-1-1C
1990 CP-3	**Population Subject Reports**	A report for each subject/ 1993	Approximately 30 reports on population census subjects such as migration, education, income, the older population, and racial and ethnic groups	Generally limited to the U.S., regions, and divisions; for some reports, other highly populated areas such as States, MSAs, counties, and large cities
		HOUSING **100-percent data**		
1990 CH-1	**General Housing Characteristics**	A report for the U.S./1992; each State and DC/1992*	Detailed statistics on units in structure, value and rent, number of rooms, tenure, and vacancy characteristics	States, counties, places of 1,000 or more inhabitants, MCDs of 1,000 or more in selected States, State parts of American Indian and Alaska Native areas, and summary geographic areas such as urban and rural
1990 CH-1-1A	**General Housing Characteristics for American Indian and Alaska Native Areas**	A single report/1992	Detailed statistics on units in structure, value and rent, number of rooms, tenure, and vacancy characteristics	American Indian and Alaska Native areas, i.e., American Indian reservations, trust lands, tribal jurisdiction statistical areas in Oklahoma, Alaska Native village statistical areas, and Alaska Native regional corporations

*Reports for Puerto Rico and the Virgin Islands of the United States are included.

TABLE 2–8 (Cont.) ▪ 1990 Census of Population and Housing Printed Reports

Series	Title	Unit of issue/projected release date	Description	Geographic areas
1990 CH-1-1B	**General Housing Characteristics for Metropolitan Statistical Areas**	A single report/1992	Detailed statistics on units in structure, value and rent, number of rooms, tenure, and vacancy characteristics	Individual MSAs and their component areas. For MSAs split by State boundaries, summaries are provided both for the parts and for the whole MSA
1990 CH-1-1C	**General Housing Characteristics for Urbanized Areas**	A single report/1992	Detailed statistics on units in structure, value and rent, number of rooms, tenure, and vacancy characteristics	Individual UAs and their component areas. For UAs split by State boundaries, summaries are provided both for the parts and for the whole UA
		Sample data		
1990 CH-2	**Detailed Housing Characteristics**	A report for the U.S./1993; each State and DC/1992–1993*	Statistics on 100-percent and sample housing subjects	States (including summaries such as urban and rural), counties, places of 2,500 or more inhabitants, MCDs of 2,500 or more in selected States, State parts of American Indian and Alaska Native areas
1990 CH-2-1A	**Detailed Housing Characteristics for American Indian and Alaska Native Areas**	A single report/1993	Statistics on 100-percent and sample housing subjects	American Indian and Alaska Native Areas, as in CH-1-1A
1990 CH-2-1B	**Detailed Housing Characteristics for Metropolitan Statistical Areas**	A single report/1993	Statistics on 100-percent and sample housing subjects	Individual MSAs and their component areas, as in CH-1-1B
1990 CH-2-1C	**Detailed Housing Characteristics for Urbanized Areas**	A single report/1993	Statistics on 100-percent and sample housing subjects	Individual UAs and their component areas, as in CH-1-C
1990 CH-3	**Housing Subject Reports**	A report for each subject/1993	Approximately 10 reports on housing census subjects such as structural characteristics and space utilization	Generally limited to U.S. regions, and divisions; for some reports, other highly populated areas such as States, MSAs counties, and large cities

*Reports for Puerto Rico and the Virgin Islands of the United States are included.

SOURCE: United States Bureau of the Census. *Census '90 Basics.* CPH-I-8 (Washington, D.C.: U.S. Government Printing Office), pp. 9–12.

TABLE 2–9 ▦ 1990 Census of Population and Housing Summary Tape Files

Summary Tape File (STF 1A, 1B, etc.) and data type (100 percent or sample)		Projected release date	Geographic areas	Description
STF 1 (100 percent)	A*†	1991–1992	States, counties, MCDs/ CCDs, places, census tracts/ BNAs, block groups (BGs)	About 1,000 cells/items of 100-percent population and housing counts and characteristics for each geographic area
	B*†	1991–1992	States, counties, MCDs/ CCDs, places, census tracts/ BNAs, BGs, blocks	
	C†	1992	U.S., regions, divisions, States (including summaries such as urban and rural), counties, places of 10,000 or more inhabitants, MCDs of 10,000+ in selected States, MSAs, UAs, American Indian and Alaska Native areas	
	D	1993	Congressional districts (CDs) by State; and within each CD: counties, places of 10,000+, MCDs of 10,000+ in selected States	
STF 2 (100 percent)	A	1992	In MSAs: census tracts/ BNAs, places of 10,000 or more inhabitants, and counties. In the remainder of each State: counties, places of 10,000+, and census tracts/ BNAs	Over 2,000 cells/items of 100-percent population and housing counts and characteristics for each geographic area. Each of the STF 2 files will include a set of tabulations for the total population and separate presentations of tabulations by race and Hispanic origin
	B	1992	States (including summaries such as urban and rural), counties, places of 1,000+, MCDs of 1,000+ in selected States, State portion of American Indian and Alaska Native areas	
	C	1992	U.S., regions, divisions, States (including summaries such as urban and rural), counties, places of 10,000+, MCDs of 10,000+ in selected States, MCDs of fewer than 10,000+ in New England MSAs, American Indian and Alaska Native areas, MSAs, UAs	

TABLE 2–9 (Cont.) ▦ 1990 Census of Population and Housing Summary Tape Files

Summary Tape File (STF 1A, 1B, etc.) and data type (100 percent or sample)		Projected release date	Geographic areas	Description
STF 3 (sample)	A*†	1992	States, counties, MCDs/ CCDs, places, census tracts/ BNAs, BGs	
	B†	1993	5-digit ZIP Codes within each State	
	C†	1993	U.S., regions, divisions, States, counties, MCDs of 10,000+ in selected States, places of 10,000+, American Indian and Alaska Native areas, MSAs, UAs	Over 3,300 cells/items of sample population and housing characteristics for each geographic area
	D	1993	Congressional districts (CDs) by State; and within each CD: counties, places of 10,000+, MCDs of 10,000+ in selected States	
STF 4 (sample)	A	1992	In MSAs: census tracts/ BNAs, places of 10,000 or more inhabitants, and counties. In the remainder of each State: counties, places of 10,000+, and census tracts/ BNAs	
	B	1992–1993	States (including summaries such as urban and rural), counties, places of 2,500+, MCDs of 2,500+ in selected States, MCDs of fewer than 2,500 in New England MSAs, State portion of American Indian and Alaska Native areas	Over 8,000 cells/items of sample population and housing characteristics for each geographic area. Each of the STF 4 files will include a set of tabulations for the total population and separate presentations of tabulations by race, Hispanic origin, and possibly selected ancestry groups
	C	1993	U.S., regions, divisions, States (including urban and rural and metropolitan and nonmetropolitan components), counties, places of 10,000+, MCDs of 10,000+ in selected States, MCDs of fewer than 10,000 in New England MSAs, American Indian and Alaska Native areas, MSAs, UAs	

*Available on microfiche (STF 1B microfiche is an extract).

†Available on laser disk (CD-ROM), (STF 1B data on CD-ROM is an extract).

SOURCE: United States Bureau of the Census. *Census '90 Basics.* CPH-I-8 (Washington, D.C.: U.S. Government Printing Office), p. 14.

▓ VITAL REGISTRATION

Historically the collection of vital registration information has been the responsibility of ecclesiastical authorities. Most cultures have some form of religious ceremony attached to each of the major vital events: baptism and birth, wedding and marriage, funeral and death. The systematic recording of vital events has been traced back to A.D. 710 in parts of Japan, while in 1497 the Archbishop of Toledo instructed parish priests to maintain vital records. In England, the Vicar General under Henry VIII instructed the clergy to record the number of baptisms, burials, and marriages that occurred in the land. In 1563 the Council of Trent made the keeping of burial and baptismal records compulsory on the part of the Roman Catholic Church.

Most of the first annals were kept by parish priests, mainly to determine the severity of the plague. Many of those early records were destroyed by age, fire, or pests long ago. Gradually, toward the end of the eighteenth century, government agencies began taking over the vital registration function. For example, national civil registration began in Sweden in 1756, in France in 1792, in England in 1837, and in Ireland in 1864. Thus, vital registration data became available at about the same time that census enumerations started appearing.

Vital Registration in the United States

The United States was one of the first countries to begin taking a regular modern census but one of the last countries to initiate the collection of vital statistics. First attempts to collect vital statistics were sporadic. As early as 1639 Massachusetts had begun collecting and maintaining records of births and deaths, but this was done only locally. Even though the model was based on English precedent, the government and not the clergy began keeping the vital records. Despite all attempts to enforce compliance with the registration system, early recordkeeping was not effective.

During the nineteenth century there was an increased awareness of the importance of vital records. Shattuch, the founder of the American Statistical Association in 1839, used that association as a forum to lobby for vital registration laws. In 1844, such laws were successfully established for Massachusetts. By 1850 the United States Census Office had invited Shattuch to help develop plans for obtaining data on births and deaths, a venture that was unsuccessful.

In 1880 the Census Office created a Death Registration Area, which included all cities and states that registered 90 percent or more of their established deaths. At that time only Massachusetts and Washington, D.C., qualified. However, there was a gradual increase in death registrations as other areas improved their record collection techniques. It has been estimated that by 1890, 31 percent of the population in the United States was included in the Death Registration Area. Part of the reason for the

TABLE 2–10 ■ Percent of Population in Birth and Death Registration Areas in the United States

Year	Birth Registration Area	Death Registration Area
1880	—	17
1890	—	31
1900	—	26
1910	—	51
1920	60	81
1930	95	95
1933 Both areas complete, with addition of Texas		

slow expansion of the Death Registration Area was the lack of a central office to encourage states to register births and deaths. The Census Office was created each ten years for the purpose of taking the decennial census, but following each census it was disbanded. Thus, there was virtually no promotion of the Death Registration Area.

In 1902 the Permanent Census Act created the Bureau of the Census, which was charged with the responsibility of collecting vital statistics along with its other duties. Subsequently the entire record collection process was accelerated somewhat.

In 1915 the Birth Registration Area was established. At that time it contained approximately 33 percent of the population. Table 2–10 shows the additions to the Birth Registration and Death Registration areas. By 1930 both areas were 90 percent complete and were finally finished with the addition of Texas in 1933. In 1957 a Marriage Registration Area was established, and in 1958 a Divorce Registration Area was added. Neither of these areas is yet complete.

It was originally the task of the Bureau of the Census to collect vital registration information; however, in 1946 the Public Health Service's National Office of Vital Statistics was authorized to collect the data. In 1960 another reorganization occurred, and the National Center for Health Statistics was formed. Its National Vital Statistics Division currently collects, publishes, and distributes information on births, deaths, marriages, and divorces. The data are collected from county courthouses, registrars, and halls of records and tabulated and recorded on monthly and annual bases.

Vital Registrations Throughout the World

Birth and death registration is now virtually complete in most of North America, Europe, and Oceania, and in certain parts of the Caribbean and Latin America. However, as Seltzer (1973, 36) noted, "In view of the basic motivational and administrative obstacles to the establishment of civil registration on a reliable basis, it is not surprising that official registration systems have been estimated as recording 40 percent or less of the live births occurring in Indonesia, Pakistan, India, the Republic of Korea, and the Philippines." Apparently death registrations are less complete than births in Asia as well, and in most cases the coverage of tropical Africa is even more deficient than that of Asia. Considerable uncertainty exists in all the developing countries with respect to the completeness of their registration systems.

Two major problems in the accuracy of vital registrations in developing countries are the following: (1) a considerable number of births and deaths are never reported and (2) whole sections or areas of countries are not part of the data-collecting system. The implications for demographic research are clear—the fertility and mortality data of developing countries is sketchy at best and cannot be considered reliable.

▨ SAMPLE SURVEYS

Because of the expense and time involved in interviewing everyone in a country, demographers frequently use sample surveys to collect information. There are four advantages of using a sample over a complete census: (1) a sample can be taken much faster than can a complete enumeration; if timeliness is important to a particular study, a sample may be the only means to collect the needed data; (2) a sample survey is much cheaper to administer than is a complete enumeration; (3) the quality and accuracy of a sample can be better than those of a complete enumeration, particularly where there are a limited number of trained personnel to conduct a complete enumeration; and (4) there is less paperwork involved, and data handling and processing can be easier.

In some nations, particularly the developing ones, a sample survey is the only economical method of collecting reliable demographic data. As Bogue (1969, 106) has commented:

> In some nations sample surveys are so widely used and have become so precise that a national census serves less to provide national totals of population composition than to provide data about smaller areas—states, cities, counties, townships, census tracts, and similar minor civil divisions—and to permit more detailed breakdown into refined categories and more elaborate cross-classifications of characteristics than do the sample surveys.

Requirements for an accurate and reliable sample survey include the following: (1) there must be an effective sampling design that will avoid biases in the selection process and (2) the sample design must lend itself to the estimation of sampling errors. It is difficult to develop and execute a sample design that is both economically feasible and scientifically correct without the help of a sampling expert.

Many variables affect the results of a sample survey, including the following: (1) characteristics of the person supplying the information, (2) characteristics of the person collecting the information, (3) salaries and benefits paid to those conducting the interviews, (4) the amount of supervision, (5) the collection procedure used, (6) the type of questions used, and (7) the actual wording of the questions used. Multiple-round surveys are becoming more important in demographic data collection. In the multiple-round survey, or longitudinal survey, information about a specific group or problem is collected on a continuing basis. It is a useful method for collecting information, particularly in areas where there is poor census coverage. According to Thomlinson (1976, 75), "Multiple-round surveys offer the triple advantages of cost reduction through sampling, keeping up-to-date by re-interviewing annually, or if desired, more frequently, and the opportunity to add and subtract questions as desired."

In the United States the Bureau of the Census regularly conducts a variety of sample surveys. Two major types of reports are published, *Current Population Reports* and *Current Housing Reports*.

▦ QUALITY AND COMPLETENESS OF POPULATION DATA

Though there are exceptions, the quality and quantity of the collected demographic data are generally related to levels of economic development. In the poorest countries demographic data usually are either absent or incomplete and of poor quality, whereas in the wealthy countries demographic data are likely to be abundant and of good quality. Censuses and vital registration systems require a considerable outlay of money, and in many of the poor countries money is simply unavailable for such purposes. For this reason sample surveys, often done with the help of the United Nations, are being conducted in many of the developing countries. They cut down on the cost and, if carefully designed and executed, can provide useful information.

Completeness of Coverage

Countries differ considerably in the number and types of questions that they include on their census forms. Most censuses include questions on age and sex; for perhaps half of the world's population, censuses also include questions on education and occupation. Although about one third of the world's people are asked questions on their language and religion, far fewer are asked about their ethnic identity. Part of the reason for the wide variation in census designs is financial; however, the variations are also affected by the political sensitivity of asking questions that some people may consider an invasion of privacy. Many people still view censuses with suspicion and resentment.

The list of questions asked in the 1990 United States Census was quite lengthy; about the only topic not dealt with was religion. On the other hand, Gambia's 1963 census consisted of only five questions: place of enumeration, tribe, age, sex, and marital status. Beyond the problem of insufficient coverage, another problem is the lack of geographical detail. Although in the United States some data are available for geographic units as small as census tracts, block groups, and even blocks, in the developing countries very few data are published for comparable minor civil divisions. Even when such data are available in developing countries, their use is often limited by a lack of maps showing the exact boundaries of the divisions used.

Another problem of geographic coverage is the failure of census takers to visit isolated areas, either because of the physical difficulties involved in travel or because of the lack of safety. In addition, the poor roads and communications systems in developing countries often means that some geographic areas will be either omitted or poorly covered.

Even for countries that have detailed modern censuses, problems arise with historical studies. Questions often disappear from the census as we go back in time.

Errors and Omissions

Occasionally census records are purposely falsified, as in the case of the 1940 Guatemalan Census. According to Whetten (1961, 20):

> The 1940 census might have been fairly adequate if the figures had not been deliberately tampered with. President Ubico, who wanted to show a large population for political purposes, issued orders to local authorities to alter the count after the census was taken. Relevant papers in the central files were carefully destroyed, but enough documentary evidence has been found in the offices of local authorities to indicate that the census results were inflated by at least 900,000 inhabitants.

Massive misreporting occurred in Nigeria in the 1962 census as political parties in different regions attempted to increase their representation in the national government. The 1962 census was officially disavowed. Fortunately, such examples of deliberate falsification of census records are rare. For the most part people attempt to answer census questions faithfully and honestly, although they often give wrong answers when they misunderstand questions or suffer lapses in memory. Most census errors are a result of omission rather than commission.

Errors in Age and Mortality Reporting

Aside from the conceptual problems related to the collection of age data, misreporting of age is believed to be quite common, especially in the developing countries. Studies of African and South Asian populations confirm this skepticism about age data. In a study in Africa, Blacker (1969, 277) noted that, "the widespread ignorance of age in the sense of numbers of completed years bedevils the collection of accurate data, and studies which have been made of reported African age distributions have revealed massive and deep-seated errors." The age situation in India has received a similar evaluation, and even in developed countries some data suggest that age is often misreported.

TABLE 2–11 ▩ Percent of Persons Enumerated Both in a Census or Census Pretest and in a Quality-check Reinterview Survey Who Were Recorded on Different Age Categories, by Age at Reinterview, Ghana, 1960 and Rawalpindi Area, 1971

Age at Reinterview	Ghana Sample, 1960		Rawalpindi Area, 1971[a]
	Males	Females	
Under 5 years	13	15	20
5–9	27	27	27
10–14	39	31	31
15–19	35	38	37
20–24	48	44	47
25–29	52	58	48
30–34	58	63	59
35–39	66	66	66
40–44	67	60	70
45–49	64	77	64
50–54	66	70	71
55–59	66	85	90
60–64	69	72	68
65–69	66	79	93
70–74	69	71	61
75 and over	41	32	53

[a]provisional and unofficial.

SOURCE: 1960 *Population Census of Ghana,* vol. 5, "General Report" (Accura: Census Office, 1964); and unpublished results of the 1971 Rawalpindi Census pretest.

The extent of age misreporting can be seen in Table 2–11. When the results for the two studies are tabulated, the percentage of people classified in different five-year age groups is 44 percent for the Rawalpindi study and 43 percent for the study in Ghana. A further evaluation (see Table 2–12) shows that among those in the 15 to 44 age brackets, the comparable percentages were 51 percent for the Rawalpindi study and 54 percent for the Ghana study. Several techniques have been used to improve the quality of age reporting; but, according to Caldwell and Igun (1971, 301), "age enumeration can be improved by allowing enumerators substantially more time than is usually the case in a national census. . . . This step, and seeing to it that the extra time is not wasted, is more important than any variation in enumeration technique."

Problems similar to those of age misreporting can be found when examining mortality records. For example, because all mortality reports involve proxy respondents, a poor accounting of deaths is common for persons living alone or living with nonrelated persons prior to their deaths.

Mortality in the developed regions is concentrated among the elderly. In contrast, in the developing areas approximately half of the deaths occur to persons less than 15 years old, and many times more deaths occur in the first year of life than among all

TABLE 2–12 ▪ Percent of Persons Enumerated in Both a Census or Census Pretest and a Quality-check Reinterview Survey Who Were Recorded in Different Five-year Age Categories, by Broad Age Group at Reinterview, Ghana, 1960 and Rawalpindi Area, 1971

Age Group at Reinterview	Ghana Sample, 1960		Rawalpindi Area, 1971[a]
	Males	Females	
All ages	42	44	44
Under 15 years	24	23	26
15–44	54	55	51
45–64	66	76	71
65 and over	76	76	76

[a]Limited in the age range 65–94 for Ghana and 65–74 for Rawalpindi study.

SOURCE: *1960 Population Census of Ghana,* vol. 5, "General Report" (Accura: Census Office, 1964); and unpublished results of the 1971 Rawalpindi Census pretest.

TABLE 2–13 ▪ Distribution of Deaths by Age and Region

	Developed Countries[a]	Developing Countries[b]
Percent of all deaths		
Under 1 year	3.0	25.4
Under 5 years	3.8	42.2
Under 15 years	4.7	48.6
15–24 years	1.5	4.0
25–64 years	26.2	24.6
65 years and over	69.0	22.9
Media age at death	72.5 years	18.6 years

[a]Median values using data for year specified in recent U.N. demographic yearbooks for England and Wales (1965), Japan (1968), Netherlands (1969), Sweden (1968), and United States (1968).

[b]Median values using data for year specified in recent U.N. demographic yearbooks for Algeria (1965), Jamaica (1964), Mexico (1969), Philippines (1967), and West Malaysia (1968).

SOURCE: Reprinted with the permission of the Population Council from *Demographic Data Collection: A Summary of Experience,* by William Seltzer (New York: The Population Council, 1973), p. 38.

of those over age 65. Table 2–13 shows the age distribution of mortality patterns in developed and developing countries. Because the mortality patterns are different, problems of measurement also differ. In the developed countries, where a larger proportion of older people are found, mortality surveys that omit the deaths of persons living alone or with nonrelatives will have a larger impact. Underreporting of deaths of the very young is common in all areas, but it has a greater impact on the developing countries who have a larger proportion of young people.

Errors in the United States Census

In such a large undertaking as the United States census, which required more than 480,000 workers in 1990, it is no wonder that errors have been made. As Kahn (1974, 44) noted:

> While the general public is sometimes surprised to hear that census figures are not beyond question, this is no news to the nation's enumerators themselves. They are among the few bureaucrats in any federal establishment who have consistently and candidly and voluntarily conceded that they make mistakes.

Among the early critics who reminded the census takers of their fallibility, George Washington remarked that:

> Returns of the Census have already been made from several of the States and a tolerably just estimate has been formed now in others, by which it appears that we shall hardly reach four millions; but one thing is certain: our *real* numbers will exceed, greatly, the official returns of them; because the religious scruples of some would not allow them to give in their lists; the fears of others that it was intended as the foundation of a tax induced them to conceal or diminished theirs; and thro' the indolence of the people, and the negligence of many of the Officers, numbers are omitted (Fitzpatrick, 1939, 329).

Fortunately the Census Bureau realized the fallibility of its information and by 1950 started to conduct regular self-analyses called Post Enumeration Surveys. In 1970 they spent over $3 million for self-evaluation; more than the total amount spent on the census a century earlier. In 1980, and again in 1990, the task was more complicated and more expensive.

In the four censuses immediately prior to 1980 in the United States there had been undercounts of 5.4 percent in 1940, 4.1 percent in 1950, 3.1 percent in 1960, and 2.7 percent in 1970 (Wolter, 1991). These figures coincide with undercounts in other developed countries. At first glance a 2.7 percent error may seem insignificant, but with a base population of over 200 million people in 1970 it meant that about 5.4 million Americans were not counted. Perhaps even more important is to consider *who* was not counted. The undercount was not distributed equally among all groups in the population. In 1970, according to the Census Bureau, there was a net under-enumeration of 6.5 percent for African-Americans and 2.2 percent for whites, similar to the 1960 undercounts of 8.3 percent for African-Americans and 2.7 percent for whites.

1980 Census. The Bureau improved its accuracy for the 1980 census. However, the most surprising result of the 1980 census was apparent by the end of 1980. The *error of closure,* the difference between the precensus estimate of the population and the actual count, was nearly 5,000,000 persons. In other words, the Census Bureau's count of 226,504,825, not counting the United States citizens living abroad, was far beyond the 1980 estimated population.

Ironically, the magnitude of the error of closure, which resulted from a combination of factors, occurred primarily because of the Census Bureau's concerted effort to provide as complete a count as possible. For the 1980 census the Census Bureau, learning from previous experiences, worked to improve such efforts as the following: (1) checking all dwellings reported as vacant; (2) verifying addresses; (3) extensive cross-checking of census rolls against other lists, such as driver's licenses; (4) more intensive canvassing of pool halls and similar areas for people who had no permanent address; and (5) more precensus advertising, much of which was aimed directly at various minority groups.

The estimated number of illegal aliens counted turned out to be a substantial 4.8 million, about 2.3 million of whom were counted in two states, Texas and California (Hauser, 1981). However, undercounts still occurred, especially for minority groups. The Census Bureau's preliminary measurements suggested an undercount of under 2.0 percent for the entire population, a figure that was gradually believed to be near 1.2 percent. Again undercounts were higher for some segments of the population; African-Americans were undercounted proportionately more than whites, for example, with the undercount for Hispanics somewhere in between. The estimated undercount for African-American males was 6.7 percent, compared to 1.5 percent for white males. An error of over 15 percent was found for African-American males between ages 20 and 55. Because the allocation of federal funds often depends on census enumerations, errors of any magnitude can have considerable political and socioeconomic consequences.

Undercounts of African-American males occur for several reasons. Many African-American men in some age categories are highly mobile, hence they are easily missed by census takers. Some other possible reasons for undercounting in certain neighborhoods were outlined in a report by an enumeration supervisor who stated:

> One of the addresses to which I obtained access had been marked in the listing book as follows: "Will not return— something thrown at me." The occupants of the house with the "vacant" apartments were a sullen group. The bleary-eyed household head of the first floor apartment had a bottle on the table and glared silently at me while his wife answered the questions. . . . My experiences apparently were prosaic compared to some I learned about from discussion with crew leaders and enumerators; e.g., the lady who blundered into the house full of dope addicts; another lady who had been chased out of a house by a threatening occupant. . . . Although this sort of experience is not a regular occurrence by any means, it need happen to an enumerator only once to be unnerving. Situations in which an enumerator is in real danger probably are rare—but cases of suspicion, sullenness, and vituperative hostility in this area are far above our expected norm. It makes the recruitment and retention of good enumerators exceedingly difficult. . . . The inevitable concomitant of these conditions is under-enumeration—both of persons and housing units (Pritzker and Rothwell, 1967, 14).

1990 Census. Preliminary evidence found that the 1990 Census once again undercounted the population, this time by a figure estimated by the Census Bureau to be between 4.3 million and 6.3 million. This estimate, based on a postcensus survey of some 165,000 households, translates into an undercount of between 1.7 and 2.5 percent, with a figure around 1.8 percent considered likely, somewhat higher than the error in 1980. As in previous censuses, the highest undercounts occurred for minority populations in metropolitan areas. African-American males were undercounted by an estimated 8.0 percent. Despite considerable pressure, especially from large cities, Robert A. Mosbacher, then Secretary of Commerce, refused to make official adjustments of the census counts.

In summary, the collection and use of all types of demographic information is important for governments, social scientists, businesses, and others. Censuses, sample surveys, and vital statistics are essential to the functioning of modern societies. As one begins to use demographic statistics, certain volumes are well worth examining. The United States Bureau of the Census publishes a detailed catalog of census materials that are available, the most recent of which is the *Census Catalog and Guide: 1992.* Also of considerable interest to those seeking population data for the United States is the Census Bureau's *Statistical Abstract of the United States,* which is published annually and contains a wealth of information. Crispell (1990) is an excellent source of information about where to get the demographic data one needs for the United States— although slanted toward business applications of these data, it is a valuable resource for anyone with demographic interests. Somewhat less useful, but still of interest for providing insight into how demographic statistics are used in marketing, is Nichols (1990).

Demographic data outside of the United States are available in a variety of different sources including the United Nations' *Demographic Yearbook,* which is published annually, *The Universal Almanac,* edited by John W. Wright, *World Resources,* an annual volume edited by the World Resources Institute and published by Oxford University Press, and, of course, the censuses of individual countries.

REFERENCES

Anderson, Margo J. (1988) *The American Census: A Social History.* New Haven, CT: Yale University Press.

Blacker, J. G. C. (1969) "Some Unsolved Problems of Census and Demographic Works in Africa," in *International Population Conference.* Vol. 1. London: United Nations.

Bogue, Donald J. (1969) *Principles of Demography.* New York: John Wiley and Sons, Inc.

Caldwell, J. and Igun, A. A. (1971) "An Experiment with Census-Type Age Enumeration in Nigeria," *Population Studies* 25:287–302.

Carr-Saunders, A. M. (1936) *World Population*. Oxford: The Clarendon Press.

Crispell, Diane. (1990) *The Insider's Guide to Demographic Know-How*. 2nd ed. Ithaca, NY: American Demographics Press.

Fitzpatrick, John C., ed. (1939) *The Writings of George Washington*. Washington, D.C.: United States Government Printing Office.

Francese, Peter K. (1979) "The 1980 Census: The Counting of America," *Population Bulletin* 34(4):1–39.

Hauser, Philip M. (1981) "The Census of 1980," *Scientific American* 245(5):53–61.

Hock, Saw Swee. (1967) "Errors in Chinese Age Statistics," *Demography* 4:859–875.

Kahn, E. J., Jr. (1974) *The American People*. Baltimore: Penguin Books, Inc.

Kaplan, Charles P. and Van Valey, Thomas L. (1980) *Census 80: Continuing the Factfinder Tradition*. Washington, D.C.: United States Government Printing Office.

Nichols, Judith E. (1990) *By the Numbers: Using Demographics and Psychographics for Business Growth in the '90s*. Chicago: Bonus Books, Inc.

Petersen, William. (1975) *Population*. 3d ed. New York: MacMillan Publishing Co., Inc.

Pritzker, Leon and Rothwell, N. D. (1967) "Procedural Difficulties in Taking Past Censuses in Predominantly Negro, Puerto Rican, and Mexican Areas," paper presented to a Conference on Social Statistics and the City.

Robey, Bryant. (1989) "Two Hundred Years and Counting: The 1990 Census," *Population Bulletin* 44(1):1–44.

Ryder, N. (1964) "Notes on the Concept of a Population," *American Journal of Sociology* 69:447–463.

Seltzer, William. (1973) *Demographic Data Collection: A Summary of Experience*. New York: The Population Council.

Shryock, H. S., Jr. and Siegel, J. *The Methods and Materials of Demography*. Washington, D.C.: United States Government Printing Office.

Thomlinson, Ralph. (1976) *Population Dynamics: Causes and Consequences of World Demographic Change*. Second Edition. New York: Random House.

United Nations. (1954) Department of Economic Affairs, Statistical Office. *Handbook of Population Methods*. Studies in Methods. Series F, No. 5. New York: United Nations.

United Nations (1967) *Manual IV: Methods of Estimating Basic Demographic Measures from Incomplete Data*. Department of Economic Affairs. Population Studies No. 42. New York: United Nations.

United Nations. (1969) *Principles and Recommendations for the 1970 Population Censuses*. Statistical Papers. Series M, No. 44. New York: United Nations.

United States Bureau of the Census. (1971) *U.S. Census of Population: 1970*. "Number of Inhabitants: United States Summary." PC(1)-A1. Washington, D.C.: United States Government Printing Office.

United States Bureau of the Census. (1990a) *Census '90 Basics*. CPH-I-8. Washington, D.C.: United States Bureau of the Census.

United States Bureau of the Census. (1990b) *TIGER: The Coast-to-Coast Digital Map Data Base.* Washington, D.C.: United States Bureau of the Census.

United States Bureau of the Census. (1992) *Census Catalog and Guide: 1991.* Washington, D.C.: United States Government Printing Office.

Whetten, Nathan L. (1961) *Guatemala: The Land and the People.* Caribbean Series 4. New Haven: Yale University Press.

Willcox, Walter F. (1940) *Studies in American Demography.* Ithaca, N.Y.: Cornell University Press.

Wolter, Kirk M. (1991) "Accounting for America's Uncounted and Miscounted," *Science* 253: 12–15.

Zelinsky, Wilbur. (1966) *A Prologue to Population Geography.* Englewood Cliffs, N.J.: Prentice Hall, Inc.

Chapter 3

Population Distribution and Composition

The analysis of spatial distributions has been a recurrent theme in geography. Determining where phenomena are located and the reasons for their particular locations traditionally has been part of the discipline of geography. In this chapter we look at the "where" of population and analyze some of the reasons behind the spatial distribution of the world's population, the age and sex structure of populations, and examples of the distribution of elderly people and major racial and ethnic populations in the United States.

It is evident that temporal changes have occurred in the world's population. Although the overall trend in population growth was one of gradual increase until approximately 300 years ago, at which time the growth rate became more rapid, there have been large fluctuations in population numbers in specific areas throughout most of human history. Uneven growth over time has been matched by a similarly uneven growth geographically; that is, growth is uneven because the populations of some countries and continents have grown more rapidly than others.

The number of inhabitants in a given area—be it a city, county, state, nation, or any other political unit—is usually one of the first population facts called for before any analysis of the area is undertaken. The numbers of people in specific geographical units are common facts needed for various administrative and research purposes. In many cases first judgments about a country or region are based upon area and size of the population. This information is more than just geographically important. According to Smith and Zopf (1976, 39):

Sociologists must have the facts relative to the numbers of inhabitants in various areas before they can compute indexes of criminality, juvenile delinquency, marriage, and so on; administrators must have them in order to determine how state and federal funds for education, agriculture, road construction, and so on, are to be apportioned among the counties, states, or other political divisions with which they are concerned.

Many other disciplines, as well as many private and public agencies, also need accurate population counts.

▨ GLOBAL DISTRIBUTION PATTERNS

An analysis of the distribution of the world's population, shown in Figure 3–1, reveals some interesting patterns. First, the majority of the earth's inhabitants live on only a small portion of the earth's total land area. Approximately 90 percent of the people live on about 10 percent of the land. Second, over 90 percent of the world's population live north of the equator and less than 10 percent live to the south; however, it must be remembered that over 80 percent of the total land area is located in the Northern Hemisphere. Third, the earth's population is concentrated on the margins of the continents. Estimates are that approximately 70 percent of the world's population live within 1,000 kilometers (600 miles) of the sea and about 67 percent live within 500 kilometers (300 miles). Fourth, population numbers generally decline with altitude. Approximately 56 percent of the world's population live below 200 meters (656 feet), whereas close to 80 percent live below 500 meters (1640 feet) (Clarke, 1972).

Four areas in the world support large population clusters: southern Asia, eastern Asia, western Europe, and east-central North America. The southern Asian cluster includes India, Pakistan, Sri Lanka, Burma, Cambodia, and Thailand, along with related areas. The eastern Asian cluster includes China, Korea, Japan, and the Philippine Islands. Together, these two clusters include over one half of the world's population. More than one person in every five lives in the People's Republic of China. The western European cluster includes most of the Commonwealth of Independent States, the United Kingdom, West Germany, and the other European nations. The last and smallest cluster includes parts of both Canada and the United States.

▨ ECUMENE AND NONECUMENE

One method of describing the distribution of the world's population is to divide the world into two areas, the ecumene and the nonecumene. The *ecumene* is the permanently inhabited portion of the world, whereas the *nonecumene* is the uninhabited or virtually uninhabited portion.

Though at first glance it may seem relatively simple to divide the world into ecumene and nonecumene, it is actually quite difficult because neither the inhabited nor the uninhabited areas of the world are represented by a continuous distribution. The permanent icecaps are relatively easy to identify as part of the nonecumene, but much of the rest of the nonecumene is isolated and either unoccupied or sparsely occupied (Trewartha, 1969). Of the total land area of the earth, approximately 30 percent is

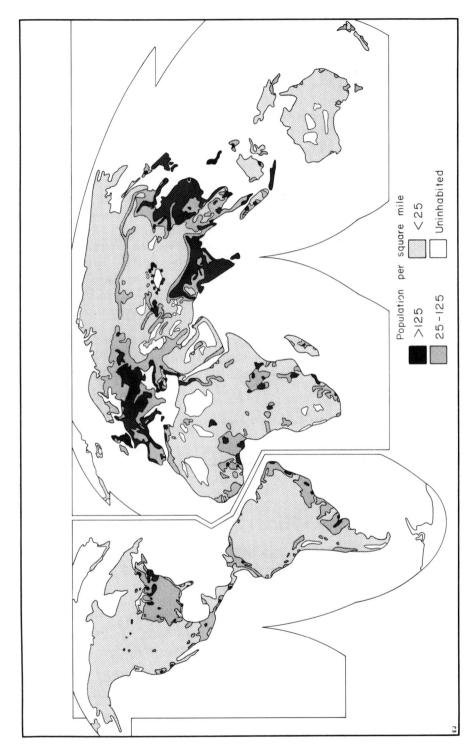

FIGURE 3-1 World Population Density. SOURCE: Data from the Population Reference Bureau. Reprinted by permission.

Population per square mile

>125

25-125

<25

Uninhabited

barren waste, without any significant human occupance. Large areas of forest are also uninhabited. The nonecumene, then, consists of perhaps 35 to 40 percent of the earth's total land area. Thus, a large portion of the earth's surface is primarily without permanent human occupance. Of course the nonecumene is smaller today than it has been in the past, because an established feature of human history has been a progressively expanding ecumene.

Further analysis of the ecumene suggests some interesting regional characteristics. The Anglo-American and western European population concentrations have many similar attributes. For example, the Anglo-American cluster was a direct result of European colonization and thus bears the stamp of European culture. Both of these clusters have advanced technology, high per capita incomes, well-developed regional specialization, and a large proportion of residents living in cities.

By contrast, the two major Asiatic concentrations, with the exception of Japan, still exist mainly in the developing world. However, this picture is changing somewhat though rapid industrialization and other signs of economic development as we move through the 1990s. During the 1980s the People's Republic of China underwent many economic reforms aimed at bettering the economic system. In addition, in the 1980s the term NIC (Newly Industrialized Country) appeared to describe such Asian nations as South Korea, Taiwan, Hong Kong, and Singapore.

Changing economic circumstances in these countries are resulting in changing demographic pictures as well, and they will continue throughout the 1990s. Even now, however, an earlier description of Asia by Trewartha (1969, 89) is still appropriate:

> Here the people are predominantly poor peasant farmers engaged in intensive subsistence agriculture. Population presses closely upon the food supply; poverty and malnutrition are omnipresent. . . . Urban population comprises a small fraction of the total. . . . What is remarkable about the Asiatic population is that it has become so vast and so dense while at the same time remaining overwhelmingly rural.

▓ POPULATION DENSITY

There are several ways to measure population density. The most common measure is a ratio that compares the total population of a place to its total area, a measure referred to as *arithmetic density*. Table 3–1 depicts the population density for the principal regions of the world for 1960, 1975, and 1988. Though Europe and Asia are the most densely settled continents, the average density of the developing countries is more than twice that of the developed countries. For example, during the 1980s the population density in Asia surpassed that in Europe, which previously had been the most densely settled continent.

Although density figures are convenient for analyzing differences in population distribution, they are often misleading. There are about 38 persons for every square kilometer on the earth's land surface. However, Oceania has only 3, Africa 20, and

TABLE 3–1 ■ Land Area and Population Density in the World and Major Area, 1960 and 1975 and 1988

Area	Land Area (1,000 km²)	Inhabitants per km² 1960	1975	1988
World total	135,779ᵃ	22.1	29.4	37.8
More developed regions	60,907	16.0	18.6	19.7
Less developed regions	74,872	27.0	39.5	52.5
Europe	4,936	86.1	96.0	100.6
USSR	22,402	9.6	11.4	12.8
U.S. and Canada	21,515	9.2	11.0	12.6
Oceania	8,509	1.9	2.5	3.1
South Asia	15,775	54.9	80.4	100.2
East Asia	11,756	67.0	85.5	110.8
Africa	30,320	9.0	13.2	20.5
Latin America	20,568	10.5	15.8	20.9

*Not including the Antarctic continent.

SOURCE: United Nations.

TABLE 3–2 ■ Population Density, 1988

	Per Sq. Kilometer	Per Sq. Mile
World Total	37.8	97.9
Africa	20.5	53.1
North America	12.6	32.6
Latin	20.9	54.0
Asia	108.1	280.0
Europe	100.6	260.5
Oceania	3.1	8.0
U.S.S.R.	12.8	33.1
Japan	329.7	854.0
U.S.	26.3	68.1
Australia	2.3	6.0
Netherlands	395.0	1023.9

SOURCE: United Nations.

North America 13, while the more densely settled continents have considerably higher figures, with 101 for Europe and 108 for Asia.

Densities obviously vary on a continental scale, but they vary to a much greater degree with a reduction in the size of areas. For example, Australia has a density of only 2 inhabitants per square kilometer, whereas the Netherlands has 330. Other examples are evident in Table 3–2. Smaller nation-states, and particularly island nation-states, often have dense populations. This fact contrasts with large nation-states like the United States and the old Union of Soviet Socialist Republics (subsequently re-configured and referred to as the Commonwealth of Independent States), which have densities of 13 and 26, respectively.

Population density values, however, have the least significance when large areas with marked environmental differences are involved. Though the average density for the former U.S.S.R. was 13 people per square kilometer, it is important to note that the density in the Asiatic portion of that country was only about 10 percent of the density in the European portion. Arithmetic density is used widely because the necessary data are easily obtained.

A somewhat more refined measure of density is the ratio of population to arable land, a measure referred to as physiological or nutritional density. Arable land is that portion of the earth's land surface that is suitable for tillage, a definition which obviously leaves out some productive areas of nonarable land, such as mining land, natural pasture, forests, and scenic regions. Nutritional density alone, however, cannot account for the great variations in productivity within arable areas that are the result of such environmental characteristics as drainage, soil, and climate. According to Trewartha (1969, 74), nutritional density provides a better indicator than does arithmetic density of the degree of crowding in a region compared with its physical potential for producing food and agricultural raw materials. Japan's arithmetic density in 1960, for example, was 655 per square mile; its nutritional density was an unbelievable 4,680, a fact which suggests the necessity for significant imports of food and vegetable raw material.

Several other density measures have been suggested, including the "standard land unit," which includes varying measures for different modes of land use, and various indices based on the calories produced by a country, the values of national income, and productivity. Some density maps give the ratio of the agricultural population to the amount of arable land, a measure that eliminates nonfarmers. As Beaujeu-Garnier (1966, 32) commented, "All of these methods have their interest in showing up this or that aspect of population density, but none is of undisputed absolute value; and, above all, none escapes from the criticism that, being applied to large and complex areas, it distorts a phenomenon which is essentially localized and variable."

▨ FACTORS IN POPULATION DISTRIBUTION

An analysis of the distribution of the world's population suggests the importance of certain fundamental factors: (1) the historical evaluation and duration of a population in a certain area; (2) the natural environment and its associated aspects such as landforms, soils, precipitation, temperature, and natural resources; and (3) the socioeconomic and technical development of a region. As we shall see, the latter factors have become increasingly important as the Industrial Revolution and modernization in its broadest sense have spread throughout the world. Given an increased technological base, natural environments have less influence on a nation's population distribution. Storm windows and natural gas help mitigate the harshness of cold winters, whereas air-conditioning has turned many desert areas into such delightfully desirable places as Palm Springs, California.

With economic development, employment structures shift from mainly employment in agriculture to increasing proportions of employment in manufacturing and services, both of which tend to concentrate populations in cities. Thus, a major redistribution of population from rural to urban areas usually accompanies modernization. We will discuss this in a later chapter.

SEX AND AGE STRUCTURE

Two of the basic characteristics of any population are sex and age. Both of these factors are important in relation to other population variables such as mortality, morbidity, marriage, fertility, and migration.

Sex Structure

The sex ratio is one of the simplest measures of population structure, and statistics on sex are usually easy to obtain and highly accurate. There is no ambiguity about the meaning of female and male and little need to misrepresent such information. The sex ratio is defined as the number of males per 100 females. For example, the sex ratio for the population of the United States in 1989 was

$$\text{Sex ratio} = \frac{\text{number of males}}{\text{number of females}} \times 100$$

$$= \frac{121,445,000}{127,317,000} \times 100 = 95.38.$$

A sex ratio of 100 indicates equal numbers of males and females in a population; a ratio above 100 indicates more males than females; and a ratio below 100 indicates more females than males. The basic factors that determine the sex ratio are (1) death rate differences between the sexes, (2) net migration rate differences between the sexes, and (3) the sex ratio of newborn infants.

All modern censuses calculate the proportions and numbers of females and males in the population. The first census in the United States determined the sex structure of the white population. Since 1820 the sex structure of all segments of the population has been tabulated. Because of the relative simplicity of the question pertaining to sex, census officials from 1930 on have concluded that the data on sex structure is the most reliable of all population data included in their tabulations.

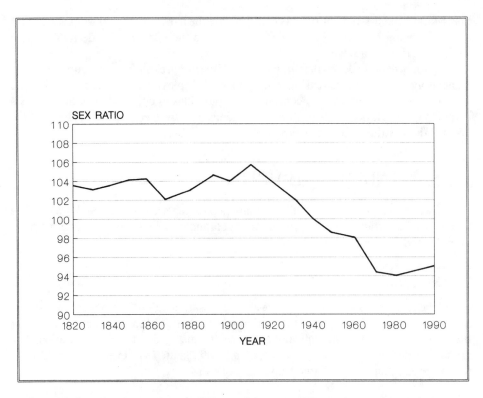

▨ **FIGURE 3–2** Sex Ratio of the Population of the United States from 1820–1990. SOURCE: Data from *Statistical Abstract of the United States*.

Examining sex ratios and correlating them with other demographic factors such as births, deaths, and migration reveal some basic facts: (1) the sex ratio at birth is relatively high (105) for the United States and for most of the rest of the world; (2) in general, females have lower death rates than males at all ages; (3) females outnumber males in migration from rural to urban areas and in other short-distance migrations; and (4) males outnumber females in long-distance moves.

The sex ratio of the U.S. population has varied greatly from place to place, time to time, and group to group. Figure 3–2 depicts the changes in the sex ratio of the United States from 1820 to 1990. The sex ratio of 94.2 in 1980 was the lowest in American history. According to Guttentag and Secord (1983, 32), "Low sex ratios, signifying a shortage of men, provide impetus for feminist movements. This is not to say that low sex ratios can bring movements about by themselves, but rather that they provide some facilitating conditions." Their work raised some challenging questions about sex ratios and society, though no geographers to our knowledge have followed up on their ideas.

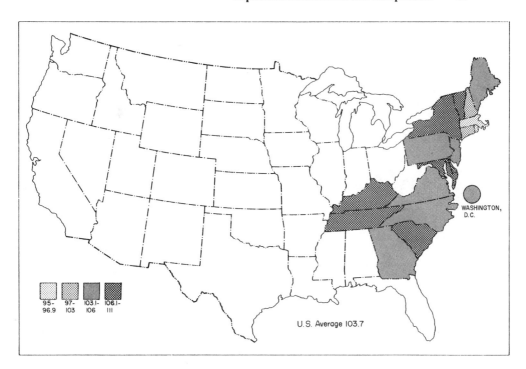

■ **FIGURE 3–3** Sex Ratios for the White Population, 1790.

Changes in the sex ratio over time in the United States are primarily due to changing immigration patterns. The all-time high of 106, which occurred in 1910, was the result of large numbers of immigrants, primarily males. The low sex ratio of 1870 was primarily due to the decline in immigration during the Civil War and the large numbers of men killed in battle.

A state-by-state analysis of the sex ratio of the United States reveals some interesting changes in spatial patterns over time. Figure 3–3 shows sex ratios for each state in 1790. These sex ratios, however, represent only the white population. The sex ratio for all of the states was 103.7. A state-by-state analysis reveals that higher sex ratios were found in what were then considered to be frontier areas, whereas the lower sex ratios were found in the more settled areas of New England.

This same pattern also appears in Figure 3–4 for 1850 although these data include both white and nonwhite residents. Once again, the frontier areas are male-dominated, whereas the more densely settled and urbanized areas have a lower sex ratio. The rush of males to the mining areas of California during the Gold Rush of 1849 is apparent in the extremely large sex ratio of that state (1222.9). It is also interesting to note that the lowest sex ratio, 95.0, is found in Washington, D.C., though in general urban areas have lower sex ratios than rural areas.

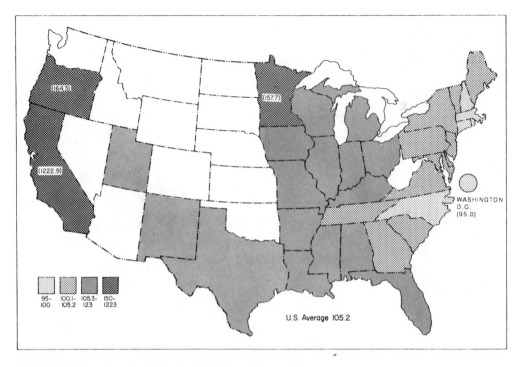

▨ **FIGURE 3–4** Sex Ratios for the Total Population, 1850.

Figure 3–5 shows sex ratios at the turn of the century. The sex ratio of the United States was still above 100, mainly because of the large influx of immigrants. Opening up the western frontier brought about significant imbalances in the sex ratio. The westward movement was largely dominated by males, making the sex ratios in several western states extremely high, whereas large numbers of females were left behind in the South and East. Washington, D.C., once again had the lowest sex ratio. Utah, although a western state, had a much lower sex ratio than the other western states, undoubtedly because of the unique settlement patterns of Utah and the role of the Mormon Church. Migration to Utah often involved families, whereas single males were most evident in early migrations to the other western states.

With the passing of the frontier came a reduction in the sex ratio for the United States as a whole, as well as a decline in sex ratios for western states, as is apparent in Figure 3–6 for 1940. Not only is there a drop in the sex ratios in the West, but also the sex ratios for various parts of the country tend to cluster close to the national average.

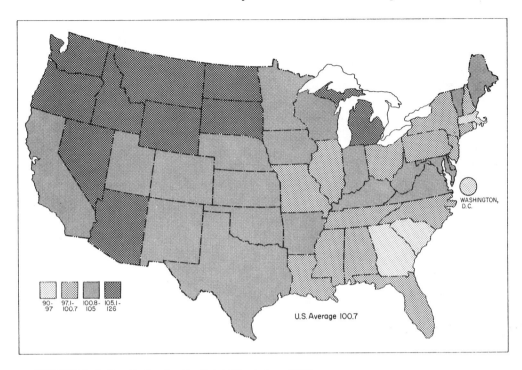

▨ **FIGURE 3–5** Sex Ratios for the Total Population, 1900.

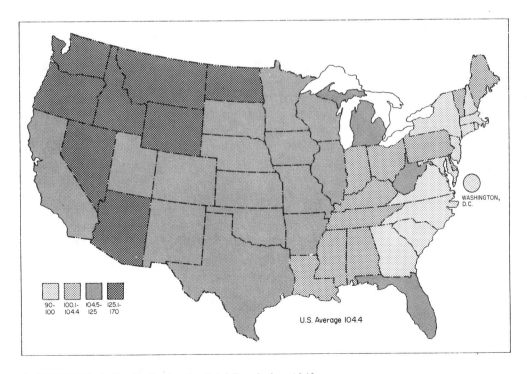

▨ **FIGURE 3–6** Sex Ratios for the Total Population, 1940.

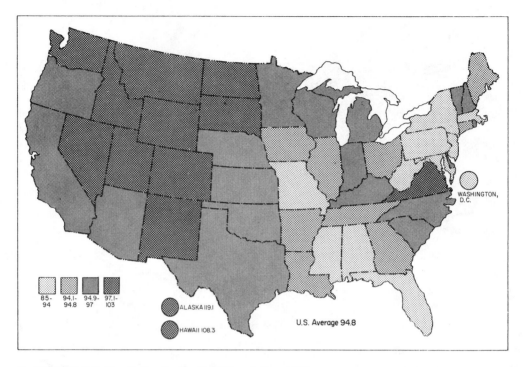

▨ **FIGURE 3–7** Sex Ratios for the Total Population, 1970.

Figure 3–7 illustrates sex ratios in 1970. It is apparent that all sections of the United States are well settled and that only relatively small regional differences exist within the country. The sex ratio for all sections of the country is close to the national average of 94.8. The only exceptions are Alaska and Hawaii, with Alaska having the highest sex ratio of all states. Alaska can be considered the last frontier; and we would expect it to have a higher proportion of males, again because of the dominance of males in migration to frontier-type areas. Although the sex ratio increased slightly between 1970 and 1990, the spatial pattern of sex ratios in 1990, as shown in Figure 3–8, differed little from the pattern in 1970.

International Variations in Sex Structure

Though males outnumber females at birth, females tend to outlive males, especially in regions providing good medical care. Thus, we would expect to find lower sex ratios in the developed countries and higher ones in the developing areas, where maternal mortality and fertility are still high.

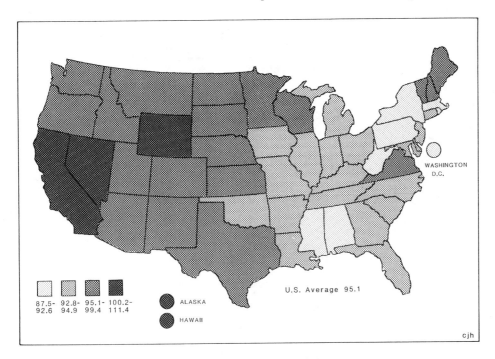

▨ **FIGURE 3–8** Sex Ratios for the Total Population, 1990. SOURCE: Data from United States Bureau of the Census.

Few countries in the world have sex ratios higher than 105 or lower than 90, as shown in Table 3–3. The reasons for high sex ratios include such variables as in-migration of males, high female mortality due to poor health facilities, undercounts of females, and high fertility, with its resulting young age composition. In some areas, such as West Malaysia, Hong Kong, and Cuba, migration and the influx of laborers have been important variables determining sex ratios. However, in other areas, such as Libya, Pakistan, India, and Sri Lanka, migration was not important; high sex ratios in these areas are probably due to higher mortality rates for females than for males.

The countries with low sex ratios are primarily found in Europe. These low ratios can be traced partly to large numbers of emigrants, mainly males, and to the heavy loss of males during World War II.

Age Structure

Much of a population's economic and social behavior is determined by the proportion of people found in various age groups. Smith and Zopf (1976, 149) suggested the following three reasons why a knowledge of the age distribution of a population is basic in nearly all population analyses.

TABLE 3–3 ▪ Sex Ratios of 105 or More

Country	Sex Ratio
Libyan Arab Republic	108
Cuba	105
Sri Lanka	108
Hong Kong	106
India	106
Iran	107
West Malaysia	106
Pakistan	111
Albania	105
Sex Ratios of 90 or less	
Malawi	90
Austria	87
German Federal Republic	89
German Democratic Republic	84
U.S.S.R.	85

SOURCE: United Nations, *Demographic Yearbook,*
27th Issue (New York: United Nations,

First, age is one of the most fundamental of one's own personal characteristics; what one is, thinks, does, and needs is closely related to the number of years since birth. Second, groups are determinants of primary social and economic importance in any society. Third, the qualified student of population must possess the technical skills needed to bring out the significant features of the age composition of a population with which he or she is concerned and also those features required to make the proper allowances or corrections the student may attempt.

It must be kept in mind that age structure is closely related to other demographic characteristics, such as the birth rate, death rate, migration rate, and marriage rate. As a result, students, researchers, and others must use caution when making comparisons and analyses involving these characteristics.

Factors Affecting Age Structure

Although many factors determine the age structure of a national population, the primary variable is the birth rate. A population with a high birth rate will have a large proportion of young people, whereas a population with a low birth rate will have a smaller proportion of young people. The role mortality plays in determining the age structure of a national population is best described by Coale (1964, 49) as follows:

Most of us would probably guess that populations have become older because the death rate has been reduced, and hence people live longer on the average. Just what is the role of mortality in determining the age distribution of a population? The

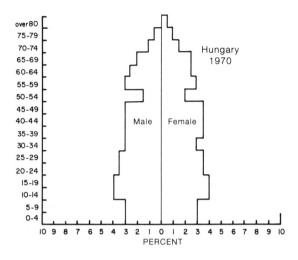

■ **FIGURE 3–9** Population Pyramid for Hungary, 1970.

answer is surprising—mortality affects the age distribution much less than does fertility, and in the opposite direction from what most of us would think. Prolongation of life by reducing death rates has the perverse effect of making the population somewhat younger.

Migration generally has little or no impact on the sex structure of national populations because most countries have restrictions on international migrations. However, for subnational populations—for example, the populations of states, counties, cities, or even particular districts within cities—migration often has a considerable impact on age structure. Migration is generally age-selective; that is, almost all types of migrations involve a large proportion of young people. An area that has experienced a great deal of out-migration usually has fewer young people in the 20 to 40 age group, whereas a region with a significant amount of in-migration may show an excess of young adults.

Catastrophes such as famine, pestilence, or war may also influence the age structure of a region. For example, war has a twofold effect on the age structure. First, many young adults are combatants in a war and are killed. Second, there is usually a sharp decline in the birth rate during a war.

Population Pyramids

A population pyramid is a useful aid in examining the age structure of a population. It also provides information about the social attributes of the population concerned.

As illustrated in Figure 3–9, a population pyramid is really two bar graphs placed back to back, with the vertical center line representing zero. The number or percentage of people in each age group, by sex, is indicated with horizontal bars, while the vertical

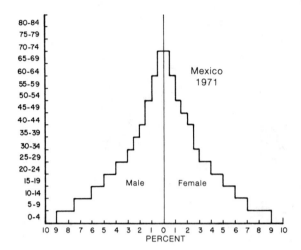

▓ **FIGURE 3–10** Population Pyramid for Mexico, 1971.

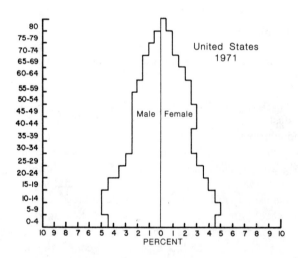

▓ **FIGURE 3–11** Population Pyramid for the United States, 1971.

axis gives the different age groups, usually in 5-year intervals. The shapes of population pyramids vary according to the country or community and the time period used. A pyramid for a particular country represents the demographic history of that country over the past two or three generations.

A national population with a large number of children, as the result of a high birth rate, would have a pyramid with a wide base, like that shown in Figure 3–10; whereas the pyramid for a population with a low birth rate would have a small base, like the pyramid for the United States in Figure 3–11. The pyramid is also affected

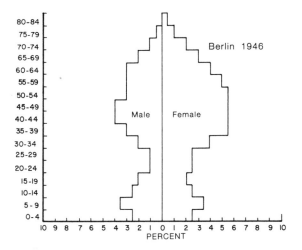

▧ **FIGURE 3–12** Population Pyramid for Berlin, 1946.

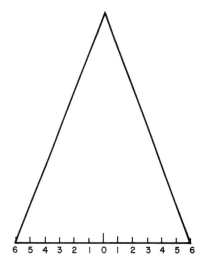

▧ **FIGURE 3–13** Population Pyramid with Regular Triangular Shape.

by death rates, though usually to a lesser extent. In wartime the death rate for certain age groups may rise considerably, and the bands representing those age groups will be shorter. For example, the population pyramid for Berlin (Figure 3–12) shows a noticeable lack of men in the 20 to 29 age brackets, most likely due to World War II and the mortality among young men who fought in the war. Finally, selective migration can also change the shape of the pyramid.

It is possible to recognize certain broad categories of population structure by comparing the shapes of pyramids for different countries. Four types of population structures can be recognized, each coinciding with a particular cultural development. The first type (Figure 3–13) is a pyramid with a regular triangular shape, typical of a country with high birth and death rates. Few countries today have this type of pyramid, but it was common for most countries during the seventeenth and eighteenth centuries.

The second type of population pyramid has a narrow top, wide base, and concave sides (Figure 3–14). This structure represents a country with a falling death rate, particularly in the youngest age category, and a high birth rate. This pyramid is typical for most of the developing countries in Africa, Asia, and Latin America.

A beehive shape characterizes a third type of population pyramid (Figure 3–15) and indicates a relatively stable population with low birth rates, low death rates, and a high median age. Most European countries have pyramids of this type; England, Wales, and Sweden are good examples. The final pyramid type (illustrated in Figure 3–16) represents a country that has had a rapid decrease in fertility, accounting for the tapered bottom of the pyramid.

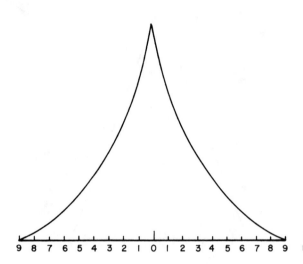

▩ **FIGURE 3–14** Population Pyramid with Concave Sides.

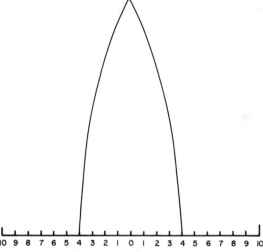

▩ **FIGURE 3–15** Population Pyramid with Beehive Shape.

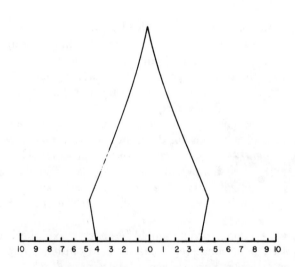

▩ **FIGURE 3–16** Population Pyramid with Tapered Base.

CENSUS TRACTS FOR PHILADELPHIA — 1970

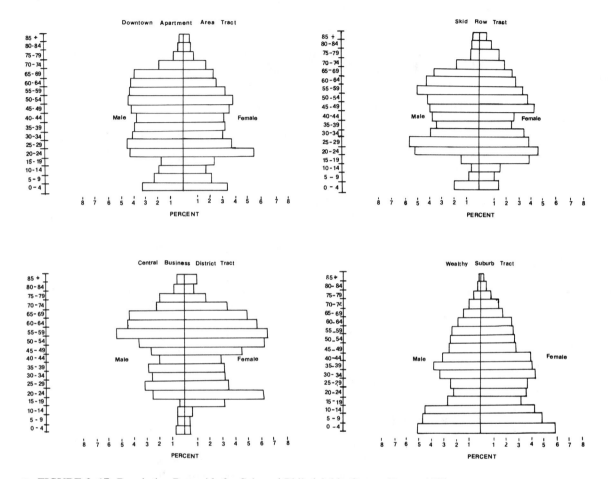

▨ **FIGURE 3–17** Population Pyramids for Selected Philadelphia Census Tracts, 1970.

Changes in birth and death rates are reflected in the shape of a population pyramid. Deviations from the normal Christmas-tree shapes can be found for areas that have few women and/or children, as shown in Figure 3–17.

Dependency Ratio

The dependency ratio is a simple statistic that measures the role of age composition on the productivity level of a population by comparing the proportion of the population in the nonproductive ages with those in the working ages. It assumes that people between ages 20 and 64 are the productive segment of the population, whereas those under 20 and over 64 years are the dependent segment of the population. It may be calculated as follows:

$$\text{dependency ratio} = \frac{\text{population under 20 plus population 65 years and over}}{\text{population 20–64 years}} \times 100$$

The purpose of the dependency ratio is to measure the number of dependents that each 100 people in the productive years must support. Thus, some nations have a high dependency ratio because of a large number of people over age 64, whereas other nations have high ratios because of a large number of children.

In the absence of comparable international data on economic activity, the dependency ratio is often used to reflect variations in economic dependency. This is the case even though some people in the dependent age range are producers, and many persons in the productive age range, particularly in Western societies, are economically dependent.

According to an analysis by the Population Reference Bureau (1977, 6):

> In general, dependency ratios are much less favorable in developing nations, due to their relatively high fertility levels; thus large population proportions are under 15 years of age. In Ghana, for example, where 47 percent of the population is under 15 and only 4 percent of the population is over 64, there are 104 persons in the "dependent ages" for each 100 persons in the "working ages." On the other hand, in the highly industrialized country of Japan, where 24 percent of the population is under 15 and 8 percent is over 64, there are only 47 persons in the "dependent ages" for each 100 persons in the "working ages."

World Patterns of Age Structure

A world view of age structure reveals some interesting patterns, as we see in Figures 3–18 and 3–19. The world's youngest populations are found in the developing nations of Africa, Asia, and Latin America, where almost half of the population in many countries is under 15 years of age. The elderly comprise only 4 percent of the entire populations of Africa, Asia, and Latin America. For example, in Tanzania, only 2 percent of the population is over 64, while 49 percent is under 15. In 1992 the following countries were among those with the highest proportions of persons under 15: Gaza (49 percent), Benin (46 percent), Ghana (45 percent), Jordan (48 percent), Syria (49 percent), Niger (49 percent), Swaziland (46 percent), Honduras (46 percent), and Nicaragua (47 percent).

Europe ranks as the world's most elderly continent with 16 percent of its population aged 65 and over. The proportion of elderly is even higher for several individual nations of Europe. For example, in 1992 the countries with the highest proportion of

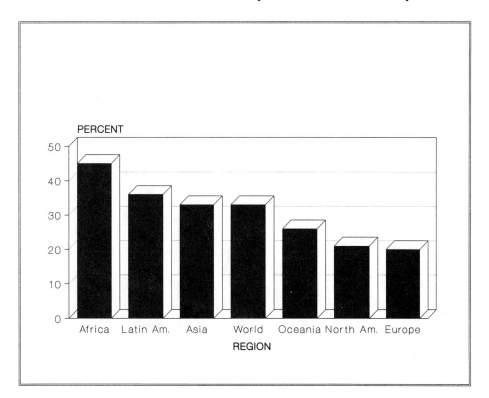

■ **FIGURE 3–18** Population Under Age 15—World and Major Regions. SOURCE: Data from *1992 World Population Data Sheet*. (Washington, D.C.: Population Reference Bureau, Inc.).

persons 65 and over included Germany (15 percent), Sweden (18 percent), Austria (15 percent), Norway (16 percent), United Kingdom (16 percent), Belgium (15 percent), France (14 percent), Switzerland (15 percent), and Denmark (16 percent).

Baby Boomers in the United States

Following World War II, the United States, as well as most European and many other countries, experienced an increase in fertility. In the United States the cohort that is generally recognized as the "Baby Boomers" includes children born between 1946 and 1964. In 1946 there were 20 percent more babies born in the United States than in the previous year, a not unexpected result of the return home of missing husbands and lovers. However, one year was apparently not enough to make up for the

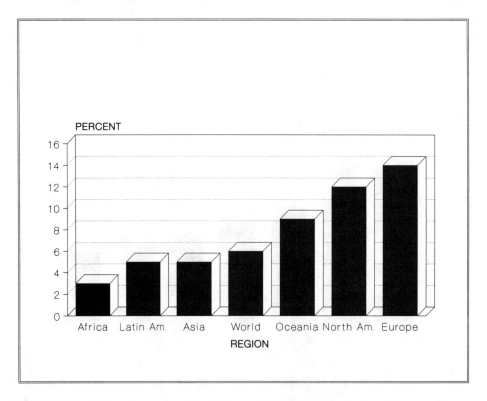

▨ **FIGURE 3–19** Population Age 65 and Over—World and Major Regions. SOURCE: Data from *1992 World Population Data Sheet.* (Washington, D.C.: Population Reference Bureau, Inc.).

war years, and Americans went on something of a fertility binge, totally unexpected by demographers and other social scientists. At the same time, it was not a return to the high fertility of earlier periods; rather, it was a larger percentage of women marrying and having two or three children.

The sustained period of earlier marriages and higher fertility, so different from what occurred in the depression years of the 1930s, was at least partly a response to better economic conditions after World War II. Bouvier and de Vita (1991, 7) also noted that "Because men's wages were rising during this period, women felt little economic pressure to enter a male-dominated work world and thus were likely to be ambivalent about the desirability of 'yet another child' and apt to 'relax contraceptive vigilance.'" Interestingly, the end of the baby boom coincides rather well with the introduction of oral contraceptives in the mid-1960s.

By the time the leading edge of the baby boom cohort began to reach public schools in the early 1950s, it was apparent that this cohort was going to create unprecedented problems. These ranged from the need for more schools during their early

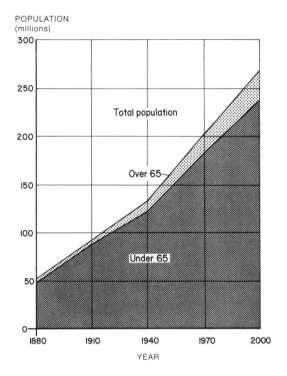

▨ **FIGURE 3–20** Population in the United States Over and Under 65 Years Old, 1880 Through 1970 and Projected to 2000. SOURCE: The Commission on Population Growth and the American Future. *Demographic and Social Aspects of Population Growth* (Washington, D.C.: U.S. Government Printing Office, 1972), pp. 52–53.

years to their retirement needs, which may become a serious problem after the turn of the century. Though the first baby boomers will not turn 65 until 2011, those taking early retirement should begin to show up in larger numbers a decade earlier.

Having been supplemented over the years by immigration, as if their numbers were not large enough, in 1990 the baby boomers numbered around 80 million, or nearly one third of the population of the United States. At that time they ranged in age from 26 to 44 and formed a prime component of everything from the workforce to the housing market.

Elderly in the United States

As we approach the twenty-first century most Americans can expect to attain the Biblical age of three score years and ten. However, an analysis of the elderly in the United States over the past 90 years shows that only recently have most Americans been able to reach this age, as is illustrated in Figure 3–20.

TABLE 3–4 ▦ Population 65 and Older in the
United States: 1900–1990

Year	Population*	Population Increase from the Preceding Decade	Percent of Population Increase from the Preceding Decade
1900	3,099		
1910	3,986	887	28.6
1920	4,929	943	23.7
1930	6,705	1,776	36.0
1940	9,031	2,326	34.7
1950	12,397	3,366	37.3
1960	16,659	4,262	34.4
1970	20,156	3,497	20.4
1980	24,830	4,674	23.2
1990	29,835	5,005	20.2

SOURCE: Leon Bouvier, Elinore Atlee and Frank McVeigh. (1975) "The Elderly
in America," *Population Bulletin,* 30(3):4, courtesy of the Population Reference
Bureau, Inc., Washington, D.C. Newest figures from the United States Bureau
of the Census.

In the United States, being elderly, or old, is usually defined according to the
Federal social security program as having reached 65 years of age. The elderly population of the United States has risen consistently since 1900, when slightly more than
3 million Americans were aged 65 and over. The elderly population increased nearly
threefold to 9 million by 1940 and to nearly 30 million in 1990 (Table 3–4). In 90 years
there was almost a 1,000 percent increase in the elderly population, compared with
just over a 325 percent increase in the total population, from 76 million to 250 million,
during the same time period.

The rapid increase in the elderly population in the United States is the result of
three major factors. First, high fertility rates occurred during the late nineteenth and
early twentieth centuries. Because of this large birth cohort, there has been an increased number of people in the 65 to 75-year age bracket. Second, a marked decline
in mortality has occurred over the past 75 years, mainly because of advances in sanitation and medicine, which allowed more people to live to age 65. Presently, around
75 percent of newborn children are expected to reach age 65, whereas in 1900 only 39
percent of newborns were expected to reach that milestone.

Third, large increases in the elderly population in recent years were due to the
high level of immigration prior to World War I. These migrants were primarily young
adults, and thus a large cohort of that age group was added to the population. Population projections by the Bureau of the Census forecast a continuing increase in the
numbers of elderly in the population until at least the year 2030. There are expected
to be 31.7 million by 2000, 34.9 million by 2010, 39.2 million by 2020, and 51.4 million

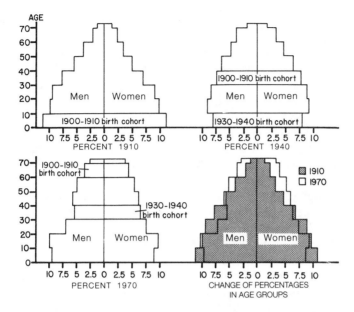

▪ **FIGURE 3–21** Age Pyramids, or Percentages in Age Groups, for the United States in 1910, 1940, and 1970. SOURCE: United States Bureau of the Census. (1972) *General Population Characteristics,* Final Report PC(1)-B1 United States Summary (Washington, D.C.: U.S. Government Printing Office), pp. 1–276.

elderly by the year 2030. These figures should be reasonably accurate projections because the future elderly have already been born, though immigration may have a significant impact on the later figures.

Not only has the total number of elderly been increasing rapidly, but the proportion of the elderly in the United States also has increased. In 1900 only about one out of every 25 Americans was 65 or older, while in 1990 about 1 out of 8 Americans was elderly. The proportion of the elderly in a population is affected by variations in the numbers of people in other age categories. The increase in the proportion of the elderly is primarily attributed to declining fertility rather than to the lowering of the death rate. Changes in the proportion of the elderly over the past 60 years are illustrated in Figure 3–21.

Spatial Distribution of the Elderly

Although the elderly population in the United States has increased dramatically within the past century, these increases have not been distributed evenly within the country. The North Central states and the Northeast region have larger proportions of the elderly than do the West and South. States with smaller proportions of the elderly either have populations with relatively high fertility (South Carolina, Georgia,

Louisiana, New Mexico, and Utah) or have received large numbers of relatively young in-migrants from other areas of the country (Maryland, Colorado, and Nevada). States with over 12 percent of their populations classified as elderly include Arkansas, Nebraska, Iowa, South Dakota, Missouri, and Florida.

Many similar states have lost a considerable number of young people due to out-migration, whereas others have an influx of retirees, which increases the proportion of the elderly. In both cases the age distribution becomes older. Nebraska and Florida are states that have similar proportions of the aged but for very different reasons. Bouvier, et al. (1975, 8) noted that in 1970, 14.6 percent of the population of Florida and 12.4 percent of Nebraska were 65 years or over. Between 1960 and 1970, however, the aged population increased by almost 80 percent in Florida but by only 12 percent in Nebraska. The high proportion of the elderly in Florida is explained by in-migration of the old; in Nebraska it is caused by the exodus of the young in addition to the longevity of the state's population.

Within America's metropolitan areas, the distribution of the elderly also presents some interesting patterns. Cowgill (1978), for example, discussed "gray ghettos" in many of the older core areas of major cities. Goodman (1987) used Lorenz curves and Gini coefficients to study the distribution of the elderly in three American cities: Baltimore, Philadelphia, and Pittsburgh. Although Pittsburgh had the largest elderly population, Goodman found that the elderly were more concentrated in the central cities of Philadelphia and Baltimore than they were in Pittsburgh. They were most concentrated in Baltimore.

However, as Soldo (1980, 13) earlier noted, "This does not reflect intentional discrimination; rather, while their children have moved to the suburbs, the elderly have stayed behind." In small towns and rural areas the elderly are also often present in relatively high proportions for the same reasons; those who left such places are typically young.

"Contrary to popular opinion," Soldo (1980, 13) noted, "relatively few Americans move during their retirement years." Most of those who do move travel only a short distance away. Those who move longer distances make areas in the Sunbelt their primary destinations, especially in California, Arizona, and Florida. Even these migration streams are selective, however, because most of the elderly people involved are the "young," more affluent elderly, those most able to make such moves (Soldo, 1980).

Race and Ethnicity in the United States

Race and ethnicity are important aspects of population composition, especially in societies that are large, diverse, and undergoing differential demographic changes. Even though the United States is hardly the only such country, it serves as a useful example. Geographers Allen and Turner (1988) have provided the most ambitious look at ethnicity in America ever undertaken. In particular they noted (Allen and Turner,

1988, p. 205) that "Differences in values, occupational directions, lifestyles, religious identities, and patterns of socializing based on ethnic background may sometimes be obvious but are more likely to be subtle and hidden from public view . . . ethnicity has played a major role in shaping social structures, patterns of political and economic competition, religion, lifestyles, food preferences, and the processes of cultural change in America."

The United States has always been shaped by changing racial and ethnic patterns, and its future will be shaped by them as well. Though less detailed than the work of Allen and Turner, McKee (1985) also has provided some useful geographic perspectives on ethnic patterns in modern America. Aside from these recent works on racial and ethnic groups in the United States by geographers, sociologists and others have much to offer as well. Some recent examples include Fuchs (1990), Gonzales (1990), and Gonzales (1991).

Any discussion of ethnicity brings with it problems of definition and measurement, many of which are beyond the scope of this brief geographic survey. For example, Glazer (1983, 234) recognized many of the definitional problems and noted:

> The term "ethnic" refers to a social group that consciously shares some aspects of a common culture and is defined primarily by descent. It is part of a family of terms of similar or related meaning, such as "minority group," "race," and "nation," and it is not often easy to make sharp distinctions between these terms. "Race" of course refers to a group that is defined by common descent and has some typical physical characteristics. Where one decides that a "race" ends and an "ethnic group" begins is not easy.

Although distinctions can be made at many scales, the Census Bureau data and classifications are used for the discussions that follow; we need to keep in mind, however, that imperfections exist in both the data and the categories. Though we wish to focus on geographic aspects of ethnicity in this section, readers should also keep in mind the following comment by Weeks (1992, 280) that "To be a member of a subordinate racial, ethnic, or religious group in any society is to be at jeopardy of impaired life chances."

Distributions of racial and ethnic groups are important and need to be studied at various scales, from national to intra-urban, but space constraints allow us here to consider only the national distributions of the three largest such groups in the United States: African-Americans, Hispanics, and Asians and Pacific Islanders. The overall racial and ethnic composition of the United States in 1990 is shown in Figure 3–22.

African-Americans. According to the 1990 Census there were almost 30 million African-Americans in the United States although as a group they were certainly undercounted. They comprise 12.1 percent of the nation's population and remain the largest minority group in the country. Their share of the United States population has changed over time, from a high of 19.3 percent in 1790 to a low of 9.7 percent in 1930.

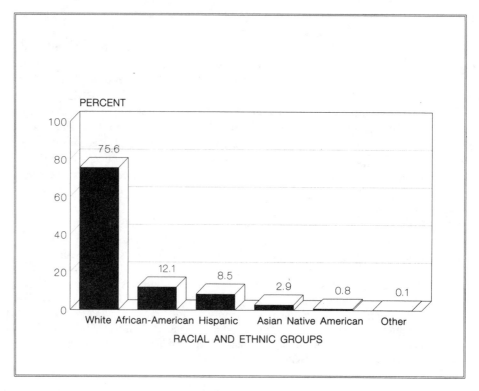

▨ **FIGURE 3–22** Population Composition of the United States, 1990, by Racial and Ethnic Groups. SOURCE: Data from *Statistical Abstract of the United States, 1991.*

Figure 3–23 shows the distribution of African-Americans in 1990. Slightly over half of all African-Americans, almost 53 percent, still live in the South. Around 57 percent live in the central cities of metropolitan areas, and their struggle for equality in America has still not been fulfilled. As Weeks (1992, 280) noted, "Being of African origin in the United States is associated with higher probabilities of death, lower levels of education, lower levels of occupational status, lower incomes, and higher levels of marital disruption than for the white population."

Although Mississippi currently has the highest proportion of African-Americans, 35.6 percent of the state's population, New York, California, and Texas, respectively, have the largest absolute populations of African-Americans—over 2 million in each state. The largest metropolitan concentrations of African-Americans are found in New York, Chicago, Los Angeles, Philadelphia, and Washington, D.C.

Hispanics. The 1990 Census counted somewhat more than 22.3 million persons of Hispanic origin in the United States, meaning they comprise about 8.9 percent of the nation's population. Though these persons are primarily of Latin American origin,

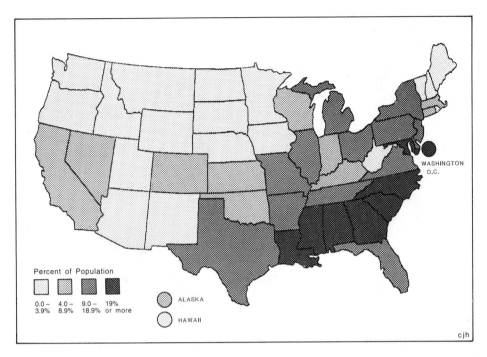

■ **FIGURE 3–23** Resident Black Population, 1990. SOURCE: Data from *Statistical Abstract of the United States, 1991*.

as a group they are far from homogeneous. More than 13 million come from Mexico, while nearly 3 million are from Puerto Rico, 1 million from Cuba, and the remaining 5 million or so from a variety of other nations. Every Spanish-speaking country in the world is represented in the count.

During the 1980s, a higher fertility for Hispanics than for non-Hispanic populations plus continued immigration raised the number of Hispanics in the United States by 53 percent. The geographical distribution of Hispanics, shown in Figure 3–24, differs considerably from that of African-Americans. The primary concentrations are in the West and Southwest (primarily of Mexican origin), New York (primarily of Puerto Rican origin), and Florida (primarily of Cuban origin). California and Texas together contain more than half of all Hispanics in the United States, with over one in every three in California alone. The major metropolitan concentrations of Hispanics are in Los Angeles, New York, and Miami.

Though average incomes for Hispanics are higher than those for African-Americans, they lag somewhat behind in education, mainly because of language problems. Hispanic fertility is above that for African-Americans, and continued immigration from Latin America is likely to sustain that differential for the foreseeable future.

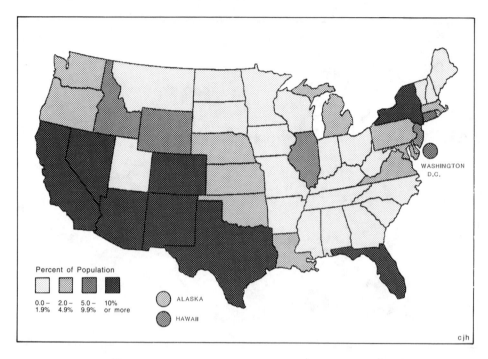

▒ **FIGURE 3–24** Resident Hispanic Population, 1990. SOURCE: Data from *Statistical Abstract of the United States, 1991.*

Asians and Pacific Islanders.   According to the 1990 Census there are slightly more than 7.2 million Asians and Pacific Islanders in the United States, and they comprise almost 3 percent of the total population. Their numbers more than doubled during the 1980s, primarily as a result of immigration. As with Hispanics, Asians and Pacific Islanders hardly form a homogeneous group; Chinese, Filipino, and Japanese, respectively, are the most numerous Asians in the United States.

Figure 3–25 shows the distribution of Asians and Pacific Islanders in the United States. Geographically, the heaviest concentrations are in the West, with the largest metropolitan concentrations in Los Angeles, San Francisco, New York, and Honolulu. As a group, Asians and Pacific Islanders have the highest median family income in the United States, along with the highest educational attainment and lowest unemployment. However, within the group there are considerable differences; Japanese, Chinese, and Koreans tend to be at the high end, whereas Indochinese refugees and some Pacific Islander groups tend to be at the low end, often living below the poverty line.

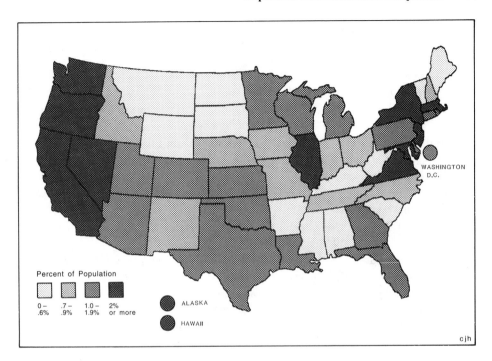

WASHINGTON
D.C.

Percent of Population

0 –
.6%   .7 –
.9%   1.0 –
1.9%   2%
or more

ALASKA

HAWAII

cjh

▩ **FIGURE 3–25** Resident Asian Population, 1990. SOURCE: Data from *Statistical Abstract of the United States, 1991.*

REFERENCES

Allen, James Paul and Turner, Eugene James. (1988) *We the People: An Atlas of America's Ethnic Diversity.* New York: Macmillan Publishing Company.

Beaujeu-Garnier, J. (1966) *Geography of Population.* New York: St. Martin's Press.

Bouvier, Leon, Atlee, Elinore, and McVeigh, Frank. (1975) "The Elderly in America," *Population Bulletin* 30(3): 1–36.

Bouvier, Leon and de Vita, Carol J. (1991) "The Baby Boom—Entering Midlife," *Population Bulletin* 46(3):1–34.

Bouvier, Leon F. (1992) *Peaceful Invasions: Immigration and Changing America.* Lanham, MD: University Press of America, Inc.

Clarke, John I. (1972) *Population Geography.* Second Edition. Oxford: Pergamon Press.

Coale, Ansley J. (1964) "How a Population Ages or Grows Younger," in Ronald Freedman, ed., *Population: The Vital Revolution*. Garden City, New York: Anchor Books, Doubleday and Co., Inc., pp. 47–58.

Cowgill, Donald O. (1978) "Residential Segregation by Age in American Metropolitan Areas," *Journal of Gerontology* 33:446–453.

Fuchs, Lawrence H. (1990) *The American Kaleidoscope: Race, Ethnicity, and the Civic Culture*. Hanover, NH: The University Press of New England.

Glazer, Nathan. (1983) *Ethnic Dilemma*. New York: Hawthorne Press.

Gonzales, Juan L., Jr. (1990) *Racial and Ethnic Groups in America*. Dubuque, Iowa: Kendall/Hunt Publishing Company.

Gonzales, Juan L., Jr. (1991) *The Lives of Ethnic Americans*. Dubuque, Iowa: Kendall/Hunt Publishing Company.

Goodman, Allen C. (1987) "Using Lorenz Curves to Characterise Urban Elderly Populations," *Urban Studies* 24:77–80.

Guttentag, Marcia and Secord, Paul F. (1983) *Too Many Women? The Sex Ratio Question*. Beverly Hills, CA: SAGE Publications.

McKee, Jesse O. (1985) *Ethnicity in Contemporary America: A Geographical Appraisal*. Dubuque, Iowa: Kendall/Hunt Publishing Company.

Morrill, Richard L. (1990) "Regional Demographic Structure of the United States," *The Professional Geographer* 42:38–53.

Population Reference Bureau. (1977) *Intercom* 5(3):6.

Smith, T. Lynn and Zopf, Paul E., Jr. (1976) *Demography: Principles and Methods*. Port Washington, New York: Alfred Publishing Co., Inc.

Soldo, Beth J. (1980) "America's Elderly in the 1980s," *Population Bulletin* 35(4):1–47.

Trewartha, Glenn J. (1969) *A Geography of Population: World Patterns*. New York: John Wiley and Sons, Inc.

Weeks, John R. (1992) *Population: An Introduction to Concepts and Issues*. 5th ed. Belmont, CA: Wadsworth Publishing Company.

Yaukey, David. (1985) *Demography: The Study of Human Population*. New York: St. Martin's Press.

Chapter 4

Theories of Population Change

Although descriptions of population growth and change are useful, we must move beyond descriptions if we want to gain a better understanding of the causes and consequences of population processes. Also, if we are ever to be able to project the future course of demographic events, we must obtain as much insight as possible into the ways that population variables interact with each other and with nondemographic variables. Furthermore, we need to understand that such interactions may differ from time to time and from place to place.

Models and theories have been developed to enhance our ability to relate demographic change to other demographic variables as well as to social and economic variables that influence population dynamics. In this chapter we consider some theories of population change, the general value of these theories, and their value in helping us to understand future demographic changes, especially in the developing countries.

Two of the most important questions about population today are (1) What will stop rapid population growth? and (2) When will it stop? Very simply, if we assume that population growth must stop, one of three things will have to occur. The birth rate must decline, the death rate must increase, or some combination of the two must happen.

Trying to predict what will stop rapid population growth and when it will stop is a difficult task. Many alternative views of future population growth have been suggested. One alternative suggests a rapid rise in population, followed by a leveling off of population growth before the earth's carrying capacity is reached. Another view proposes a rapid rise in population that overshoots the carrying capacity. This overshoot leads to an increase in the death rate due to lack of food; the increased death rate then leads to a decline in population numbers below the carrying capacity. A similar alternative to the previous one would be an overshoot followed by a long period of continuing fluctuation of population above and below the carrying capacity. Perhaps the most catastrophic consequence of rapid population growth would be an alternative where a rise in population growth leads to a degradation of the earth's carrying capacity, which then brings about a drastic reduction in population size. One final alternative suggests a continual increase in the earth's carrying capacity that stays ahead of population growth most of the time. In a few instances, for relatively short periods of time, population growth may overtake the carrying capacity, but new innovations quickly increase the carrying capacity again. Which of these alternatives will be most appropriate for the future is certainly a matter of speculation. However, several theories and models about population growth have been formulated to explain changes in birth and death rates.

▨ THE ROLE OF THEORY

Theory is an overworked term that often means different things to different people. However, for our purposes a *theory* is a formal conceptual structure composed of laws and rules that bind together the otherwise disparate facts that come from empirical research.

When compared with the physical sciences, the fields of population geography, demography, and other social sciences have been relatively unsuccessful in developing theories, though theory building has rapidly accelerated in the past several decades. According to Abler, Adams, and Gould (1971, 45), "theory is the matrix of all science, and the science with an underdeveloped theoretical arm is very much like a ship without a rudder; it drifts rather aimlessly and gets nowhere except by sheer good fortune."

Geographers, demographers, and others interested in population dynamics share this concern for theory building because it is valuable as a guide in helping them explain existing data and in predicting as yet unobserved data. Achieving such goals, however, has not been easy. As Teitelbaum and Winter (1989, 3–4) reminded us:

> Explanation entails causality, which in turn requires comment on a range of variables hard to define or measure. These variables of necessity include the differential resource endowment across nations; and the character of social conflict along gender, ethnic, national, religious, or class lines. When such issues enter the argument, so does political and philosophical language, replete with moral assumptions and a priori beliefs. Since the discussion of population and resources must entail explanation as well as description, the distinction between ideology and science has never been easy or clear. This is inevitable given the nature of the issues involved and the inordinate difficulty in isolating them from political questions of all kinds.

Classification of Theories

Population theories can be divided into primary and secondary theories. *Primary theories* are those that have been developed mainly for the purpose of explaining demographic behavior, whereas the main purpose of *secondary theories* is the analysis of a much broader class of phenomena that have demographic implications.

For example, a researcher's main interest may be in the area of social class, economic behavior, or some other nondemographic phenomenon; however, the theory that results from the study may have demographic significance. Such a theory would be considered a secondary theory. If our intention is to identify specific factors related to fertility, mortality, or migration, our theory is then a primary one. Because of the relatively recent scientific interest in population, most of the primary theories are largely post-Malthusian. Prior to the late eighteenth century the study of population received little specialized attention and most of the theories related to population were secondary in nature.

Any population theory, either primary or secondary, can be placed into one of two categories: environmental or naturalistic. *Naturalistic* explanations emphasize the role of biological processes and often fail to consider people's adaptive capacities. *Environmental* theories seek explanations of demographic behavior through a variety of processes that may themselves vary in time and space (Thomlinson, 1976).

Emphasis today is placed on environmental theories in which the term environmental refers to both the physical and cultural environment. Though the role played by heredity is recognized, the predominant view is that more human events are controlled by culture. According to Thomlinson (1976, 33), "The simplicity of naturalistic explanations and their implications that we are not responsible for what happens are tempting, but rigorous research has brought us around to more complicated, as well as more realistic, social explanations."

Early Population Theories

It is not surprising that few major philosophers paid much attention to the topic of human population. Most early views on population and the factors affecting fertility originated as folklore. People often thought, according to Eversley (1958, 281), that "high living causes sterility . . . intellectual pursuits and gallantry diminish powers of procreation . . . and idiots breed like rabbits." Such notions as these were held by many throughout history, and similar notions are still held today by a considerable number of people.

Perhaps the most common belief about population prior to Malthus was that population growth was good and decline was bad. As Tomaselli (1989, 8) commented in writing about population concerns in the eighteenth century, "Playing on the fear of population decline in attacking any given social, legal, or political practice or, conversely, emphasizing the extent to which a reform would bring about an increase in population were such standard rhetorical ploys, that it is often difficult to assess the real importance which was given to the issue of population in and of itself."

Wealth and material progress were largely dependent on manual labor, and a growing labor force was viewed as a way to prosperity. With the high mortality rates that prevailed throughout most of human history, it was necessary to have many children in order to overcome the negative effects of the "grim reaper." Hernandez (1974, 146) pointed out that:

> . . . another important legacy from premodern times has been the persistence of the utopian dream: an optimum population in an ideal state, according to Plato and Aristotle; medieval notions of a harmonious balance of the material and spiritual; the Renaissance belief in the perfectibility of art and life; and the modern scientism that offers unlimited horizons for human betterment.

It was partially in response to such a utopian dream that Malthus wrote his famous essay on population.

▒ MALTHUS

Perhaps more than any other population theorist, Thomas Robert Malthus (1766–1834), both an economist and a clergyman, has had a profound impact on attitudes and ideas concerning population growth. His name still appears in most discussions of population prospects and seems ineradicably associated with the topic of population. However, demographers are not all in agreement that Malthus made a significant contribution to the scientific study of population.

Malthus was born in England in 1766 in a rather well-to-do family and lived during a time of political and industrial revolution. For most of the preceding time, people in Europe had been conditioned to expect and to accept a bitter lot and a short life. This fatalism was conditioned by a belief that there were not enough material resources to go around. The major economic thought of the day was Mercantilism, an economic system with strong government policies directed toward the accumulation of wealth. Poverty was associated with the merits of man and the will of God, and the earth was viewed as a place of testing and punishment. Mercantilist population policies were mainly pronatalist because more births meant more workers, hence more aggregate wealth.

At the same time, as Wrigley (1989, 31) noted, Malthus and the two other great classical economists, Adam Smith and David Ricardo, were in complete agreement that, "The secular tendency of real wages was likely to be flat, if not tending downward, because any increase in the funds available to pay wages would be matched by a proportional rise in the number of wage earners."

However, during Malthus's time industrialization was accelerating and ideas were rapidly changing; the acceptance of deprivation was being challenged strongly. Liberty, equality, and fraternity became the new watchwords. Rapidly increasing production and increased trade suggested that resources might not be so limited after all. Rather, abundance might be possible.

Out of this background a rash of utopian schemes, wild dreams, and visions of the future were forthcoming. The future was seen as a time when poverty, misery, vice, want, greed, and even death itself might be eliminated. With a little bit of luck, and a few changes, the perfect society could evolve. Malthus's father was caught up by these new ideas concerning the perfectibility of man and society. He invited many utopians to his home for discussions, but in these discussions the young Malthus took a position opposite to that of his father.

The first edition of Malthus's famous population essay, published in 1798, was entitled, *An Essay on the Principle of Population as it affects the future improvement of society; With remarks on the speculations of Mr. Godwin, M. Condorcet, and other writers*. It was written neither as a text in demography nor as an exposition of some new law of population growth. Rather, its intent was to refute some of the utopian ideas that were then gaining currency. His chief targets were the authors mentioned in his title. Commenting upon Condorcet, Malthus (1959, 3) wrote: "I have read some of the speculations on the perfectibility of man and of society with great pleasure. I have been warmed and delighted with the enchanting pictures which they hold forth. I ardently wish for such happy improvements. . . ." Unfortunately, Malthus then argued, the road to utopia would always be blocked because he believed that humans would always press up against the limit of subsistence.

Malthus's first edition of the *Essay* was rather simple. His "principle" of population was the result of two postulates and one assumption. The first postulate was that "food is necessary to the existence of man," and the second was that "the passion between the sexes is necessary and will remain in its present state." Malthus assumed that population would always tend to increase at a geometric rate, whereas food production could only be increased at an arithmetic rate. In his own words:

> Population, when unchecked, increases in geometric ratio. Subsistence increases only in an arithmetical ratio. A slight acquaintance with numbers will show the immensity of the first power in comparison of the second . . . the human species would increase as the numbers 1, 2, 4, 8, 16, 32, 64, 128, 256, and subsistence as 1, 2, 3, 4, 5, 6, 7, 8, 9. In two centuries the population would be to the means of subsistence as 256 to 9; in three centuries as 4,096 to 13; and in two thousand years the difference would almost be incalculable.

According to Malthus, population growth would always press against the means of subsistence unless the process was prevented by some powerful and obvious checks. These checks, according to Malthus, could be categorized as either *positive* or *preventive*.

Preventive checks were those that affected the birth rate. In his view moral restraint was the only acceptable one although Malthus recognized that "vices" such as homosexuality and birth control could also have an impact. The positive checks were those that affected the death rate, including misery, disease, famine, and war. Thus, Malthus felt that there was no way to escape the positive checks and that Godwin's argument that things would become perfect if we could simply eliminate government and private property was wrong. The "Principle of Population" was inflexible, inexorable, and inescapable. No exercise of reason could remove its effect, he argued, producing his own dismal view of the future of humankind and helping to saddle economists forever with the description of their discipline as the "dismal science."

From today's perspective a number of weaknesses can be identified in Malthus's thinking. He emphasized land as the major limiting variable on expanding food supplies, yet other inputs such as improved crop rotation patterns, fertilizers, and new hybrid strains of seeds have been, and continue to be, major factors in increasing food supplies. Furthermore, food is not our only necessity. Clothing, shelter, and other items are essential to at least some degree; and industrialization, well underway in his own era, certainly increased the availability of many of these items more rapidly than the rate of population growth. He failed to consider the major changes that transportation systems would undergo, as well as the expansion of trade that would accompany such changes. Because of his clerical leaning, he also failed to foresee the possibility that contraceptives would be widely accepted or to even imagine that couples would decide to limit the sizes of their families in response to changing socioeconomic conditions.

Though considerable discussion and controversy appeared after the publication of Malthus's book in 1798, his theory went out of favor by the middle of the nineteenth century. By then the Industrial Revolution had created ways to reduce the pressure of population, including emigration to the New World, and to raise wages above the subsistence level for more workers.

However, the rapid increase in population during the mid-twentieth century, coupled with considerable malnourishment in many areas, has revived an interest in Malthus's ideas. Many "neo-Malthusians" still feel that population growth will outrun the food supply and that the world will not be able to continue supporting a growing population. Strangeland (1904, 356) summarized Malthus's contribution as follows:

> Malthus's work was a great one, written in an opportune time, and though it cannot lay claim to any considerable originality as far as theories presented are concerned, it was successful in that it showed more fully, perhaps more clearly, and certainly more effectively than had any previous attempt, that population depends on subsistence and that its increase is checked by want, vice, and disease as well as by moral restraint or prudence.

▨ THE NEO-MALTHUSIANS

Neo-Malthusians continue to argue that population growth is problematic. Not only do they state, as Malthus did, that population growth creates problems relative to food supplies, but they go beyond that to relate population growth to environmental problems as well. They see the consequences of rapid population growth not just in mass poverty but also in the deteriorating quality of the earth itself as a home for humans. At the same time they go far beyond Malthus's "moral restraint" as a means of controlling population growth, supporting family planning, contraceptives of every sort, and even abortion.

Two major voices for neo-Malthusianism are biologists Paul Ehrlich and Garrett Hardin. Both generated considerable public interest in the problems of population growth in the late 1960s, and both have pursued those themes since. Ehrlich's 1968 book, *The Population Bomb,* set forth the central themes of rapid population growth, uncertain and inadequate food supplies, and environmental degradation.

Ehrlich and Ehrlich (1990, 225) revisited the population issue and its relationship to environmental and other problems, and concluded that, "A central problem facing us now is finding ways to convince national and international leaders and the world's people that opportunities for action to assure global environmental security are fast slipping away . . . it's the top of the ninth and humanity has been hitting nature hard . . . we must always remember that nature bats last!" The writings of Ehrlich, Hardin, and other neo-Malthusians are discussed in detail in Chapter 10.

▧ BOSERUP

In 1965 Danish economist Ester Boserup proposed an argument regarding the relationship between population growth and food supply that was in many ways directly opposite that of Malthus. Rather than arguing that population growth "depends" on agriculture, treating it as a dependent variable as Malthus did, she began her investigation by stating that, "population growth is here regarded as the independent variable which in its turn is a major factor determining agricultural developments." (Boserup, 1965, 11)

In essence, she argued that population growth and critical population densities could stimulate agricultural innovation and change. As a starting point, she suggested replacing the distinction between cultivated and uncultivated land with the concept of frequency of cropping. Given definitions of land use and patterns of tool adoptions in agrarian societies that she outlined, she was able "to define the concept of intensification in agriculture in a new way, namely as the gradual change towards patterns of land use which make it possible to crop a given area of land more frequently than before" (Boserup, 1965, 43).

Faced with population growth in an agrarian society, people would be confronted with a threat to their standard of living. Whereas Malthus would argue that death rates would rise to curtail the population growth and restore equilibrium, Boserup saw another possibility, namely an intensification of the agricultural system. She argued that by working more hours and adopting more intensive ways of growing crops, people could cope with a growing population. The primary trade-off that they would be forced to make is one of leisure for work.

Boserup envisioned a succession of increasingly more intensive agricultural practices as population growth continued, ranging from forest-fallow to bush-fallow, through short-fallow and annual cropping, to multi-cropping, the most intensive of the five systems. She noted that "Under the pressure of increasing population there has been a shift in recent decades from more extensive to more intensive systems of land use in virtually every part of the underdeveloped regions." (Boserup, 1965, 16)

Boserup (1981) broadened her arguments somewhat but continued to argue that population growth acted as a stimulant to technological change, at least under some conditions. However, she recognized also that high rates of population growth could overload systems. Agricultural intensification has continued to occur throughout the underdeveloped world; however, in some cases, despite total growth in agricultural production, per capita growth has remained constant or even declined as populations grew at unprecedented rates. Such conditions have occurred in various parts of Africa in recent decades.

Though Boserup provided some compelling arguments for treating population growth as an independent variable that in turn drives agricultural intensity and technological innovation, she is not without her critics as well. One frequent argument against her work focuses on population growth itself and asks why, if food was scarce to begin with, a population would begin to grow, especially since slow or no growth has been typical for most of human history. Another criticism is that she treats agrarian societies as closed systems, whereas migration may act as a safety valve for population growth in many cases even though that role has certainly become more limited with the rapid expansion of population in the twentieth century.

▒ MARX AND ENGELS

Down through the years several theorists have disagreed with the basic Malthusian ideas. Foremost among Malthus's critics was Karl Marx, who argued that no such thing as overpopulation existed. Marx believed that Malthus was a bourgeois, chauvinist clergyman who upheld the established order of social inequality. Furthermore, Malthus was accused of copying the writings and ideas of the classical school of economic theorists, who proposed unrestricted competition, self-interest, private property, and individualism as solutions to Europe's population explosion. Malthus was branded as an easy target for revolutionary criticism and an archenemy of the worldwide socialist movement, because he was considered a literary oppressor of the underprivileged and an apologist for the exploiting class.

In the *Communist Manifesto* and in other works, Marx expounded the familiar class struggle theory that an uprising by the proletariat would eventually lead to a classless society without private property and that an egalitarian ethic would prevail. He believed that the output of food and resources was outstripped by population growth not because there was a natural law that subsistence could not keep pace with population growth, but because poor people, under the capitalist system, were denied access to the control of food and resources.

Furthermore, he argued, if poor people were given control over the means of subsistence—equipment, knowledge, land, and an adequate share of the wealth—their production of goods and services would far surpass the growth of population. Exploitation by the rich and private ownership of the means of production blocked this solution. In essence, Marx felt that there was no population problem; the problem was a maldistribution of resources.

Communists and socialists have generally agreed with the concept that it is not growth but the maldistribution of resources that is the basis of the population problem. However, there is a basic difference between the socialists and the communists, as demographer Ralph Thomlinson (1976, 44) noted in his statement that "whereas communists prefer to deny the existence of population problems, socialists acknowledge the problems but turn to revision of the social order for a solution." In the former communist countries, however, birth control was often widely practiced (Brackett, 1968). Of course, in the remaining communist countries, such as the People's Republic of China, the reasons given for birth planning are often improved health, better education for the next generation, and improved conditions for women, not direct control of population size (Jaffee and Oakley, 1978).

▦ THE DEMOGRAPHIC TRANSITION: AN OVERVIEW

The original demographic transition theory, or model, was based on historical observations of demographic changes in western European countries. The gap between the birth rate and death rate in Europe was closed by a declining birth rate, not by a rising death rate as Malthus had predicted. A new kind of demographic stability was reached, first in northwestern Europe and then elsewhere. This transition from a relatively stable demographic regime with high birth rates and death rates to a similarly stable regime with low birth rates and death rates is known as the *demographic transition*.

The basic *demographic transition model* postulates a deterministic causal link between modernization on the one hand and both mortality and fertility reduction on the other. Conceptually it can be viewed as an idealized sequence of stages through which a given population passes, and the end result is a stable demographic regime with low birth and death rates. The data upon which the transition model is based came primarily from the demographic experience of northwestern Europe, principally England and Wales. Figure 4–1 illustrates the changes in vital rates that have taken place in England since 1700 and provides the idealized view of this descriptive model.

Prior to its industrialization in the eighteenth century, England generally experienced high birth and death rates, though not as high as those currently being experienced in many Third World countries. The result was a relatively stable population in which births were approximately balanced by deaths. A decisive break occurred around the middle of the eighteenth century, when the death rate started a long-term decline. The reasons for this initial decline are still not completely understood, though most experts agree that it was probably due to unusually good harvests at the time.

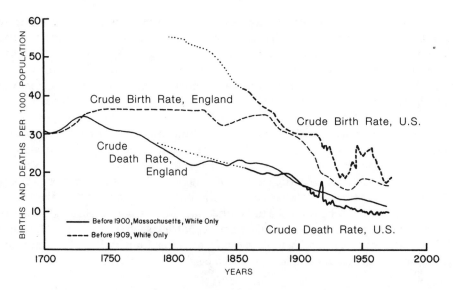

■ **FIGURE 4–1** Mortality and Fertility Transition in the United States and England. SOURCE: Abdel R. Omran. (1977) "Epidemiologic Transition in the United States: The Health Factor in Population Changes in the Eighteenth Century," *Population Bulletin* 32(2):15. Courtesy of the Population Reference Bureau, Inc., Washington, D.C.

The good harvests were a result of such agricultural improvements as crop rotation and advances in animal husbandry.

There was also a slight rise in the death rate in the early nineteenth century, probably associated with the growth of factory towns and their squalid, unhealthy living conditions. However, after a few decades the death rate resumed its decline, which has continued until today.

In England following 1700 the birth rate initially increased slightly as a result of the Industrial Revolution. With industrialization and the disappearance of the apprentice system, unskilled young people could get factory jobs and did not have to endure long apprenticeships before they received compensation. Thus, young people could marry earlier and start families at younger ages. Improved living conditions may also have added slightly to the birth rate.

Fertility stayed relatively constant for the next one hundred years, then started its major decline around 1870. The primary reason for the decline was not a change in marriage patterns, but a redefinition of the ideal family size within marriage. Several reasons for this decline in ideal family size have been suggested. First, the contribution of children to family welfare was declining. In the preindustrial period children contributed a great deal to family welfare. Because the overwhelming majority of people were involved in agricultural pursuits, children were useful in weeding crops, fetching water, and gathering wood. In the early textile factories and mines children served an important economic function because they worked at a much cheaper rate than adults.

Children were also a form of social security; they were often the only means of support for their parents when the parents became unable to work. However, as more restrictions were put on child labor practices in the middle and late nineteenth century and as populations generally became more urbanized, children became more of a burden to parents. The state began to take on a welfare function and to provide for older citizens. With increasing industrialization, the number of people engaged in farming dropped significantly and the role of children as producers was diminished.

A second reason for the redefinition of ideal family size had to do with rising expectations. The Industrial Revolution produced a tremendous volume of goods and services. People could shift increasingly from satisfying needs to satisfying wants. Luxuries increasingly became viewed as necessities; social mobility and the attainment of riches were easier if one had fewer children. With the growth of knowledge came more favorable attitudes toward family planning. The result was a significant decline in the birth rate.

Though Figure 4–1 illustrates the demographic experience of England, the general trends were viewed the same for most of the Western world. The timing of the transition varied from place to place, but the results were essentially the same, at least when viewed at the national scale. The new balance of vital rates represented an improved condition of human efficiency and health, as well as a level of material well-being that had never before been achieved.

In the typical experience of demographic transition, the decline in birth rates lagged behind the decline in death rates and occurred after industrialization was well along. Obviously the demographic transition was not foreseen by Malthus, who believed that a population equilibrium would be reached by a rise in the death rate rather than a lowering of the birth rate.

The general pattern of the demographic transition can be associated with different areas of the world today. Figure 4–2 represents an idealized demographic transition model. Stage A indicates an area with a high birth rate and a high death rate, equivalent to the preindustrial era in Europe. No major world region remains in this stage although a few African countries, such as those of the Sahel, probably still do. Stage B represents a population with a high birth rate and a declining death rate. Many of the African nations are now in this stage. Parts of Asia, excluding at least Japan, China, Hong Kong, and Taiwan, may also fit into this category.

Stage C includes nations with high birth rates and low death rates, such as most of tropical Latin America and some African nations, where populations are growing at the fastest rates in the world. Kenya, for example, had a crude birth rate of 45 and a crude death rate of 9 in 1992, yielding an annual population growth rate of 3.7 percent.

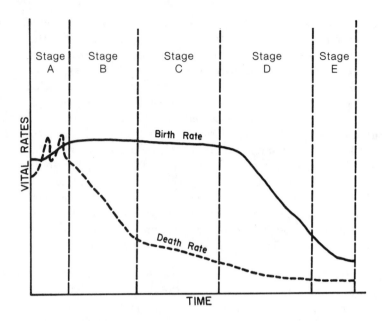

▪ **FIGURE 4–2** Stages of the Demographic Transition.

Countries in stage D have declining birth rates and low death rates. Examples of this would include countries in temperate Latin America, such as Argentina and Uruguay, as well as the People's Republic of China, Taiwan, and South Korea. In the decades following 1970, birth rate declines in developing countries became more common, somewhat slowing the world's overall growth rate. The final category, Stage E, depicts a population with low birth and death rates and includes the countries of the Western world and Japan.

If we accept the demographic transition model and believe that there is a causal link between modernization and a decline in both vital rates, then the obvious solution to rapid population growth is to modernize the world as rapidly as possible. However, if there is progressive step-wise movement from stage A to stage E, then the speed at which nations move through these stages is critical. The nations in stage D are heading in the right direction and in a short time should reach an equilibrium between births and deaths. Although the nations in stage C are experiencing a rapid increase in population, they are going in the right direction and should soon experience a decline in birth rates and a concomitant decrease in population growth.

The critical nations are those found in stages A and B. They have yet to reach their greatest rates of demographic increase and still must pass through stage C, the period of most rapid population growth. Africa and Asia contain the largest populations, and if they follow the European experience, they will experience a tremendous increase in numbers. However, the People's Republic of China appears to be experiencing a rapid decline in fertility. As early as 1982 the Chinese were officially encouraging the one-child family, a drastic demographic measure.

Clearly the demographic transition model is not a simple one which, once stated, is applicable to all places or all times. As Beaver (1975, 9) commented:

> In general, the theory of the demographic transition is not well explicated, but is weighted down with numerous supplementary arguments drawn from different disciplines. The only clear implication of this theory is the prediction that socioeconomic development will lead to natality decline, and that this will tend to occur sometime after a major decline in mortality.

▨ RELEVANCE OF THE TRANSITION MODEL

Though the demographic transition model has received considerable attention in recent years, its relevance is increasingly in doubt. Whether the transition model is useful in explaining the population changes that are occurring in the developing countries is an important issue. Conditions in today's developing countries differ considerably from those that prevailed in the Western nations as they moved through the demographic transition.

Policy formulation in developing countries often depends on the concepts of the transition model, and to the degree that these concepts are validated they will be useful in guiding policy development. However, questions need to be raised about the degree to which the developing countries will duplicate the experience of the developed countries upon which the demographic transition model is based. Some time ago Teitelbaum (1975, 422) noted:

> . . . the situation is a mixed one; in some respects the different circumstances in developing countries suggest great obstacles to the timely completion of the transition by means of a "natural" decline in fertility along the European pattern. In other respects these differences provide reasons to anticipate an unusually rapid completion of the transition in these countries.

It is important to see that differences between the European experience and the likely experience of today's developing countries may both favor and operate against rapid movement through the demographic transition. Some of the differences and their possible influences on demographic change in the developing countries are discussed below.

Population Growth

As we have already seen, population growth in the developing countries is occurring at unprecedented rates. Africa is the world's fastest growing region with a 3.0 percent rate of natural increase in 1992. Zambia was growing at 3.8 percent in 1992, making it the fastest growing country in Africa and probably in the world, followed closely by Kenya, Uganda, and Togo. The impact of such growth becomes apparent if you remember that at an annual growth rate of 3.5 percent a population would double in only 20 years and would increase 32-fold in a century. By comparison, when most European countries were undergoing their demographic transitions, the average doubling time was in the area of 85 to 95 years and few countries experienced annual growth rates of more than 1.5 percent.

One of the obvious problems associated with rapid population growth is the related growth in demand for goods and services and for social investment. Whereas the European and North American countries were not much affected by these difficulties, most of the developing countries today face severe problems and find that population growth increases the difficulty of raising the levels of living. (Kindleberger and Herrick, 1977)

To make matters even worse, it will be much more difficult to halt the rapid growth of the developing countries than it was to slow down the growth in European countries during their demographic transition. The younger age structures in the modern developing countries, the result of much higher fertility, add a great momentum for further growth, a compelling *demographic inertia*. Even if the fertility rate in the developing countries declined to replacement level within the next decade, a highly unlikely event, they would still continue to grow for another 60 years or more and would nearly double in size. For a country like India, even a doubling of population would present considerable problems.

Mortality Declines

One of the reasons for rapid population growth in the developing countries is the rapid decline in mortality that has occurred as modern medicines and public health programs have been introduced. The European countries experienced a gradual decline in mortality that was related to the economic and social forces of industrialization and economic development. In many developing countries today mortality rates have declined much more rapidly. As a consequence, the developing countries have mortality levels considerably below those that prevailed in Europe during early stages of industrialization. Further mortality declines are likely, especially in Africa.

Fertility Levels

The fertility levels of most of the developing countries today are higher than those that prevailed in Europe before the European countries began their demographic transitions. Many African countries had crude birth rates of 45 or more in 1992, and a few were still over 50. Among such countries were Liberia, Mali, Malawi, Togo, Uganda and Kenya. The 1992 crude birth rate for Africa was 43. By comparison, the crude birth rate in early nineteenth century Britain was estimated to be around 35. The major reason for the discrepancy is the difference in marriage patterns. Extensive nonmarriage and late marriage were typical in nineteenth century Europe, whereas the practice in most developing countries today is early and nearly universal marriage.

Although high birth rates prevail in the developing countries as a result of current marriage patterns coupled with low rates of contraceptive usage, some hopeful signs are appearing as well. For one thing, it may be possible to reduce fertility in the developing countries today by altering the marriage patterns and by introducing more effective contraceptive practices. Part of the recent fertility declines in the People's Republic of China have resulted from such efforts. For example, raising the legal marriage age reduces the number of years women may possibly conceive.

Of course, motivation toward smaller families is going to be necessary before significant declines in fertility are recorded in most of the developing countries. The "demonstration effect" of the European transition and the predominance of small families in Europe and the United States has spread recently to most of the developing world as a result of expanded trade and better communication systems.

The role of governments and various international agencies may also aid in bringing about rapid fertility declines. Family planning programs are most likely to be effective if they are supported by the government. Governments today are more apt to be involved in many forms of planning than were their nineteenth-century counterparts. Furthermore, many developing countries today have social scientists and planners who actively participate in the formulation and execution of national policies for economic development and social change. Such planning was almost nonexistent in the European countries during their periods of demographic transition and industrialization. Also, financial and technical assistance for both development and family planning programs is available from such organizations as the United Nations and the United States Agency for International Development.

Migration

Migration undoubtedly played a significant role in the stabilization of population in parts of nineteenth-century Europe. International migration operated as a "safety valve" and softened the effect of rapid population growth. Millions of European citizens moved to Oceania and the Americas during the nineteenth century. However, this potential "safety valve" for releasing population pressure is no longer available for large numbers of people because of current economic and political realities.

During the European demographic transition, the growing rural population was able to find opportunities for gainful employment in urban areas as industry rapidly expanded. New skills and occupations were acquired as people moved from rural to urban areas. In the developing countries today, however, industrialization is unable to create jobs in the cities fast enough to absorb the rapidly growing labor force—thus encouraging fertility to remain high. In some countries attempts are being made to slow down the rate of rural-urban migration.

Education and Economic Development

Economic development and modernization for many developing countries has proceeded more rapidly than in nineteenth-century Europe. To the extent that a direct correlation exists between modernization and fertility decline, it suggests a possibility for a more rapid fertility decline in the developing countries and a quicker completion of the demographic transition. However, education also has an impact on fertility; in general, lower fertility is associated with higher educational levels. Rapid population growth in the developing countries, together with the large proportions of people in the younger age groups, means a rapidly increasing demand for educational facilities. The developing countries usually cannot keep up with this demand, and the result is most likely to be deferment of the goal of universal education along with its potential effect of lowering fertility.

However, care must be taken in trying to forecast the demographic consequences of modernization. Caldwell (1976, 358) commented:

> . . . the major implication of this analysis is that fertility decline in the Third World is not dependent on the spread of industrialization or even on the rate of economic development. It will of course be affected by such development in that modernization produces more money for schools, newspapers, and so on; indeed, the whole question of family nucleation cannot arise in the nonmonetized economy. But fertility decline is more likely to precede industrialization and to help bring it about than to follow it.

We are still a long way from understanding the specific interactions between socioeconomic and demographic changes. Undoubtedly other differences between the transition experience of the European countries and the likely course of demographic events in the developing countries also could be identified. Changes in the composition of the labor force in the developing countries would have a downward effect on fertility if more women found occupations outside the home, for example. Once women have opportunities for fulfillment outside of the traditional role of housewife and mother, they will be motivated to have smaller families. In addition, once women have outside incomes, a part of the cost of having children will be the income foregone during pregnancy and following pregnancy. This opportunity cost may be enough to discourage parents from having as many children.

Some Final Comments on the Relevance of the Transition Model

The demographic transition model has held a respectable position for many years. Recently, however, critics have increasingly questioned its validity, especially with regard to its applicability to developing countries.

From around the middle of the eighteenth century onward in Europe, marital fertility underwent a sustained decline; it was mainly associated with the modernization that was sweeping the area. At a general level the transition model appears compatible with the events that occurred. However, when causal links are established in a model and that model is then used to predict the course of fertility decline in today's countries, its success may be quite limited. Most likely the course of events will differ significantly from the earlier patterns.

Furthermore, the ability of the demographic transition model to explain the demographic changes that occurred in Europe during the transition is being called into question. Freedman (1979, 64) wrote, ". . . detailed empirical work has been unable to establish combinations of development variables at specific levels which were systematically related to the European fertility declines." In some countries fertility declines began in less advanced regions, rather than in the more advanced ones. Also, Freedman (1979, 64) noted that "detailed study of the European fertility transition has shown that many areas that were culturally similar, for example, in language or ethnicity, also demonstrated similar fertility patterns, without prime reference to socioeconomic developmental indices critical to transition theory."

Although it appears that spatial and temporal variations in fertility decline were probably more complicated than we have believed, the new evidence does not necessarily invalidate the demographic transition model. It does suggest, however, that we need to look more closely than ever at the model, especially with respect to its predictive ability. We cannot specify neat causal relationships. For example, we cannot state that a 10 percent rise in a nation's level of urbanization will result in a specified decrease in fertility.

Recent studies of the demographic transition in Europe have highlighted another problem, one associated with the way in which fertility is usually measured. The usual way to chart the transition is to look at crude rates. However, as van de Walle and Knodel (1980, 15) pointed out, "France and Ireland around 1900 had almost the same crude birth rate." But, they went on to say, "this result was obtained in France by family limitation (within marriage) and in Ireland by high proportions of single persons in the reproductive ages." Thus, historical demographers are now breaking down overall fertility into the various components that comprise it. The major component, of course, is marital fertility, for which an index has been developed. Related data for selected countries are shown in Table 4–1.

After reviewing several studies of European fertility decline, van de Walle and Knodel (1980, 20–21) provided the following useful summary:

> 1. The past was largely characterized by natural fertility, that is, the deliberate practice of family limitation was mostly absent (and probably unknown) among most of the population prior to a fairly recent time. This was true, even though a substantial proportion of births may have been unwanted. High infant and child mortality may have reflected unconscious efforts to eliminate unwanted children.

TABLE 4–1 ▪ Index Numbers of Marital Fertility: Selected European Countries, 1850–1910

(lg in 1880 = 100)

Country	Date						
	1850	**1860**	**1870**	**1880**	**1890**	**1900**	**1910**
Belgium	109	109		100	89	71	59
Denmark	99	94	96	100	97	89	77
England-Wales	100	99	102	100	92	82	69
Germany			103	100	96	90	73
Ireland			99	100	101	100	101
Italy		105	100	100	99	98	95
Netherlands	100	98	102	100	97	90	78
Norway			93	100	98	93	90
Scotland		101	103	100	95	86	—
Sweden	96	101	101	100	96	91	80
Switzerland		107	102	100	96	91	76

SOURCE: Etienne van de Walle and John Knodel. "Europe's Fertility Transition. New Evidence and Lessons for Today's Developing World." *Population Bulletin* 34, No. 6 (February, 1980), p. 18.

2. The transition from high to low fertility represented a shift from natural fertility to family limitation, occurred rapidly, and was an irreversible process once underway.
3. The onset of long-term fertility decline was remarkably concentrated in time and took place under a wide variety of socioeconomic and demographic conditions.
4. Differences in the start and in the speed of the fertility decline seem to have been determined more by the cultural setting than by socioeconomic conditions.

During the 1980s considerable attention was given to refining and reinterpreting the European experience of the demographic transition. One shift in focus has been from the role of individual choice in fertility decline to that played by relatives, friends, and neighbors in influencing local fertility behavior (Coale and Watkins, 1986). Watkins (1990, 242) argued the need for paying more attention to the role played by ". . . members of the community with whom individuals interact on a day-to-day basis, as well as the members of . . . 'imagined communities' . . . I assume that in the end it is individuals who act in the privacy of their bedroom; I propose, however, that even when the couple is literally alone in the bedroom, the echoes of conversations with kin and neighbors influence their actions."

Watkins (1990) focused on the diversity of marriage and marital fertility both within and among the countries of western Europe during two different time periods, 1870 and 1960, and found that between the these periods diversity increased to a maximum and then decreased to below what it had been in 1870. She also discovered that variations in fertility during the former period were closely related to linguistic diversity. She found that national social integration ultimately diminished demographic diversity within nations, even though at the same time demographic diversity among nations became more pronounced. She identified the following variables as most important in reducing within-nation demographic diversity: (1) the integration of national markets, (2) the expansion of state functions, and (3) nation-building.

Before leaving the subject of demographic change, two more theories need to be discussed regarding fertility. These theories enhance our understanding of past demographic changes and suggest some additional factors to consider when projecting future demographic change.

▓ MULTIPHASIC RESPONSE AND DEMOGRAPHIC DEVELOPMENT

As we have seen, countries that have achieved a reasonable modernization level also have experienced a decline in birth rates and death rates. Moreover, the decline in birth rates, with the possible exception of France, has lagged behind the decrease in death rates. What is not explicit is the causal mechanism, the direct linkage between modernization and the declines in birth and death rates.

Modernization is a complex process involving sweeping changes in the socioeconomic fabric of societies as they are transformed from primarily rural-agricultural societies to primarily urban-industrial societies. Somewhere in this complex of changes there are reasons for the observed declines in vital rates, but their specification is elusive. The search for a better explanation of this phenomenon continues, and two theories have been proposed: multiphasic response and demographic development.

Theory of Multiphasic Response

Davis argued that the demographic transition model was perhaps too simplistic, mainly because it considered only changes in vital rates. In so doing, the transition model ignores other possible demographic responses. Davis (1963, 345) stated that the process of demographic change and response not only is continuous but also reflexive and behavioral—reflexive in the sense that a change in one component is eventually altered by the change it has induced in other components; behavioral in the sense that the process involves human decisions in the pursuit of goals with varying means and conditions. Thus, the subject of demographic change is complex. Davis attempted to incorporate the complexities in an analysis of demographic change in the industrialized, or developed, countries.

He entered the subject with a discussion of demographic change in Japan, the only non-Western country so far to industrialize. One of the major demographic responses to modernization in Japan was abortion. Both abortion rates and birth rates

TABLE 4–2 ▓ Births and Abortions in Japan

	Births	**Annual Totals (000's) Abortions**	**Sum**	**Sum per 1,000 Population**
1949	2,697	102	2,798	34.4
1950	2,338	320	2,658	32.1
1951	2,138	459	2,596	30.8
1952	2,005	798	2,803	32.8
1953	1,868	1,067	2,935	33.9
1954	1,770	1,143	2,913	33.1
1955	1,727	1,170	2,897	32.6
1956	1,665	1,159	2,825	31.4
1957	1,563	1,122	2,686	29.6
1958	1,653	1,128	2,781	30.4
1959	1,626	1,099	2,725	29.5

SOURCE: Kingsley Davis, "The Theory of Change and Response in Modern Demographic History," *Population Index,* No. 4 (October, 1963), p. 347. Used by permission.

are well documented and appear in Table 4–2. As Davis argued, abortions have also been common in many other areas of the world, but their numbers have not been so well documented. Other demographic responses in Japan included the increased use of contraceptives, sterilization, emigration, and postponement of marriage. For example, in 1920, 17.7 percent of females aged 15 to 19 were married. By 1955, however, this figure had dropped to 1.8 percent. Of the Japanese situation Davis (1963, 349) stated:

> It is the picture of a people responding in almost every demographic manner then known to some powerful stimulus. Within a brief period they quickly postponed marriage, embraced contraception, began sterilization, utilized abortions, and migrated outward. It was a determined multiphasic response, and it was extremely effective with respect to fertility.

The stimulus to this multiphasic response was not population pressure and the prevalence or threat of dire poverty. Japanese industrial output grew more rapidly between 1913 and 1958 than did that of Germany, Italy, and the United States. Rather, according to Davis (1963, 352), the stimulus was "in a sense the rising prosperity itself, viewed from the standpoint of the individual's desire to get ahead and appear respectable, that forced a modification of his reproductive behavior."

Davis went on to further test these ideas in agricultural areas of northwestern Europe. With sustained population growth in these areas, it was observed that families tended to remain large. Birth rates were not decreasing. However, another response was occurring: migration. High birth rates could be sustained only if there were sufficient outflows from the population. Presently, however, with international migration restricted as it is, emigration is unlikely to solve the pressures generated by population growth.

Theory of Demographic Development

One of the shortcomings of the theory of demographic transition is its weak predictive ability. Its validity is dependent on the acceptance of two propositions. First, the pattern was characteristic of the now developed countries, and second, the experience of these countries is applicable to today's developing countries.

As Tabbarah (1976) mentioned, still another observation, that crude birth rate increases are associated with economic development, is unexplained by the demographic transition model. Rises in birth rates have occurred in parts of Latin America, Africa, and Asia. Tabbarah suggested that the demographic transition model also fails to explain *why* a fertility decline occurred and *when* fertility in a country will decline. He offered another model, *the model of demographic development,* to explain some of these observations.

Two variables are central to Tabbarah's model. One is C_m, the maximum number of children an average couple can expect to have in its completed family. The other is C_d, the number of children the couple desires to have in its completed family. C_d can only be determined through interviews. C_m can be calculated from demographic statistics using the formula

$$C_m = B_m (1-D),$$

where B_m equals the maximum number of live births the average couple can expect to have in its completed family (B_m is then total natural fertility); and $(1-D)$ is the survival rate of these live births to maturity given the mortality rate, D, to the age of maturity. The age of maturity could be set at perhaps 18 to 20. Available data on these variables for several groups of countries appear in Table 4–3. Tabbarah suggested the following four stages of demographic development.

In stage 1 C_m is less than C_d. In this stage most couples are unable to have their desired number of children. Both fecundity and the survival rate of children are low, hence the low value of C_m. At the same time, socioeconomic conditions are relatively poor, a situation that leads to a high value of C_d.

In stage 2 C_m is approximately equal to C_d. Under these circumstances couples are having children in about the desired number. This situation is a result of a combination of raising C_m somewhat, due to increasing fecundity and survival rates, and of lowering C_d, the desired family size.

In stage 3 C_m exceeds C_d, but only by a relatively small amount, whereas in stage 4 C_m exceeds C_d by a relatively large amount. Figure 4–3 follows trends in desired and maximum achievable family size as they occur over time and at different stages of demographic development. Time is plotted on the X axis and development is assumed to be associated with time. The number of children is plotted on the Y axis. Tabbarah (1976, 198) described the interpretation of Figure 4–3 as follows:

A couple at t_1 (stage 1 of demographic development) desires to have C_d number of children in its completed family, and for this it needs to have $B_d{}^1$ number of births ($B_d{}^1 - C_d{}^1$ children are eliminated by mortality). However, the desired number of

TABLE 4–3 ▧ Ranges of Fertility and Mortality Variables in Selected Regions, 1960s

Region	B	$^{o}e_{o}$	I–D	C_m	C_d
Black Africa	3–7	30–50	55–75	2–5	5–15
North Africa and Asia	5–8	35–55	60–75	3–6	4–8
Korea and Taiwan	6–9	60–68	85–95	5–9	3–6
Europe and North America	9–12	65–75	90–100	8–12	2–4

SOURCE: Reprinted with the permission of the Population Council from "Population Education as a Component of Development Policy," by Riad B. Tabbarah, *Studies in Family Planning 7*, no. 7 (July 1976):198.

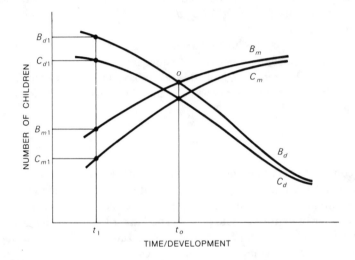

▧ **FIGURE 4–3** Trends in Desired and Maximum Achievable Family Size at Various Stages of Demographic Development. SOURCE: Reprinted with the permission of the Population Council from "Population education as a component of development policy," by Riad B. Tabbarah. (1976) *Studies in Family Planning,* 7(7):198.

births cannot be attained by the couple since its fecundity level permits it to have only B_m births (which results in C_m number of children in its completed family). It is clear that as long as curve $B_d - B_m$, that is, as long as couples desire more births than their fecundity permits, they will aim at maximum reproduction and hence follow curve B_m. This situation exists until point o, corresponding to time to (stage 2), is reached. After that point (stages 3 and 4), the desired number of births can be attained by the average couple and fertility can now follow the curve B_d. Therefore, under conditions of optimal knowledge and control, fertility will follow the line B_m—o—B_d.

Tabbarah's model is an aid to understanding changes in fertility behavior over time. Its main contribution is the explicit introduction of ideal family size into the model.

The importance of this contribution was noted by Beaver (1975, 9), who, following a discussion of factors related to fertility declines— urbanization, education, nonkinship institutions, and consumption levels, stated:

> Usually these variables are thought to mediate between socioeconomic development and "desired or ideal family size." The latter are hypothetical constructs which appear, though often implicitly, in most explanations. This is not a necessary assumption; even in developed societies family size is not always the result of planned, conscious decision. Of course this problem can be avoided by making "desired or ideal family size" a norm, and thus avoiding the assumption of individual decision.

However, further testing of the demographic development model is necessary if it is to prove its value. Refinements may be necessary. Even though ideal family size is explicit in the model, the factors that influence ideal family size must still be identified and causally linked together if the model is to have predictive value.

REFERENCES

Abler, Ronald, Adams, John S., and Gould, Peter. (1971) *Spatial Organization: The Geographer's View of the World.* Englewood Cliffs, N.J.: Prentice Hall, Inc.

Beaver, Steven E. (1975) *Demographic Transition Theory Reinterpreted.* Lexington, Mass.: Lexington Books.

Boserup, Ester. (1965) *The Conditions of Agricultural Growth: The Economics of Agrarian Change under Population Pressure.* Chicago: Aldine Publishing Company.

Boserup, Ester. (1981) *Population and Technological Change: A Study of Long-Term Trends.* Chicago: The University of Chicago Press.

Brackett, James W. (1968) "The Evolution of Marxist Theories of Population: Marxism Recognizes the Problem," *Demography* 5:157–173.

Caldwell, John C. (1976) "Toward a Restatement of Demographic Transition Theory," *Population and Development Review* 2:321–366.

Coale, Ansley J. and Watkins, Susan Cotts, eds. (1986) *The Decline of Fertility in Europe.* Princeton, NJ: Princeton University Press.

Coleman, David and Schofield, Roger. (1986) *The State of Population Theory: Forward from Malthus.* Oxford: Basil Blackwell.

Davis, Kingsley. (1963) "The Theory of Change and Response in Modern Demographic History," *Population Index* 29:345–366.

Ehrlich, Paul. (1968) *The Population Bomb.* New York: Ballantine Books.

Ehrlich, Paul R. and Ehrlich, Anne H. (1990) *The Population Explosion.* New York: Simon and Schuster.

Eversley, David R. (1959) *Social Theories of Fertility and the Malthusian Debate.* London: Oxford University Press.

Freedman, Ronald. (1979) "Theories of Fertility Decline: A Reappraisal," in Philip M. Hauser, ed., *World Population and Development: Challenges and Prospects.* Syracuse: Syracuse University Press, pp. 63–79.

Hernandez, Jose. (1974) *People, Power, and Policy: A New View on Population.* Palo Alto, California: National Press Books.

Jaffee, Frederick S. and Oakley, Deborah. (1978) "Observations on Birth Planning in China," *Family Planning Perspectives* 10:101–108.

Kindleberger, Charles P. and Herrick, Bruce. (1977) *Economic Development.* 3d ed. New York: McGraw-Hill Book Company.

Malthus, Thomas Robert. (1959) *Population: The First Essay.* Ann Arbor: The University of Michigan Press.

Merrick, Thomas W., with PRB Staff. (1986) "World Population in Transition," *Population Bulletin* 41(2):1–51.

Strangeland, Charles E. (1904) *Pre-Malthusian Doctrines of Population.* New York: Columbia University Press.

Tabbarah, Riad B. (1976) "Population Education as a Component of Development Policy," *Studies in Family Planning* 7:197–201.

Teitelbaum, Michael S. (1975) "Relevance of Demographic Transition Theory for Developing Countries," *Science* 188:420–425.

Teitelbaum, Michael S. and Winter, Jay M. eds. (1989) *Population and Resources in Western Intellectual Traditions.* Cambridge: Cambridge University Press.

Thomlinson, Ralph. (1976) *Population Dynamics: Causes and Consequences of World Demographic Change.* 2d ed. New York: Random House.

Tomaselli, Sylvana. (1989) "Moral Philosophy and Population Questions in Eighteenth Century Europe," in Teitelbaum, Michael S. and Winter, Jay M., eds. *Population and Resources in Western Intellectual Traditions.* Cambridge: Cambridge University Press, pp. 7–29.

van de Walle, Etienne; and Knodel, John. (1980) "Europe's Fertility Transition: New Evidence and Lessons for Today's Developing World," *Population Bulletin* 34(6):1–43.

Watkins, Susan Cotts (1990) "From Local to National Communities: The Transformation of Demographic Regimes in Western Europe, 1870–1960," *Population and Development Review* 16:241–272.

Weeks, John R. (1992) *Population: An Introduction to Concepts and Issues.* 5th ed. Belmont, California: Wadsworth Publishing Company.

Woods, Robert. (1982) *Theoretical Population Geography.* London: Longman.

Wrigley, E. A. (1989) "The Limits to Growth: Malthus and the Classical Economists," in Teitelbaum, Michael S. and Winter, Jay M., eds. *Population and Resources in Western Intellectual Traditions.* Cambridge: Cambridge University Press, pp. 30–48.

Chapter 5
Mortality: Patterns and Trends

...u three basic population processes, mortality is in many ways the easiest to discuss. Death occurs only once, and it is usually clearly defined although recent medical technologies have complicated the picture in many ways. Moral and legal issues surrounding the definition of death have drawn more attention in the last decade, as organ transplants and life-support systems have become commonplace.

MEASURES OF MORTALITY

The crude death rate was introduced earlier and was defined as the annual number of deaths per 1000 people in the midyear population. The rate is considered to be "crude" because the total population is included in the denominator, whereas the probability of dying in a particular time period is not equal for everyone. Thus, more refined mortality measures attempt to correct for the age structure of the population.

Age-Specific Death Rate

The probability of dying within a given time interval is closely related to age. The age-specific death rate, then, takes age into consideration and may be defined as

$$\text{ASDR} = \frac{D_a}{P_a} \times 1000,$$

where D_a = number of deaths of people in the age group a, usually either a one- or five-year age group, and
P_a = midyear population in age group a.

Generally, death rates are lowest for adolescents and young adults. The typical J-shaped mortality curve is shown, separately for males and females, in Figure 5–1.

Infant Mortality Rate

The infant mortality rate is defined as

$$IMR = \frac{D}{B} \times 1000.$$

where D = annual number of deaths of infants between birth and age one year, and
B = annual number of births.

Infant mortality is unevenly distributed throughout the first year of life, with most infant deaths occurring in the first six months. In areas where infant mortality rates are low, a high portion of infant deaths occur within the first 28 days of life. These early infant deaths often result from congenital defects or injuries at birth, deaths that modern medicine may be able to do little to prevent.

Neonatal Mortality Rate

The neonatal mortality rate reflects the influence of congenital and birth-related problems on infant mortality and is calculated

$$NMR = \frac{D_j}{B} \times 1000,$$

where D_j = number of deaths to infants between birth and 28 days of age in
a given year, and
B = number of births in that year.

As Thomlinson (1976, 157) noted, "neonatal mortality . . . varies remarkably little from country to country, and has shown little susceptibility to reduction under pressure from modern medical science."

▨ THE LIFE TABLE

Though various mortality rates are useful in describing mortality conditions, they tell us nothing directly about life expectancy at different ages nor about the numbers of people who will survive to different ages. Yet such information is extremely valuable. Life tables, on the other hand, are based on observed mortality, usually by age and sex,

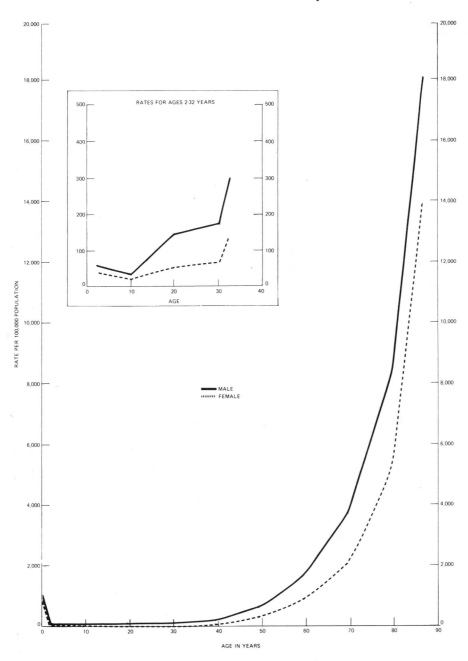

■ **FIGURE 5–1** Death Rates by Age and Sex: United States, 1984. Source: U.S. Department of Health and Human Services, *Vital and Health Statistics, Series 20. No. 15, Death Rates by 10-year Age Groups, Race, and Sex: United States, 1970 and 1972–84.* (Washington, D.C.: U.S. Government Printing Office, 1987), p. 9.

and provide us with information on life expectancy and survivorship. A detailed discussion of life tables, as well as birth, death, and migration rates, may be found in Barclay (1958). The following discussion considers only an abridged form of the life table and its associated functions. It is abbreviated in the sense that not all functions of the life table are used.

Coefficients in the Abridged Life Table

Four important coefficients are used in our abridged life table: (1) the life table mortality rate, (2) the survival table, (3) the number dying, and (4) the average remaining life.

Life Table Mortality Rate.   The life table mortality rate is the primary coefficient in the life table. It gives the probability of dying within a given age interval and is represented by the symbol $_nq_x$, which gives the probability of dying between age x and age x + n. If n equals 1 and x = 0, then $_1q_0$ would be the probability of dying between birth and age 1. A graph of the life table mortality rate has the same J-shape discussed earlier for the age-specific death rate.

Survival Table.   The survival table gives us the numbers of people who survive to different ages. Usually the life table begins with 100,000 people at birth (regardless of the actual size of the population) and then shows the number who will survive to each age. The symbol 1_x is the number of people surviving to exactly age x.

Number Dying.   This column shows the number of people dying in each successive interval and is designated $_nd_x$.

Average Remaining Life.   The average remaining life, or expectation of life, designated by e_x, is the average number of years still to be lived by those who survived to age x. Table 5–1 shows an abridged life table for the United States, both for the total population and separately for males and females. Notice that a graph of either $_nq_x$ or $_nd_x$ would be a J-shaped curve.

Though the life table is of considerable value in demography, it seldom enters into geographic studies of population. However, the life table is a valuable resource for students of population, regardless of disciplinary focus.

▨ MAJOR DETERMINANTS OF MORTALITY

Mortality varies both from time to time and place to place. To understand these variations it is necessary to consider the determinants of mortality. Ideally, vital registration data on mortality in which deaths are recorded by age, sex, and cause is the most useful. In reality, however, most information from developing countries is far less

TABLE 5–1 ■ Abridged Life Tables by Race and Sex: United States, 1988

Age Interval Period of life between two exact ages stated in years, race, and sex	Proportion dying Proportion of persons alive at beginning of age interval dying during interval	Of 100,000 born alive		Average remaining lifetime Average number of years of life remaining at beginning of age interval
		Number living at beginning of age interval	Number dying during age interval	
(1)	(2)	(3)	(4)	(7)
x to $x + n$	$_nq_x$	l_x	$_nd_x$	e_x
ALL RACES				
0–1	0.0100	100,000	999	74.9
1–5	.0020	99,001	198	74.7
5–10	.0012	98,803	120	70.8
10–15	.0014	98,683	134	65.9
15–20	.0044	98,549	431	61.0
20–25	.0058	98,118	565	58.3
25–30	.0061	97,553	596	51.6
30–35	.0074	96,957	717	46.9
35–40	.0096	96,240	924	42.2
40–45	.0126	95,316	1,204	37.6
45–50	.0189	94,112	1,777	33.0
50–55	.0300	92,335	2,766	28.6
55–60	.0473	89,569	4,238	24.4
60–65	.0728	85,331	6,208	20.5
65–70	.1055	79,123	8,344	16.9
70–75	.1568	70,779	11,096	13.6
75–80	.2288	59,683	13,654	10.7
80–85	.3445	46,029	15,858	8.1
85 and over	1.0000	30,171	30,171	6.0
MALE				
0–1	.0110	100,000	1,104	71.5
1–5	.0022	98,896	220	71.3
5–10	.0014	98,676	138	67.5
10–15	.0017	98,538	165	62.5
15–20	.0062	98,373	615	57.6
20–25	.0087	97,758	854	53.0
25–30	.0089	96,904	865	48.4
30–35	.0107	96,039	1,024	43.8
35–40	.0134	95,015	1,276	39.3
40–45	.0170	93,739	1,592	34.8
45–50	.0245	92,147	2,261	30.3
50–55	.0385	89,886	3,457	26.0

TABLE 5–1 (Cont.) ▓ Abridged Life Tables by Race and Sex: United States, 1988

Age Interval	Proportion dying	Of 100,000 born alive		Average remaining lifetime
Period of life between two exact ages stated in years, race, and sex	Proportion of persons alive at beginning of age interval dying during interval	Number living at beginning of age interval	Number dying during age interval	Average number of years of life remaining at beginning of age interval
(1)	(2)	(3)	(4)	(7)
x to $x + n$	$_nq_x$	l_x	$_nd_x$	e_x
MALE				
55–60	.0610	86,429	5,273	22.0
60–65	.0941	81,156	7,639	18.2
65–70	.1360	73,517	9,996	14.9
70–75	.2022	63,521	12,842	11.8
75–80	.2931	50,679	14,852	9.1
80–85	.4239	35,827	15,189	6.9
85 and over	1.0000	20,638	20,638	5.1
FEMALE				
0–1	.0089	100,000	890	78.3
1–5	.0018	99,110	175	78.0
5–10	.0010	98,935	101	74.2
10–15	.0010	98,834	100	69.2
15–20	.0024	98,734	240	64.3
20–25	.0028	98,494	272	59.4
25–30	.0033	98,222	321	54.6
30–35	.0041	97,901	405	49.8
35–40	.0058	97,496	567	45.0
40–45	.0084	96,929	817	40.2
45–50	.0135	96,112	1,293	35.5
50–55	.0219	94,819	2,077	31.0
55–60	.0347	92,742	3,217	26.6
60–65	.0537	89,525	4,810	22.5
65–70	.0793	84,715	6,716	18.6
70–75	.1210	77,999	9,435	15.0
75–80	.1843	68,564	12,640	11.7
80–85	.2981	55,924	16,671	8.7
85 and over	1.0000	39,253	39,253	6.3

SOURCE: United States Department of Health and Human Services. *Vital Statistics of the United States, 1988,* Vol. II, Section 6, *Life Tables* (Rockville, MD: National Center for Health Statistics, 1988), pp. 3–5.

complete. The United Nations has estimated that only 68 percent of deaths are recorded in Latin America, 15 percent in Asia, and less than 1 percent in Africa (Ruzicka and Lopez, 1990).

Progress has been made in the past decade regarding the use of sample surveys to ascertain both birth and death rates in different regions. Although there are still many gaps and limitations in mortality data, international agencies like the World Bank and the United Nations Population Division have been able to publish estimates of vital rates for most countries of the world (World Bank, 1991).

Mortality, Morbidity, and the Epidemiologic Transition

Morbidity, or sickness, may or may not result in death. The case fatality rate is a measure of the proportion of sick persons who die. Basically, diseases may be classified as communicable or degenerative. The role of these diseases in overall death rates has changed over time, leading to the development of an "epidemiologic transition" theory, first described by Abdel Omran (1977, 4) as follows:

> This theory focuses on the shifting web of health and disease patterns on population groups and their links with several demographic, social, economic, ecologic, and biological changes. Many countries have experienced a significant change or transition from high to low mortality accompanying either social development (as occurred in the West with the Industrial Revolution) or a combination of medical development and early social change (which was the story in many developing countries when antibiotics, insecticides, sanitation, and other medical technology were introduced after World War II). Common to all these countries is a clear shift in the kinds of diseases and causes of death that are prevalent at a fixed point in time: the Old World epidemics of infection are progressively (but not completely) replaced by degenerative diseases, diseases due to stress, and man-made diseases. Thus typhoid, tuberculosis, cholera, diphtheria, plague, and the like decline as the leading diseases and causes of death, to be replaced by heart diseases, cancer, stroke, diabetes, gastric ulcer, and the like, together with increased mental illness, accidents, disease due to industrial exposure, and, now, diseases which can be traced to a deteriorating environment.

Accompanying this epidemiologic transition, of course, has been a significant rise in the average life expectancy of those involved. For the world as a whole, average life expectancy has risen from about 30 years in 1900 to around 64 years in 1992. Worldwide, however, there are still great variations from nation to nation, as is apparent in Figure 5–2. Life expectancy at birth today ranges from a low of 41 years in Afghanistan to a high of 79 in Japan. More than 300 million people live in nations where the average life expectancy is less than 50 years. In many of these countries one of every ten newborns dies before age one (United Nations Development Programme, 1990).

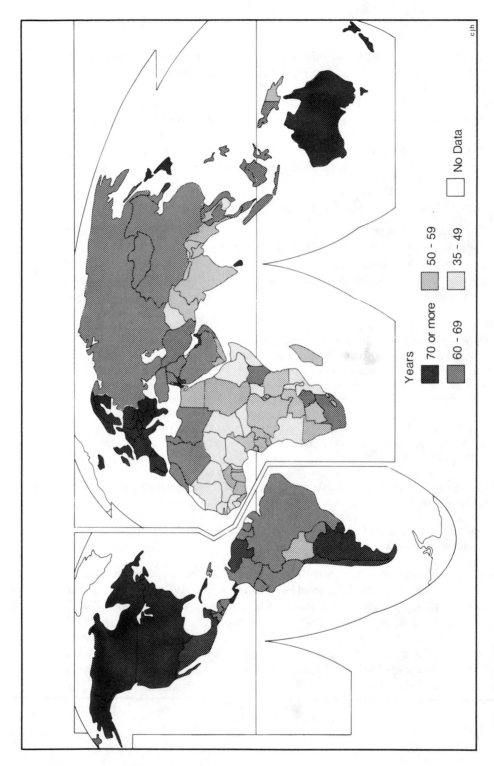

FIGURE 5–2 Life Expectancy at Birth in 1991. SOURCE: Data from *World Population Data Sheet 1991.* (Washington, D.C.: The Population Reference Bureau, Inc.).

Years

70 or more
60 - 69
50 - 59
35 - 49
No Data

Life expectancy tends to be generally related to the level of economic development, as is apparent on the map in Figure 5–2.

The gains in life expectancy in the past four decades have not been shared equally among the world's nations. A wide gap still exists between life expectancies in the developing nations in Africa, Asia, and Latin America and those in the more developed nations.

Within the developing world itself there have also been divergent trends. Eastern Asia, dominated by China, had a remarkable gain of 26 years in life expectancy from 1950–1990, surpassing both the Commonwealth of Independent States and Latin America (Mosely and Cowley, 1991, 7). With a gain of only 14 years in life expectancy, Africa showed the least improvement over this 40-year period. There are also great disparities among industrial countries, with Japan making the greatest gain among them. The gap between the countries with the lowest life expectancies in 1992 and those with the highest is approaching 40 years.

To gain a better understanding of the importance of the epidemiological transition theory, we must return to Omran's study, in which he introduced four concepts. One is especially important at this point and it was stated by Omran (1977, 9) as follows:

> During the transition, a long-term shift occurs in mortality and disease patterns whereby pandemics of infection are gradually displaced by degenerative and man-made diseases as the chief forms of morbidity and primary causes of death. Typically, mortality patterns distinguish three major successive stages of the epidemiologic transition: 1. *The Age of Pestilence and Famine,* when mortality is high and fluctuating, thus precluding sustained population growth. In this stage the average life expectancy at birth is low and variable, vacillating between 20 and 40 years. 2. *The Age of Receding Pandemics,* when mortality declines progressively; the rate of decline accelerates as epidemic peaks become less frequent or disappear. The average life expectancy at birth increases steadily from about 30 to about 50 years. Population growth is sustained and begins to take off exponentially. 3. *The Age of Degenerative and Man-Made Diseases,* when mortality continues to decline and eventually approaches stability at a relatively low level. The average life expectancy at birth rises gradually until it exceeds 70 years. It is during this stage that fertility becomes the crucial factor in population growth.

Furthermore, Omran suggested that, because of variations in the timing of the transition, there are three basic models of the epidemiologic transition: (1) the classic or Western model, (2) the accelerated model, and (3) the delayed model.

The classic or Western model describes the epidemiologic transition as it occurred in Western societies over the past 200 years, a transition in which crude death rates decreased from around 30 to under 10. The mortality decline occurred gradually in response to a mosaic of economic, social, and environmental improvements. In the early stages of this mortality decline, medical practices were relatively unimportant, while today downward shifts in mortality are strongly influenced by modern medicine (McKeown and Brown, 1969).

The accelerated model is descriptive of the mortality transition as it occurred in Japan, Eastern Europe, and the former Soviet Union. The transition was socially determined at the outset, but it benefited from the revolution taking place in medical science.

The delayed model may be applied to the observed conditions in most developing countries today, where rapid declines in mortality have occurred since the end of World War II. Mortality declines in the developing countries have been the result of modern medicine, the use of insecticides, and organized disease eradication programs.

Arguments about the relationship between mortality and economic development have attracted considerable attention. Some people argue that advances in mortality conditions in developing countries today are not closely related to economic development, as they have been in the past; others argue that economic development is still a major determinant of mortality conditions. In a study of health care in the Third World, Phillips (1990, 51) argued that "the epidemiological transition is therefore apparently a concept that needs to be applied with caution in many Third World countries. Only . . . where health services are on the whole more uniformly available and data more reliable, can the concept be used with much confidence for present and future health care planning."

At first glance it seems that a nation's income is an essential factor in determining mortality levels. Populations in the United States and in the nations of Northern and Western Europe, with per capita incomes around $20,000, have a life expectancy of 75 years, whereas people in many nations in Africa, with per capita incomes around $600 per year, have a life expectancy of only 53 years. Although most wealthy countries have high life expectancy rates, there are a number of low-income countries that have life expectancy rates approaching those of the wealthier countries. Conversely, some countries with relatively high per capita incomes rate relatively low on measures of health and survival (Mosley and Cowley, 1991, 31).

Table 5–2 lists five countries (Category A) that have relatively high life expectancy rates with low rates of gross national product (GNP) per capita. Most noteworthy are China and Sri Lanka, which have incomes below $500 per capita yet have life expectancy rates approaching that of most developed countries. Most countries in that income range have life expectancies in the 40s and low 50s. These five countries, however, have several features in common. They all have relatively high literacy rates for both men and women, an indication of an investment in education, with particular attention to equity for women. These nations also have relatively low fertility rates.

The countries listed in Category B (Table 5–2) have per capita incomes over $2,000 but life expectancy rates under 65 years. All but one of these nations is in North Africa. In general, the literacy rates for these nations are lower than those in Category A, and there is also a greater disparity between men and women. Total fertility rates for these nations are high as well, indicating that women do not participate broadly in these societies. The role of women in many Islamic countries is limited to childbearing and childrearing.

TABLE 5–2 ■ Life Expectancies Relative to GNP Per Capita—1991

Category A. High Life Expectancy with Low GNP Per Capita		
Country	**GNP/capita** **U.S. dollars**	**Life** **Expectancy**
China	$ 360.	69 years
Sri Lanka	430.	70
Jamaica	1,260.	74
Costa Rica	1,790.	77
Cuba	—	76
Category B. Lower Life Expectancy with High GNP/Per Capita		
Saudi Arabia	$6,230.	63
Oman	5,220.	64
Gabon	2,770.	52
Algeria	2,170.	64

SOURCE: *World Population Data Sheet 1991.* (Washington, D.C.: The Population Reference Bureau, Inc.). Reprinted by permission.

According to Mosley and Cowley (1991, 32), "The per capita public expenditures for health services in Saudi Arabia ($248.) and Libya ($163.) are 20 to 50 times greater than those in China ($5.) or Sri Lanka ($7.), suggesting that good health is not necessarily produced by spending money on sophisticated hospital care." In an effort to find out how some of these poor nations have managed to achieve these remarkable gains in health, the U.S.-based Rockefeller Foundation sponsored an international conference in Bellagio, Italy. The conference concluded that poor countries can achieve higher health standards and life expectancies if they have a political commitment to equality and if their programs focus on wide access to education, food, and basic health services (Halstead, et al., 1985).

However, there still is at least some tendency toward a relationship between income and mortality, though it is apparently weaker now than it was during the epidemiologic transition in the Western nations.

▓ CAUSES OF DEATH

The epidemiologic transition helps explain minor shifts in causes of death from various diseases although other causes of death must also be considered. Table 5–3 shows leading causes of death in the United States for 1988. Diseases of the heart were the first major cause of death, accounting for 35 percent of all deaths in the United States in 1988. In 1900 the leading causes of death in the United States were influenza and pneumonia. Malignant neoplasms were the second major cause of death in 1988,

TABLE 5–3 ▨ Mortality from 15 Leading Causes of Death: United States, 1988

(Rates per 100,000 population. Numbers after causes of death are category numbers of the Ninth Revision International Classification of Diseases, 1975.

	Cause of Death and Rank Order	Rate	Percent of Total Deaths
	All Causes	882.0	100.0
1	Diseases of heart (390–398, 402, 404–429)	311.3	35.2
2	Malignant neoplasms, including neoplasia of lymphatic and hematopoietic tissues (140–206)	108.3	22.4
3	Cerebrovascular diseases (430–438)	61.2	6.9
4	Accidents and adverse effects (E800–E949)	39.5	4.5
	. . . Motor vehicle accidents (E810–E825)	20.0	2.3
	. . . All other accidents and adverse effects (E800–807, E826–E949)	19.5	2.2
5	Chronic obstructive pulmonary diseases and allied conditions (490–496)	33.7	3.8
6	Pneumonia and influenza (480–487)	31.6	3.6
7	Diabetes mellitus (250)	16.4	1.9
8	Suicide (E950–E959)	12.4	1.4
9	Chronic liver disease and cirrhosis (571)	10.7	1.2
10	Atherosclerosis (440)	9.0	1.0
11	Nephritis, nephrotic syndrome, and nephrosis (580–589)	9.1	1.0
12	Homicide and legal intervention (E960–E978)	9.0	1.0
13	Certain conditions originating in the perinatal period (760–779)	7.4	.8
14	Septicemia (038)	8.5	1.0
15	Congenital anomalies (740–759)	5.2	.6
	. . . All other causes	119.7	13.6

SOURCE: *Statistical Abstract of the United States, 1991.* (Washington, D.C.: U.S. Government Printing Office), Table 116, p. 79.

accounting for just over 22 percent of all deaths. Thus, almost 60 percent of all deaths in the United States in 1988 resulted from two causes: heart disease and malignant neoplasms.

Mortality conditions in the United States prior to 1900 are not well documented, though it is safe to assume that mortality was well above what it has been in most of the twentieth century. Most likely, mortality conditions during the eighteenth and nineteenth centuries in the United States were similar to those experienced in Western Europe during the same period. Wars, famines, and epidemics caused fluctuations in year-to-year death rates.

TABLE 5-4 ▪ Life Expectancy at Specified Ages, Massachusetts, 1850 to 1900–1902

Year	At Birth		Age 20		Age 40		Age 60	
	Male	Female	Male	Female	Male	Female	Male	Female
1850	38.3	40.5	40.1	40.2	27.9	29.8	15.6	17.0
1855	38.7	40.9	39.8	39.9	27.0	28.8	14.4	15.6
1878–82	41.7	43.5	42.2	42.8	28.9	30.3	15.6	16.9
1890	42.5	44.5	40.7	42.0	27.4	28.8	14.7	15.7
1900–02	46.1	49.4	41.8	43.7	27.2	28.8	13.9	15.1

SOURCE: United States Bureau of the Census (1975) *Historical Statistics of the United States, Colonial Times to 1979.* Part 1 (Washington, D.C.: U.S. Government Printing Office), p. 56.

TABLE 5-5 ▪ Life Expectancy at Birth by Race and Sex, U.S., 1900–1990

Year	White Male	White Female	Nonwhite Male	Nonwhite Female
1900	46.6	48.7	32.5	33.5
1910	48.6	52.0	33.8	37.5
1920	54.4	55.6	45.5	45.2
1930	59.7	63.5	47.3	49.2
1940	62.1	66.6	51.5	54.9
1950	66.5	72.2	59.1	62.9
1960	67.4	74.1	61.1	66.3
1970	68.0	75.6	61.3	69.4
1980	70.7	78.1	65.3	78.6
1985	71.8	78.7	67.2	75.2
1990	72.7	79.6	67.5	75.7

SOURCE: National Center for Health Statistics. *Vital Statistics of the United States, 1970,* Vol. 2, Mortality, Part A, Table 5-5 and *Statistical Abstract of the United States, 1991.* (Washington, D.C.: U.S. Government Printing Office), Table 105.

Early data for Massachusetts suggest that some improvement in mortality conditions probably occurred in the nineteenth century, as is apparent in Table 5–4. These data suggest that improvements affected mainly infant and childhood mortality, because major gains in life expectancy appear only for life expectancy at birth. Undoubtedly, during this period considerable regional variations in death rates could be observed, as well as differences for whites and nonwhites. Life expectancy during the twentieth century also changed dramatically in the United States, as is apparent in Table 5–5.

Though mortality and morbidity have been studied by geographers for a long time, most of those studies have been on national and international scales. However, the study of disease in cities, although not entirely new, seems to be gaining in popularity. In one case detailed maps were used to study an outbreak of cholera that occurred in London during the 1850s (Stamp, 1964). It was found that a close correlation existed between sources of contaminated water and the incidence of cholera. Pyle and Rees (1971) used factor analysis to study health statistics, housing, and social composition in Chicago. The incidence of several diseases were found to be linked to poverty and to population density.

Condran and Cheney (1982) studied the decline in mortality that occurred in Philadelphia between 1870 and 1930. They found that explanations of mortality decline were often dependent on definitions. "Medical treatment," according to Condran and Cheney (1982, 119), "will account for much less of the decline in mortality if it is defined as chemotherapy, specific immunization, or surgery than if the definition is broadened to include the work of public physicians and nurses in isolating patients or in feeding sick infants during the summer months." Such emphases, they argue, have underestimated the impact of medical activities on declines in death rates. Condran and Cheney (1982, 119) noted also that, "the declines of typhoid fever in Philadelphia and elsewhere emphasize the fact that great progress has been made against disease not only by isolating the disease-producing organism, but also by identifying the environmental sources of the disease." Finally, they argued that no single factor alone could explain the dramatic decline that occurred in Philadelphia's mortality. This generalization certainly is also true of other cities, regions, and nations. However, as they also argue (1982, 120), "future research on the origins of the mortality transition will profit from careful attention to individual cities and the changes occurring in small areas within cities."

In another study of urban mortality, Cotter and Patrick (1981) focused their attention on the spatial pattern of cholera in 1849 in Buffalo, New York. They found that ethnicity, socioeconomic status, and neighborhood all influenced the direction and timing of the spread of the disease, as did the urban physical environment. They also found that diffusion of the disease was limited by cultural and physical isolation of various segments of the urban population, especially immigrants, who suffered the worst during the epidemic. "Cholera moved in limited circles," wrote Cotter and Patrick (1981, 49), "because interaction within groups was more frequent and of greater intensity than was interaction between groups."

Poor immigrants, mainly Irish, were the first to be affected by the epidemic, because their circumstances favored both entry and spread of the disease. Because many other neighborhoods did not interact with the Irish ones, cholera diffusion was restricted. In the city's Fifth Ward only a few people contracted cholera because conditions were not conducive to the disease's spread. According to Cotter and Patrick (1981, 49), "Not only did topography, low population density, and superior economic status combine to protect this ward, so also did its lack of interaction with the immigrant groups among whom cholera circulated." Thus, the diffusion of cholera in Buffalo was greatly affected by neighborhood locations and their established patterns of interaction.

Crimmons (1981) suggested that American mortality between 1940 and 1977 could be divided into three distinct periods characterized by differences in both age-specific and course-specific mortality rates. In the first period, from 1940 until the mid-1950s, American mortality declined rapidly. In the second period, from the mid-1950s until 1968, the pace of mortality decline leveled off, leading many to argue that mortality may be about as low as it can get. However, in the third period, beginning in 1968, mortality began another rapid decline. As Crimmins (1981, 251) noted:

> . . . much of the recent decline is accounted for by decreases in cardiovascular diseases. This is the first time in history that mortality declines have been dominated by decreases in diseases of old age or degenerative diseases. Because this is so, we may be beginning a new era of mortality decline, which, if it continues, will lead to large increases in life expectancy at older age.

▓ MORTALITY DIFFERENTIALS

It is one of the givens of demographics that not everyone is equally likely to die in a given time interval. The risk of death differs with age, sex, race, income, and rural versus urban residence, among other things.

Age Differentials

As noted previously, the typical J-shaped curve shows that under normal circumstances the probability of dying is relatively high for infants in the first year of life; is very low for children, adolescents, and young adults; and then rises more rapidly in the older ages. We have noted as well that improvements in mortality tend to be concentrated heavily within the infant and early childhood age groups although other age groups also have benefited.

In addition, significant differences are evident between the developing and the developed countries. In the developing countries children under age 5 account for half of all deaths, primarily caused by infectious diseases. Only 5 percent of the deaths in these nations are among the elderly older than age 75. Some African villages, for example, have reported deaths among infants and young children at ten times the rate of the aged.

In the developed nations, on the other hand, only 2 percent of deaths are among children under age 5, whereas almost two-thirds occur to those over 75 years of age.

Infant Mortality in the United States

Infant mortality in the United States has consistently decreased from a level of 100 or more at the turn of the present century (as is apparent in Figure 5–3) to 9.1 in 1991. Figures for infant mortality rates during the eighteenth and nineteenth centuries are unavailable, but most likely they were always in excess of 100 and may at times

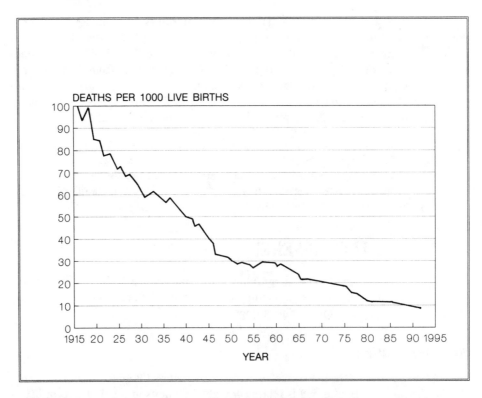

■ **FIGURE 5–3** Infant Mortality Rate: United States, 1915–1992. SOURCE: Data from *Vital Statistics of the United States, 1984,* Vol. II, Mortality Part A, Section 2, Table 2.1 and *1992 World Population Data Sheet.*

have been twice that. Data for Massachusetts provide a somewhat better perspective on the transition in infant mortality, as Table 5–6 clearly shows.

It is noteworthy that significant disparities in infant mortality rates exist within the United States today. A recent study reported that the infant mortality rate among African-Americans was 17.6 per 1000, which was more than double the rate for whites of 8.5 per 1000 (National Center for Health Statistics, 1990). The nation's capital, Washington, D.C., had an infant mortality rate of 21.2 per 1000, a rate greater than less developed countries such as Cuba, Chile, and Costa Rica.

The reason for the discrepancy in infant mortality along racial lines is primarily because African-Americans have a variety of social disadvantages. African-American mothers are less likely to receive prenatal care and their infants are twice as likely to be of low birth weight. Significant cost-effective programs to overcome these problems are available, but recent funding by the Reagan/Bush administrations has not kept pace with the growing number of eligible women and children (Paige and Davis, 1986).

TABLE 5–6 ▪ Infant Mortality Rate,
Massachusetts, 1851–1854 to 1950–1954

Period	Rates
1851–54	131.1
1855–59	122.9
186)–64	142.5
1865–69	146.3
1870–74	170.3
1875–79	156.3
1880–84	161.3
1885–89	158.5
1890–94	163.2
1895–99	153.2
1900–04	141.4
1905–09	134.3
1910–14	116.7
1915–19	100.2
1920–24	78.7
1925–29	67.6
1930–34	53.9
1935–39	43.2
1940–44	34.3
1945–49	28.4
1950–54	22.8

SOURCE: United States Bureau of the Census.
(1975) *Historical Statistics of the United States,
Colonial Times to 1970.* Part 1 (Washington, D.C.:
U.S. Government Printing Office), p. 57.

Infant Mortality in Other Parts of the World

Despite the affluence and advanced technology in the United States, infant mortality conditions here are not as good as they are in a number of other countries (see Table 5–7), although they are improving.

Worldwide the pattern of infant mortality is as shown in Figure 5–4. Infant mortality rates range from a low of 4.5 in Japan to a high of 182 in Afghanistan. Among major world regions infant mortality is highest in Africa, with an overall rate of 102. Asia is next highest with an overall rate of 68. Western Europe is the lowest with a rate of only 7, though North America with 9 is very close behind.

Infant and child mortality is primarily a problem associated with the developing countries. In 1990 approximately 98 percent of the deaths among children less than 5 years of age occurred in the developing countries. The tragedy, according to UNICEF estimates, is that 95 percent of the estimated 14.5 million infant and child deaths in

TABLE 5–7 ▨ Twenty-three Countries with
Lowest Infant Mortality Rates, 1991

Country	Deaths per 1000 Live Births
Japan	4.5
Iceland	5.3
Finland	5.8
Sweden	5.8
Taiwan	6.2
Singapore	6.6
Netherlands	6.8
Canada	7.2
France	7.2
Switzerland	7.3
Hong Kong	7.4
Ireland	7.5
Germany	7.5
Australia	7.7
Austria	7.9
Norway	8.0
Spain	8.3
Denmark	8.4
United Kingdom	8.4
Belgium	8.6
Italy	8.8
United States	9.1
Luxembourg	9.9

SOURCE: *World Population Data Sheet 1991*. (Washington, D.C.: The Population Reference Bureau, Inc.). Reprinted by permission.

developing countries in 1990 were preventable (Grant, 1990). Even in the developed countries, where only 300,000 children less than age 5 died (mostly in Eastern Europe and the former Soviet Union), more than 60 percent of those deaths were potentially preventable as well.

It has been estimated that 24 percent of the world's newborns died before age 5 in 1950; by 1990, however, the infant and child mortality rate (ICMR) had declined more than 55 percent to 10.5 percent. Perhaps the most impressive decline occurred in China, where the rate went from 26.6 percent to 4.1 percent, an 85 percent reduction. Japan also had an impressive drop from 7.5 percent to 0.8 percent, a drop of 89 percent.

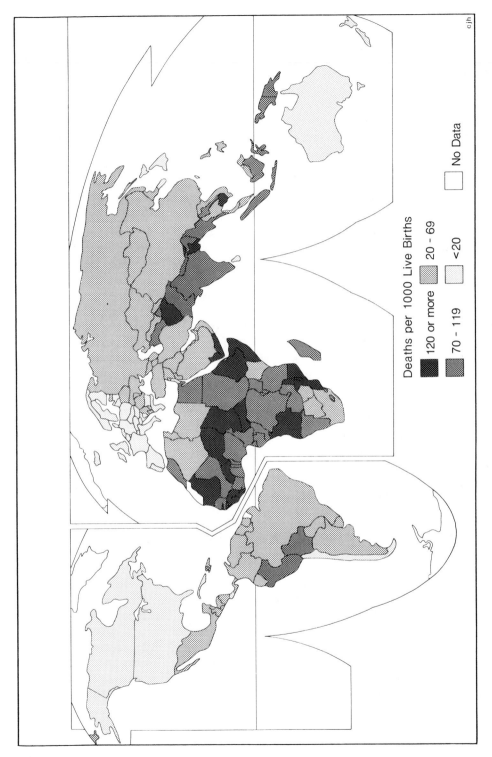

■ **FIGURE 5–4** Infant Mortality in 1992. SOURCE: Data from *1992 World Population Data Sheet.* (Washington, D.C.: The Population Reference Bureau, Inc.).

Deaths per 1000 Live Births

120 or more
70 - 119
20 - 69
<20
No Data

Researchers have identified several factors that are thought to be related to infant mortality risks. High-risk babies include those born to mothers who are adolescents, are over age 40, or have had more than seven births and when the interval between births is less than 7 years (Mosley and Cowley, 1991, 10). National policies aimed at discouraging early marriage and childbearing, along with aggressive family planning programs, can prevent births to high-risk mothers and substantially reduce infant and child mortality (Rutstein, 1991).

In almost every country studied, the infant and child mortality rate fell as the education of mothers improved. Figure 5–5 depicts changes in mortality rates for children less than age 5 as these changes relate to the mothers' education for selected countries. According to Mosley and Cowley (1991, 11), "Maternal education appears to affect child health in a number of ways. . . . The more educated a mother is, the more likely she is to use maternal and child health services—specifically prenatal care, delivery care, childhood immunizations, and oral rehydration therapy for diarrhea."

A few major diseases are responsible for a large proportion of deaths among children under 5 years of age (Table 5–8). These diseases, for the most part, are preventable at a relatively low cost. Oral Rehydration Therapy (ORT) has been effectively used to combat childhood diarrhea. UNICEF estimates that in 1990 more than 1.0 million diarrhea deaths were prevented by ORT, although another 2.5 million preventable deaths still occurred from diarrhea. Immunization coverage also has greatly increased in the past decade, even though it varies widely in the developing world from 95 percent in China to only 53 percent in sub-Saharan Africa (Grant, 1991).

Another, more intractable problem is that of childhood malnutrition. Although malnutrition is not listed in many cases as a cause of death, estimates are that it is a contributing factor in up to 40 percent of child deaths. An estimated 177 million children in the developing world are malnourished (Carlson and Wardlaw, 1990).

Sex Differentials

Sex differences in mortality have been of considerable interest to demographers. The risk of death appears to be greater for males at all ages. Even among fetal deaths males are more likely to die. No simple explanation of these sex mortality differentials has been accepted.

Some people have argued that the female is biologically superior to the male. Support for this argument comes from reported sex differentials favoring females among other species, including rats, and from the higher fetal mortality for males in humans.

Madigan's study of mortality among religious teaching orders of brothers and sisters also supported the idea of female biological superiority (Madigan, 1957). His sample of religious communities was an attempt to control for sociocultural differences that influence mortality and to view mortality under conditions that were as similar as possible for both sexes. Both sexes were found to have greater life expectancies than

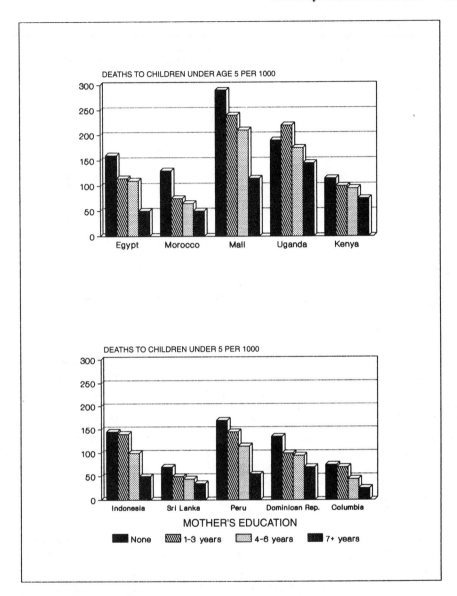

■ **FIGURE 5–5** Under-Five Mortality Rates and Mother's Education. Results from Selected Demographic and Health Surveys. SOURCE: W. Henry Mosley and Peter Cowley. (1991) "The Challenge of World Health," *Population Bulletin* 46:10. Courtesy of The Population Reference Bureau, Inc.

TABLE 5–8 ▨ Causes of Death to Children under Age 5 in Developing Countries

Causes of Death	Number (thousands)	Percentage of deaths
Diarrheal diseases	4,000	27.4
Immunizeable diseases	3,700	25.3
Measles	2,000	13.7
Whooping cough	600	4.1
Tuberculosis	300	2.1
Neonatal tetanus	775	5.3
Polio	25*	0.2
Acute respiratory infections	2,375	16.3
Malaria	750	5.1
Other infections/parasitic diseases	450	3.1
Perinatal causes	2,425	16.6
Injuries	200	1.4
Other causes	700	4.8
Total	14,600	100.0

*Polio causes about 250,000 paralytic cases annually, of which about 10 percent die.

SOURCE: W. Henry Mosley and Peter Cowley. (1991) "The Challenge of World Health," *Population Bulletin* 46:11.

the general population, but the differences in life expectancy between the sexes was as apparent for this sample as for the entire population. That demographers are not generally convinced of this argument is apparent in the following comment from Thomlinson (1976, 148):

> Although some persons believe that women are biologically superior to men, this conclusion cannot be properly deduced from the factually supportable premises. One piece of contrary evidence is the higher mortality rates among underdeveloped areas and in some nonliterate societies. Although the evidence is insubstantial, what we can learn from excavations of ancient burial sites implies a higher mortality among women.

An alternative explanation of mortality sex differences is to attribute them to differentials in occupation, status, and role. Males are employed in more hazardous occupations than are females. Military deaths are primarily male. Males are believed by some to be under greater stress than females; males generally smoke more, drink more, and even drive more than females; and they are more often murdered. All of these factors are likely to raise male mortality rates. At the same time, as societies move through the demographic transition, women may benefit differentially because fewer childbirths undoubtedly increase the probability of living longer. However, both social and biological differences probably contribute to observed sex differentials.

Indications of mortality sex differentials, as well as changes in these differentials, may be seen in Tables 5–9 and 5–10 and are certainly worth some attention at this point.

TABLE 5–9 ▧ Selected Life Table Values: 1959–1988 (Prior to 1960, excludes Alaska and Hawaii. Beginning 1970, excludes deaths of nonresidents of the United States. See also *Historical Statistics, Colonial Times to 1970,* series B, pp. 116–125)

Age and Sex	Total[1]					White					Black		
	1959–1961	1969–1971	1979–1981	1985	1988	1959–1961	1969–1971	1979–1981	1985	1988	1979–1981	1985	1988
Average expectation of life in years													
At birth: Male	66.8	67.0	70.1	71.2	71.5	67.6	67.9	70.8	71.9	72.3	64.1	65.3	64.9
Female	73.2	74.6	77.6	78.2	78.3	74.2	75.5	78.2	78.7	78.9	72.9	73.5	73.4
Age 20: Male	49.8	49.5	51.9	52.7	53.0	50.3	50.2	52.5	53.3	53.6	46.4	47.4	47.0
Female	55.6	56.6	59.0	59.3	59.4	56.3	57.2	59.4	59.8	59.9	54.9	55.3	55.1
Age 40: Male	31.4	31.5	33.6	34.3	34.8	31.7	31.9	34.0	34.7	35.2	29.5	30.2	30.3
Female	36.6	37.6	39.8	40.1	40.2	37.1	38.1	40.2	40.4	40.6	36.3	36.6	36.6
Age 50: Male	23.0	23.1	25.0	25.6	26.0	23.2	23.3	25.3	25.8	26.3	22.0	22.5	22.0
Female	27.7	28.8	30.7	30.9	31.0	28.1	29.1	31.0	31.1	31.2	27.8	27.9	28.0
Age 65: Male	13.0	13.0	14.2	14.6	14.9	13.0	13.0	14.3	14.6	14.9	13.3	13.3	13.4
Female	15.8	16.8	18.4	18.6	18.6	15.9	16.9	18.6	18.7	18.7	17.1	17.0	16.9

SOURCE: *Statistical Abstract of the United States, 1991.* (Washington, D.C.: U.S. Government Printing Office), Table 106.

TABLE 5–10 ▧ Men per 100 Women by Age and Race, 1900–1990

Age and Race	1900	1930	1960	1970	Projection 1990
All Races:					
Over 65	102	100.4	82.6	72.1	67.5
Over 75	96.3	91.8	75.1	63.7	57.8
White:					
Over 65	101.9	100.1	82.1	71.6	67.7
Over 75	97.1	92	74.3	63.2	58.4
Black:					
Over 65	102.9	105.7	30.1	79.8	68.2
Over 75	89.6	89.6	87.6	74.7	62.6

SOURCE: Leon Bouvier, Elinore Atlee, and Frank McVeigh. (1975) "The Elderly in America," *Population Bulletin,* 30(3):9. Courtesy of the Population Reference Bureau, Inc., Washington, D.C.

Color and Class Differentials

Many, if not most, racial and ethnic mortality differentials reflect differences in socioeconomic status. No convincing evidence of significant biological differences in the resistance to diseases can be identified among different racial and ethnic groups although a few diseases are largely restricted to certain groups. Probably the best example of such a disease is sickle-cell anemia, which is mainly restricted to African-Americans.

Crude death rates for the United States in 1988 for whites and nonwhites appear in Table 5–11. They suggest heavier mortality rates among whites, especially among white females. However, keep in mind that the crude death rate can be deceptive. Age-specific death rates reveal a different picture entirely, as is apparent in Table 5–12. Nevertheless, for most groups, nonwhite mortality is considerably above white mortality. Table 5–12 also illustrates sex differentials of mortality.

In most countries, social status and mortality are related although the degree of the relationship varies in different types of political and economic systems. One example of this relationship is shown in Table 5–13. However, such class differentials have probably increased as countries passed through the epidemiological transition. As Pressat (1970, 37) commented:

> It is certainly true that, until recent times, social inequality did not too seriously aggravate the risks of mortality among the lower classes. Because of the ineffectiveness of medical care, the poor lost very little by not being able to take advantage of it. The great epidemics spared no one and the standard of hygiene at the court of Versailles was probably no higher than in country districts. The crisis of subsistence was probably the only plague which did not affect the rich, whose dietary habits could be disastrous anyway.

Today many differences in mortality may be attributed to differences in socioeconomic factors, but many other differences also are important and should not be overlooked.

▨ MEDICAL GEOGRAPHY

Medical geography, the study of the spatial aspects of health and illness, is an area of geographic inquiry that has seen a considerable amount of recent research activity. Its focus has been twofold: (1) on disease ecology, the "manner and consequences of interaction between the environment and the causes of morbidity and mortality" (Birdsall, 1991, 392) and (2) on the health care delivery system and its spatial aspects.

The mapping of disease has received much attention in the past few years. Studies such as those on the techniques of mapping cancer by Boyle, et al. (1989) and Clayton and Kaldor (1989) have provided useful geographic insights into that disease. A more traditional atlas and compendium of analytical techniques was developed by Cliff and Haggett (1988).

TABLE 5–11 ■ Crude Death Rates by Color and Sex, United States, 1989

Population	Crude Death Rate	
	White	Nonwhite
Total	9.1	7.6
Males	9.5	8.7
Females	8.6	6.5

SOURCE: *Statistical Abstract of the United States, 1991.* (Washington, D.C.: U.S. Government Printing Office).

TABLE 5–12 ■ Death Rates by Age, Color, and Sex, United States, 1988

Color and Sex	Rates per 1000 in Each Age Group										
	Under 1 Year	1–4 Years	5–14 Years	15–24 Years	25–34 Years	35–44 Years	45–54 Years	55–64 Years	65–74 Years	75–84 Years	85 Years and Over
White											
Total	8.3	0.5	0.2	1.0	1.2	1.9	4.4	11.7	26.7	62.8	158.8
Male	9.3	0.5	0.3	1.4	1.7	2.6	5.6	15.3	35.0	82.0	188.1
Female	7.3	0.4	0.2	0.5	0.6	1.2	3.2	8.5	19.1	51.3	147.6
Nonwhite											
Total	17.5	0.7	0.3	1.3	2.4	4.1	7.8	16.8	32.5	66.9	127.9
Male	18.1	0.8	0.4	2.0	3.5	5.9	10.7	21.9	41.8	84.0	145.5
Female	16.0	0.6	0.3	0.6	1.3	2.6	5.5	12.7	25.5	56.3	119.6

SOURCE: United States Department of Health and Human Services. *Vital Statistics of the United States, 1988,* Vol. II, Mortality—Part A (Washington, D.C.: U.S. Government Printing Office), Table 1–3, pp. 3–4.

TABLE 5–13 ■ Death Rates in 1975 by Size of Landholdings, Companiganj, Bangladesh

Size of Land Holding (acres)	Death Rate
None	35.8
.01–.49	28.4
.50–2.99	21.5
3.00+	12.2

SOURCE: Lester R. Brown. (1976) *World Population Trends: Signs of Hope, Signs of Stress.* Worldwatch Paper No. 5 (Washington, D.C.: Worldwatch Institute) October, p. 20. Used by permission.

The analysis of geographical variations in health care provision and consumption is another area of concern to geographers. Analytical models in this area have focused on both the individual level (Senior and Williamson, 1990) and on the national level (Mohan, 1988). According to Jones and Moon (1991, 443), writing in a recent review about the progress made in medical geography, "Sophisticated modelling of this nature, together with informed qualitative work, provides medical geography with a means to complement its traditional regional-scale analyses. In disease mapping, modeling allows the assessment of environmental effects, taking into account individual characteristics. In health-care geography it provides a basis for in-depth analyses of the relationship between need and provision/consumption."

▨ ACQUIRED IMMUNE DEFICIENCY SYNDROME (AIDS)

The past decade has seen an alarming rise in mortality attributable to AIDS. In many ways AIDS is like the bubonic plague of medieval times. Both diseases were initially incurable; currently, almost everyone who contracts AIDS will eventually die from opportunistic infections and neoplasms.

Data from the World Health Organization point out that over 500,000 AIDS cases were reported worldwide by mid-1987, and between 5 million and 10 million people worldwide had been infected by the virus (Marx, 1987, 1523). By the end of 1986, 32,560 cases had been reported in the Western Hemisphere, with 90 percent of them in the United States. In 1983 a little over 2,000 AIDS cases were reported by the United States Centers for Disease Control (CDC). By 1988 this number had surpassed 30,000.

Although the exact origin of the AIDS virus has not been determined, most researchers believe that the retrovirus responsible for AIDS originated in Africa. Six years before its identification in the United States, the disease had been isolated in central Africa. Since its initial recognition in Africa around 1972, the disease has diffused to most other parts of the world.

AIDS in the United States

In the United States the initial appearance of AIDS had three prominent foci—the metropolitan areas of San Francisco, Los Angeles, and New York City. According to a study by Dutt, et al. (1987, 457–458), "Prior to 1983, 67 percent of the AIDS victims in the country were confined to these areas." The rate map for 1988 (Figure 5–6) shows the emergence of another focal point in Florida, probably the result of its close connections with both the Caribbean countries and New York City, where the disease was prevalent.

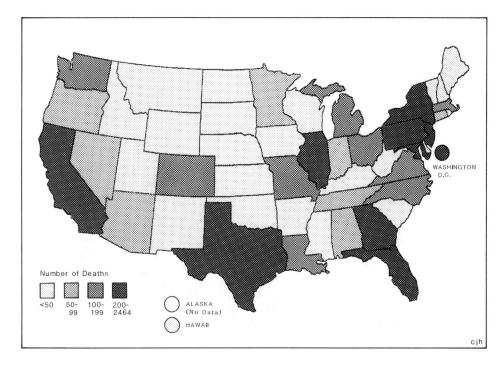

▩ **FIGURE 5–6** Deaths Among AIDS Cases, 1989. SOURCE: Data from Centers for Disease Control, Center for Infectious Diseases, AIDS Program.

The number of people diagnosed as having AIDS rose sharply in the 1980s (Figure 5–7). In 1981 only 318 persons were diagnosed as having AIDS; but by 1989, that figure had increased to over 35,000. Between 1981 and 1988, over 30,000 persons contracted AIDS.

An analysis of AIDS victims by age and gender points out some interesting relationships. Most AIDS victims are between the ages of 13 and 49, but almost half of them are in the 30 to 39 age cohort. Only 9.7 percent of AIDS victims are over age 50 and about 1.4 percent below age 13. Most of these younger victims contracted the disease through blood transfusions. AIDS victims are predominantly male. Currently, only 7.4 percent of American AIDS victims are female. These age and gender characteristics are similar throughout the nation and changed little between 1981 and 1987 (Dutt, et al., 1987, 487). In the early 1990s some evidence suggested an increasing incidence of AIDS among women, mainly prostitutes and those in relationships with heterosexual or bisexual IV drug users.

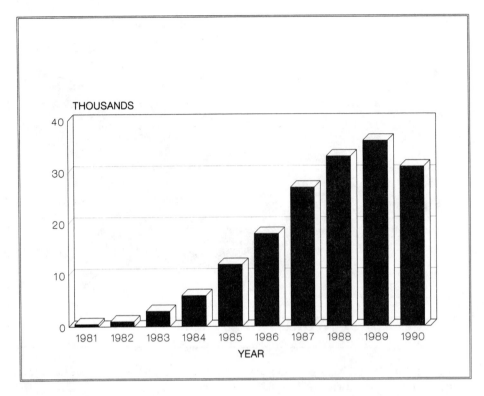

■ **FIGURE 5–7** AIDS in the United States, Cases Diagnosed, 1981–1990. SOURCE: Data from Centers for Disease Control, Center for Infectious Diseases, AIDS Program.

AIDS is a viral disease that attacks the human immune system, leaving victims virtually defenseless against infection and other disorders. As a result, victims do not actually die from the virus itself but rather from such opportunistic infections as pneumonia, tuberculosis, influenza, and Karposi's sarcoma, a relatively rare form of cancer. The syndrome is fatal to almost everyone who contracts it. An analysis of mortality rates among different racial groups shows that deaths have been more numerous among Hispanics and African-Americans than among whites. These differences are probably due to the fact that more and better health-care facilities are available to whites than are within reach of African-Americans and Hispanics.

Although AIDS first appeared in the metropolitan areas of San Francisco, Los Angeles, and New York, it has now spread to other large metropolitan areas as well as to small cities and towns. According to Dutt, et al. (1987, 471), "Once confined to the peripheries of the country, the disease has now spread to its heartland. AIDS is also becoming more prevalent among heterosexuals, who constitute the overwhelming bulk of the sexually active Americans. If this trend continues, the disease will intensify and no part of the country, indeed no group in it, will be AIDS-free in the near future. AIDS has no racial, political, social, or physical barriers. Without the development of a curative drug or preventive vaccine, the potential for destruction from the spread of AIDS cannot be measured or predicted. It is not an overstatement to assert that humanity is in danger."

In an effort to understand the spatial dimensions of the diffusion pattern of AIDS, Gould, et al. (1991, 80) have developed modeling techniques to portray the geographic dimensions of AIDS diffusion and have attempted to "predict the next maps, not just numbers down the time line." A time-series of maps was produced for the State of Pennsylvania (Figure 5–8) and, according to Gould et al. (1991, 86), "If you know your human geography of Pennsylvania, you can see the hierarchical diffusion, the jumping from city to city; you can see the spatially contagious diffusion, the wine stain on the tablecloth; and you can also see the way in which the structure of the human landscape, the major turnpikes and roads, channels the epidemic." Similar maps have also been developed for the spread of AIDS in the western United States from 1981 to 1988 (Gould, 1991).

▨ PATTERN OF WORLD MORTALITY

The current world pattern of mortality is shown in Figure 5–9. Any interpretation of this pattern must be approached very cautiously because the crude death rate served as the measure of mortality, and the crude death rate is greatly affected by the age structure of a population. For example, the crude death rate in the United States is higher than that of Mexico; yet few people would expect mortality conditions to be better in Mexico. Two other measures, life expectancy at birth and the infant mortality rate, are better indicators of actual mortality conditions. For Mexico the infant mortality rate is more than four times higher than that of the United States, and the life expectancy at birth in Mexico is less than that of the United States.

Maps of both world infant mortality rates and world life expectancy at birth have been discussed previously in this chapter. The main reason for now considering a map of world crude death rates is that it provides us with a look at one of the two rates used to calculate the rate of natural increase. Areas of low crude death rates, if they also have high crude birth rates, may be areas of rapid population growth. Areas with high crude death and birth rates are potential areas for fast growth in the future, as typically crude death rates have fallen earlier and faster than crude birth rates.

In 1992 the estimated crude death rate for the world was 9. Death rates of 9 or less are found in many developed countries, from the United States to Australia, as well as in some of the developing countries of Latin America. Most of Western Europe and Asia, along with parts of North Africa, have death rates between 10 and 20. The highest death rates, those above 20, are found in Africa, as well as in Afghanistan.

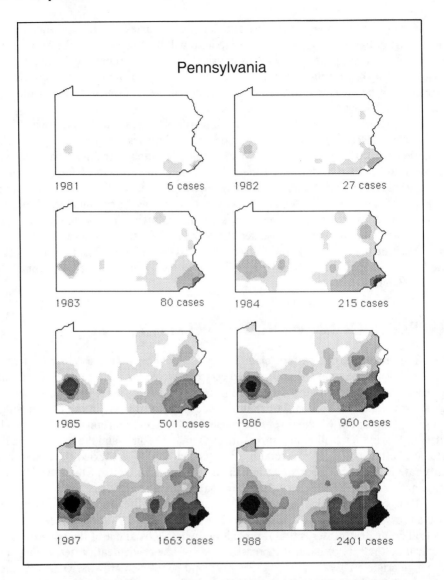

■ **FIGURE 5–8** Diffusion of AIDS in Pennsylvania, Taken from a Colored and Animated Sequence Made for Television. Grey Tones Increase Geometrically, 1, 3, 9, 27, 81, 243, etc.
SOURCE: Reprinted by permission of Peter Gould, "AIDS: Predicting the Next Map," *INTERFACES,* Volume 21, Number 3, May-June 1991. Copyright © 1991 by the Operations Research Society of American and The Institute of Management Sciences, 290 Westminster Street, Providence, Rhode Island 02903 USA.

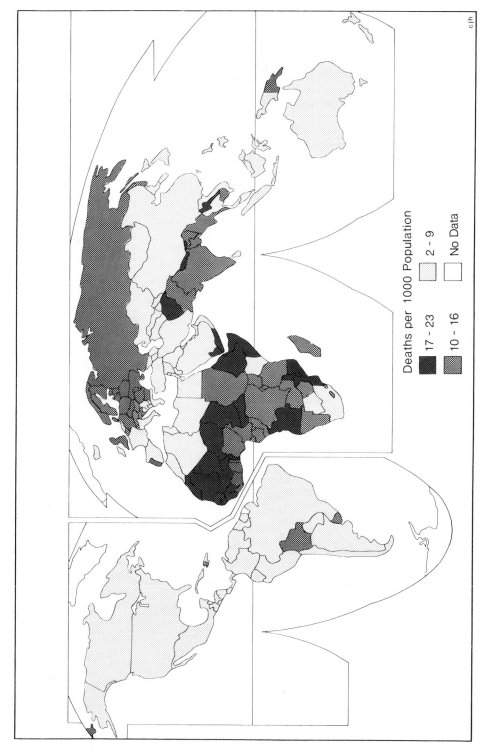

Deaths per 1000 Population

■ 17 - 23
▨ 10 - 16
▨ 2 - 9
☐ No Data

■ **FIGURE 5-9** World Crude Death Rates, 1992. SOURCE: Data from *1992 World Population Data Sheet.* (Washington, D.C.: Population Reference Bureau, Inc.).

TABLE 5–14 ■ Death Rate in
Matlab Bazar, 1966/67 to 1974/75

Year	Death Rate
1966/67	15.0
1967/68	16.6
1968/69	15.0
1969/70	14.9
1970/71	14.8
1971/72	21.4
1972/73	16.2
1973/74	14.2
1974/75	19.8

SOURCE: Lester R. Brown. (1976) *World
Population Trends: Signs of Hope, Signs
of Stress.* Worldwatch Paper No. 8
(Washington, D.C.: Worldwatch Institute)
October, p. 19. Used by permission.

Barring major catastrophes, such as widespread famines, epidemics, and nuclear holocaust, it is likely that the epidemiological transition will continue to reduce world mortality rates. However, some signs of checks on the downward trend in death rates are appearing. In discussing the decreasing world growth rate, Brown (1976, 6) commented:

> . . . tragically, the slowdown in population growth is not due entirely to falling birth rates. In some poor countries population growth is being periodically checked by hunger-induced rises in death rates. These recent upturns in the national death rates represent a reversal of postwar trends, one which political leaders in the affected countries are not eager to discuss.

Food scarcity tends mainly to increase the death rates for infants and the elderly although other age groups also can be affected. One of those countries where food scarcity is severe is Bangladesh. In one district, Matlab Bazar, records of births and deaths are quite accurate, and the trend for that district may be seen in Table 5–14. Death rate increases have occurred in parts of India and in Africa's Sahel since 1970, again mainly as a result of food shortages. In Ethiopia alone 200,000 lives were lost to famine.

The world food situation is discussed in more detail in Chapter 11. The impact of rising death rates from starvation and malnutrition need to be mentioned here, however. It is especially worthwhile to consider Brown (1976, 25), who stated that although death rates measure the principal demographic effect of prolonged hunger, they do not measure the social impact. For every person who dies, scores or even hundreds may suffer and lie close to death. The true social cost of food shortages must take into account these hapless individuals, as well as the millions of infants and children who somehow survive prolonged periods of semi-starvation only to suffer irreparable brain damage in the process.

No one wishes to see death rates increase anywhere, but clearly the planet is becoming more strained in its ability to deal with population growth, most of which is occurring in the developing countries of the Third World. Given that some balance between birth rates and death rates must be achieved in order to curtail world population growth, we continue to believe that lowering fertility rates is much preferable to raising death rates. As we move on to a discussion of fertility, however, it will become obvious that we are moving neither far enough nor fast enough to prevent the world's population from at least doubling again during the next century. At the same time, despite its important connections to economic, social, and environmental problems around the globe, population growth was virtually absent from the agenda at the Earth Summit that was held in Rio de Janeiro in June of 1992.

REFERENCES

Barclay, George W. (1958) *Techniques of Population Analysis*. New York: John Wiley and Sons, Inc.

Birdsall, Stephen. (1991) "Medical Geography," in H. J. deBlij and Peter O. Muller, *Geography: Regions and Concepts*. 6th ed. New York: John Wiley and Sons, Inc., pp. 392–393.

Boyle, P., Muir, C. S., and Grundman, P., eds. (1989) *Mapping and Cancer: Recent Results in Cancer Research 114*. Berlin: Springer Verlag.

Brown, Lester R. (1976) *World Population Trends: Signs of Hope, Signs of Stress*. Worldwatch Paper No. 8, Washington, D.C.: Worldwatch Institute.

Carlson, Beverly A. and Wardlaw, Tessa M. (1990) *A Global, Regional, and Country Assessment of Child Malnutrition*. New York: UNICEF.

Clayton, E. C. and Kaldor, J. (1989) "The Role of Advanced Statistical Methods in Cancer Mapping," in Boyle, et al., *Mapping and Cancer*. Berlin: Springer Verlag.

Cliff, A. D. and Haggett, P. (1988) *Atlas of Disease Distributions*. Oxford: Basil Blackwell.

Condran, Gretchen A. and Cheney, Rose A. (1982) "Mortality Trends in Philadelphia: Age- and Cause-Specific Death Rates 1870–1930," *Demography* 18:94–124.

Cotter, John V. and Patrick, Larry L. (1981) "Disease and Ethnicity in an Urban Environment," *Annals of the Association of American Geographers* 71:40–49.

Crimmins, Eileen M. (1981) "The Changing Pattern of American Mortality Decline, 1940–77, and Its Implications for the Future," *Population and Development Review* 7:229–254.

Dutt, Ashok K., Monroe, Charles B., Dutta, Hiran M., and Prince, Barbara (1987) "Geographical Patterns of AIDS in the United States," *The Geographical Review* 77(4):456–471.

Gould, P., Kabel, J., Gorr, W., and Golub, A. (1991) "AIDS: Predicting the Next Map," *Interfaces* 21:80–92.

Gould, P. (1991) "Editorial Report," *Science* 234:1022.

Grant, James P. (1990) *The State of the World's Children 1990.* New York and Oxford: Oxford University Press for UNICEF.

Gwatkin, Davison R. and Brandel, Sarah K. (1982) "Life Expectancy and Population Growth in the Third World," *Scientific American* 246(5):57–65.

Halstead, Scott B., Walsh, Julia A., and Warren, Kenneth S., eds. (1985) *Proceedings of a Conference held at the Bellagio Conference Center, Bellagio, Italy, 29 April–3 May 1985.* New York: The Rockefeller Foundation.

Jones, Kelvyn and Moon, Graham. (1991). "Medical Geography," *Progress in Human Geography* 15:437–443.

Madigan, Francis C. (1957) "Are Sex Mortality Differentials Biologically Caused?" *Milbank Memorial Fund Quarterly* 35:202–223.

Marx, Jean L. (1987) "Probing the AIDS Virus and Its Relatives," *Science* 230(19 June 1987):1523.

McKeown, Thomas and Brown, R. G. (1969) "Medical Evidence Related to English Population Changes in the Eighteenth Century," in Michael Drake, ed., *Population in Industrialization.* London: Methuen and Co., Ltd.

Mohan, J. (1988) "Restructuring, Privitisation and the Geography of Health Care Provision in England 1983–1987," *Transactions of the Institute of British Geographers* 13:449–465.

Mosley, W. Henry and Cowley, Peter. (1991) "The Challenge of World Health," *Population Bulletin* 46:1–39.

National Center for Health Statistics. (1990) "Advance Report of Final Natality Statistics, 1988," *Monthly Vital Statistics Report* 39(4):Supplement.

Omran, Abdel R. (1977) "Epidemiologic Transition in the U.S.: The Health Factor in Population Changes in the Eighteenth Century," *Population Bulletin* 32(2):1–42.

Paige, David M. and Davis, Lenora. (1986) "Fetal Growth, Maternal Nutrition, and Dietary Supplementation." *Clincal Nutrition* 5:191–198.

Phillips, David R. (1990) *Health and Health Care in the Third World.* New York: John Wiley and Sons, Inc.

Pressat, Roland. (1970) *Population.* Baltimore: Penguin Books.

Preston, Samuel H. (1976) *Mortality Patterns in National Populations.* New York: Academic Press.

Pyle, G. F. and Rees, P. H. (1971) "Modeling Patterns of Death and Disease in Chicago," *Economic Geography* 47:475–488.

Rutstein, Shea O. (1991) "Levels, Trends, and Differentials in Infant and Child Mortality in the Less Developed Countries" Paper presented at the seminar on Child Survival Interventions: Effectiveness and Efficiency at The Johns Hopkins University School of Hygiene and Public Health, Baltimore, MD.

Ruzicka, Ldao T. and Lopez, Alan D. (1990) "The Use of Cause-of-Death Statistics for Health Situation Assessment: National and International Experiences," *World Health Statistical Quarterly* 43:249–257.

Senior, M. and Williamson, S. (1990) "An Investigation into the Influence of Geographical Factors on Attendance for Cervical Cytology Screening," *Transactions of the Institute of British Geographers* 15:421–434.

Stamp, L. Dudley. (1964) *The Geography of Life and Death*. Ithaca, NY: Cornell University Press.

Thomlinson, Ralph. (1976) *Population Dynamics: Causes and Consequences of World Demographic Change*. 2nd ed. New York: Random House, Inc.

United Nations Development Programme. (1990) *Human Development Report 1990*. New York: Oxford University Press.

World Bank. (1991) *World Development Report 1991*. New York: Oxford University Press.

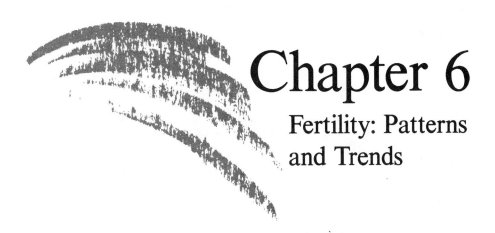

Chapter 6

Fertility: Patterns and Trends

The causes and consequences of fertility patterns are of major concern in today's world. At one time relatively high reproductive rates were characteristic of most societies, mainly as a response to prevailing high death rates. However, with death rates low or falling in most regions today, fertility patterns differ considerably from place to place. Explanations of spatial variations in fertility are drawn from many sources and differ from place to place as well as from time to time. As Robertson (1991, 24) noted, ". . . the processes and values of reproduction are inextricably tied up with the processes and values of economic production and political control."

▓ MEASURES OF FERTILITY

Before proceeding, it is necessary to distinguish between two terms that are sometimes confused, namely fertility and fecundity. *Fecundity* refers to the biological capacity for reproduction, whereas *fertility* refers to actual reproductive behavior. One measure of fertility has already been introduced, the crude birth rate. Others now need to be considered.

Child-Woman Ratio

The child-woman ratio is an indirect measure of fertility that is used to estimate fertility in situations where birth records are deficient or nonexistent, mainly in the underdeveloped countries. It is "indirect" in the sense that it does not use births in the measure at all. It is calculated as

$$CWR = \frac{P_{0-4}}{F_{15-44}} \times 1000,$$

where CWR = child-woman ratio,

P_{0-4} = the total number of children under five years of age, and

F_{15-44} = the total number of females between 15 and 45 years of age. This age group is considered to be the child-bearing age group sometimes the 15–49 age group is used instead.)

The child-woman ratio, then, indicates the number of children under 5 years of age per 1000 females in their child-bearing years. One disadvantage of using this ratio as a measure of fertility is that the number of surviving children is affected by prevailing mortality rates.

General Fertility Rate

The general fertility rate is a more refined measure of fertility than either the crude birth rate or the child-woman ratio. As with the crude birth rate, actual numbers of births are used in the numerator. In the denominator, however, the total population is replaced by the total number of females in the child-bearing age group, usually considered to be 15 to 44 years of age. The general fertility rate is calculated as

$$GFR = \frac{B}{F_{15-44}} \times 1000,$$

where B = total number of births in a one-year period, and

F_{15-44} = total number of females between the ages of 15 and 45 at midyear.

The general fertility rate gives the annual number of live births per 1000 women in the child-bearing age group.

Age-Specific Birth Rate

Age-specific birth rates are useful because child-bearing varies considerably with age. The age-specific birth rate is analogous to the general fertility rate, but instead of having the total number of females in the child-bearing age group as the denominator, it has the total number of women in a smaller age group, such as a one-year or five-year age group. The numerator, then, is the total number of children born in any given year to mothers in that specified age group. Normally five-year age groups are used. There are six or seven age groups, depending upon the upper age used. In generalized form the calculation of age-specific birth rates is

$$ASBR = \frac{B_a}{F_a} \times 1000,$$

where B_a = the number of births to females in the age group designated by "a" (e.g., a = 15–19 years old), and

F_a = the total number of females in the age group "a" at midyear.

If the child-bearing ages of 15 to 44 are used in five-year age groups, then there are six age-specific birth rates, one for each of the age groups 15 to 19, 20 to 24, . . . 40 to 44. Often a seventh is added for the age group 45 to 49. For many countries sufficient data for calculating the age-specific birth rates are not available. Births occurring to women who are outside of the normal child-bearing age range are arbitrarily assigned to either the 15 to 19 year age group if they occurred to females below age 15, or to the 45 to 49 year age group if they occurred to females more than 50 years of age. For most populations there are relatively few births outside of the 15 to 49 age range.

Total Fertility Rate

The total fertility rate is a useful way to summarize the age-specific birth rates for a population. It is the average number of children a woman would have *if* she were to have children at the prevailing age-specific rates as she passed through her reproductive years. The total fertility rate is calculated as

$$\text{TFR} = 5 \sum_{a=1}^{7} \frac{B_a}{F_a}$$

where B_a = the number of births to females in age group "a" in a one-year period,
  F_a = the midyear number of females in age group "a," and
  a = five-year age groups as follows: 15–19, 20–24, 25–29, 30–34, 35–39, 40–44 and 45–49, for a total of 7 different age groups.

The 5 preceding the summation sign is there because we are using five-year age groups. If one-year age groups were used, the 5 would disappear from the equation.

In the United States in 1992 the total fertility rate was 2.0, somewhat below the 2.1 that is considered to be "replacement" level, but above the 1.8 that it had been only five years earlier. In 1992 the world's total fertility rate was estimated to be 3.3. Figure 6–1 provides some idea of the range of values that countries show for total fertility rates. Countries that maintain a total fertility rate of less than 2.1 for a sustained period of time will experience negative population growth, as we saw earlier in our discussion of different population projections for the United States. Both the causes and consequences of negative population growth have received considerable attention in recent years (Examples include Teitelbaum and Winter, 1985, and Davis, Bernstam, and Ricardo-Campbell, 1987).

Gross Reproduction Rate

The gross reproduction rate is the same as the total fertility rate except that only female births are counted. Thus, it gives the average number of daughters that a woman would have *if* she passed through her entire reproductive life at the prevailing age-

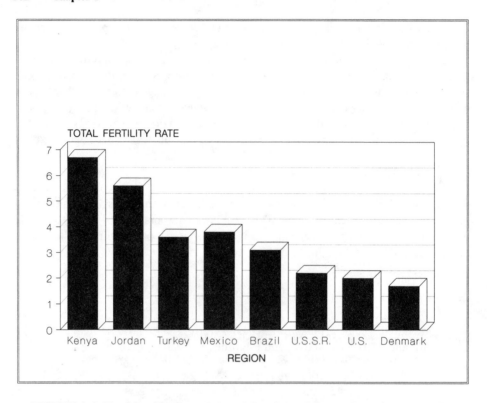

▨ FIGURE 6–1 Total Fertility Rate: Selected Countries. SOURCE: Data from *1992 World Population Data Sheet*. (Washington, D.C.: Population Reference Bureau, Inc.).

specific birth rates. The gross reproduction rate can be found by multiplying the total fertility rate by the proportion of births that is female. The gross reproduction rate is calculated as

$$GRR = 5 \sum_{a=1}^{7} \frac{FB_a}{F_a}$$

where FB_a = the number of female births to females in age group "a" in a one-year period,

F_a = the midyear number of females in age group "a," and

a = five-year age groups.

Net Reproduction Rate

The net reproduction rate is the same as the gross reproduction rate except that it is reduced somewhat to allow for the fact that not all women will live through their entire reproductive period. A net reproduction rate of 1.0 would indicate that on the average females are exactly replacing themselves.

▨ MAJOR DETERMINANTS OF FERTILITY

The reproductive behavior of a population results from a complex of biological, social, and economic factors that operate differently from place to place as well as from time to time. To explain spatial and temporal variations in fertility, it is necessary to consider its determinants.

Biological Determinants of Fertility

As noted earlier, we must distinguish between fertility, actual reproductive performance, and fecundity, the biological capacity for reproduction. However, they are obviously related. Fecundity may be affected by a number of physical factors including age, health and nutritional status, and even the physical environment.

Age and Fecundity. In most societies reproduction is accomplished mainly by young adults. In calculating fertility rates, the female reproductive years are generally assumed to be ages 15 to 44 or 15 to 49.

Puberty marks the onset of reproductive capacity. For females, menarche, or the beginning of menstruation, denotes puberty. The change from being infecund to fecund is not a sudden change from one state to another but rather a more gradual increase through a period of adolescent subfecundity to a mature fecundity, reached at roughly ages 26 to 30 (Doring, 1969). The female fecund period ends with menopause, when menstruation ceases. For males puberty also marks the beginning of reproductive capacity; however, the end of the male reproductive period is not so clearly marked.

Health, Nutritional Status, and Fecundity. A person's health may affect fecundity for varying periods of time. In general, good health and fecundity go together. A variety of diseases may impair fecundity either temporarily or permanently. The most important diseases in this respect are venereal diseases, which may, if left untreated, cause permanent sterility. Nutritional status affects fecundity as well, especially in cases of severe malnutrition, which may even lead to temporary infecundity.

In turn, a woman's health may be adversely affected by reproduction, especially if she was already experiencing health or nutritional problems. As the National Research Council (1989, 15) noted, "By avoiding pregnancy, women with health problems may substantially improve their own chances for survival and good health."

Environment and Fecundity.   Most of the literature on environment and fertility is concerned with the effect of various environmental factors on sexual activity and related behavior rather than on fecundity. One environmental variable thought by some to be related to fecundity is the effect of altitude, though the evidence so far is inconclusive (James, 1966).

Social Determinants of Fertility

Given a normally fecund population, fertility will be determined to a considerable degree by variations in social variables, including at least the following: marriage patterns, contraceptive practices, and abortions. Davis and Blake (1956) provided a framework that pointed out "intermediate variables" through which various social factors operate to affect fertility.

They identified three sets of such variables under the following headings: (1) factors that affect exposure to intercourse, (2) factors that affect exposure to conception, and (3) factors that affect gestation and successful parturition. Fertility variations among nations, then, can be explained by understanding how social differences are being translated into fertility behavior through these "intermediate variables." Major sources of such variations include those discussed subsequently.

Marriage and Fertility.   In most societies today marriage is the socially recognized union within which procreation occurs. However, marriage is obviously not a necessary prerequisite for reproduction, thus illegitimacy and variations in cultural norms from place to place also must be considered when possible. The formation of any sexual union, however temporary or permanent, can potentially result in reproduction, though data for unions other than marriage are often difficult to obtain. As Robertson (1991, 6) commented, "The way we reproduce seems to make the family a logical necessity, but the enormous variation in family patterns around the world is a reminder that these elementary relations of reproduction may be organized in many different ways." Nonetheless, whatever the nature of sexual unions may be, entering into them is a prerequisite for reproduction.

In particular, in populations where contraceptives are not widely used, the age at which females marry or enter into sexual unions of any kind is an important determinant of fertility. Assuming that the ages 15 to 44 are the child-bearing years for most women, it is logical that those who marry later will have fewer children on the average, providing that there are few illegitimate births. Typically, in the developing countries today the average age at marriage is fairly low, especially in comparison with the pattern in most of the developed countries. In some nations, such as Panama, Honduras, and Bolivia, the legal marriage age is as low as 12 for females and 14 for males.

In areas where women marry young and practice little or no contraception, fertility is likely to be high unless other factors operate to lower it. In preindustrial European countries the average age at marriage was also relatively low although there was a rise in the age at marriage beginning as early as the eighteenth century (Hajnal, 1965).

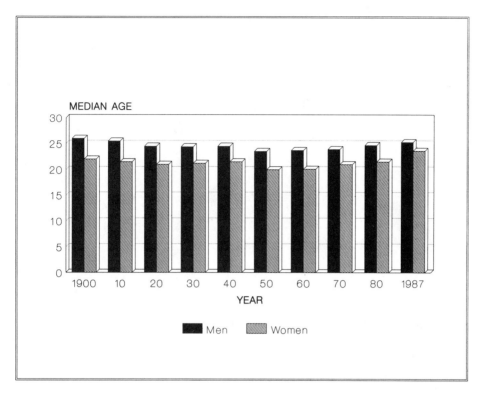

▪ **FIGURE 6–2** Median Age at First Marriage by Sex for the United States. SOURCE: Data from *Statistical Abstract of the United States, 1991*, p. 87.

In the United States the median age at first marriage has not changed considerably during the last one hundred years although it has moved gradually upward since World War II, as is apparent in Figure 6–2. This rising age at first marriage has also been associated with an increase in the percentage of those never married by given ages, as is shown in Figure 6–3.

One of the steps that the People's Republic of China has taken to decrease fertility has been to encourage people to postpone marriage, ideally to around age 25 for females and 28 for males. Coupled with strong sanctions against premarital sex, there is little doubt that the higher age at marriage has been a factor in China's recent fertility decline. However, it is far from being the only factor.

Another determinant of the fertility of a population is the percent of the population that marries. A high rate of celibacy is unusual in most populations, though there are a few exceptions, such as Ireland.

Related to marriage patterns, and also influencing fertility to varying degrees in different societies, is the amount of time spent between marriages after a divorce, separation, or death of a spouse. In general the rate of dissolution of marriages is lower

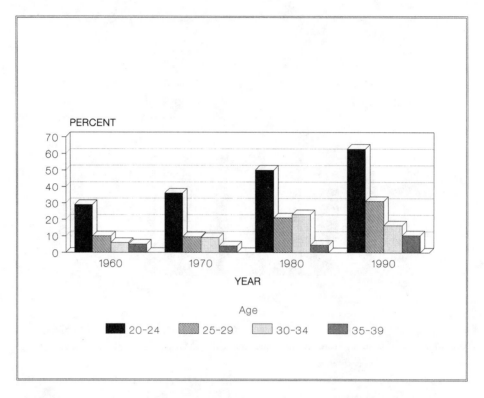

▩ **FIGURE 6–3** Percent of Females Never Married by Age for the United States. SOURCE: Data from United States Bureau of the Census, *Marital Status and Living Arrangements: March 1990,* Current Population Reports, Population Characteristics, Series P-20, No. 450.

in preindustrial societies than in advanced ones, with such exceptions as the Islamic peoples. Societies have varying attitudes toward the remarriage of widows.

Given exposure to sexual intercourse within marriages or other types of sexual unions, fertility is then influenced primarily by sexual behavior and contraceptive practice. Both the frequency of intercourse and abstinence for varying periods of time may have effects on fertility. Periodic abstinence may result from sickness or other reasons. Furthermore, some societies forbid intercourse during certain times, for example, while a woman is breast-feeding a child (Saxton and Serwada, 1969). Such practices would tend to increase the spacing between children and reduce fertility. Geographers have seldom studied variations in sexual behavior although a pioneering study by Ford and Bowie (1989) provided evidence that such studies would be a rewarding addition to the literature in population geography.

Contraception and Fertility.   A major determinant of fertility today is the degree to which contraception is practiced. Contraceptive practice is most common in the industrialized nations; however, with the increasing influence of family planning programs in many countries, more people are beginning to control their fertility, as noted some time ago by Nortman (1977, 3):

> Among the most far-reaching and visible developments going on in the world today is the change in contraceptive knowledge, attitudes, and practices—popularly known as the "KAP" of contraception. The past decade has seen a rapid acceleration in the historical trend to ever-increasing adoption and use of contraception. Contraception is now being practiced where it never was before, and people everywhere are turning to new and much more efficient methods.

Nortman estimated that around one third of the married couples in the world now practice some form of contraception, and that percentage is likely to rise during the 1990s and beyond. Contraceptives may be classified into the following groups: (1) those that prevent the entry of sperm, (2) those that avoid or suppress ovulation, and (3) those that prevent implantation (Segal and Nordberg, 1977, 24). Included in the first group are coitus interruptus (withdrawal), condoms, spermicides, douches, and diaphragms, along with sterilization. The second group includes both "rhythm" methods and oral contraceptives. The third category is that of the intrauterine device, or IUD. Abortions are in a separate category because they are used only after conception has occurred; they can serve as a backup to contraceptive failure.

Though contraceptive technology has lagged considerably since the innovations of the 1960s, there are some new contraceptive methods currently under investigation including Norplant, an implant for females that releases minute doses of progestin to inhibit ovulation for up to five years; two types of vaccines designed to block sex-related hormones, one of which could be used by both males and females; pharmacologic suppression of the corpus luteum; long-acting forms of contraception steroids; pharmacologic contraception for males; and a vaginal-ring that provides time-release of both estrogen and progestin to inhibit ovulation.

The most controversial recent innovation has been RU 486, synthesized in 1980 and distributed in France during the 1980s (Ulmann, Teutsch, and Philibert, 1990). Given to females in tablet form along with a small dose of prostaglandin, RU 486 has the ability to terminate pregnancies, even though it was not initially developed for that purpose. It is controversial not because of questions about its safety, but because it aborts rather than prevents pregnancies.

The use of various contraceptives in the United States is shown in Figure 6–4. By far the most popular method is the oral contraceptive, although sterilization is the most popular method for couples where the wife is in the 30 to 44 age group.

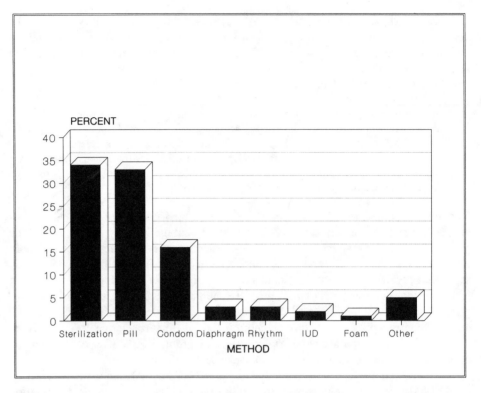

▧ **FIGURE 6–4** Contraceptive Usage in the United States, Married Women Ages 15–44, 1988. SOURCE: Data from *Statistical Abstract of the United States, 1991,* p. 70.

Abortion and Fertility. Sometimes considered a contraceptive, but actually a backup measure when pregnancy has already occurred, abortion has been and continues to be an important determinant of fertility. The role of abortion as a supplement to contraception is apparent in many places. Nortman (1977, 24) commented:

> Studies in Japan, Latin America, and elsewhere have demonstrated that when societies are motivated to begin to control their fertility, the incidence of abortion (again, legal or illegal) tends to rise initially along with the use of contraception, but as contraception becomes more efficient, widespread, and available, abortion wanes, to be used only when contraception fails.

Figure 6–5 provides information on legal abortions in selected European countries. Estimates of the total annual number of abortions in the world range from 30 million to 55 million. However, such figures are speculative and based on sometimes highly questionable country estimates.

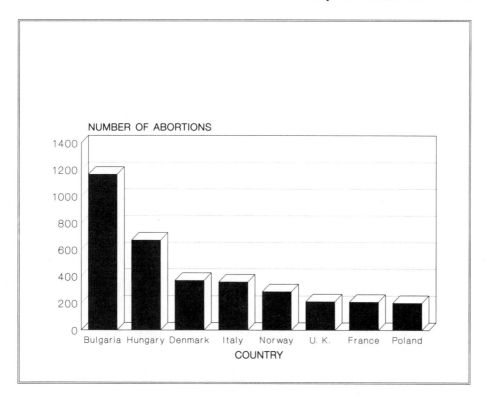

NUMBER OF ABORTIONS

■ **FIGURE 6–5** Legal Abortions per 1000 Live Births: Selected European Countries. SOURCE: Data from United Nations, *Demographic Yearbook,* 1988. (New York: United Nations).

The impact of a sudden change in abortion laws is illustrated in Figure 6–6. Abortion was legalized in Romania in 1956 and then severely restricted in 1967. Following the restriction, a rapid rise in fertility occurred.

In the United States, prior to 1970, it was relatively difficult for a woman to obtain a legal abortion. In the period 1972–1974 there were 2,229,070 legal abortions performed (Tietze, 1977). Despite two major Supreme Court decisions in 1973, *Doe v. Bolton* and *Roe v. Wade,* uniform abortion practices in all states are not yet implemented. Tietze and Murstein (1975, 7) commented:

> By late 1975, the decision of the Supreme Court had not yet been fully implemented throughout the United States. Under severe political pressure from a well-organized and well-financed "right to life" movement, legislatures and various law enforcement officers in several states, as well as many hospital boards and hospital administrators, have taken a variety of actions designed to prevent, or at least limit or

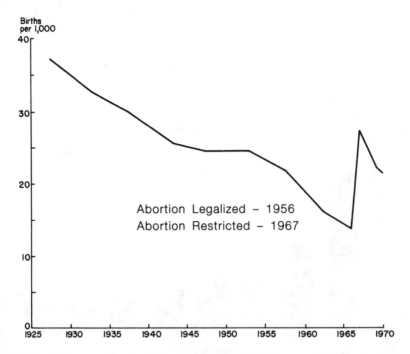

■ **FIGURE 6–6** Romania: Crude Birth Rates, 1925–1970. SOURCE: "A Decade of Growth: World Population in the 1960s," *Population Profile* (Washington, D.C.: The Population Reference Bureau, Inc.), p. 4. Reprinted by permission of the Population Reference Bureau, Inc.

delay, implementation. Some of these actions have already been challenged and declared unconstitutional by the courts. At the same time, efforts were made in the Congress of the United States to initiate a constitutional amendment that would nullify the decision of the Supreme Court. Few issues have so divided such disparate groups of people in the United States, and contentiousness between pro-life and pro-choice groups continues to grow and to affect politics at every scale from national to local.

The spatial pattern of abortion rates in the United States may be seen in Figure 6–7, and it is clear that substantial differences remain among the states with respect to abortion practices. In the 1980s, debates about legal abortions in the United States were still going on, but the original Supreme Court decision remained in effect although many have begun to argue that *Roe v. Wade* is dead. Nonetheless, abortion remains an important political issue, and anti-abortion sentiment still plays a role in the conservative agenda in the United States. There are currently about 1.6 million abortions annually despite such opposition.

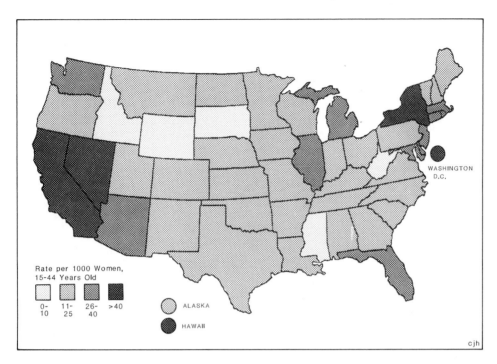

■ **FIGURE 6–7** Rate of Abortions in the United States, 1988. SOURCE: Data from *Statistical Abstract of the United States, 1991,* p. 72.

Economic Determinants of Fertility

It has often been suggested that fertility decline in the industrialized countries occurred as a response to economic development with its concomitant changes in social mobility and population redistribution. Modernization remains the driving force behind the demographic transition model, and, as Robertson (1991, 70) reasonably noted, "The more acutely people are aware of economic constraints, the more likely they are to exert control over reproduction." As Figures 6–8 and 6–9 indicate, at least for the countries shown, there is a general relationship between crude birth rates and both GNP per capita and the level of urbanization, variables that serve at least to some degree as measures of the level of development.

One current area of fertility research is concerned with developing an economic theory of fertility. Espenshade (1977, 3) pointed out:

> . . . children are valuable. Most fundamentally, they provide for the continuation of the human species. If births were to cease, mankind would become extinct within the span of our lifetime. But this reason for wanting children is usually not uppermost in the minds of parents. To them, children are sources of joy and happiness,

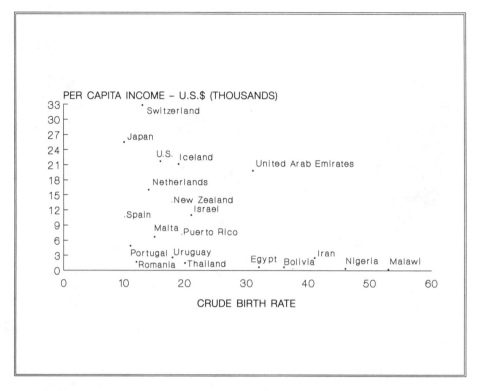

PER CAPITA INCOME – U.S.$ (THOUSANDS)

▩ **FIGURE 6–8** The Relationship Between Per Capita GNP and Crude Birth Rates. SOURCE: Data from *1992 World Population Data Sheet*. (Washington, D.C.: Population Reference Bureau, Inc.).

companionship, and pride. In some circumstances, children may also be prized because they are a potential means of support and security once parents are no longer able to provide for themselves. At the same time, children are costly. They put added pressure on family resources, and they can in other ways curtail the activities and opportunities of parents.

The essence of an economic theory of fertility is that a couple's decision to produce, or not to produce, a child is based on the costs and benefits of the child, as perceived by the couple. Such a theory, then, begins with a consideration of the costs and benefits of children. Costs and benefits have both economic and noneconomic components.

Value of Children. Hoffman and Hoffman (1973, 20) suggested that the value of children may be thought of as "the functions they serve or the needs they fulfill for parents." A variety of terms for this concept have been used in the literature, including satisfaction, benefits, utilities, rewards, gains, gratifications, advantages, and positive

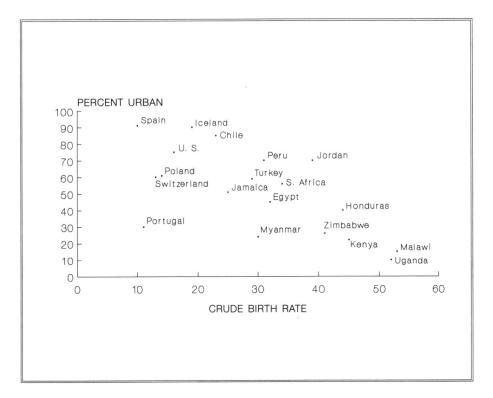

■ **FIGURE 6–9** The Relationship Between Level of Urbanization and Crude Birth Rates. SOURCE: Data from *1992 World Population Data Sheet*. (Washington, D.C.: Population Reference Bureau, Inc.).

general values. As Espenshade (1977, 4) commented, "the value of children is used to mean that collection of good things parents receive from having children."

Children may have both economic and noneconomic values. The noneconomic values are mainly psychological in nature and include the psychic satisfactions that parents derive from having and rearing children. Among these noneconomic values are the following: adult status and social identity; expansion of the self; morality; primary group ties; stimulation, novelty, and fun; creativity and accomplishment; power and influence; and social comparison and competition.

Two types of economic benefits of children are the following: (1) children as a source of financial security in old age and in emergencies and (2) the value of children as productive agents (Leibenstein, 1963). Espenshade (1977, 5) stated:

> . . . there is a tendency to assume that the economic values of children are most salient in the developing countries, especially in rural areas. In fact, it is widely believed that this is the major reason parents in such regions want large families.

As a society modernizes and achieves higher levels of economic and social development, the economic value of children declines in importance. The extension of compulsory schooling and the enactment of child labor laws reduce the economic contribution from children. Similarly, to the extent that social security becomes institutionalized in such programs as public health and welfare measures, pension plans, and private annuity and life insurance programs, parents can relax their dependence on children as a source of old-age support.

More than two decades ago Mahmood Mamdani (1972, 113) made the importance of children in Third World countries clear in the following discussion of the failure of birth control in Manupur, a small village in India's Punjab:

> To Hakika Singh, the solution to his financial troubles is not to reduce the size of his family he has to support, but to *increase* it. It is the family that will support him, will even be his salvation. Admittedly, he must take one chance: the next baby may be a girl instead of a boy. But since he is faced with utter financial disaster if he does anything else, Hakika Singh is willing to take that chance. Even with a number of sons, he may fail; yet they are his only hope. Even if the chances for success are low, his sons are his only route to success. As we concluded our conversation, his parting words were: "A rich man invests in his machines. We must invest in our children. It's that simple."

Cost of Children.   Costs may be considered as the disadvantages of children. Among the terms used for the costs of children are dissatisfactions, disadvantages, disvalues, penalties, and negative general values. These costs may be both economic and noneconomic.

Among the noneconomic costs are included the emotional and psychological problems that children impose on parents. Any parent is aware that raising children causes anxieties about such matters as the child's health and behavior.

Among the economic costs are (1) direct maintenance costs and (2) opportunity costs. Direct maintenance costs are actual monetary outlays required for the support of children. These costs include food, clothing, housing, educational expenses, and medical expenses. Opportunity costs measure opportunities that parents must sacrifice to have and raise children.

According to Espenshade (1977) three types of opportunity costs may be recognized. First, a lower standard of living may result as certain consumption expenditures are foregone. Second, children may reduce a family's ability to save and invest. Third, and of increasing importance in the United States as well as elsewhere, the wife may sacrifice her earnings. Espenshade (1977, 6) noted:

> . . . the relative importance of the three kinds of economic opportunity cost is likely to vary according to the level of economic development. In the less developed countries, for example, there is a tendency to think that children scarcely affect consumption standards or the ability to save and invest. But whether or not this is actually the case depends on the level of aspirations among the population.

The costs and benefits of having children vary from time to time and place to place. In very general terms, in preindustrial, primarily agrarian societies, the perceived costs of having and rearing children are low, whereas the perceived benefits are high. Thus, in such societies couples will tend, all else being equal, to have large families.

With economic development, industrialization, and urbanization underway in a society, the perceived costs and benefits of having and rearing children may be altered. As people increasingly become urban dwellers, and more frequently pursue nonagricultural jobs, they may begin to see that the costs of children appear to be rising and the benefits seem to be diminishing. Families in urban areas may find housing, education, and medical costs all more expensive. At the same time they may find more goods available to them. Thus, they may discover that children are not as attractive to them as they are to their rural counterparts.

In the developed countries a large percentage of the population is urban, and most of the labor force is employed in the secondary, tertiary, and quaternary sectors of the economy. Females usually find more job opportunities outside the home in these developed countries, and their participation in the labor force has increased greatly during the last two decades. The costs of having and rearing children are likely to be quite high. With the costs of children high and their perceived benefits low, the modern couple in an urban area of an industrialized country is likely to desire a small family. Figure 6–10 shows the direct costs of raising a child to age 18 in the United States. Add on to that a substantial figure for sending a child to college, and it is not surprising that most couples today in the United States are opting for small families.

One final consideration of an economic view of fertility is what we might learn about population growth itself and the likelihood of controlling it. McKenzie and Tullock (1989, 97) argued that:

> Economists are in general agreement that the optimum quantity produced of anything is that quantity at which the marginal cost of the last unit is equal to the marginal benefits of it. This will be the case if all costs and benefits are actually considered by the individual making the decision on the output. And this rule of thumb holds for the production of children.

They go on to note, however, that seldom do couples have to assume the total costs of their fertility decisions—some of those costs are born by others, either directly in such forms as increased congestion or indirectly through taxes for such things as schools. At the same time, they go on to note that population growth will be controlled in response to changes that are likely to occur in the child production process, including the following: (1) resource scarcity will force up the costs of children, (2) less favorable tax structures and the availability of contraceptives and abortion, and (3) greater incentives for improved contraceptive technology with the rising costs of children.

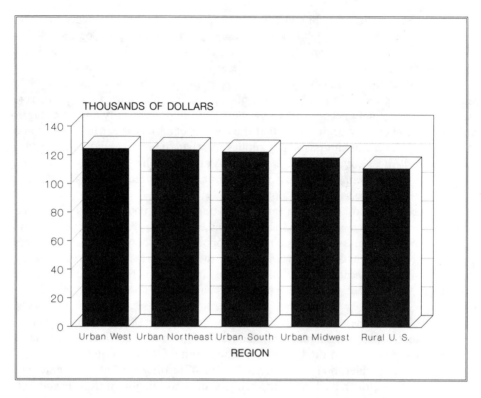

THOUSANDS OF DOLLARS

▨ **FIGURE 6–10** Expenditures on a Child to Age 18, Middle Income Husband–Wife Families, 1990. SOURCE: Data from *Family Economics Review* 1991, 4(1):33.

▨ KENYA: A LOOK AT HIGH FERTILITY

With a total fertility rate of 8.0 in 1988, Kenya began the new decade with the dubious distinction of having the highest fertility level of all countries in the world. According to a study, Mott and Mott (1980, 7) noted that "tribal loyalties and the high value placed on children by Kenya's vast population majority of rural families, and especially its women, combine to dampen national efforts to reduce population growth." Kenyans perceive that the relative place of a tribe in the political arena is primarily a function of tribal size, a situation that frustrates efforts to lower fertility.

According to Mott and Mott (1980, 7), "Tribal pressures affect Kenyan's behavior more than pronouncements arriving from the national seat of government, but what ultimately counts is what an individual perceives in his or her own best interest." In a country in which the vast majority of the people work on the land, children are viewed as essential. They are the key to survival and are closely tied to status. They are a ready supply of labor, especially during peak times in the agrarian life cycle.

Because much of the farm work is done by females, they perceive children as the major way in which the burden of farm chores can be relieved. Thus, to them the benefits of children are clear and tangible, whereas the costs are minimal. Of course, children also represent a major source of security for both males and females. Again, according to Mott and Mott (1980, 9), "the vast majority of rural parents must still look to children for financial—and physical—support in old age."

To rural Kenyans, children have a considerable prestige value as well. More children increase the chances that at least one of them will turn out to be a success or to marry well. This reinforces the tendency for women to have many children. In addition, because opportunities outside of the home are extremely limited for rural Kenyan women, the opportunity cost of having children remains low. Low actual costs and low opportunity costs, combined with high perceived benefits of children, lead to a perpetual cycle of high fertility. Nonetheless, in 1992 Kenya's total fertility rate had dropped to 6.7 as couples were apparently responding to changing perceptions about the costs and benefits of children and to an increasing availability of information about family planning and contraceptives.

▓ FERTILITY DIFFERENTIALS

The fertility of a particular population results from a complex of different factors; in addition, different groups within a population may respond to similar factors in various ways. Thus, different groups within a population are likely to display varied fertility levels. Such differential fertility within a nation may in turn help explain regional fertility patterns. Important observed fertility differentials include rural-urban, income, education, and ethnic factors.

Rural-Urban Fertility Differentials

As noted already, fertility tends to be related to the level of urbanization when viewed at the world scale. Differential fertility between rural and urban areas within a nation is also common. In the United States in 1986, for example, the general fertility rate was 70.3. However, in metropolitan areas the general fertility rate was only 67.4, compared with a rate of 81.5 in nonmetropolitan areas. Furthermore, within metropolitan areas the general fertility rate was 68.2 in the central cities and 66.8 in the areas outside of the central cities.

Similarly, in a study of fertility differentials for Japanese women by place of residence, Matsumoto, Park, and Bell (1971, 18) found that "as expected, within each sample area, fertility decreases with increasing urbanization."

Income Differentials

Previously we observed that fertility tended to be related to levels of economic development, as measured by GNP per capita for a sample of countries. Within a nation, fertility differences also tend to exist for various income groups.

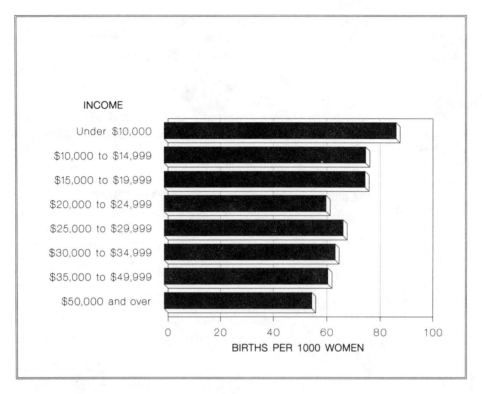

INCOME

BIRTHS PER 1000 WOMEN

▪ **FIGURE 6–11** Births Per 1000 Women in the United States by Family Income. SOURCE: United States Bureau of the Census, *Fertility of American Women: June 1990,* Current Population Reports, Population Characteristics, Series P-20, No. 454.

In general, fertility tends to be highest for the lowest income groups and to decrease with increasing income levels although occasionally it will rise again at very high income levels. Part of the economic explanation for this rise is that those at high income levels can afford more of everything, including children. Data for the United States appear in Figure 6–11. These data show a somewhat more complex pattern of relationships between fertility and income, though fertility is still highest for the lowest income group.

Educational Differentials

Like income, education tends to be negatively related to fertility. As Hawthorn (1970, 92) commented, "It is true of all societies that awareness of methods of birth control varies directly with urban background or residence, a higher than average education, and a higher than average income. . . ." However, beyond the knowledge of contraceptives, education may motivate couples to limit family size because of their

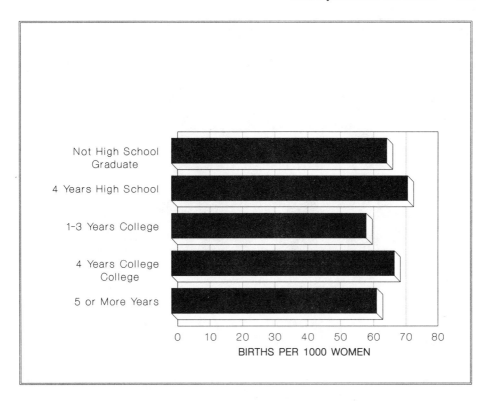

▧ **FIGURE 6–12** Births Per 1000 Women in the United States by Educational Attainment, 1990. SOURCE: Data from United States Bureau of the Census, *Fertility of American Women: June 1990,* Current Population Reports, Population Characteristics, Series P-20, No. 454.

greater awareness of the costs and benefits of children. Also, for more educated females the opportunity costs of having and rearing children are likely to be higher than for their less-educated counterparts, and they are likely to marry at somewhat later ages. Figure 6–12 shows the relationship between educational attainment and fertility for 1990 in the United States.

Racial and Ethnic Differentials

Different racial and ethnic groups often have different fertility levels than the national populations of which they are a part. For example, in the United States African-Americans, American Indians, and Mexican-Americans tend to have higher fertility rates than do whites. Such differentials tend to exist in most nations where there are significant numbers of the national population who belong to different racial or ethnic groups. Figure 6–13 provides information for such differentials in the United States in 1990.

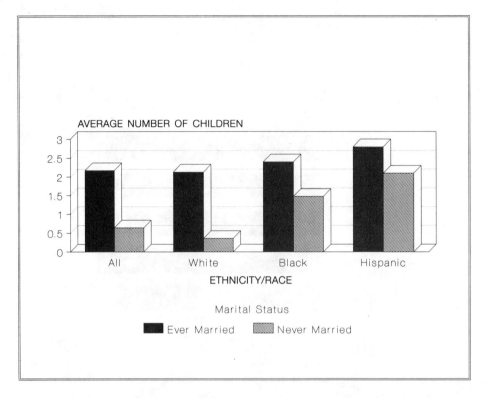

▨ **FIGURE 6–13** Average Number of Children Ever Born to Families Ages 40–44 by Race, Ethnicity, and Marital Status, 1990. SOURCE: Data from United States Bureau of the Census, *Fertility of American Women: June 1990,* Current Population Reports, Population Characteristics, Series P-20, No. 454.

Age Differentials

Women of child-bearing age in a society are not equally likely to have children at any given age. In most societies fertility is more concentrated in certain age groups, as is apparent for the United States in Figure 6–14.

Fertility differentials are useful and important for explaining spatial and temporal differences in fertility. We must keep in mind, however, that fertility differentials of different types are probably not independent. Educational differences in fertility, for example, may also be reflecting income differences as well. Ethnic differentials also reflect income and educational differences. Furthermore, some patterns, once established, may be self-perpetuating. For example, Kahn and Anderson (1992, 54) found that ". . . it appears that both teen marriage and childbearing behaviors tend to be reproduced across generations." Finally, statements about the causes of fertility differentials should be made with care. Many other fertility differentials can be noted, such as religious and occupational factors.

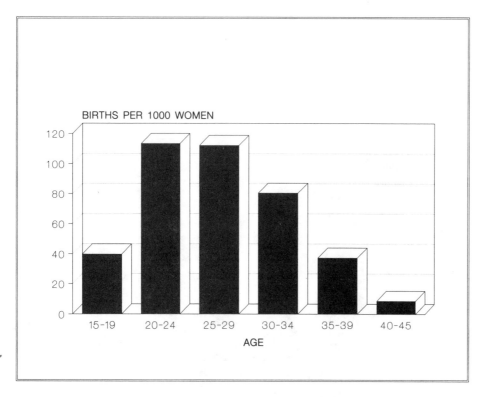

▩ **FIGURE 6–14** Births Per 1000 Women by Age for the United States, 1990. SOURCE: Data from United States Bureau of the Census, *Fertility of American Women: June 1990,* Current Population Reports, Population Characteristics, Series P-20, No. 454.

▦ SPATIAL FERTILITY PATTERNS AND TRENDS

Fertility varies in both space and time. Such variations result from similar variations in the determinants of fertility, as well as variations in the response to particular determinants. The map in Figure 6–15 shows the recent spatial pattern of crude birth rates in the world. The rates vary from a high of 53 in Malawi to a low of 10 in Greece, Italy, and Spain. In general, the world fertility pattern reflects the pattern of economic development, as shown in Figure 6–16. Lutz (1989) has carefully examined fertility differences among nations.

Africa has a crude birth rate of 43, and most African nations have crude birth rates of at least 40. Among the major exceptions are Tunisia and South Africa, with crude birth rates of 27 and 34, respectively. Bledsoe (1990) provided a detailed look at how marriage patterns and fertility in much of Africa are related and how education and other variables are changing traditional marital arrangements.

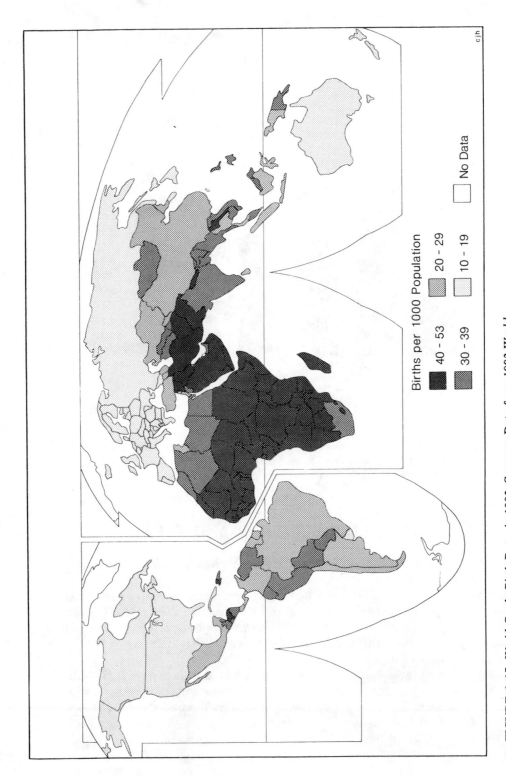

■ **FIGURE 6–15** World Crude Birth Rates in 1992. SOURCE: Data from *1992 World Population Data Sheet*. (Washington, D.C.: Population Reference Bureau, Inc.).

Births per 1000 Population

40 - 53
30 - 39
20 - 29
10 - 19
No Data

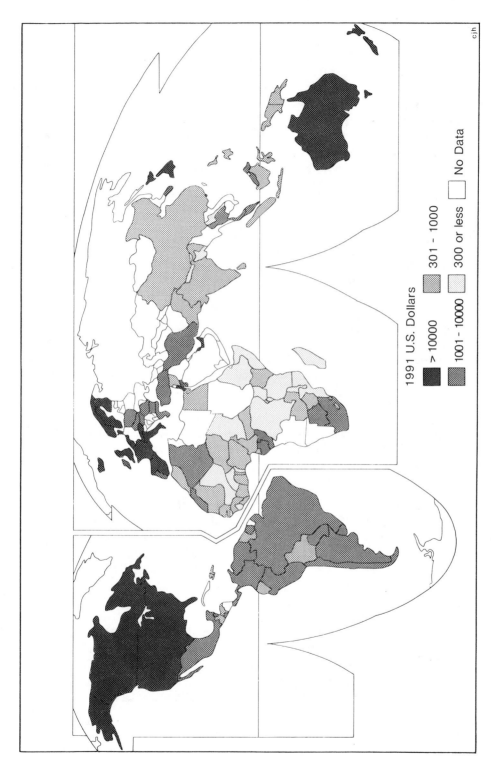

■ **FIGURE 6–16** World Per Capita GNP in 1992. SOURCE: Data from *1992 World Population Data Sheet*. (Washington, D.C.: The Population Reference Bureau, Inc.).

1991 U.S. Dollars

- > 10000
- 1001 – 10000
- 301 – 1000
- 300 or less
- No Data

For Asia, with close to 60 percent of the world's population, the fertility pattern is more varied than it is in Africa. Asia has a crude birth rate of 26, and the highest Asian crude birth rates are found in southern and western Asia. The United Arab Emirates is one of many examples where our generalization about an inverse relationship between income and fertility fails to hold. Per capita GNP in this tiny country in 1992 was $19,860, close to that of the United States, yet the crude birth rate was 31. Similar examples include Kuwait and Saudi Arabia. This is true for several oil-rich nations, where the sudden wealth has not yet been followed by general modernization. As a result, a sharp contrast exists between extreme wealth (often concentrated in a few hands) and the traditional socioeconomic fabric of the majority of residents.

In broad regional terms, East Asia, with a crude birth rate of 19, stands in marked contrast to Southwest Asia. Even here fertility varies from a crude birth rate of 36 in Mongolia to one of only 10 in Japan. Of major importance in this highly populated region is the recent decline of fertility in the People's Republic of China, which in 1992 had a crude birth rate of 20, a figure that represents a slight increase from the beginning of the 1980s. However, estimates of China's population and vital rates differ considerably. There is little doubt among researchers that Chinese fertility has fallen since the beginning of the 1970s; but with insufficient data the actual rate is unknown, probably even to the Chinese. Extremely low crude birth rates have been reported in many urban areas. When discussing Chinese population, despite its major demographic significance, we are still left at a point described by Orleans (1976, 56) as follows:

> It is easy to sympathize with anyone who has to choose a particular population figure or series of figures for China, but unfortunately one can offer little more than consolation. It is possible to agree or disagree with some of the assumptions and conclusions and to support either a particular estimate or a divergent point of view, but there is no way to prove that one set of figures is more accurate or more reliable than another.

In Southern Asia the crude birth rate is 33. India, Asia's other population giant, has a crude birth rate of 30. According to Mauldin (1976, 245), "the evidence is unmistakable that fertility has fallen significantly in India during the past 15 years even though the level of fertility is not known with precision." With an annual rate of natural increase of 2.0 in 1992 India continued to grow steadily, despite three decades of attempts to control fertility there. Krishnan (1989) found that there were widespread differences in fertility within India, with crude birth rates ranging from only 20.4 in Goa to 39.7 in Rajasthan.

In 1992 Latin America had a crude birth rate of 28 and, like Asia, showed considerable regional variations in fertility. According to Palloni (1990, 143), "Most Latin American countries are currently undergoing what could be considered the third revolution in their demographic patterns . . . the downward shift in fertility." In Central America the crude birth rate is 31, with a high of 40 in Honduras and 39 in Guatemala.

Panama has the lowest crude birth rate in Central America, 24, a figure that is down from recent years. Only in temperate South America and parts of the Caribbean do crude birth rates get much lower. Growth rates are high throughout most of Latin America because of the prevalence of low crude death rates; however, declining birth rates should reduce growth rates during the 1990s and have already done so in many countries.

In North America, Canada has a crude birth rate of 15 and the United States has one of 16. The annual rate of natural increase for the two together is around 0.80 percent. Though these growth rates are slow compared to those in the developing countries, growth in the United States and Canada contributes substantially to the growth in demand for the world's energy and other resources.

Similarly, Europe has an overall crude birth rate of 12. Crude birth rates within Europe vary from a low of 10 in Greece, Italy, and Spain, to a high of 25 in Albania, which also has the lowest per capita GNP in Europe. In general, crude birth rates are lower in Western Europe and higher in Eastern Europe although such differences are not large.

In Oceania the crude birth rate is 20. Within the region, the rate varies from a low of 15 in Australia to a high of 41 in the Solomon Islands. Again, the rates tend to reflect differences in economic development.

Clearly, despite several exceptions, fertility patterns at the world scale reflect the spatial distribution of economic development. Within the realm of the developed countries crude birth rates have fallen to quite low levels, sometimes even below crude death rates, as in Germany and Austria. Total fertility rates are currently below replacement level in many developed countries, including the United States, Denmark, Sweden, Norway, Hungary, and Switzerland.

Fertility also has begun to decline in a number of developing countries, including the People's Republic of China, Hong Kong, Taiwan, South Korea, Panama, Costa Rica, and Mexico. Without a doubt, during the 1990s more developing countries will be added to the list of those with declining levels of fertility. Everyone interested in population keeps an eye on China, because of its size if for no other reason. In 1979 the Chinese government decided to promote the one-child family in a dramatic effort to bring population growth to a halt, even though Chinese fertility had dropped during the 1970s. By 1992 China's crude birth rate was 20, a very low figure considering that country's low income level but up somewhat from what it had been in 1980. However, the rate of annual increase was still 1.3 percent, which is considered problematic because of the base population of more than one billion people.

Though the one-child policy seems acceptable in urban areas, a greater concern in the early 1980s was the considerable resistance to it that was apparent in rural areas. Goodstadt (1982, 53) noted, "In the countryside, the government's measures to solve chronic agricultural bottlenecks have led to more income for the larger family; and the family itself has considerable survival power because even urban China has not developed economic and social substitutes that offer better safeguards for the individual against old age and the other hazards of life."

In 1992 the Population Reference Bureau reported a world population of 5,420,000,000, a figure that was well beyond the 1990 high variant projection of the United Nations, namely, 5,327,000,000. As the Population Reference Bureau (1988, 3) noted, "The differences in these absolute numbers mean far less than the actual progress of rates, in particular the total fertility rate (TFR), or average number of children per woman. The increase in fertility in China in 1986 and 1987, along with a slower than projected decrease in fertility in India, has led to a slightly higher than projected total fertility rate."

REFERENCES

Bledsoe, Caroline. (1990) "Transformations in Sub-Saharan African Marriage and Fertility," *Annals of the American Academy of Political and Social Science* 510:115–125.

Bumpass, Larry L. (1990) "What's Happening to the Family? Interactions Between Demographic and Institutional Change," *Demography* 27:483–498.

Cherlin, Andrew. (1990) "Recent Changes in American Fertility, Marriage, and Divorce," *Annals of the American Academy of Political and Social Science* 510:145–154.

Cho, Lee-Jay. (1973) *The Demographic Situation in the Republic of Korea.* Papers of the East-West Population Institute. Number 29. Honolulu: East-West Center.

Davis, Kingsley and Blake, Judith. (1956) "Social Structure and Fertility: An Analytic Framework," *Economic Development and Cultural Change* 4:211–235.

Davis, Kingsley, Bernstam, Mikhail S., and Ricardo-Campbell, Rita, eds. (1987) *Below-Replacement Fertility in Industrial Societies: Causes, Consequences, Policies.* Cambridge: Cambridge University Press.

Doring, Gerhard K. (1969) "The Incidence of Anovular Cycles in Women," *Journal of Reproduction and Fertility,* Supplement 6:77–81.

Espenshade, Thomas J. (1977) "The Value and Cost of Children," *Population Bulletin* 32(1): 1–47.

Ford, Nicholas and Bowie, Cameron. (1989) "Urban-Rural Variations in the Level of Heterosexual Activity of Young People," *Area* 21:237–248.

Goodstadt, Leo F. (1982) "China's One-Child Family: Policy and Public Response," *Population and Development Review* 8:37–58.

Hajnal, J. (1965) "European Marriage Patterns in Perspective," in David V. Glass and D. E. C. Eversley, eds., *Population in History.* Chicago: Aldine Publishing Company, pp. 101–143.

Hawthorn, Geoffrey. (1970) *The Sociology of Fertility.* London: Collier-Macmillian Limited.

Hoffman, Lois W. and Hoffman, Martin L. (1973) "The Value of Children to Parents," in James W. Fawcett, ed., *Psychological Perspectives on Population.* New York: Basic Books, pp. 19–76.

Isaacs, Stephen L. and Holt, Renee J. (1987) "Redefining Procreation: Facing the Issues," *Population Bulletin* 42:(3):1–37.

James, W. H. (1966) "The Effect of Altitude on Fertility in Andean Countries," *Population Studies* 20:97–101.

Jones, Elise F., et al. (1989) *Pregnancy, Contraception, and Family Planning Services in Industrialized Countries.* New Haven, CN: Yale University Press

Jones, Elise F. and Forrest, Jacqueline Darroch. (1992) "Underreporting of Abortion in Surveys of U.S. Women: 1976 to 1988," *Demography* 29:113–126.

Kahn, Joan R. and Anderson, Kay E. (1992) "Intergenerational Patterns of Teenage Fertility," *Demography* 29:39–57.

Krishnan, Gopal. (1989) "Fertility and Mortality Trends in Indian States," *Geography* 74: 53–56.

Leibenstein, Harvey. (1963) *Economic Backwardness and Economic Growth.* New York: John Wiley and Sons, Inc.

Lightbourne, Robert, Jr., Singh, Susheela, and Green, Cynthia. (1982) "The World Fertility Survey: Charting Global Childbearing," *Population Bulletin* 37(1):1–54.

Lutz, Wolfgang. (1989) *Distributional Aspects of Human Fertility: A Global Comparative Study.* New York: Academic Press.

Mamdani, Mahmood. (1972) *The Myth of Population Control: Family, Caste, and Class in an Indian Village.* New York: Monthly Review Press.

Matsumoto, Y. Scott, Park, Chai Bin, and Bell, Balla Z. (1971) *Fertility Differentials of Japanese Women in Japan, Hawaii, and California.* Working Papers of the East-West Population Institute. Honolulu: East-West Center.

Mauldin, W. Parker. (1976) "Fertility Trends: 1950–1975," *Studies in Family Planning* 7:242–248.

McKenzie, Richard B. and Tullock, Gordon. (1989) *The Best of the New World of Economics . . . and Then Some.* 5th ed. Homewood, Illinois: Richard D. Irwin.

Mott, Frank L. and Mott, Susan H. (1980) "Kenya's Record Population Growth: A Dilemma of Development," *Population Bulletin* 35(3):1–43.

National Research Council. (1989) *Contraception and Reproduction: Health Consequences for Women and Children in the Developing World.* Working Group on the Health Consequences of Contraceptive Use and Controlled Fertility. Washington, D.C.: National Academy Press.

Nortman, Dorothy. (1977) "Changing Contraceptive Patterns: A Global Perspective," *Population Bulletin* 32(3):1–37.

Orleans, Leo A. (1976) "China's Population Figures: Can the Contradictions Be Resolved?" *Studies in Family Planning* 7:52–57.

Palloni, Alberto. (1990) "Fertility and Mortality Decline in Latin America," *Annals of the American Academy of Political and Social Science* 510:126–144.

Population Reference Bureau. (1988) "A Billion more People per Decade?" *Population Today* 16(5):3.

Robertson, A. F. (1991) *Beyond the Family: The Social Organization of Reproduction.* Berkeley and Los Angeles: University of California Press.

Saxton, G. A., Jr. and Serwada, D. M. (1969) "Human Birth Interval in East Africa," *Journal of Reproduction and Fertility* Supplement 6:83–88.

Segal, Sheldon J.; and Nordberg, Olivia Schieffelin. (1977) "Fertility Regulation Technology: Status and Prospects," *Population Bulletin* 31(6):1–25.

Teitelbaum, Michael S. and Winter, Jay M. (1985) *The Fear of Population Decline.* Orlando, FL: Academic Press.

Tietze, Christopher. (1977) "Legal Abortions in the United States: Rates and Ratios by Race and Age, 1972–1974," *Family Planning Perspectives* 9:12–15.

Tietze, Christopher and Murstein, Marjorie Cooper. (1975) "Induced Abortion: 1975 Factbook," *Reports on Population/Family Planning* No. 14, Second Edition: 75 pages.

Ulmann, Andre, Teutsch, Georges, and Philibert, Daniel. (1990) "RU 486," *Scientific American* 262(6):42–48.

Chapter 7

Population Policy and Family Planning Programs

In this chapter we consider population policies in general, but concentrate primarily on policies and programs that have been designed to reduce fertility. Such policies were almost unknown 40 years ago.

Family planning programs and national policies regarding population issues were a new phenomenon in the early 1960s. India was the only country in 1960 that had such a program. The last 40 years has seen a significant increase in support for family planning activities in both the developed and developing countries. Today, the majority of people live in nations that have formulated and adopted national policies to reduce population growth. In a study of family planning programs, Nortman (1985, 32) determined that 76 percent of the population in the less developed countries lived in countries with official policies and national family planning programs to reduce population growth.

The global diffusion of family planning practices has been the result of efforts by both public and private organizations. In the early 1960s only about 18 percent of the women of childbearing ages in the developing nations were practicing family planning. The total fertility rate was slightly over 6.0 children per woman in the developing world compared with 2.7 children for the industrialized nations. Today, the total fertility rate for the less developed countries has dropped to 3.9 while that for the developed nations is 1.9 children per woman. One half of all couples of childbearing age in the developing world and 70 percent in the developed world use some means of birth control (United Nations, 1990).

In 1951 India became the first country to adopt an official policy to support family planning and slow population growth. In the early 1960s four more countries (Table 7–1), primarily in Asia, announced population growth control policies. Since the mid-1960s, many more developing countries have adopted policies, although 50 developing

TABLE 7–1 ▦ First Governments to Support Family Planning and Slower Population Growth

Country	Year Policy Adopted	Annual Growth Rate	
		1960–1965	1985–1990
India	1951	2.26	2.07
Pakistan	1960	2.69	3.44
Republic of Korea	1961	2.64	0.95
China	1962	2.07	1.45
Fiji	1962	3.27	1.78
Egypt	1965	2.51	2.39
Mauritius	1965	2.64	1.17
Singapore	1965	2.81	1.25
Sri Lanka	1965	2.43	1.33
Turkey	1965	2.49	2.08

SOURCE: Peter J. Donaldson and Amy Ong Tsui. (1990) "The International Family Planning Movement," *Population Bulletin* 45:5.

countries (39 percent of the total) do not have specific policies to lower fertility and another 18 (14 percent) have policies to maintain or raise fertility. The countries are mostly small nations and represent only about 18 percent of the developing world's population (Figure 7–1).

Two terms that are often misused interchangeably need to be introduced and defined—namely, the terms *policy* and *program*. A national population *policy* is an official government strategy or set of guidelines specifically designed to affect the size and growth rate of a population, the distribution of a population, or its composition. The important feature of such a policy is that the government *intentionally* plans to control one or more demographic variables. As the United Nations (1969, 178) noted:

> All governments design policies, adopt administrative programmes, and enact laws which intentionally or unintentionally directly influence the components of population growth—fertility, mortality, and international migration—as well as the internal redistribution of the nation's inhabitants. However, such measures represent national population policy only when implemented for the purpose of altering the natural course of population movements.

Once a government policy is adopted and a set of objectives has been specified, a population *program* may be initiated. The program includes the various means and measures that must be utilized in order to achieve the objectives of the population policy. For example, a government establishes a policy of lowering fertility. A family planning program may then be established to provide information and methods for controlling conception.

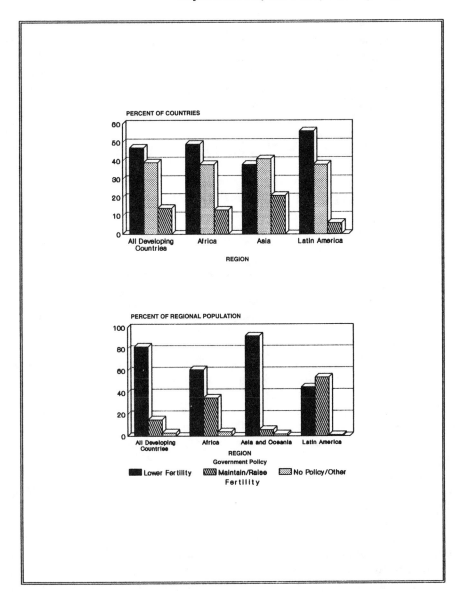

▓ **FIGURE 7–1** Government Policies on Fertility Levels in Developing Regions, 1989.
SOURCE: Peter J. Donaldson and Amy Ong Tsui. (1990) "The International Family Planning Movement," *Population Bulletin* 45(3):6. Courtesy of the Population Reference Bureau, Inc.

Explicit population policies are aimed at changing selected demographic variables. However, these demographic variables may also be influenced indirectly by other economic and social policies—such as tax laws, public education, welfare, health, and various development programs. Furthermore, not all governments adopt national population policies; however, they may, as in the case of the United States, support or at least permit population-related programs.

▨ BASES AND OBJECTIVES OF POPULATION POLICY

Most national population policies, especially in the developing countries, have been designed to decrease the prevailing high rates of population growth. The central focus of such policies is on decreasing fertility. However, some earlier population policies in the developed countries were designed to encourage higher birth rates. As Schroeder (1976, 6–7) noted:

> Declining fertility led governments to proscribe abortion and contraception, and to adopt measures aimed at promoting large families, early marriages, and increased immigration. In most countries, the decision to promote more rapid population growth was reinforced by other factors—religious, military, or economic.

Examples of attempts to encourage higher birth rates include egalitarian and welfare measures in Sweden, the pronatalist policy of Hitler's Germany, and family subsidies in France. Similarly, for the former Soviet Union, Thomlinson (1976, 604) commented that "worries over the low birth rate and consequent slow rate of population increase were among the reasons that led Soviet leaders to revoke legalization of abortions in 1936. . . ." Although changes in some of these earlier policies have occurred in recent years, many developed countries still have policies, direct or indirect, that could be described as pronatalist.

Between 1976 and 1989 the number of governments that limited access to modern methods of birth control fell from 15 to 6 (Table 7–2). The only nations that currently restrict access to modern birth control methods are Iraq, Kampuchea, Laos, Mongolia, Saudi Arabia, and the Vatican. The number of nations that do not directly support modern birth control fell from 28 to 20 countries. However, most recent policy trends are increasingly antinatalist, especially in the developing countries. Attention will be given to such policies in a subsequent section.

Government policies designed to reduce mortality are virtually universal. The bases of such programs are mainly economic, but they are also humanitarian in nature. Programs for carrying out death control policies are many and varied. Examples include disease control programs, worker-safety programs, and medical care programs.

Government immigration policies also are common in most countries although they are designed for different purposes in different places. Their impact is mainly on the composition of the national population.

TABLE 7–2 ▨ Trends in Government Policies Regarding Modern Methods of Birth Control, 1976–1989

Date of Assessment	Total	Access Limited	No Support Provided	Access Not Limited	
				Indirect Support Provided	Direct Support Provided
Number of Governments					
1976	158	15	28	18	97
1978	158	13	27	20	98
1980	165	11	27	22	105
1983	168	7	32	28	101
1986	170	6	18	24	122
1989	170	6	20	20	124
Percentage of Governments					
1976	100	9	18	11	61
1978	100	8	17	13	62
1980	100	7	16	13	64
1983	100	4	19	17	60
1986	100	4	11	14	72
1989	100	4	12	12	72

SOURCE: United Nations. (1989) *Trends in Population Policy,* Population Studies No. 114 (New York: United Nations), Table 16.

The development of population policy is usually slow and is often fraught with difficulties. The international Population Council has suggested a series of eight steps that might characterize the sequential development of a policy to limit fertility (Nortman, 1973, 11):

1. Government interest in population as it impinges on development planning;
2. A pronouncement on population matters by some responsible public official;
3. The establishment of a commission to study the demographic situation;
4. Surveys to determine the extent of knowledge, attitude, and practice of contraception (KAP surveys); the establishment of pilot population projects; and course work in demography at the university level;
5. The allocation of a new or increased budget for family planning, usually through official health programs;
6. The elaboration of specific demographic targets and time frames;
7. Establishment of a family planning apparatus somewhere in the government to implement programs;
8. Integration of all previously existing population related programs and development of subsidiary activities such as public information and evaluation.

It should be apparent that the path to government adoption of a fertility control policy, as well as the development of programs designed to meet the goals of that policy, is a lengthy and controversial one. Still, the increasing awareness of such policy needs is helping to create the necessary atmosphere in which to adopt and implement growth control policies.

Out of the adoption of fertility control policies has come the need for family planning programs. These programs are normally government supported and administered. Their primary purpose is to provide birth control information and services on a voluntary basis to people who desire such information. The difficulties of the task set out for family planning programs are many, but the perceived need seems to justify their existence. Some time ago Berelson (1972, 201) made the following comment on the state of family planning: "In my view, the present state is simultaneously impressive, frustrating, uneven, inadequate, and doubtful or unknown. The prospects are promising and dubious." Berelson suggested that the difficulties facing family planning programs could be classified as political, bureaucratic, organizational, economic, cultural, religious, and personal, along with the problem of the sheer size of the program required in many countries.

▓ FAMILY PLANNING PROGRAMS

With a continual lowering of the world's death rate, the only humane path to slowing population growth is to lower fertility. Those countries that have not yet completed the demographic transition need to do so. As we have already seen, modernization in the developing countries, as important as it is, may not be sufficient to bring about needed fertility declines. Though family planning programs seem relatively new, their history is not.

Brief Historical Sketch

Perhaps the earliest attempt to advocate openly the use of contraceptives to control family size occurred early in the Industrial Revolution in England with the publication of *Illustrations and Proofs of the Principle of Population* by Francis Place in 1822. Place's argument in favor of controlling family size was purely economic. Workers could receive higher wages and better working conditions if only they could limit the supply of laborers available. Following Place, similar books were published in England and in the United States. However, during the 1870s legal attempts to suppress such literature were made in both countries.

In the United States, the "Comstock Law," which forbade the dissemination by mail of information about birth control, was passed by Congress in 1873. Similar laws against the distribution of birth control literature were also passed by many states and the importation of such literature was outlawed in 1890.

In America the chief voice in the early campaign for family planning was that of Margaret Sanger. Following the efforts of Sanger and others, the Comstock Laws were finally repealed. However, the last of the Comstock Laws was not repealed until 1966 in an action taken by the Massachusetts legislature.

In 1916, the same year the Comstock Law was repealed, Margaret Sanger opened America's first birth control clinic in Brooklyn, New York. A similar clinic, aimed at serving poor women, was opened five years later by Marie Stopes in England. By the mid-1930s, the medical profession voiced its acceptance of family planning through the qualified endorsement of birth control by the American Medical Association (AMA). The history of landmark events in the international family planning movement is outlined in Table 7–3.

After World War II, there was a significant increase in both the stature and the number of private groups that promoted family planning activities. The International Planned Parenthood Federation (IPFF) was established, the United Nations established the Population Commission, and John D. Rockefeller, 3rd, established the Population Council.

According to Donaldson and Tsui (1990, 10), "The IPFF is the most prominent and widely recognized private sector effort to support family planning internationally. Its objectives were (and are) to promote family planning and population education, to support family planning services, and to stimulate and disseminate research on fertility regulation. In 1990, IPFF had 107 family planning member affiliates representing 150 countries."

Recent Developments in Family Planning Programs

A surge of activity and rapid expansion of the family planning movement occurred during the 1960s and 1970s. This support was evident in both the developing and the industrialized nations. In 1968 the United States Congress specifically allocated funds to support family planning activities. Family planning became a central component of the United States Agency for International Development (AID) program. In the next two decades AID contributions to population and family planning assistance throughout the Third World totaled $3.9 billion, making it the largest single donor of population aid (Gillespie and Seltzer, 1990, 562).

Another important event during this period was the establishment of the United Nations Fund for Population Activities (UNFPA) in 1967. The goals of UNFPA are "to provide an awareness of population problems and their relationship to social and economic development, the implementation of population policies, and the spread of family planning to better the health and well-being of the individual, family, and community" (Donaldson and Tsui, 1990, 11).

Americans became more aware of population issues through the publication of Paul Ehrlich's book *The Population Bomb*, and a number of organizations were founded to publicize the problems associated with rapid population growth (Zero Population

TABLE 7–3 ▪ Landmark Events in International Family Planning

Early Advocates

1860   Malthusian League founded in England to spread information on birth control.

1873   Comstock law in the United States enacted to prohibit advertising or prescription of contraception (later repealed in 1916).

1916   First free birth control clinic opened in Brooklyn, New York, by Margaret Sanger.

1921   First birth control clinic opened in England by Marie Stopes.

1937   American Medical Association gives qualified endorsement to birth control.

Post-World War II Developments

1946   United Nations Economic and Social Council establishes a population commission representing member governments and a population division within the secretariat.

1951   India adopts family planning as part of its economic program.

1952   John D. Rockefeller, 3rd establishes the Population Council

            Constitution for the International Planned Parenthood Federation (IPPF) drafted at an international conference in Cheltenham, England (ratified in 1953).

Rapid Program Expansion

1960   Oral contraceptives are introduced.

1961   Plastic IUDs become available.

1967   The trust fund for the United Nations Fund for Population Activities (UNFPA) is created.

1968   United Nations International Conference on Human Rights issues the Teheran proclamation of which article 16 states: "Parents have a basic human right to determine freely and responsibly the number and spacing of their children."

            Pope Paul VI issues *Humanae vitae* banning the use of artificial contraception.

            Paul Ehrlich publishes *The Population Bomb*.

            U.S. Congress first allots foreign aid funds for family planning.

1969   First non-eugenic, non-restrictive sterilization laws are passed in Singapore and the state of Virginia, U.S.A.

1973   U.S. Supreme Court upholds *Roe v Wade* decision, limiting the right of states to interfere in the private decision of a woman and her doctor to terminate a pregnancy.

1974   United Nations holds first world conference on population in Bucharest. The United States urges countries to adopt policies aimed at slowing growth, primarily through family planning.

1979   The People's Republic of China begins campaign for "one child for one couple."

Political Realignments and New Technologies

1984   The Second UN World Conference on Population is held in Mexico City. Most third world countries favor slower population growth and family planning. The United States shifts its position, stating that population growth is a neutral phenomenon.

1985   A law is enacted that prohibits the U.S. government from supporting any organization that supports or participates in the management of a program of coercive abortion or involuntary sterilization. Support for the UNFPA and IPPF is suspended.

1988   RU-486 is approved for terminating early pregnancy in France.

SOURCE: Peter J. Donaldson and Amy Ong Tsui. (1990) "The International Family Planning Movement," *Population Bulletin* 45:8. Courtesy of the Population Reference Bureau, Inc.

TABLE 7–4 ▩ Government Support for UNFPA, 1984–1989

Ten Largest Donor Governments	1984 Millions of US $	Ten Largest Donor Governments	1989 Millions of US $
United States	$38.0	Japan	$40.2
Japan	19.8	Netherlands	24.5
West Germany	12.5	West Germany	21.1
Norway	10.9	Norway	19.6
Netherlands	9.5	Sweden	17.6
Canada	8.8	Finland	14.9
Sweden	5.7	Denmark	11.6
Denmark	4.5	Canada	9.8
United Kingdom	3.9	United Kingdom	8.7
Italy	1.8	Switzerland	4.4
Other governments	7.0		7.1
Total contributions	122.4		179.5
Percentage from 10 largest donors	94		96

SOURCE: UNFPA, 1984 and 1989 *Annual Reports* (New York: United Nations).

Growth, Population Crisis Committee, Population Institute). Population studies also increased at the nation's academic institutions. Population studies programs were started or expanded at a number of Universities including Brown, Chicago, Michigan, North Carolina, Pennsylvania, and Princeton.

The last decade has seen many new developments regarding population and family planning. According to Donaldson and Tsui (1990, 12), "This period has been characterized by the increasing commitment of the public and policymakers in the Third World to family planning, both to slow population growth and to improve the health of women and children. The period has also witnessed the waning of U.S. government concern about the effects of rapid population and of its support for family planning."

A new political conservatism in the United States, led by President Ronald Reagan, brought about a drastic change in United States policy relative to population issues. This change in policy led the United States to withdraw its financial support for UNFPA and the IPFF.

Fortunately for UNFPA and the IPFF, the cutting of funds by the United States was more than matched by additional funding support from the nations of Scandinavia, Western Europe, and Japan. A comparison of support and changes from 1984–1989 are shown in Table 7–4.

▥ IMPLEMENTING FAMILY PLANNING PROGRAMS

For family planning programs to be successful, they must have ongoing financial support as well as strong public and political support, and good management and organization. These family planning programs have been described as "organized efforts to assure that couples who want to limit family size and space their children have access to contraceptive information and services and are encouraged to use them as needed" (Simmons, 1986, 175).

Five types of activities have been particularly successful in the development of family planning activities, particularly in the developing nations. These are (1) demonstration projects that established that the demand existed for family planning services and that these services could be delivered in a medically safe and culturally acceptable manner; (2) the provision of contraceptives such as the IUD, condoms, spermicides, or the pill; (3) the support of training programs in population and family planning; (4) assistance with surveys and national censuses; and (5) other technical assistance, including methods to help the staff of family planning programs improve counseling on contraceptive side effects, expand the types of contraceptive methods offered, or conduct clinical trials to evaluate new contraceptive methods (Donaldson and Tsui, 1990, 18–20).

▥ FAMILY PLANNING IN DEVELOPING COUNTRIES

Family planning programs in developing countries, for the most part, have sprung up in the last 30 years. Family planning services were originally introduced in developing countries in the 1940s and 1950s by private physicians and private groups to women who were self-motivated. By the late 1950s and early 1960s, however, governments became aware of rapid population growth and its socioeconomic consequences and became concerned with family planning.

Government support of family planning programs is now widespread among the developing nations. The number of men and women using contraception has grown more than sixfold since the 1960s, with over 400 million of the estimated 850 million to 880 million married couples now using contraception. Nearly 70 percent of these couples live in the developing world.

Recent estimates (Figure 7–2) are that approximately 50 percent of married women of childbearing age in the developing nations use some form of family planning. There is considerable regional variation ranging from a low of 17 percent in Africa to a high of 75 percent in East Asia.

This rapid increase in contraceptive use is primarily the result of increases in sterilization and the use of modern contraceptives such as the pill and the IUD. The

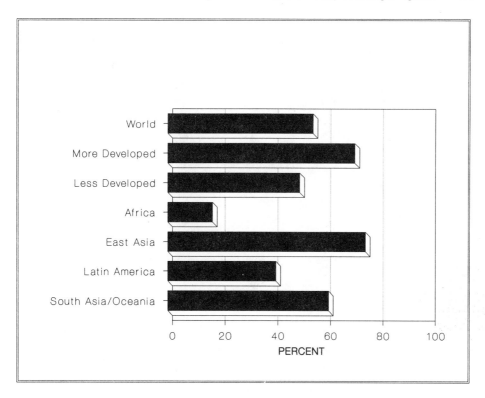

▨ **FIGURE 7–2** Contraceptive Use in World Regions, 1990 Estimates. SOURCE: Peter J. Donaldson and Amy Ong Tsui. (1990) "The International Family Planning Movement," *Population Bulletin* 45(3):20. Courtesy of the Population Reference Bureau, Inc.

most widely used form of contraception in the world today is sterilization (Table 7–5). In almost 45 percent of Third World couples who use birth control, one partner has been sterilized. Female sterilization outnumbers male sterilization in Third World countries by almost three to one. The second most prevalent type of contraceptive in the Third World is the IUD, used by over 70 million women, followed by the pill, used by 38 million women.

Methods of contraceptive use vary regionally throughout the world (Table 7–5). Almost one half of the birth control practiced in Asia and the Pacific is through sterilization, whereas the comparable figure in Latin America is a little over one third and less than 8 percent in Africa. Latin America also relies heavily on the pill, which is almost as popular as sterilization. In Africa, 38 percent of contraceptive users rely on the pill, with a fairly significant proportion, 23 percent, relying on traditional methods.

TABLE 7–5 ▪ Contraceptive Users and World Regional Estimates by Method, 1987

Method	Percent Using Each Method[a]					
			Developing Countries			
	Total	Developed Countries	Total	Africa	Latin America	Asia and the Pacific
Sterilization	35	15	44	8	39	48
Female	25	10	33	8	39	34
Male	10	5	12	0	1	14
Pill	15	20	13	38	30	9
Injectable	2	0[b]	2	8	3	2[b]
IUD	19	8	23	15	9	26
Condom	10	19	6	8	3	6
Vaginal methods	2	4	1	1	1	1
Traditional methods[c]	18	35	11	23	15	9
Total percent	100	100	100	100	100	100
Total number	437	133	304	14	35	255

[a]Married women age 15–49 in millions.

[b]Users of injectables in this region are usually combined with pill users.

[c]Traditional methods include rhythm, withdrawal, abstinence, and other methods.

Percents may not total to 100 because of rounding.

SOURCE: United Nations. (1989) *Levels and Trends of Contraceptive Use as Assessed in 1988* (New York: United Nations), Table 13.

In an effort to look at regional variations in family planning programs within the Third World, Freedman (1990) divided these countries into three categories: (1) less developed countries with rapid development, (2) countries with moderate development, and (3) countries with relatively little development. In the countries with rapid development, such as Korea, Taiwan, Mexico, and Singapore, fertility rates have fallen rapidly.

For example, in Taiwan in 1960, just before both family planning and development programs started, the total fertility rate was about 6 and contraceptive use was at low levels. By 1986, according to Freedman (1990, 37), "only 26 years later, the fertility rate had fallen by 70 percent to 1.7—below replacement levels—and virtually all women were using contraception before the end of their childbearing years." Although Taiwan's family planning program coincided with rapid social and economic development, it is "unlikely that the disadvantaged masses—the poor, rural, and illiterate—would have adopted family planning so rapidly without the family planning program" (Freedman, 1990, 37).

Freedman's second category, those countries with moderate development, included China, Indonesia, and Thailand. In these countries rapid fertility declines have taken place under initially unfavorable social and economic conditions. Freedman attributes this decline of fertility and increased use of contraception to a variety of factors, including the mobilization of the bureaucratic infrastructure and the ability of governments to incorporate the village masses into family planning programs.

The third category includes those countries with little socioeconomic development and weak infrastructure. Most of the countries of sub-Saharan Africa, as well as India, Pakistan, Bangladesh, and the smaller countries of Southwest Asia, are in this category. Although some of these countries have family planning programs, they have not been very successful in increasing contraceptive use enough to make a major decrease in fertility. Freedman believes that the reason for this lack of success is because "the family planning system is weak, with poor-quality services provided in ways that are inappropriate for the local culture" (Freedman, 1990, 39).

Although there are continuing debates about the efficacy of family planning programs, increasing evidence suggests that they are having a significant impact on fertility in many places. Most of the debate focuses on whether economic development and its concomitant social and economic transformations are a necessary precondition for fertility decline. Family planning advocates argue that an increase in the supply of birth control information and services can bring about significant fertility reductions without substantial economic development.

A variety of studies have attempted to evaluate the role of family planning in fertility decline. For example, Lapham and Mauldin (1987) measured the quality of national family planning programs in 91 less developed countries. They concluded that high-quality family planning programs play a significant role in contraceptive use and fertility decline, independent of social and economic change. Another significant conclusion from their study was that family planning goes hand in hand with steady economic development and that higher levels of contraceptive use and larger, more rapid birth rate declines were a joint product of the two forces (Table 7–6).

Family planning programs cannot take all the credit for fertility declines, but in many places they have had an impact. Other factors in recent fertility declines probably include improvements in literacy, improvements in the status of women, rural development programs, income redistribution, and population education programs.

Improved communications are important in determining the effectiveness of family planning programs. Various barriers to communication, from cultural sensitivities to language differences, have impeded the family planner's ability to get the message across. Various forms of communication have been tried, from traditional means to mass media approaches. Posters showing small, happy, healthy families have been common in several countries, for example India, Taiwan, and Jamaica. In one study Worrall (1977) suggested that family planning communication tended to proceed at stages that were dependent on the government's attitude and policy.

After seeing that fertility rates are coming down in a number of developing countries, and after discussing improvements in communicating family planning activities, it is useful to look at the implications of these fertility trends for future contraceptive use in the developing world. Estimates of the number of women using contraception in selected future years were made by Bongaarts (1986, 131) and appear in Table 7–7. In 1984 approximately 256 million women were practicing contraception; of that

TABLE 7–6 ■ Contraceptive Prevalence and Crude Birth Rate Decline by Socioeconomic Setting and Family Planning Program Effort

Socioeconomic Setting in 1970	Program Effort[a]				
	Strong	Moderate	Weak	Very Weak or None	All Levels
Contraceptive Prevalence Rate, 1977–1983					
High	60	58	50	36	55
Upper middle	63	42	25	11	30
Lower middle	48	27	8	6	12
Low	—	19	4	3	4
All settings	59	44	23	7	26
Crude Birth Rate Decline, 1965–1980					
High	34	31	27	11	27
Upper middle	43	23	11	3	13
Lower middle	—	18	7	2	5
Low	—	—	0	1	1
All settings	36	26	13	3	11

Note: Contraceptive prevalence based on data from 91 countries; birth rate declines based on data for 73 countries. Each country was weighted equally, not by population size.

[a]Program effort in 1982 for contraceptive use, during the 1972–1982 period for crude birth rate decline.

SOURCE: Peter J. Donaldson and Amy Ong Tsui. (1990) "The International Family Planning Movement," *Population Bulletin* 45:38. Courtesy of the Population Reference Bureau, Inc.

TABLE 7–7 ■ Estimated Number of Married Women Practicing Contraception, by Region, for Selected Years from 1984–2025

Region	Women Practicing Contraception (millions)				
	1984	1990	2000	2010	2025
Africa	11	16	35	74	168
Latin America	32	41	58	73	90
East Asia*	132	160	180	184	171
South Asia	81	120	190	250	307
Developing countries	256	337	462	581	736

*Excluding Japan.

SOURCE: John Bongaarts. (1986) "The Transition in Reproductive Behavior in the Third World," in Jane Menken, ed. *World Population and U.S. Policy: The Choices Ahead.* (New York: W. W. Norton and Company), Table 7, p. 131. Used by permission.

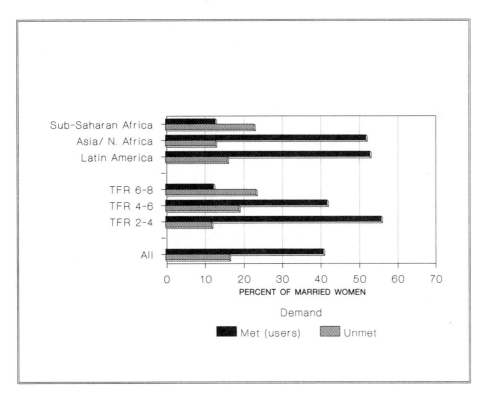

▩ **FIGURE 7–3** Total Demand for Contraception by Region and Fertility Level. SOURCE: Reprinted with permission of The Population Council, from John Bongaarts, "The KAP-Gap and the Unmet Need for Contraception," *Population and Development Review* 17 no. 2 (June 1991): 310.

number more than half lived in East Asia (China). Estimates are that by the year 2025 there will be a threefold increase to 736 million. The largest percentage of increase is projected to be in South Asia (from 81 to 307 million) and in Africa (from 11 to 168 million). According to Bongaarts (1986, 131), "These projections make clear that a rapid expansion of family planning services provided by both the public and private sectors will be required for at least the next several decades. This need for additional services is greatest in South Asia and Africa."

In a more recent study Bongaarts (1991) analyzed the unmet need for contraceptive services. The total unmet need was strongly correlated with the fertility level (Figure 7–3). The average total demand was nearly 60 percent, of which 42 percent represents unmet use and the remainder, 17 percent, is unmet need. According to Bongaarts (1991, 311):

> Differences by region and level of fertility in these variable are as expected: the total demand in sub-Saharan Africa and in countries with high fertility is lower than elsewhere. In these countries the unmet need actually exceeds the current level of

contraceptive use by a substantial margin. The unmet need represents a smaller but still important proportion of total demand in the Asian and Latin American populations and in countries with low fertility.

A variety of factors are responsible for this unmet need, including poor quality family planning services, limited access to these services, lack of contraceptive knowledge, weak motivation, and opposition from spouses. Although exact figures are unavailable, perhaps 100 million couples or unmarried individuals in Third World countries have an unmet need for contraceptive services.

Before going on to family planning in the developed countries, one further note should be made about programs in the developing countries, namely, that funding for family planning is increasingly a problem. International aid has accounted for one third of the funds while the less developed countries themselves have supplied the remaining two thirds of the funding. The developing countries will be expected to increase their financial contributions in the future. The contribution by AID in the 1990s is lower in real dollar terms than it was in the late 1970s. More significant, however, is the increasing demand and desire to practice family planning by people throughout the world. Third World countries continue to increase their commitment and support for family planning efforts while support from the largest international donor, the United States, is waning.

India

Among the developing countries, India is generally believed to be the one whose government first favored lowering the rate of population growth. The country's anti-natalist policy dates back to 1952, and was subsequently incorporated into the first Indian Five-Year Plan. However, in the early years family planning tended to be poorly financed. After a slow start, followed by occasional lapses, the program was revitalized in 1965.

In 1965 the Indian Government established the Department of Family Planning. This new department was under the authority of the Ministry of Health and Family Planning. The Indian program is funded by the Central Government; however, most of the organization and operation of the program is left to the various states.

Until 1976, participation in the family planning program was voluntary. In that year, however, compulsory sterilization was introduced in India in the state of Maharashtra. From 1975–1977 Prime Minister Indira Gandhi suspended civil liberties, and both the number of sterilizations and abuse of the program reached its peak. According to Singh (1990, 127), "Public sector employees needed to show a vasectomy certificate to get a transfer, promotion, food license, or an allocation of a house or medical care."

Until the introduction of involuntary sterilization, the mainstay of the voluntary program had been sterilization, coupled with traditional contraceptives, especially IUDs and condoms. In the 1970s the Indian program attempted to improve communications and motivation. A need for convincing people of the advantages of smaller families was obvious.

A major element in Indian programs during the 1970s was a package of incentives. The major incentive was a financial award offered to men or women, with two or more children, who underwent a sterilization operation. The amount of the incentive was inversely related to the number of children. The maximum cash award was 150 rupees, more than a month's wages for the average agricultural worker. Beyond this cash incentive from the national government, the various states added other incentives, such as salary increases for sterilization, and such disincentives as denying women maternity leave for children beyond the second one.

When the Janata Party assumed power in 1977, the family planning program was not dismantled. However, the program's emphasis was shifted considerably; only noncoercive methods were considered to be acceptable to the new government. Also, a new emphasis was placed on family welfare. Monetary incentives for sterilizations and IUD insertions were retained, with new rates of 100 rupees for a vasectomy and 120 rupees for a tubectomy, irrespective of the acceptor's current family size (Visaria and Visaria, 1981). Unfortunately, under the Janata Party people involved in the family planning program became demoralized and program achievements fell to low levels as well.

Between 1978 and 1981, however, the program gradually recovered. In 1979 the Working Group on Population Policy set a new long-range goal: India should reach replacement-level fertility by 1996. In the same year the government planned for an increase in international family planning assistance for the 1980–1985 period.

An analysis of data on contraception reveals some interesting changes (Table 7–8). Approximately one third (34.9 percent) of the total eligible couples in 1985–1986 were using effective contraceptive methods. Fifteen years earlier, in 1970–1971, the comparable figure was 10.4 percent. The ineffectiveness of the program, however, becomes clear when birth rate statistics are analyzed. The decline in the birth rate during the same time period was very small, from 36.8 per 1000 population in 1970–1971 to 33.9 per 1000 in 1985.

The principal contraceptive method was sterilization, especially vasectomy, and it has proved ineffective. According to an analysis of a village program by Singh (1990, 128–129):

> The implementation of the sterilization program left much to be desired for reducing fertility. The pressure of meeting quotas must have resulted in the sterilization of persons who were old or otherwise marginal to fertility reduction such as grandfathers, or unmarried older uncles. A father who voluntarily opts for sterilization usually does so after he has reached his desired family size, five or six children, with a sufficient number of sons.

TABLE 7–8 ▦ Effective Methods of Contraception Used by Eligible Couples
in India (percentages)

Year	Sterilization	IUD	Other Methods	All Methods
1970–71	8.0	1.4	1.0	10.4
1971–72	9.7	1.3	1.2	12.2
1972–73	12.2	1.1	1.2	14.5
1973–74	12.2	1.0	1.5	14.7
1974–75	12.6	1.0	1.2	14.8
1975–76	14.2	1.0	1.7	17.0
1976–77	20.7	1.1	1.7	23.5
1977–78	20.1	0.9	1.5	22.5
1978–79	19.9	0.9	1.6	22.4
1979–80	19.9	1.0	1.4	22.3
1980–81	20.1	1.0	1.7	22.8
1981–82	20.7	1.1	2.0	23.7
1982–83	22.0	1.4	2.5	25.9
1983–84	23.7	2.2	3.7	29.5
1984–85	24.9	2.9	4.4	32.1
1985–86	26.5	3.7	4.7	34.9

SOURCE: Compiled from the *Yearbooks* of the Department of Family Welfare, Ministry of Health and
Family Welfare, Government of India, New Delhi.

According to Freedman (1990, 39), there is probably a consensus among most Indian
and foreign observers that the program has been poorly executed and ineffective for
several reasons: (1) an obsession with unreasonably high targets for the program has
demoralized personnel; (2) there has been too much emphasis on sterilization linked
to a controversial incentive program; (3) there has been little continuity of family
planning program personnel; and (4) officials within the program have been out of
touch with the realities of Indian village life. As Roberts (1990, 88) stated, "In India,
where states function relatively independently and represent a range of religious and
ethnic groups, the national coercive effort to reduce birth rates proved impossible to
implement."

▦ TWO SUCCESS STORIES: KOREA AND THAILAND

Two family planning programs that have achieved a great deal of success are
those in Korea and Thailand. The national program in Korea was adopted in 1961 and
has been one of the most successful in the developing world. The achievements of the
family planning program went hand in hand with impressive economic growth. Between 1962 and 1988, per capita income increased from $62 to $3,600, and the proportion of women who completed secondary school increased over 65 percent between
1965 and 1987 (World Bank, 1990).

Although these economic changes influenced people's views on family size, the
family planning program also played a significant role in shaping people's perceptions

of childbearing and family size. In the early 1960s family planning was practiced by less than 10 percent of the women at risk of pregnancy; the nation's total fertility rate was 5.4. By 1991 the total fertility rate had fallen to 1.6, and the percent of married women using contraception had risen to 77 percent.

The government family planning program that contributed to this impressive change in reproductive behavior was, according to Donaldson and Tsui (1990, 40), "based on a system of targets that established performance standards for the country's family planning outreach workers who were responsible for visiting women in their homes and encouraging them to begin to use contraception." Recent changes in the Korean program have placed the emphasis on family planning as a way to improve both maternal and child health.

Thailand is another nation that has had a very successful family planning program. Between 1965 and 1991 the proportion of married women of reproductive age using a contraceptive increased from 15 to 68 percent. The total fertility rate also declined dramatically, from 5.7 in the mid-1960s to 2.2 in 1991.

The national family planning program was aimed at providing information about contraceptive use to all citizens, especially those in rural areas. Nonphysicians, mostly secondary school graduates and auxiliary midwives, were trained to distribute a wide variety of contraceptives. Thailand was one of the first nations to permit the use of DMPA, an injectable contraceptive. Recently the contraceptive implant NORPLANT has been introduced.

The Thai program also successfully linked national and international resources, as well as bringing together both public and private sector programs. These efforts were strongly supported by the country's economic development and by the cultural environment in which the family planning activities took place (Knodel, et al., 1987).

▦ FAMILY PLANNING IN DEVELOPED COUNTRIES

Because of the smaller populations in developed countries, along with their lower rates of population growth, less emphasis is generally placed on discussions of family planning programs in developed countries. Though the nature of population problems in the developed countries differs from that of such problems in the developing countries, it still deserves, and is receiving, increasing attention (Berelson, 1974).

Earlier we pointed out that population policies in the developed countries were generally pronatalist in the past. However, current policies in most developed countries are more likely to favor lower fertility. Low fertility is characteristic of these countries, all of which have more-or-less completed their demographic transitions and the use of contraceptives is widespread (Figure 7–4).

Although the United States has no explicit population policy, it does have a concern with family planning services. In 1970 the Family Planning and Population Research Act was passed. Laws governing abortions have been liberalized as well although recent changes supported by the Reagan and Bush administrations have increasingly tried to restrict access to abortion, especially for the poor. As Table 7–9 shows, large numbers of American women use contraceptives in a variety of methods.

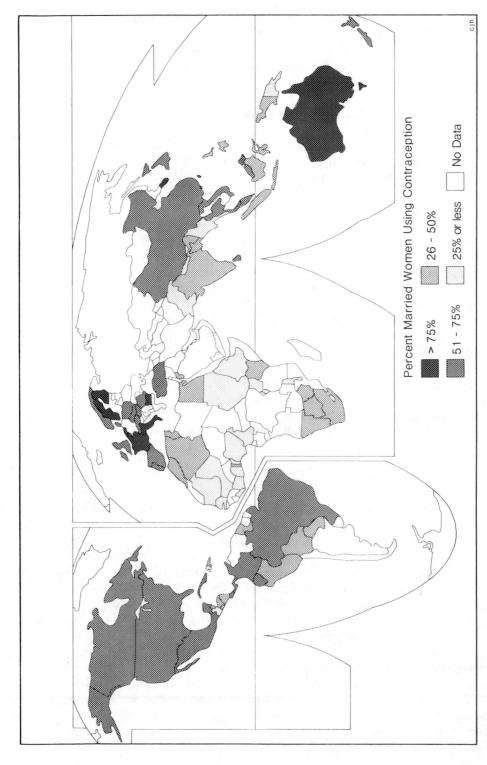

■ **FIGURE 7–4** Percent of Married Women Using Contraception, 1992. SOURCE: Data from *1992 World Population Data Sheet.* (Washington, D.C.: The Population Reference Bureau, Inc.).

TABLE 7–9 ■ Contraceptive Use by Women, 15–44 Years Old, by Age, Race, Marital Status, and Method of Contraception: 1982 and 1988

[Based on the 1982 and 1988 National Survey of Family Growth]

Contraceptive Status and Method	All Women, 1982	1988								
		All Women[1]	Age			Race		Marital Status		
			15–24 Years	25–34 Years	35–44 Years	White	Black	Never Married	Currently Married	Formerly Married
All Women (1,000)	54,099	57,900	18,592	21,726	17,582	47,077	7,679	21,058	29,147	7,695
Percent Distribution										
Sterile	27.2	29.7	3.1	27.0	61.3	30.5	29.6	5.2	44.0	42.6
Surgically sterile	25.7	28.3	2.4	26.0	58.7	29.2	27.8	4.3	42.4	40.9
Noncontraceptively sterile[2]	6.6	4.7	0.2	2.7	12.0	4.7	5.7	0.9	6.2	9.7
Contraceptively sterile[3]	19.0	23.6	2.2	23.3	46.7	24.5	22.1	3.4	36.2	31.3
Nonsurgically sterile[4]	1.5	1.4	0.7	0.9	2.7	1.3	1.8	1.0	1.6	1.7
Pregnant, postpartum	5.0	4.8	5.0	7.6	1.1	4.8	5.0	2.4	7.1	2.5
Seeking pregnancy	4.2	3.8	2.7	5.8	2.4	3.7	3.9	1.3	6.0	2.0
Other nonusers	26.9	25.0	45.7	16.7	13.5	23.8	26.9	52.5	4.8	26.6
Not sexually active[5]	19.5	19.0	37.9	10.3	8.5	18.1	16.7	43.5	0.3	19.5
Sexually active[5]	7.4	6.5	7.8	6.4	5.0	5.7	10.2	9.0	4.5	7.1
Nonsurgical contraceptors	36.7	36.7	43.5	43.0	21.6	37.2	34.6	38.5	38.1	26.3
Pill	15.6	18.5	29.7	21.6	3.0	18.4	21.6	24.7	15.1	14.5
IUD	4.0	1.2	0.1	1.4	2.1	1.1	1.7	0.6	1.5	2.1
Diaphragm	4.5	3.5	1.3	4.8	4.1	3.8	1.1	2.1	4.6	3.0
Condom	6.7	8.8	9.5	9.1	7.7	9.2	5.8	8.2	10.6	3.4
Foam	1.3	0.6	0.3	0.8	0.8	0.6	0.6	0.2	1.0	0.5
Rhythm[6]	2.2	1.4	0.6	1.7	1.8	1.4	1.2	0.6	2.1	1.1
Other methods[7]	2.5	2.6	2.0	3.6	2.2	2.5	2.6	2.1	3.2	1.7

[1]Includes other races, not shown separately.

[2]Persons who had sterilizing operation and who gave as one reason that they had medical problems with their female organs.

[3]Includes all other sterilization operations, and sterilization of the husband or current partner.

[4]Persons sterile from illness, accident, or congenital conditions.

[5]Those having intercourse in the last 3 months before the survey.

[6]Periodic abstinence and natural family planning.

[7]Withdrawal, douche, suppository and less frequently used methods.

SOURCE: United States Department of Commerce. (1991) *Statistical Abstract of the United States.* (Washington, D.C.: U.S. Government Printing Office), Table 101.

In Europe several nations have reached, or are close to reaching, zero population growth. Most of these countries have permissive policies with respect to contraceptives and abortions, but no official antinatalist policies. In some cases, for example France, even permissive policies are of recent origin. As Schroeder (1976, 24) noted:

> France—historically one of the most aggressively pronatalist countries of Western Europe—has recently made some sweeping changes in its posture toward family planning. These include a law passed in 1974 permitting distribution of contraceptives financed by the social security system, plus a comprehensive public information campaign and the provision of free medical examinations and family planning counseling.

In the Commonwealth of Independent States (formerly the Soviet Union) population policy is concerned mainly with population distribution. Higher fertility is being encouraged in selected areas where growth rates are currently low. Both contraceptives and abortion, however, are readily available.

In Asia, Japan, the largest developed country in the region, has a widely accepted family planning program. Family planning services are available through more than 800 health-care centers throughout the country. Abortions are readily available as well. Throughout the industrialized world, low fertility is common, even though explicit policies toward low fertility are not. A major element in low fertility has obviously been the effect of high and rising socioeconomic status, coupled with urbanization. Family planning programs often aid in the maintenance of low fertility levels.

Eastern Europe: A Modern Dilemma

Oddly enough, in a world in which China, India, and others struggle to alter birth rates downward through various policies and programs, the countries of Eastern Europe discovered that social and economic policies there during the Cold War years led to undesirably low fertility levels. During the past 30 years, fertility in Eastern Europe has followed a downward trend, in large part because of abortion.

In Eastern Europe, then, governments have tried to encourage couples to have more children. "Prior to the adoption of explicitly pronatalist goals," according to David (1982, 32), "most of the countries already had a complicated structure of programs and policies that worked both directly and indirectly to ease the financial burden of large families." Included were maternity leave, monthly payments to families with children, lump-sum payments for the birth of a child, price supports for children's needs, tax breaks for parents, and a host of other features that would appear to encourage couples to have large families.

Unfortunately, the desired results failed to materialize. David (1982, 32) pointed out that "while these measures did lessen the economic burden of childbearing, they were not powerful enough to overcome the physical and psychological burden which childbearing posed to women holding full-time jobs—as socialist policy decrees they must—and also faced with inadequate housing and chronic shortages of consumer goods and services and childcare facilities." As van de Kaa (1987, 52) noted in a study of European population changes "collective and individual interests do not seem to coincide . . . Eastern European countries appear incapable of overcoming individualistic desires and raising fertility to replacement level."

Understanding fertility trends in Eastern Europe requires an appreciation of the status of women in these formerly socialist countries. Although Marxist ideology gave women equal status with men, reality was not always in accord with ideology. David (1982, 39) noted that in Eastern European countries "laws have not eradicated the vestiges of male chauvinism or changed the economic conditions which still make childbearing a particularly heavy burden for women, whatever financial incentives governments might devise to encourage them to bear children."

The recent democratic revolutions in Eastern Europe have brought monumental changes to the political and economic structure of these nations. It will be interesting to follow these changes and to watch what impact they may have on demographic behavior.

▦ LAW AND POPULATION POLICY

Policies designed directly to affect demographic variables are often politically and emotionally sensitive issues. They may involve significant changes in preexisting laws, especially those that have controlled the dissemination of knowledge concerning contraceptive devices. Table 7–10 outlines a Law and Population Classification Plan that includes the broad variety of legal issues associated with population and family planning (Lee, 1990, 8–9).

Looking into the future, it seems that family planning programs are likely to expand to reach an increasing number of couples. Laws governing the sale of contraceptives will most likely change also in favor of increasing their availability. Governments probably will increase their support for family planning programs and population policies designed to slow rates of population growth. If all goes well, the decline in the world's population growth rate will continue, and the next century should see a world population that is nearly stable in size.

▦ SUMMARY

Fertility control policies and family planning programs are of special interest to us because they are so closely related to the future growth of the world's population, as well as to the geographic distribution of population growth. Though population policies are also concerned with mortality and migration, both internal and international, our focus is primarily on fertility.

Until recently everything seemed rather simple, because we assumed that future fertility trends could be predicted, at least in general terms, from the demographic transition model. Given sufficient time and sustained development in a country, we

TABLE 7–10 ▓ Law and Population Classification Plan

---

100 Fertility regulation
    110 Sterilization
    120 Contraception
    130 Abortion
200 Family status and welfare
    210 Marriage
    220 Termination of marriage
    230 Extended family obligations
300 Children and child welfare
    310 Support of children generally
    320 Protection of children
    330 Artificial insemination
    340 Legitimacy of children
    350 Registration of births
400 Criminal offences penology
    410 Criminal law treatment of sexual activity
    420 Penology (as affecting ability of prisoners to continue family relations)
500 Public welfare
    510 Family allowances generally
    520 Housing assistance programs
    530 Maternity leaves and benefits
    540 Old age and retirement benefits
    550 Death benefits to survivors
    560 Labour protection and employment standards
    570 Personal status and integrity
    580 Personal mobility (internal and external migration)
600 Public health
    610 Health insurance and medical assistance
    620 Hospital insurance and public clinics
    630 Control of medical facilities
    640 Medical profession (licensing, education, and regulation)
    650 Drugs and pharmaceuticals
    660 Food distribution and control
    680 Environmental protection programs (efforts to control population growth as a means of protecting the environment)
700 Education
    710–720 Compulsory education
    730 Literacy programs
    740 Adult education programs
    750 Financial assistance to education
    760 Educational opportunities for women
    770 Education affecting population directly (health, sex, marriage, contraception, and population)

TABLE 7–10 (Cont.) ■ Law and Population Classification Plan

800	Property and economic factors	
	810	Income distribution measures generally
	820	Taxation
	830	Land tenure and land improvement programs
	840	Distribution of decedents' property
	850	Employment guarantee and public works programs
	860	Guaranteed wage and income subsidies
900	Miscellany	
	910	Military service
	920	Religious law
	930	Other

SOURCE: From POPULATION POLICY: CONTEMPORARY ISSUES by Godfrey Roberts, ed. Pp. 8–9. Copyright © 1990 by Praeger Publishers, an imprint of Greenwood Publishing Group, Inc., Westport, CT. Reprinted with permission.

could expect fertility to decline. However, few demographers were very specific about when the decline would occur, how much the decline would be, or which developmental variables were most clearly related to changes in fertility. As van de Walle and Knodel (1980, 38) commented in their summary of literature on fertility declines in Western Europe, "there is only a loose relationship between the level of socioeconomic development and fertility decline." Economic development is no longer viewed as a necessary precondition for fertility decline.

Certainly some changes associated with modernization may facilitate fertility declines, as also may family planning programs. Reducing infant and childhood mortality; expanding educational opportunities, especially for girls and women; improving the status of women; providing a more equitable distribution of the benefits of development; and raising the legal marriage age may all contribute to reducing fertility levels in the developing countries. All of these variables can be related to the decision to have a child, though specifying mathematically precise relationships is tenuous, if not impossible.

However, few researchers doubt that an essential ingredient in lowering fertility is motivation. Until people are strongly motivated to have smaller families, no amount of propaganda and no supply of contraceptive methods will bring about a significant change. "Whether or not a family planning program will meet with success," wrote van de Walle and Knodel (1980, 39), "will be determined by how receptive couples are to the idea of reducing their fertility once the knowledge and means of birth control are available."

REFERENCES

Berelson, Bernard. (1972) "The Present State of Family Planning Programs," in Harrison Brown and Edward Hutchings, eds. *Are Our Descendants Doomed? Technological Change and Population Growth.* New York: The Viking Press, pp. 201–236.

Berelson, Bernard, ed. (1974) *Population Policy in Developed Countries.* New York: McGraw-Hill Book Company.

Bongaarts, John. (1986) "The Transition in Reproductive Behavior in the Third World," in Jane Menken, ed. (1986) *World Population and U.S. Policy.* New York: W.W. Norton, pp. 105–132.

Bongaarts, John. (1991) "The KAP-gap and the Unmet Need for Contraception," *Population and Development Review* 17:293–313.

David, Henry P. (1982) "Eastern Europe: Pronatalist Policies and Private Behavior," *Population Bulletin* 36(6):1–48.

Donaldson, Peter J. and Tsui, Amy Ong. (1990) "The International Family Planning Movement," *Population Bulletin* 45:1990.

Ehrlich, Paul R. and Ehrlich, Anne H. (1972) *Population, Resources, Environment: Issues in Human Ecology.* 2d ed. San Francisco: W. H. Freeman and Company.

Freedman, Ronald. (1990) "Family Planning Programs in the Third World," *The Annals of the American Academy of Political and Social Science* 510:33–43.

Gillespie, Duff G. and Seltzer, Judith R. (1990) "The Population Assistance Program of the U.S. Agency for International Development," in Helen M. Wallace and Kanti Giri, eds. *World Population and U.S. Policy.* New York: W. W. Norton and Company, pp. 75–206.

Knodel, John, Chamrathrithirong, A., and Debavalya, Nibhon. (1987) *Thailand's Reproductive Revolution: Rapid Fertility Decline in a Third World Setting.* Madison, WI: University of Wisconsin Press.

Lapham, Robert J. and Mauldin, W. Parker. (1987) "The Effects of Family Planning on Fertility: Research Findings," in Robert J. Lapham and George B. Simmons, eds. *Organizing Effective Family Planning Programs.* Washington D.C.: National Academy Press, pp. 647–680.

Lee, Luke T. (1990) "Law, Human Rights, and Population Policy," in Godfrey Roberts, ed. *Population Policy: Contemporary Issues.* New York: Praeger.

Nortman, Dorothy. (1973) "Population and Family Planning: A Factbook," *Reports on Population/Family Planning.* New York: The Population Council.

Nortman, Dorothy and Hofstatter, Ellen. (1976) "Population and Family Planning Programs," *Reports on Population/Family Planning.* No. 2, 8th ed. New York: The Population Council.

Nortman, Dorothy. (1985) *Population and Family Planning Programs: A Compendium of Data Through 1983.* New York: Population Council.

Roberts, Godfrey, ed. (1990) *Population Policy: Contemporary Issues*. New York: Praeger.

Schroeder, Richard C. (1976) "Policies on Population Around the World," *Population Bulletin* 29(6):1–36.

Simmons, George. (1986) "Family Planning Programs," in Jane Menken, ed. *World Population and U.S. Policy*. New York: W. W. Norton and Company, pp. 175–206.

Singh, Harbans. (1990) "India's High Fertility Despite Family Planning: An Appraisal," in Godfrey Roberts, ed. *Population Policy: Contemporary Issues*. New York: Praeger.

Thomlinson, Ralph. (1976) *Population Dynamics: Causes and Consequences of World Demographic Change*. 2d ed. New York: Random House.

United Nations. (1969) "World Population Situation," Note by the Secretary General. Geneva, Switzerland: United Nations Population Commission.

United Nations. (1989) *Trends in Population Policy*. Population Studies No. 114, New York: United Nations.

United Nations. (1990) *1990 Revision of World Population Prospects: Computerized Data Base and Summary Tables*. New York: United Nations.

van de Kaa, Dirk J. (1987) "Europe's Second Demographic Transition," *Population Bulletin* 42(1):1–57.

van de Walle, Etienne and Knodel, John. (1980) "Europe's Fertility Transition: New Evidence and Lessons for Today's Developing Countries," *Population Bulletin* 34(6):1–43.

Visaria, Pravin and Visaria, Leela. (1981) "India's Population: Second and Growing," *Population Bulletin* 36(4):1–55.

Worall, Robert P. (1977) "Communicating Population and Family Planning," *Population Bulletin* 31(5):1–39.

World Bank. (1990) *World Development Report 1990*. New York: Oxford University Press.

Chapter 8
Migration and Mobility

One of the most distinguishing characteristics of humans is their propensity to migrate. The distance of these movements and their frequency are distinctive. This mobility is evidenced by the linguistic, social, and nationalistic mixing of much of the world's population. Although the human population has always been mobile, its mobility has accelerated with economic and technological progress, particularly with progress in the fields of communications and transportation. Cultural adaptability has allowed humans to adjust to major ecological changes by employing mental abilities and technological skills.

Migration differs from fertility and mortality in several ways. First, the biological processes of birth and death are uniform, discrete, and distinct events. Because migration is not a biological event, it does not have a uniform process. Although there is no upper limit to migration, there is an upper limit to the number of children a woman can have. Goldscheider (1971, 49) remarked that "the total migration of communities or societies would not imply their demise, but their removal to another location." For example, the ghost towns of the American West were created when people left after the inducement that drew them there in the first place, typically minerals such as gold or silver, disappeared.

Second, because migration involves leaving one place and entering another, two populations must be considered: the population of the area of origin and the population in the area of destination. Changing mortality and fertility affect an area in a relatively simple way, whereas migration involves two areas; thus, to understand the migration process fully, both areas must be studied.

Finally, births and deaths are considered universals; that is, societies must have reproduction and some control over the inevitability of death in order to survive. On the other hand, migration is not a universal. Migration does not occur to everyone; it is a selective process that effectively has no upper limit. Some societies experience a great deal of migration, whereas others experience very little. In addition, migration can be repeated and even reversed.

▦ MEASURES OF MIGRATION

At first glance it may seem that defining the term "migrant" would be relatively simple. However, several problems can be identified. For example, if a migrant is simply defined as someone who "moves," then several questions must be answered. What constitutes a move? Must the move be permanent or do transients classify as migrants? Many people, such as commuters, shoppers, and tourists, change their geographical position, but should they be considered migrants? There are no definitive answers to all these questions. According to Thomlinson (1976, 267–268), "Demographers thus define persons as migrants if they change their place of normal habitation for a substantial period of time, crossing a political boundary."

Demographers distinguish between movers and migrants according to a single criterion. Movers are persons who change their place of residence; migrants are those whose change of residence takes them into a new political unit. Thus, all migrants are movers, but not all movers are migrants.

Thomlinson also pointed out that getting information for all moves made by all persons is almost impossible, but it is usually possible to obtain a record of moves where people cross political boundaries. Also, crossing a political boundary can be significant, particularly if one moves from one country to another, even if the distance involved in such a move is short.

Geographer Curtis Roseman (1971) provided a different and conceptually useful way of describing migration. He distinguished between *partial displacement* migration and *total displacement* migration. His differentiation was made by considering a household's *activity space,* the set of places such as schools, work, stores, and recreational facilities with which the household interacts on a regular basis. Partial displacement moves are those that disturb only a portion of a household's activity space. For example, a family moves to a different part of town. The husband and wife keep the same workplaces, but the children go to a different school and the family shops in a different shopping center. In contrast, total displacement migration, which involves longer distances, requires moving the entire activity space as well as the place of residence.

Basic Concepts

A standard set of migration concepts has evolved gradually over time. They are useful in testing various hypotheses and to facilitate the collection of data. To understand the migration literature, we need to understand the terminology and concepts.

Gross Migration.   The total sum of all the people who enter and leave an area is considered gross migration. Thus, this measurement indicates the total volume of population turnover in a community.

Net Migration.   During any specific time, a region may be receiving migrants from one region and losing migrants to another region. The difference between the arrivals and departures is called net migration. When more people leave an area than move into that area, net migration is said to be negative. Positive net migration, on the other hand, occurs when more people enter than leave an area.

Out-Migration and In-Migration.   Each migratory event involves two actions: leaving one place and arriving at another. Leaving the place of origin is referred to as out-migration, whereas arriving at the place of destination is referred to as in-migration.

Areas of Origin and Destination.   The area of origin is the place from which a migrant leaves, whereas the area of destination is the place at which the migrant arrives.

Migration Rates.   The relative frequency of migration is called the migration rate. It is the number of migratory events divided by the population exposed to the chance of migrating. Donald Bogue (1969, 758) defined four such rates.

$$\text{Out-migration rate: } \frac{O}{p} \times k$$

$$\text{In-migration rate: } \frac{I}{p} \times k$$

$$\text{Net-migration rate: } \frac{I - O}{p} \times k$$

$$\text{Gross-migration rate: } \frac{I + O}{p} \times k$$

where O is the number of out-migrants from an area,
I is the number of in-migrants to an area,
p is the average or mid-interval population of the area, and
k is a constant, usually 100 or 1000.

These migration rates can be computed as specific rates if both the numerator and denominator refer to the same particular substratum of the population. There can be specific rates for age, occupation, income, race, sex, or any other particular subgroup for which data are available.

Migration Interval.   Because migration is a time-specific process, it is necessary to specify the time interval over which migration is studied or observed. All other things being equal, the longer the time interval, the smaller the average size of the annual number of migrants, because a significant proportion of migrants return rather quickly to their places of origin. Even though migration data may have been computed on an average annual basis for two sample groups, if the migration intervals involved are not the same, then the data may not be comparable.

Migration Streams and Counterstreams.   Migrants who move from a particular origin to a particular destination over the same migration interval are considered part of a migration stream. Migrants who return to that origin during the same period are part of a counterstream.

Differential Migration.   The study of the selectivity of migration and of the differing rates among various social, demographic, and economic groups is referred to as differential migration. This term is also used when studying the differences in the population composition of migration streams.

Emigration and Immigration.   A person who changes residence from one country to another is considered an emigrant relative to the country of origin and an immigrant relative to the country of destination.

International Migration and Internal Migration.   International migration involves a change of residence from one country to another, whereas internal migration refers to change of residence within a country. Because some territories have characteristics similar to those of nation-states, the distinction between international and internal migration is not always clearcut. For example, difficulties arise when trying to designate migration between Puerto Rico and the United States. The migration literature not only can be broadly categorized into international versus internal, but internal migration can be categorized further into rural-urban, inter-urban, and even intra-urban.

Types of Migration

It is clear that migration can take many forms. Although most people in the United States think of migration streams as comprised of individuals, or perhaps families, moving freely from place to place, this has not always been the typical migration pattern. Several types of migration have been defined, including (1) primitive migration, (2) group or mass migration, (3) free-individual migration, (4) restricted migration, (5) and impelled or forced migration. Most of these types were first recognized by a noted demographer, William Petersen (1958).

Primitive Migration.   This type of migration is associated with groups who are unable to cope with natural forces in their physical environments. One method of coping with the deterioration of the physical environment of an area is to move away from it. This is generally done by a group of people, and many times it is related to hunting or to gathering food.

Thus, when there is a disparity between the produce of the land and the number of people that must subsist from that land, a primitive migration takes place. According to Petersen (1975, 320), "this can come about either suddenly, as by drought or an attack of locusts, or by the steady pressure of growing numbers on land of limited area and fertility."

Group or Mass Migration.   Most of the major population movements, certainly until the seventeenth century, consisted mainly of the movement of groups of people. Group migration refers to the migration of a clan, tribe, or other social group that is larger than a family. Throughout history entire societies left their original domiciles and laid claim to or invaded other areas. In some cases armies invaded other areas and some of the soldiers settled in the region of conquest. After an invasion, the native population was either assimilated or displaced.

Another type of mass or group migration is colonization. The early stages of the colonization process involve group migration; but during later stages, most migration is by individuals or families (Simkins, 1970).

Free-Individual Migration.   Free-individual migration has been described by Fairchild (1925, 20) as the following:

> The movement of people, individual, or in families acting on their own individual initiative and responsibility without official support or compulsion, passing from one well-developed country (usually old and thickly settled) to another well-developed country (usually new and sparsely settled) with the intention of residing there permanently.

A great deal of international migration since the seventeenth century has been characterized as this type, particularly migration to Australia, New Zealand, and the Americas.

Migration from Europe to the United States has been particularly important. Since the founding of the early colonies in the United States, it has involved some 30 to 40 million people. Much of the growth of the population of the United States is attributable to these immigrants. For example, Gibson (1975, 158) estimated that "about 98 million, or 48 percent, of the 1970 population (203 million) is attributable to the estimated net migration of 35.5 million in the 1790–1970 period." Similar percentages would probably apply to the counts provided by the 1980 and 1990 censuses.

Restricted Migration. Free migration has slowly been replaced by restricted migration. Since the turn of the century, numerous laws have been enacted to restrict the migration of people between countries. In some cases the restrictions involve a complete ban on all movement of certain types of people, whereas in other countries migration quotas have been set up to curtail movement.

Restrictions on international movements to the United States in the twentieth century have primarily been the result of increasing numbers of immigrants who desired to move to the United States, as well as the changing nature of the immigrants themselves—from Anglo-Saxon Protestants of northern and western Europe to Catholics of southern and eastern Europe. Immigration to the United States has been curtailed since 1921, when barriers were set up to restrict both the numbers and the types of migrants. A similar situation exists in other countries, such as Australia and Canada, countries that originally opened their doors to all immigrants but have since restricted immigration.

It was ironic that as the following words of Emma Lazarus' poem, "The New Colossus," were being inscribed and dedicated on the Statue of Liberty, the United States was about to impose racial barriers on migration and was soon to establish a quota system:

> Not like the brazen giant of Greek fame,
> With conquering limbs astride from land to land;
> Here at our sea-washed, sunset gates shall stand
> A mighty woman with a torch, whose flame
> Is the imprisoned lightning, and her name
> Mother of Exiles. From her beacon-hand
> Glows world-wide welcome; her mild eyes command
> The air-bridged harbor that twin cities frame.
> "Keep ancient lands, your storied pomp!" cries she
> With silent lips. "Give me your tired, your poor,
> Your huddled masses yearning to breathe free,
> The wretched refuse of your teeming shore.
> Send these, the homeless, tempest-tost to me,
> I lift my lamp beside the golden door!

Presently, restrictive policies in most countries present difficulties for prospective international migrants. These people must either stay where they are or find illegal methods of overcoming restrictions. According to Thomlinson (1976, 288), "two results of all these confining ordinances are that an enormous potential is being pent up in certain areas, and inequalities in the distribution of scarce goods and the standard of living are being aggravated."

Pressures for more international migration continue to increase, particularly as developed countries continue to have low rates of population growth while developing countries are growing at medium to high rates. Although the ratio of earnings in the richest countries to those in the poorest countries keeps increasing, the fraction of the world's population enjoying that wealth continues to decline. No one currently believes that containing international movements will continue to be possible, at least not without committing an ever-expanding pool of resources toward that end.

Impelled and Forced Migration. When the state or some other political or social institution is the activating agent in migration, the movement is referred to as impelled or forced migration. There is a rather simple distinction between these two types: with impelled migration the migrant holds some degree of choice, whereas with forced migration the migrant has no power or control over the situation. For example, the Nazi policy between 1933 and 1938 that encouraged Jewish emigration by various anti-Semitic laws and acts would be considered impelled migration, whereas the policy that followed, with the actual forcing of Jews to leave their homes and in many cases actual extermination, would be considered a forced migration policy (Petersen, 1975, 321).

Forced migration generally serves one of two purposes. First, it can be used to remove a potentially hostile group from a country. Second, it can be used to furnish an unskilled labor force for certain areas. The slave trade was a forced migration. According to Bouvier, Shryock, and Henderson (1977, 16):

> Forced migration, the most tragic of group movements, has meant flight and often enslavement for untold millions of human beings. Yet, despite the involuntariness of the act, this represents a major form of migration that has been prevalent throughout much of history. . . . The millions upon millions of 20th century refugees represent today's variation of "forced migration," which can be expected to continue as long as mankind insists on waging war or exercising total ethnic domination.

Tempting though it is to believe that slavery and the slave trade is a thing of the past, confined to the pages of history books, that is hardly the case. Tyler (1991), for example, pointed out that there are more slaves in the world today than at any time in the past, perhaps as many as 200 million, though most of today's slaves are either bonded laborers or child laborers not chattel slaves.

Even the latter are still with us, however, as children are sold in slave markets in Thailand, the Sudan, and a few other countries (Tyler, 1991). These children are in turn used for everything from sex slaves and child laborers to fodder for "religious" sacrifices. A grim article in *Stern*, for example, suggested that as many as 10 million youngsters worldwide are involved in child prostitution (Oberlander, 1992).

▓ MIGRATION THEORY

Migration, particularly that between nations, is one of the most striking changes that can occur in a person's life. According to Bogue (1969, 801):

> In a high proportion of such moves the person not only changes his national loyalties, but also forsakes his native language, his cultural heritage and customs, his relatives and lifelong friends, and his occupation. So drastic is the change that many adults never make a complete adjustment in their lifetime, and it is only their children or grandchildren who are fully integrated into the receiving society.

Yet people have always made such moves.

The reasons why people migrate are varied, and several theories have been developed to help explain migration patterns. The pioneer effort in migration theory was developed by Ravenstein in the 1880s and set down in his "Laws of Migration." He studied population movements in Great Britain and related migration to population size, density, and distance. He had a minimum of records of migrants in England, but in a fairly short time he extracted the essentials from those records and published a series of generalizations, most of which still hold true today. Some of Ravenstein's generalizations were the following: (1) most moves cover only a short distance, (2) females predominate among short-distance movers, (3) for every stream there is a counterstream, (4) movement from the hinterland to the city is most often made in stages, and (5) the major motive for migration is an economic motive. With respect to the latter, Ravenstein (1889, 286) stated that "bad or oppressive laws, heavy taxation, an unnatural climate, uncongenial social surroundings, and even compulsion . . . all have produced and are still producing currents of migration, but none of these currents can compare in volume with that which arises from the desire inherent in most men to 'better' themselves in material respects. . . ." It is surprising that from Ravenstein's day until now, relatively few attempts have been made to extend his generalizations, or to devise additional ones, or to gather his generalizations into a theoretical framework.

One important conceptual framework, accompanied by a set of hypotheses about the volume, streams, and characteristics of migrants, was proposed by Lee (1966). He began by classifying the elements that influence migration into the following groups: (1) factors associated with a migrant's origin; (2) factors associated with a migrant's destination; (3) obstacles between the two that the migrant must overcome, which Lee calls intervening obstacles; and (4) personal factors.

People move for a variety of reasons, including job changes, marriages, divorces, graduations, retirements, and trouble with the law. People may move because of conditions in their area of origin, conditions at their destination, or some combination of the two. Not all people in a particular area perceive conditions the same way, thus they may respond differently to the same stimuli. Lee suggested that a good climate was almost universally attractive, whereas a bad climate was undesirable. However, not everyone agrees on exactly what is or is not desirable. Recently some researchers have focused on the role of environmental preferences and migration patterns.

Lee summarized his ideas with the schematic diagram shown in Figure 8–1. The circles representing the places of origin and destination have pluses, zeros, and minuses. The pluses indicate elements to which potential migrants respond favorably, whereas the minuses are elements to which they react negatively. Zeros stand for elements to which potential migrants are indifferent.

A potential migrant adds up the pluses and minuses for both the origin and one or more possible destinations then decides whether the balance of pluses and minuses favors moving or staying. "Push-pull" models of migration derive from the observation

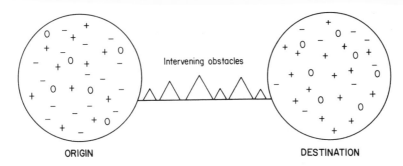

FIGURE 8–1 Lee's Migration Model. SOURCE: By Everett S. Lee in "A Theory of Migration." From *Demography:* Vol. 3, No. 1, 1966, page 50. Used by permission.

that some elements of an origin may "push" people to migrate, whereas some elements of a destination may "pull" migrants toward it. However, before the migrant decides to move, another set of circumstances must be considered—Lee's intervening obstacles. These include such things as the actual cost of making the move, which is obviously related to distance, and psychic costs, such as the necessity of breaking ties with family, friends, and community, especially when long distances are involved. Furthermore, many personal factors may also influence a migration decision, for example, health, age, marital status, and number of children. Clearly, a person's decision to migrate depends upon many considerations. Some of these considerations require further elaboration.

Reasons for Migrating. In a theoretical economic sense migration is the mechanism by which human resources move to their highest valued use; however, this ideal often goes unrealized. Among the major determinants of migration are distance, income, and information.

Repeatedly it has been shown that most migration takes place over short distances. The distance itself, however, is related to other factors that also inhibit migration. For example, distance is related to both the economic and psychic costs of moving. Furthermore, distance can determine the ease or difficulty with which one can collect reliable information about alternative destinations. Several studies have suggested that the psychic costs of leaving friends and relatives may be significant although they are difficult to measure.

Factor Mobility View. A simple economic theory of migration is based on wage rate differentials, which in turn reflect geographic variations in the supply and demand for labor, one of the major factors of production. We could argue that migrants move up the wage rate gradient; that is, they move from low-wage areas to high-wage areas. In a *perfect* world, migration would then serve as an equilibrium mechanism.

As people left low-wage areas, the smaller remaining labor supply would drive wages upward. At the same time, the growing supply of labor in the high-wage area would tend to depress wages. In ideal conditions migrants would move between the areas until wage rates were equal in both places.

However, imperfections exist in the market mechanism, and people are not perfectly mobile. For example, many Appalachians have chosen to stay in Appalachia despite low wages and high unemployment rates, partly because they have had deep attachments to the region and partly because they have been unaware of opportunities elsewhere.

Some important findings of a study by the United States Department of Labor (1977) are worth considering at this point. First, the study found that household-level unemployment or job dissatisfaction does operate as a "push" factor in migration. People who are recent arrivals in an area and who fail to find employment immediately, are especially likely to move again. Second, local economic conditions, such as unemployment rates, do affect out-migration, but only among those who are unemployed.

Third, unemployed individuals and others currently seeking work are more responsive to such economic determinants as family income, local wage rates, and expected earnings increases than are persons who are satisfied with their current jobs. Fourth, families are much more likely to move in a given time period if they moved in the recent past, mainly because of a tendency for people to return to places that they recently left. Fifth, families that have moved several times are more likely to move again than are families that have made only one or no moves recently, if the multiple moves were nonreturn moves. Such people are often referred to as *chronic movers*.

Sixth, wives are not passive, secondary migrants but have a significant influence on the family's decision to move. Also, contrary to the results of some studies, families with working wives are not necessarily less likely to move than are families in which wives do not work. These families will seek locations that maximize both incomes. Finally, and somewhat surprisingly, the study found that age and education, typically found to be among the strongest correlates of the propensity to migrate, appear to be relatively unimportant in explaining the migration of married couples when other migration determinants, many of which vary with age and education, are held constant.

Human Capital Model. First developed by Sjaastad (1962) and nicely summarized in Clark (1986), it is an alternative economic model. Because individuals seek to improve their incomes over the long run, movements take place when individuals or families decide that the benefits of a move outweigh the costs. The model is in many ways an improvement over the more simplistic factor mobility approach, though it is not unrelated to it conceptually. Clark (1986, 67) identified the following advantages of the human capital model over competing models: (1) benefits occur over a period of time, which helps explain why migration rates drop with age and (2) psychic as well as monetary costs and benefits can be included.

Role of Information.   Information is also important in the decision to migrate, especially information about alternative destinations. People are hesitant to move to areas about which they know little or nothing. Nelson (1959) found that friends and relatives who had previously moved from one place to another were especially good sources of information about their current location. Often this "friends and relatives effect" leads to chain migration, exerting a directional bias on movers who leave a particular place. What we find, then, is that the distribution of past migrants tends to be a good predictor of future migration patterns (Greenwood, 1975). Migration streams, once established, are likely to be perpetuated for a long period of time.

Behavioral View of Migration.   Among geographers, Julian Wolpert (1965) was one of the first to approach migration by concentrating on individual behavior rather than on aggregate data. He argued that understanding and explaining migration patterns was dependent on sorting out constants in migration behavior. He identified three central concepts of migration behavior: (1) place utility, (2) field theory approach to search behavior, and (3) life-cycle approach to threshold formation.

According to Wolpert (1965, 162), place utility "refers to the net composite of utilities which are derived from the individual's integration at some position in space." Dissatisfaction with one's current location, then, is the major stimulus for beginning a search for another location. Place utility may be either positive or negative, depending upon how an individual perceives his or her location. Of considerable importance, then, is how the individual perceives the utility of his or her current place relative to the perceived utility of other places. According to Wolpert (1965, 162):

> The utility with respect to these alternative sites consists largely of anticipated utility and optimism which lacks the reinforcement of past rewards. This is precisely why the stream of information is so important in long-distance migration—information about prospects must somehow compensate for the absence of personal experience.

Subsequently, Wolpert (1966) suggested that the study of residential mobility should be viewed in terms of stresses in the current place of origin and the potential migrant's threshold for stress. Thus, the decision to move may be viewed as being dependent on both the alternatives available at a given time and a person's ability to cope with stress. Somewhat earlier, Rossi (1955) had noted that residential complaints and dissatisfaction were important determinants of the decision to move. Wolpert proposed that a person's tolerance for stress could be measured by a "threshold function." Once a person's stress threshold is surpassed in a particular location, that person is likely to move.

Despite the many reasons individuals choose to change their places of residence, it is generally agreed upon by researchers that the study of movement behavior should focus on two major decisions: (1) the decision to seek a new residence and (2) the search for and selection of a new residence (Moore, 1972). Roseman (1977) also emphasized the need for considering separately the decision to move and the decision about where to move.

Residential Preferences and Migration.   According to Schwind (1971, 150):

> Patterns of migration presumably are functions of, and should therefore contain
> information on, both the total magnitude of population systems and the aggregate
> preferences of migrants for relevant characteristics of regions. Migrants, however,
> probably respond not so much to factual statistical information about regions as to
> rather general perceptions of regional attractiveness.

Although geographers have accomplished a great deal in studies of place preferences,
most of the work specifically relating to urban migration and city size preferences has
been done by sociologists. Changing migration patterns in the United States since 1970
have stimulated researchers to seek explanations of migration patterns outside of the
standard wage theory and its derivatives.

Studies of city size preferences are often concerned with the question of the need
for a population distribution policy in the United States. Numerous proposals have
been made, including those designed to aid depressed rural areas, such as Appalachia;
to focus migrants on cities in the medium-sized range, thus decreasing in-migration to
the most congested cities; and to guide the overall development of the American urban
system. Fuguitt and Zuiches (1975, 491) noted that:

> An important element figuring in this discussion is concern about public preferences
> and attitudes on desirable places to live. A policy that provides community and
> housing options compatible with preferences should have a greater chance of success
> and could be expected to lessen any discrepancy between the actual and ideal dis-
> tribution of the population.

Geographer Gundars Rudzitis (1991, 81) noted that, "Today, there is an increasing
recognition of the need to incorporate noneconomic variables or surrogates into migration and regional growth models." He went on to note the importance of climate,
trade-offs between climate and income, and the importance of what he called the
"location-specific amenities model."

One criticism of many studies of city size preferences is that they failed to include
an indication of the relative locations of cities, especially those in the smaller size categories. For many people a considerable difference in attractiveness exists between an
isolated small town and a small town located within easy driving distance of a major
city. Puzzled by the apparent contrast between survey results and actual migration
patterns, Fuguitt and Zuiches (1975) added to a city size questionnaire a question
asking those who preferred small towns whether they preferred those towns to be within
30 miles of a large city. What the distance-qualifying question showed was that a majority of those respondents who preferred small towns and rural areas said that they
would like to live within 30 miles of a city of at least 50,000. Thus, we must be careful
in interpreting the results of preference surveys that fail to include a distance-
qualifying question.

It appears that the perceived quality of life in small towns is their major attraction, however romantic the perception may be, whereas the lack of employment acts as a constraint on movement to them. As we have mentioned already, migration into small towns often destroys the very characteristics that attracted migration in the first place. Fuguitt and Zuiches (1975) concluded that if all people could move to the places they preferred, no mass exodus to remote areas would occur. Most people seem to prefer the best of both worlds, a quiet bucolic residential location and the opportunities and amenities that can be provided only by a metropolitan area.

More recently, Rudzitis (1991, 86) commented that there is a ". . . need for imagination rooted in regional historical reality if we are to better understand and promote the vitality of nonmetropolitan areas." He also suggested the need for geographers to consider such concepts as "sustainable development" in rural areas and small towns and the need for incorporating aspects of the relationship between local vitality and the natural environment in such areas. In concluding, Rudzitis (1991, 86) also argued that, "A major shortcoming is the lack of studies of place, a comparative base from which to measure what might be expected. . . . A place, the world is what people take it to be, lying scattered openly on the surface, not as we social scientists often regard it, concealed beneath deceptive appearances." As geographer Peirce Lewis noted in his Presidential Address to the Association of American Geographers, "Good intellectual description provokes strong thought" (Lewis, 1985, 469).

▓ SELECTIVITY OF MIGRATION

Migration is a selective process. Trewartha (1969, 137) stated:

> Assuming a sedentary population with an inducement to move, typically some individuals will leave and others remain where they are. But those who leave do not represent a random distribution of the biological and cultural characteristics of humanity in either the region of exit or entrance, for certain elements of the population tend to be more migratory than others. This is termed *migratory selection*.

Probably the most important and universally accepted migration differential is age. In movements within countries, as well as those between countries, it is older adolescents and young adults who predominate in most areas, as is apparent for the United States in Figure 8–2. Young people can generally adapt more easily to new conditions and, because they have only recently entered the labor force, they can change jobs more easily. Because of the age selectivity of migrants, we generally find that areas that have experienced a great deal of in-migration have a young age structure, whereas areas that have experienced a lot of out-migration are generally older in their population composition.

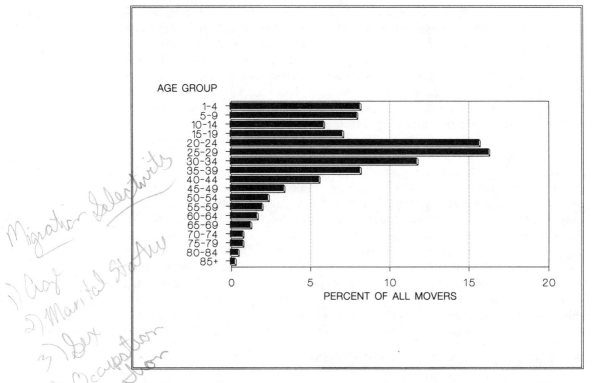

▧ **FIGURE 8-2** Total Mobility by Age of Movers, United States, 1989–1990. SOURCE: United States Bureau of the Census.

Marital status also has a bearing on migration selectivity. In the developing areas of the world, migration is usually undertaken by young, single adults. This was also probably true of the developed world in past times. However, in the developed countries today, married couples seem to be almost as mobile as the single.

Another facet of migration is sex selectivity, but whether the migration stream is male- or female-dominated depends upon a variety of factors. For example, in nineteenth-century Europe the movement from farm to city was primarily accomplished by young farm girls who went to work in the cities as domestic servants. On the other hand, the frontier towns in America were largely male dominated. According to Trewartha (1969, 138):

. . . there is some validity, no doubt, in the generalization that in less-developed countries migrants are predominantly male. . . . All the large commercial and industrial cities of India show a strong male predominance. The same is true in the newer settlements and mining towns of Negro Africa. . . .

Occupation and education are other variables involved with migration selectivity. Unskilled workers are less likely to be migratory than the skilled and semiskilled, and professional people are typically the most mobile occupational group.

A considerable amount of research has been done on the relationship between education and migration selectivity. These studies have focused on the similarities and differences between the well educated and the poorly educated in regard to distances, rates, and direction of migration. Also, several studies dealing with education levels at the places of origin and destination of migrants have been undertaken.

In general, migrants have higher levels of education than nonmigrants, particularly over long distances. Folger and Nam (1967, 210) found that "persons with higher levels of education are more migratory than persons with lower levels of education, and the difference in migration rates between poorly educated and well-educated persons increases for longer-distance moves." Similarly, data on migration in the United States between 1965 and 1970 points out the same pattern. For example, during this period, although the college-educated group made up only 11 percent of the nation's total population aged 25 and over, they accounted for 25 percent of the people who migrated between noncontiguous states. Similar conclusions were reached with older age groups of the college-educated population.

The above data and conclusions refer to relatively long-distance moves. An analysis of short-distance moves, such as from one house to another within the same county, reveals that in the United States the most poorly educated are somewhat overrepresented; they tend to make more short-distance moves.

With regard to changes in the educational status at the places of origin and destination, the data suggest relatively few significant changes at either place. In summarizing several studies, Folger and Nam (1967, 185) concluded that "the effects of interregional migration on the educational attainment of the resident population are small."

Although there appears to have been relatively little effect on educational levels at places of origin and destination relative to internal migration in the United States, there has been a significant impact on the international scene. Educational self-selection, operating in the form of the so-called "brain drain," has become an international issue of concern. The developing countries feel that the brain drain is hindering their cultural and economic development. Perhaps the most significant aspect is the migration of trained medical personnel to the developed countries. A report by the United States Agency for International Development (1973, 112) found:

> . . . there are not enough medical and paramedical personnel in Haiti to meet the ordinary needs of the people. In relation to population, available personnel are equivalent to one physician for every 12,000 people, one nurse for every 12,000, and one paramedic for every 6,200. Nor is the medical situation improving. There has been an exodus of health professionals from the island. It is said that all medical school graduates in 1969 left Haiti because of the lack of economic opportunity.

There are those, however, who argue that the brain drain does not necessarily have an adverse effect on the poorer countries. For example, they argue that discoveries made in one area will eventually benefit all areas and that scientists and other highly educated persons should be in those areas where they can be the most productive. Though this may be true, there is little doubt that most developing countries are in dire need of trained professionals if they are to proceed with economic and social development programs.

▓ CONSEQUENCES OF MIGRATION

Because migration is a selective process, it produces changes in both the areas of origin and destination. The magnitude of these changes depends upon several variables. Because migrants are largely young, areas of high out-migration will experience an aging of their populations. We see this in parts of the Great Plains area of the United States, as well as in parts of Appalachia. In turn, as the age structure of an area becomes older, death rates increase and birth rates decrease. In receiving regions, the opposite impact results. Thus, the effect of migration is not just a matter of numbers.

Migration and its concomitant mixing of peoples have a variety of effects. There is a complex pattern of interaction between geographic, demographic, social, and economic factors, the consequences of which are therefore varied. Of particular significance to geographers is the impact of migration on space and numbers, an impact that takes on two forms: (1) if the reception areas absorb large numbers of people, the cities and towns expand and, with the filling of the countryside, new lands open up, affecting the population distribution and density of the receiving area and (2) conversely, the source areas for these migrants experience a decrease in population and a decline in density. Both population growth and decline produce far-reaching socioeconomic consequences.

Good examples of the impact of migration are the changes that took place in the United States and Ireland since the first third of the nineteenth century. Ireland has probably been more affected by emigration than any other country. Currently, the combined population of the Republic of Ireland and Northern Ireland is approximately 4.5 million people. In 1841 the Irish population was 8.2 million. Since that time almost 5 million Irish have migrated to the United States, and millions more have settled in Australia, Canada, and England.

An analysis of the Irish situation by Meenan (1958) pointed out that emigration has rarely been viewed as a beneficial force. Meenan (1958, 80) also noted some self-perpetuating features of the Irish situation and stated that:

> In each generation it is a movement of the younger sons and daughters. It is not an emigration of whole families and it never has been, except perhaps at the time of the famine. If it had been such, it might well have come to an end decades ago when the removal of families had led to a redistribution of farm holdings and the establishment of a new rural equilibrium. As things are, emigration enables those who are left to marry and rear families whose members will in their turn seek a living abroad. Certainly this is not all the story: A vicious circle is created whereby emigration causes underdevelopment, which in turn leads to further emigration.

Many researchers believe that emigration can be advantageous to areas of dense populations. Studies of Italy's post-World War II emigration have shown that the economically disadvantaged regions, where most of the population were engaged in agricultural pursuits, provided most of the overseas emigrants. Population transfers relieved pressure on resources in these regions and made it possible for disadvantaged areas to increase their per capita incomes. Another factor noted in the study of Italy was that Italians living abroad sent money back to their homeland, thus reducing Italy's adverse trade balance. Similar circumstances have existed in other countries as well and may have helped to diminish the differences between the poor and the prosperous nations.

▓ INTERNATIONAL MIGRATION

There are many ways to classify the complex and diverse movements of human populations, but perhaps the most common simple division is to divide movements into two basic categories: international migration and internal migration. As Clark (1986, 74) has noted:

> International migration has a two-part structure: On one hand, it is composed of the labor streams seeking jobs in foreign countries; on the other, it is composed of the increasing flows of refugees from war and political disruption. However, neither of these flows takes place in a vacuum. The labor streams are inextricably woven together with changing urban development and there are increasingly dramatic social and economic impacts from global refugee migrations.

Each of these deserves at least some attention here.

Changing Nature of International Migration

Although international movements of people are as old as history, little useful information existed on the volume and nature of such movements before the nineteenth century. Archaeological evidence suggests that even the earliest ancestors of humans were wanderers. A progenitor of modern humans, *Homo erectus,* has been traced through fossil evidence to such widely separated places as China, Africa, Europe, and Java (Howell, 1965). The first "Americans" were most likely people who migrated from Siberia to Alaska over a land bridge that existed at various times during the Pleistocene Era. A Biblical example of migration was the movement of the Children of Israel out of Egypt to the Promised Land under the leadership of Moses. Many other examples of early migrations exist, and there is little doubt that all of human history has been dramatically affected by such movements.

One of the largest migrations in human history was the emigration from Europe that began in the sixteenth century and continued into the early twentieth century. Estimates are that over 60 million Europeans were involved in this migration. The primary places of origin for migrants were Germany, Russia, Poland, Spain, Austria, Hungary, Italy, Portugal, Sweden, the Netherlands, and the British Isles. The primary destinations for the emigrants were the United States, Canada, Australia, New Zealand, Brazil, Argentina, the British West Indies, and South Africa.

TABLE 8–1 ■ Estimated Numbers of
Expatriate Chinese in Asia, About 1969

(Outside the People's Republic of China, Taiwan, Hong Kong, and Macao)		
	Numbers (000s)	**% of Total Population**
Thailand	4,930	14
Indonesia	4,800	4
Malaysia	3,602	34
South Vietnam	2,661	15
Singapoe-Malacca	2,200	98
Cambodia	2,000	30
Burma	500	2
Philippines	376	1
Laos	61	2
Japan	54	—
Korea	26	—
India	16	—
Pakistan	3	—
Ceylon	1	—
Total	21,229	14

SOURCE: Leon F. Bouvier with Henry S. Shryock and
Harry W. Henderson, "International Migration:
Yesterday, Today, and Tomorrow," *Population Bulletin,*
Vol. 32, No. 4 (September, 1977), p. 7. Courtesy of the
Population Reference Bureau, Inc., Washington, D.C.

The flow of migrants out of Europe was relatively slow until the nineteenth century. Because of declining death rates in Europe during the early nineteenth century, the European population was growing rapidly. Also, Europeans began to feel that life was perhaps more rewarding abroad and that the overseas lands looked attractive. At the same time new technological improvements, such as the steamship, made migration easier. This is not to say that emigration from Europe was not fraught with dangers. As Beaujeu- Garnier (1966, 172) pointed out:

> . . . the exiles, often very poor, made lengthy journals on the deck or in the hold of a wretched vessel. Of the starving Irish who quitted their country in the famine of 1845, 6 percent died at sea, and counting also those who died soon after arrival, one in five of these unhappy creatures failed to make a home on the welcoming continent.

International migration from Asia was relatively small compared with the massive movement out of Europe. For example, Table 8–1 gives the estimated numbers of expatriate Chinese in Asia, amounting to a total of over 21 million people who emigrated from China to other Asian regions. These data can be compared with data for

TABLE 8–2 ■ Immigrants from Europe to Principal Overseas Destinations, 1956–1970[a]

Country or Region	(In thousands)			
	1956–1960	1961–1965	1966–1970	1956–1970
Australia	524.9	588.8	764.8	1,878.5
New Zealand	70.9	86.1	70.4	227.4
Canada	672.9	365.2	589.9	1,628.0
United States	700.1	531.6	600.6	1,832.3
South Africa	45.2	78.6	149.7	273.5
Latin America[b]	490.0	226.3	131.0	847.3
Total	2,504.0	1,876.6	2,306.4	6,687.0

[a]Based on statistics of receiving countries.

[b]From Italy, Portugal, and Spain only, based on statistics of the sending countries. Migrants from these three countries constituted about 95 percent of all European migrants to Latin America.

SOURCE: United Nations, *International Migration Trends, 1950–1970*, Conference Background Paper, E/CONF .60/CBP/18, May 22, 1974, Table 8.

other areas of the world, such as Africa, which received only 94,000 ethnic Chinese; Oceania, which received 99,000; the Americas, which received 643,000; and Europe, which received 89,000.

Migration from Africa was significantly different from movements out of other regions of the world. The huge exodus of Africans was primarily involuntary. Slaves were taken from Africa and brought to the New World from the sixteenth century to the nineteenth century. Approximately 10 million slaves were imported into slave-using areas between 1451 and 1870. The number of slaves actually taken from Africa has been estimated at over 11 million, since perhaps 25 percent of the slaves died en route to their destination. In terms of both numbers of people moved and distance traveled, this was the greatest slave migration in history.

International Migration Since 1940

Recent international migration has taken several forms. Refugee movements have been a primary facet of migration since 1940. There have been two major movements: (1) population transfers within the Indian subcontinent between India and Pakistan and (2) the uprooting of Eastern and Central Europeans that represented a drastic solution to the problems of ethnic minorities in these regions prior to World War II. These forced migrations were not of a selective nature because entire communities were uprooted and moved.

Not all of the post-World War II migration movements were as dramatic or tragic as these forced migrations. The movement of Europeans from 1956 to 1970 is shown in Table 8–2. These data show that almost 7 million Europeans moved to Australia, New Zealand, Canada, the United States, South Africa, and Latin America. In some countries, like South Africa and Australia, the data reflect the special efforts of those countries to attract Europeans.

TABLE 8–3 ■ Migration Balances Between Principal Sending and Receiving
Countries of Europe, 1960–1970

	(In thousands) Receiving Countries					
Sending Countries	Total	West Germany	France	Switzerland	Belgium	Netherlands
Greece	250	240	a	a	a	a
Italy	500	230	100	150	12	a
Portugal	510	40	450	a	a	a
Spain	640	150	330	100	40	20
Yugoslavia	490	400	55	25	a	a
Total	2,390	1,060	940	280	70	40

aLess than 10,000

SOURCE: United Nations, *International Migration Trends, 1950–1970,* Conference Background Paper,
E/CONF .60/CBP/18, May 22, 1974, Table 4.

TABLE 8–4 ■ Estimated Net Migration
Balances for Major World Regions,
1946–1957 and 1960–1970

	(In millions)	
Region	1946–1957	1960–1970
Africa	+0.5	−1.6
Asia	−0.5	−1.2
Europe	−5.4	−0.3
Latin America	+.09	−1.9
North America	+3.4	+4.1
Oceania	+1.0	+0.9

SOURCE: United Nations, *International Migration
Trends, 1950–1970,* Conference Background Paper,
E/CONF. 60/CPB/18, May 22, 1974, Table 5.

The large decline in migrants moving to Latin America reflects the increase in
job opportunities for Southern Europeans in countries closer to home, as well as the
measures taken by Latin American countries to slow down immigration. Recent migratory movements within Europe are reflected in Table 8–3. In total, the United Nations estimates that Western and Northern Europe gained 2.6 million people through
migration from Southern Europe from 1960 to 1970. More recent studies of European
migration by geographers include Salt (1985) and White (1985).

In summary, the balance of international migration since the end of World War
II has increasingly shifted toward North America and Oceania. According to the data
shown in Table 8–4, these were the only two major regions of the world to record a net

TABLE 8–5 ▩ Estimates of Net Migration in Selected Countries of Europe, Northern America, and Oceania, 1950–1970

Region and Country	Net Migration (000s)	Region and Country	Net Migration (000s)
Europe	−3,028	*Northern Europe*	−698
Western Europe	+8,748	Denmark	−32
Austria	−103	Finland	−214
Belgium	−211	Ireland	−558
West Germany	+4,780	Norway	−10
France	+3,258	Sweden	−297
Luxembourg	+22	United Kingdom	−181
Netherlands	−50		
Switzerland	+630		
		Northern America	+8,698
Southern	−7,301	Canada	+1,802
Europe	−651	United States	+6,896
Greece	−1,958		
Italy	−81		
Malta	−1,952		
Portugal	−1,377	Oceania	+1,857
Spain	−1,282	Australia	+1,712
Yugoslavia		New Zealand	+145
	−3,777		
Eastern Europe	−178		
Bulgaria	−174		
Czechoslovakia	−2,488		
East Germany	−161		
Hungary	−526		
Poland	−250		
Romania			

SOURCE: United Nations, *International Migration Trends, 1950–1970*, Conference Background Paper, E/CONF .60/CBP/18, May 22, 1974, Table 6.

immigration from 1960 to 1970. Also, emigration from Europe dropped significantly, from 5.4 million between 1946 and 1957 to 300,000 between 1960 and 1970. Detailed estimates of historical net migration in selected countries of Europe, North America, and Oceania for the 1950–1970 period are shown in Table 8–5.

Immigration in the United States

Immigration has played a key role in the social and economic development of the United States. If there had been no immigration to the United States during the nineteenth and early twentieth centuries, then population growth would have been much slower; and the ethnic composition of the United States' population would be substantially different.

TABLE 8–6 ■ U.S. Immigration from Europe, 1820–1976

Country of Origin	Number of Immigrants (000s)	Country of Origin	Number of Immigrants (000s)
Germany	6,960	Spain	248
Italy	5,278	Belgium	201
Great Britain	4,8636	Romania	168
Ireland	4,722	Czechoslovakia	137
Austria and Hungary	4,313	Yugoslavia	109
U.S.S.R.	3,362	Bulgaria	68
Sweden	1,270	Finland	33
Norway	856	Lithuania	4
France	744	Luxembourg	3
Greece	638	Latvia	3
Poland	506	Albania	2
Portugal	422	Estonia	1
Denmark	363	Other Europe	55
Netherlands	357		
Switzerland	347	Total	36,033

SOURCE: Leon F. Bouvier with Henry S. Shryock and Harry W. Henderson, "International Migration: Yesterday, Today, and Tomorrow," *Population Bulletin* Vol. 32, No. 4 (September, 1977), p. 17. Courtesy of the Population Reference Bureau, Inc., Washington, D.C.

Immigration history in the United States can be divided into four distinct periods: colonial, old immigration, new immigration, and restricted immigration. The first three periods could be considered times of free-individual moves, whereas the last period involved significant restrictions on immigration.

The immigrants who came to the United States during the colonial period were confronted with a situation that was significantly different from that experienced by later arrivals. Most were of British ancestry although other ethnic groups such as the Dutch, Swedes, Germans, French, and Spanish were also represented.

The period of old immigration was approximately 1800 to 1880 and involved a considerable increase in immigration. The overwhelming majority, about 95 percent, of these immigrants came from western and northern Europe. Though the largest proportion of these immigrants came from England, large numbers of them were from France, Germany, Scotland, and Ireland.

The period of new immigration started around 1880 and was marked by a shift in the source of immigrants from western and northern Europe to eastern and southern Europe. This new wave of immigration was much larger than the old, and in the first decade of the twentieth century approximately 9 million immigrants entered the United States. A breakdown of total immigration from Europe is outlined in Table 8–6.

Since 1921 immigration to the United States has no longer been free. Restrictions on both the number and types of migrants are in effect. The changing nature of the patterns of immigration for the United States over time is illustrated in Figure 8–3.

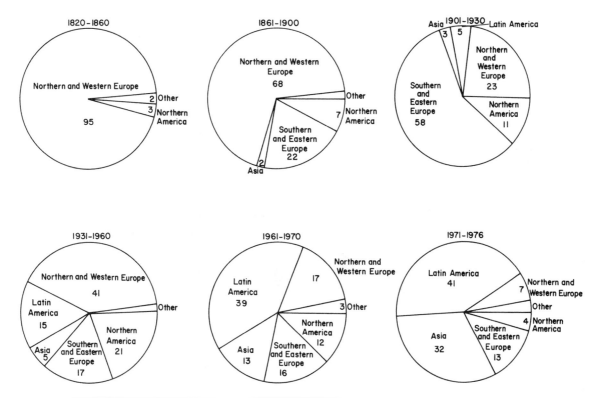

▪ **FIGURE 8–3** U.S. Immigrants by Region of Origin, 1820–1976. SOURCE: Leon F. Bouvier with Henry S. Shryock and Harry W. Henderson. (1977) "International Migration: Yesterday, Today, and Tomorrow," *Population Bulletin* 32(4):24–25. Courtesy of the Population Reference Bureau, Inc., Washington, D.C.

Undocumented Immigration

Since the establishment of migration quotas, there has been relatively little concern about the origin of present-day legal immigrants to the United States. There is, however, increasing concern over the presence of immigrants who have entered the United States illegally. Many of the factors that help explain legal migration also apply to illegal migration. The attributes of places of origin and destination hold true for undocumented immigrants as well as for legal immigrants. The undocumented immigrant is confronted by unfavorable conditions in his or her place of origin and tries to overcome these difficulties by emigrating.

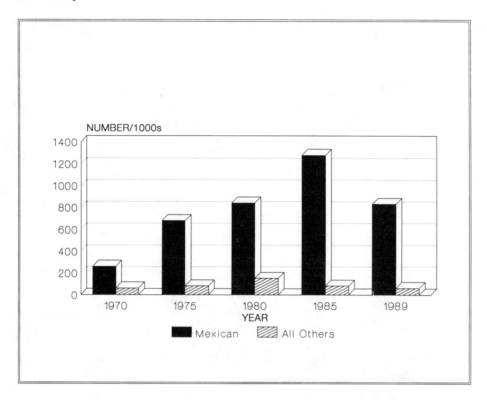

▨ **FIGURE 8–4** Deportable Aliens Located in the United States. SOURCE: Data from *Statistical Abstract of the United States,* 1991.

The problem of undocumented immigration is not just associated with the United States. Similar problems exist in Latin America, Asia, and Europe. In a study of immigration in Europe, King (1974, 82) noted:

> Increasingly restrictive immigration policies in Europe had made it more difficult to migrate legally to Western Europe, with the result that by the summer of 1973 it was estimated that there were more than half a million foreigners illegally working or living in Europe, mainly engaged in activities such as road construction, building, agriculture, hotels, and the public services.

More recently France, Germany, and Austria have experienced rightward political shifts as voters have become increasingly concerned with the presence of immigrants, especially those who have, or are at least perceived to have, entered illegally.

Presently the United States attracts the largest number of illegal migrants. There is no actual count of the number of illegal migrants in the United States, but estimates range from 6 million to 10 million. In addition, although no exact count of illegal aliens exists, there are data on the number who have been apprehended. Data from 1970 to 1989, shown in Figure 8–4, suggest approximately a 400 percent increase in the apprehension of illegals during that period. It has been estimated that only one out of every three or four persons attempting to enter illegally is caught.

The largest proportion of undocumented immigrants come from Mexico, as is shown in Figure 8–4. Of the 1,346,300 illegal aliens located in the United States in fiscal year 1985, 1,267,000, or about 94 percent, were from Mexico. Economic conditions in Mexico provide a "push" to migrate to the United States for employment, and the estimated growth of the Mexican labor force at about one million annually during the 1990s is a virtual guarantee that this particular migration stream will continue.

In the past many migrants stayed close to the border after illegal entry. However, recent data show that large numbers are now scattering throughout the nation, to New York, Houston, Chicago, Miami, San Antonio, and Los Angeles. The problem of illegal aliens is complex. Many interest groups are involved with both sides of the issue. Labor unions are fearful that jobs that could be held by United States citizens are being taken by illegal aliens. Those who favor limited or zero population growth see the influx of illegal aliens as a stumbling block in achieving a stable population. On the other hand, there are those who are against efforts to curb immigration, including agricultural interest groups that benefit economically from the cheap labor supply of illegals. Also, some Hispanic rights groups, as well as the United States Catholic Bishops, fear increased discrimination against Mexican-Americans.

Immigration Reform and Control Act of 1986 (IRCA)

After years of political bickering, the Congress of the United States finally passed legislation designed to deal more realistically with immigration and the problems resulting from illegal immigration. This bill contained two key provisions. First, there was an amnesty program for aliens who had lived and worked in the United States since before January 1, 1982. Second, there were sanctions for employers who knowingly hire unauthorized workers.

To qualify for amnesty under this act a person must have proved that he or she entered the United States before January 1, 1982, and had resided in the United States continuously since that time of entry. Proof of eligibility required such records of long-term residence as health and school records, employment records, and utility receipts. The deadline for applications ended early in May, 1988, at which time approximately 1.5 million people had applied.

Special provisions were made for agricultural workers so they could be given temporary status if they had worked for at least 90 days between May 1, 1985, and May 1, 1986. After two years of temporary status they can then apply for permanent residency. After November 6, 1993, all applicants who successfully qualified for amnesty will begin to qualify for citizenship.

Employers are to be enforcers of the new program because of their responsibility for not hiring illegal aliens. Severe penalties will be given out to those who violate the new law. Employers are required to screen applicants, who must provide documentation of their status in the form of a passport from the United States, certification of

United States citizenship, an alien registration receipt card, or a foreign passport with a work authorization stamp. If they have none of these items, then they must have either a birth certificate showing that they were born in the United States or a social security card plus proof of identification in the form of a valid driver's license or state identification card. Though employers can not be held responsible for the authenticity of each of the above items, they must keep them on file for a period of at least three years once they have been submitted.

One unplanned result has been the development of a cottage industry in document production in the border states. Another effect has been a change in the traditional pattern of circular and repeat migration from Mexico to the United States. As Vernez and Ronfeldt (1991) noted, "Mexican immigration to the United States can no longer be characterized by the persistent image of the Mexican immigrant as a temporary worker staying here for a short period of time and leaving his or her family behind, if it ever could be so characterized." This change will have considerable impact on states in the southwest, especially California and Texas. Bean, Edmonston, and Passel (1990) provides coverage of many of the implications of undocumented immigration since IRCA for those who would like to pursue this topic further.

Immigration Act of 1990

Despite polls that regularly show Americans are concerned about the level of immigration (Page and Shapiro, 1992), Congress passed legislation to increase the number of legal immigrants who would be accepted each year. The result of that legislation was the Immigration Act of 1990. The impact will be to increase legal immigration from a level of some 500,000 annually to around 700,000 annually, with some adjustments made after 1993, when a required review of immigration will be made.

Part of this revised legislation is designed to increase the immigration of skilled and educated people, as well as more wealthy people. Up to 10,000 slots per year will be available to investors who are willing to put at least $1,000,000 into an American business that employs ten or more workers. Only half of that amount is required if the investment is made in a rural or depressed area. Another 40,000 slots were set aside in a lottery for potential immigrants from 34 countries, mainly European, that felt neglected under previous legislation. Of those, 40 percent were set aside for Irish immigrants.

Refugees

Estimates of the number of refugees worldwide vary from 12 million to 15 million although no one knows with any degree of certainty. What is known, however, is that in recent decades, as a result of wars and famines, refugees have increased in numbers. At the same time, geographers have shown an increased interest in refugees in recent years. In one article, Kliot (1987) noted that since the beginning of the twentieth century more than 100 million people have become refugees. As with other forms of migration, refugees affect both the region they leave and the one to which they move. Refugees often flee one form of conflict only to precipitate another.

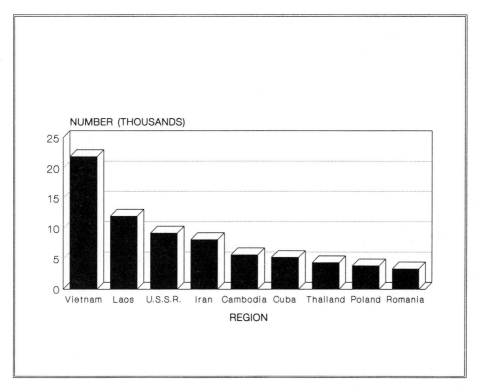

■ **FIGURE 8–5** Estimated Refugee Arrivals to the United States. SOURCE: Data from *Statistical Abstract of the United States,* 1991.

Kliot (1987) argued that among the major causal agents of current and future refugee movements are the following: (1) ethnic, racial, and religious problems within countries; (2) local and regional wars, from South Africa and the Middle East to the breakup of what only a short time ago was Yugoslavia; and (3) changing racial policies of many governments in Africa and Asia. In another recent study, geographer Richard Black (1991, 281) noted an important point, ". . . geographers must draw links between this field and their own longstanding interests in issues such as migration, 'natural' and other disasters, and the politics of conflicts which are often the immediate cause of refugee flows."

Since the end of its involvement in the Vietnam War, the United States has admitted numerous refugees from Southeast Asian countries under a special refugee act. Figure 8–5 shows the source regions for refugees into the United States for 1989, and the predominant sources are still countries in Southeast Asia, primarily Vietnam and Laos.

Originally the government of the United States encouraged a refugee distribution policy that spread Southeast Asian refugees across the United States. However, subsequent migration patterns for these groups has redistributed their numbers considerably, and, like other Americans, they have been moving to the sunbelt. As a result, concentrations of Asian refugees have developed in many areas, especially in Southern California, where Long Beach has the largest settlement of Cambodians outside of Cambodia and where nearby Westminster has gained the nickname "Little Saigon" as a reflection of the concentration of Vietnamese in that city. The redistribution of Indochinese refugees within the United States was carefully studied by Desbarats (1985), who found that refugees were concentrating in states that offered some combination of high public assistance benefits, lenient eligibility requirements for receiving those benefits, mild climates, reasonable employment opportunities, and large Asian communities.

Though we have looked only briefly at refugees here, primarily the recent experience in the United States, geographers are now studying refugees in many places. Rogge (1991), for example, has looked at the uncertain future for refugees in Southeast Asia, and Everitt (1991) considered the refugee problem in Middle America since the 1970s. Luciuk (1991, 197) ended his study of refugees in Afghanistan by saying that "Since even the most optimistic estimates suggest that many years of economic, political, and social rehabilitation will be required before the land and its peoples recover from what has been described as a genocidal war, it seems evident that Afghanistan will remain a deeply troubled region of the world, and, as such, a source area of refugees and displaced persons, well into the foreseeable future." In surveying the refugee situation in Africa, Kenzer (1991, 200) concluded that the situation was "horrible at best."

▓ INTERNAL MIGRATION

A large proportion of migrants never cross national borders but move only within their own countries. Internal migration is more difficult to assess, and only those countries that keep a complete dossier on each citizen can accurately reconstruct the exact nature of internal migration. However, in countries such as the United States, census information can be used to trace internal migration patterns.

Some generalizations can be made about internal migration. One of the major movements in modern times has been the movement of people from rural to urban areas. This movement has been the result of many complex interactions, especially the shift of employment away from rural agricultural pursuits and toward urban industrial and service occupations. As Zelinsky (1971, 236) noted, "The onset of modernization . . . brings with it a great shaking loose of migrants from the countryside."

The conquest of new territory has been an important force in the settlement of many countries. The movement of the frontier in the United States, from the original thirteen colonies to the Pacific Ocean, has its parallels elsewhere; for example, the westward push of the pioneer fringe in Brazil, the northwestward expansion across Canada, the northward movement in Australia, and the movements of peoples from the Andes to the coastal plain and interior forests of South America.

Nomadism is still another type of internal movement. Even in this final decade of the twentieth century, there are still people who are constantly moving about, often with little regard for international boundaries. Many nomads still are found today in the Sahel region of Africa, for example, and in the high latitudes of both Europe and North America.

Internal Migration in the United States

Approximately 4 million Americans lived in a narrow belt along the Atlantic Ocean in 1790. One hundred years later the United States occupied an area that extended to the Pacific Ocean. Movements during the twentieth century have been primarily westward and coastward, with a loss of population in rural areas and a concentration of people in cities and suburbs although recently there was a brief revival of growth in nonmetropolitan areas.

Because of the large gains in population in the western states, as well as in Florida, Texas, and other states in the Southwest, the center of population for 1990 was farther west and somewhat south of its 1980 location, as is apparent in Figure 8–6. The United States is indeed a nation of migrants. Since the annual mobility sample studies were first begun in 1947, about one fifth of the American population has changed residence each year.

The United States has entered a new era with respect to both the distribution of population and economic activities (Fosler, et al., 1990). Capital and people are increasingly being attracted away from the old industrial heartland and toward the South, Southwest, and West. Forces not only in the national economy but increasingly in the global economy as well are constantly at work changing locational advantages, economic landscapes, and consequent patterns of internal migration. The essence of American mobility was captured in the following comment by geographer Paul Simkins (1978, 204): "Although it does not appear as such in any of the state seals or flags, the wheel in many ways may be considered a symbol of America; the wagon or train wheel which early carried the nation westward, or the automobile wheel that moves it now increasingly to and from metropolitan centers." Americans have always sought to better their lot in life, whether they were pioneers seeking "elbow room" or folks in twentieth-century rural Iowa seeking the perpetual sunshine of Southern California.

At the forefront of motives for migration, of course, has been the hope of material gain, though the recent rise of the Sunbelt as a center of attraction for migrants suggests that other motives are also important, especially such amenities as mild climates. Many seek to escape the long cold winters of the cities of the Northeast, as well as their smog, traffic congestion, and even high crime rates. Though an overview of migration patterns can deal only with aggregates of people, we need to remember that the motives for migration differ for various age groups and for other characteristics of people as well.

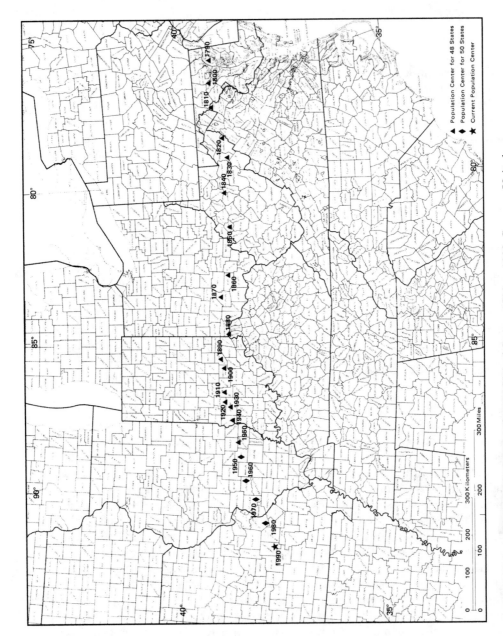

■ **FIGURE 8–6** Center of Population for the United States: 1790 to 1990. Source: United States Bureau of the Census.

Despite the rural-urban migration that characterized the redistribution of people throughout the United States during the twentieth century, Americans have never been in unanimous agreement that cities, especially large ones, were desirable places. Industrialization concentrated people in cities, primarily for economic reasons. Urban locations often meant lower costs for industries, as well as better access to service needs and to local markets for goods. However, from the worker's viewpoint, industrial concentration in urban areas meant more jobs and higher wages, so to the cities they moved.

Once in the cities, however, most groups have tried to work their way outward again, giving rise to suburbanization. Many problems in the cities today are at least in part related to suburbanization because it, like other migration processes, is selective.

Two noticeable and interesting migration trends that emerged in the 1970s are still of special interest and may have possible long-range implications for the redistribution of people, jobs, and wealth in the United States: (1) movement to the "Sunbelt," and (2) the "Rural Renaissance." Though movement to the Sunbelt continued throughout the 1980s and on into the 1990s, the Rural Renaissance was more ephemeral. During the 1980s, metropolitan areas again grew faster than nonmetropolitan areas.

Movement to the Sunbelt

The Sunbelt states are those of the South and Southwest, along with California, though there is not complete agreement from one list of Sunbelt states to the next. Colorado, for example, is sometimes included because of its growth pattern rather than its climatic claims. Furthermore, within the Sunbelt itself there is considerable variation in the growth and attractiveness of different states. Mississippi, for example, has hardly had the same experience during the 1980s that Texas or Florida has had.

Since 1970, a dramatic shift of population away from states in the North Central and Northeast and toward the Sunbelt states has occurred. A disproportionate share of recent population growth in the United States has occurred in only three states: California, Florida, and Texas. In the 1980s the Sunbelt states with the highest rates of growth were Nevada, Arizona, Florida, New Mexico, Hawaii, and Texas. Not only people, but also industry, are increasingly attracted to the Sunbelt.

Regional growth during the 1970s and 1980s was highest in the West. Reductions in population growth rates were occurring in many states in the Midwest and Northeast. People are increasingly moving away from the older areas of the North Central and Northeastern states, partly in response to environmental preferences and partly as a result of aggressive economic development in many of the Sunbelt states. Many people also are being attracted both to the Rocky Mountain states, even though new energy development no longer offers as many job opportunities as it did in the 1970s, and to the Pacific Northwest, especially to Portland and Seattle, although early in the 1990s opportunities were limited in those cities and unemployment was high. Nevertheless, Biggar (1979, 27) still may be right in his comment:

> . . . the Sunbelt migration, then, is part of a larger radical change in the South and the West. It is closely related to the industrial development which typifies most states in the "Southern Rim." It is a reflection of changing American lifestyles. It is part of the equalization of U.S. regions which has brought the South more in line with the rest of the nation.

The Rural Renaissance

During the 1970s, for probably the first time in American history, more people were leaving metropolitan areas than entering them. The long-established pattern of rural-urban migration underwent a reversal during the 1970s. As you might imagine, not all nonmetropolitan areas were equally pleased with the prospect of increased population growth and "rural urbanization." Conflicts often arise between growth advocates and those who seek to limit growth. Land use conflicts are also common.

Many small-town residents fear that growth will destroy the very features that attract people to small towns. For example, they point to increasing crime rates, traffic congestion problems, and even smog as inevitable results of small-town growth. It is interesting to note that quite often it is the newcomer who is most vocal about limiting further growth and change.

The sudden reversal of long-term urbanization in America caught many people, including demographers and geographers, by surprise. Many had thought that most of the nonmetropolitan growth was just spillover from expanding metropolitan areas; however, even nonmetropolitan areas far from urban centers were participating in the new trend. Spillover, of course, has been commonplace in recent decades, but a new pattern seemed to be at hand. Among its major causes were (1) changes in communication and transportation technology that have taken away, or at least mitigated, the necessity of urban concentration, and (2) the expansion of highways that allow easy access to urban areas. However, regional variations in the rates of both metropolitan and nonmetropolitan growth rates may be observed.

The growth of retirement and recreational communities has also been a factor in nonmetropolitan growth. Early retirement, coupled with better benefits for retirees, frees an increasing number of people to seek locations based on personal preferences rather than economic necessities. Wherever the elderly choose to go, of course, services are required; thus, jobs are created and further growth is stimulated. Not only Florida and the Southwest but also the Ozarks, the Texas hill country, and California's "Gold Country" in the western foothills of the Sierra Nevada are experiencing growth from influxes of retirees. In the 1990s retirees may be looking in new directions as well. From Hanover, New Hampshire, to Sequim, Washington, retirees are seeking out smaller, less expensive, less crime-ridden areas; and they may be willing to trade some sunshine for peace and quiet.

Just as social scientists were getting comfortable with the idea of the Rural Renaissance, it came to an end. By the early 1980s metropolitan areas were again growing faster than nonmetropolitan ones. Richter (1985, 260) wrote that "the turnaround from negative to positive net migration in nonmetropolitan areas was sustained throughout the 1970s . . . nevertheless a slowdown in the growth of nonmetropolitan areas (occurred) in the late 1970s." Richter (1985, 261) went on to suggest that "the validity of the turnaround and the evidence for a slowdown in nonmetro growth by the end of the decade may be incorporated into new theories of urban-rural migration." These theories need to explain changing mobility patterns in "post-industrial" societies, and they must include the effects of innovations in communication and transportation technology.

The Canadian experience has been similar, as noted by Keddie and Joseph (1991). Though they found less concrete evidence of a rural turnaround during the 1970s in Canada, they did find that ". . . the data for the early 1980s point toward a return to the urban-dominated growth scenario prevalent in the 1960s" (Keddie and Joseph, 1991, 378). They also noted that changes in rural population trends generally were a good indicator of the economic fortunes of different regions.

Although during the 1980s and early 1990s nonmetropolitan areas have grown more slowly than they did in the 1970s, many of them are still definitely attracting migrants. Hopefully, studies of the patterns that emerged in the late 1970s and 1980s will help to illuminate more clearly the underlying causes of changing mobility patterns in the United States.

Finally, it is worth noting here that national and regional trends often obscure underlying patterns that may be seen for particular subgroups of the population, from retirees to ethnic groups. These various patterns are important as well and do receive considerable attention in the migration literature. Examples of such studies include Robinson (1986), who wrote about the reversal in the 1980s of the previous pattern of African-American net migration out of the South, and McHugh (1989), who studied the internal redistribution of Hispanics within the United States.

▓ FUTURE MIGRATION TRENDS

What will happen to migration patterns in the United States in the future is a matter for speculation; however, some current trends in all likelihood will continue. The volume of migration should keep increasing, as will the westward and southwestward movements. Migration between cities and from central cities to suburbs can be expected to continue. Cities that are service centers, or that perform political or commercial functions, will grow more rapidly than manufacturing cities. Also, amenities such as climate and scenery will become increasingly important factors in people's decisions to migrate.

Elsewhere, the nature and extent of future migration will be primarily a function of environmental quality and population growth. There are no longer any large open areas or "safety valve" spaces available. With a combination of scarce resources and increasing population pressure, there most likely will be continued migration in even larger numbers of people in search of shelter, food, and a better lifestyle.

At the international level, free migration is no longer possible in most instances because of conflicts between the interests of a society and the rights of the individual. Continued population growth, the exploitation of resources at an unprecedented rate, vast differences in living standards from place to place, and political instability are all related to migration processes, however. We can be assured that the restless movements of people at all levels will continue as individuals and groups seek ways to better their lives in this increasingly complex and interrelated global society of the 1990s.

REFERENCES

Bean, Frank D., Edmonston, Barry, and Passel, Jeffrey S., eds. (1990) *Undocumented Migration to the United States: IRCA and the Experience of the 1980s.* Santa Monica, CA: Rand Corporation.

Beaujeu-Garnier, J. (1966) *Geography of Population.* New York: St. Martin's Press.

Berry, Brian J. L. (1991) "How 'Sticky' is Urbanward Migration? Evidence for the United States, 1850–1980," *Urban Geography* 12(3):283–290.

Biggar, Jeanne (1979) "The Sunning of America: Migration to the Sunbelt," *Population Bulletin* 34(1):1–42.

Black, Richard. (1991) "Refugees and Displaced Persons: Geographical Perspectives and Research Directions," *Progress in Human Geography* 15:281–298.

Bogue, Donald J. (1969) *Principles of Demography.* New York: John Wiley and Sons, Inc.

Bouvier, Leon F. (1992) *Peaceful Invasions: Immigration and Changing America.* Lanham, MD: University Press of America.

Bouvier, Leon F., Shryock, Henry S., and Henderson, Harry W. (1977) "International Migration: Yesterday, Today, and Tomorrow," *Population Bulletin* 32(4):1–42.

Clark, W. A. V. (1986) *Human Migration.* Beverly Hills: SAGE Publications.

Conner, Roger L. (1989) "Answering the Demo-Doomsayers: Five Myths About America's Demographic Future," *The Brookings Review* 7(4):35–39.

DeJong, Gordon F. and Sell, Ralph R. (1977) "Population Redistribution, Migration, and Residential Preferences," *Annals of the American Academy of Political and Social Science* 429:130–144.

Desbarats, Jacqueline. (1985) "Indochinese Resettlement in the United States," *Annals of the Association of American Geographers* 75(4):522–538.

Everitt, John. (1991) "Refugees on Mainland Middle America," *The Canadian Geographer* 35(2):194–195.

Fairchild, Henry P. (1925) *Immigration.* New York: The Macmillan Company.

Findlay, Allan. (1989) "Skilled International Migration: A Research Agenda," *Area* 21(1): 3–11.

Folger, John K. and Nam, Charles B. (1967) *Education of the American Population.* A 1960 Census Monograph, Washington, D.C.: United States Government Printing Office.

Fosler, R. Scott, et al. (1990) *Demographic Change and the American Future.* Pittsburgh: University of Pittsburgh Press.

Fuguitt, Glenn V. and Zuiches, James J. (1975) "Residential Preferences and Population Distribution," *Demography* 12:491–504.

Gibson, Campbell (1975) "The Contribution of Immigration to United States Population Growth: 1790–1970," *International Migration Review* 9:157:177.

Goldscheider, Calvin. (1971) *Population, Modernization, and Social Structure.* Boston: Little, Brown and Company.

Gordenker, Leon. (1987) *Refugees in International Politics.* New York: Columbia University Press.

Greenwood, Michael J. (1975) "Research on Internal Migration in the United States: A Survey," *Journal of Economic Literature* 12:397–433.

Hamilton, Nora and Chinchilla, Norma Stoltz. (1991) "Central American Migration: A Framework for Analysis," *Latin American Research Review* 26:75–110.

Howell, Clark F. (1965) *Early Man.* New York: Time-Life Books.

James, Daniel. (1991) *Illegal Immigration: An Unfolding Crisis.* Lanham, MD: University Press of America.

Keddie, Philip D. and Joseph, Alun E. (1991) "The Turnaround of the Turnaround? Rural Population Change in Canada, 1976 to 1986," *The Canadian Geographer* 35:367–379.

Kenzer, Martin S. (1991) "The African Refugee Crisis in Context," *The Canadian Geographer* 35(2):197–200.

King, Michael C. (1974) "The Malaise of Migrant Workers in Western Europe—with Special Reference to Switzerland," *Migration Today* 18:82–93.

Kliot, N. (1987) "The Era of Homeless Man," *Geography* 72:109–121.

Kosinski, Leszek A. and Prothero, R. Mansell, eds. (1974) *People on the Move: Studies on Internal Migration.* London: Methuen and Co., Ltd.

Lee, Everett S. (1966) "A Theory of Migration," *Demography* 3:47–57.

Lewis, Peirce. (1985) "Beyond Description," *Annals of the Association of American Geographers* 75:465–477.

Luciuk, Lubomyr Y. (1991) "A Landscape of Despair: Comments on the Geography of the Contemporary Afghan Refugee Situation," *The Canadian Geographer* 35(2):195–197.

McHugh, Kevin E. (1989) "Hispanic Migration and Population Redistribution in the United States," *Professional Geographer* 41(4):429–439.

Meenan, J. F. (1958) "Eire," in Brinley Thomas, ed. *Economics of International Migration.* London: Macmillan.

Moore, Eric G. (1972) *Residential Mobility in the City*. Resource Paper No. 13. Washington, D.C.: Association of American Geographers.

Nelson, P. (1959) "Migration, Real Income, and Information," *Journal of Regional Science* 1:43–74.

Oberhauser, Ann M. (1991) "The International Mobility of Labor: North African Migrant Workers in France," *Professional Geographer* 43(4):431–445.

Oberlander, Hans. (1992) "Mord an der Seele," *Stern* 14(26.März):20–32.

Page, Benjamin I. and Shapiro, Robert Y. (1992) *The Rational Public: Fifty Years of Trends in Americans' Policy Preferences*. Chicago: The University of Chicago Press.

Petersen, William (1958) "A General Typology of Migration," *American Sociological Review* 23:256–265.

Petersen, William (1975) *Population*. Third Edition. London: The Macmillan Company.

Plane, David A. and Rogerson, Peter A. (1991) "Tracking the Baby Boom, the Baby Bust, and the Echo Generations: How Age Composition Regulates US Migration," *Professional Geographer* 43(4):416–430.

Ravenstein, Edward G. (1889) "The Laws of Migration," *Journal of the Royal Statistical Society* 52:241–305.

Richter, Kerry. (1985) "Nonmetropolitan Growth in the late 1970s: The End of the Turnaround?" *Demography* 22:245–264.

Robinson, Isaac. (1986) "Blacks Move Back to the South," *American Demographics* 8(6): 40–43.

Rogge, John R. (1991) "Refugees in Southeast Asia: An Uncertain Future?" *The Canadian Geographer* 35(2):190–193.

Roseman, Curtis C. (1971) "Migration as a Spatial and Temporal Process," *Annals of the Association of American Geographers* 61:589–598.

Roseman, Curtis C. (1977) *Changing Migration Patterns Within the United States*. Resource Papers for College Geography No. 77–2. Washington, D.C.: Association of American Geographers.

Rossi, Peter. (1955) *Why Families Move*. Glencoe, Illinois: Free Press.

Rudzitis, Gundars. (1991) "Migration, Sense of Place, and Nonmetropolitan Vitality," *Urban Geography* 12(1):80–88.

Salt, John. (1985) "Europe's Foreign Labour Migrants in Transition," *Geography* 70:151–158.

Schwind, Paul J. (1971) "Spatial Preferences of Migrants for Regions: The Example of Maine,"*Proceedings of the Association of American Geographers* 3:150–156.

Simkins, Paul D. (1970) "Migration as a Response to Population Pressure: The Case of the Philippines," in Wilbur Zelinsky, Leszek A. Kosinski, and Mansell R. Prothero, eds. *Geography and a Crowding World*. New York: Oxford University Press, pp. 259–267.

Simkins, Paul D. (1978) "Characteristics of Population in the United States and Canada," in Glenn T. Trewartha, ed. *The More Developed Realm: A Geography of Its Population*. Oxford: Pergamon Press, pp. 189–220.

Sjaastad, L. A. (1962) "The Costs and Returns of Human Migration," *The Journal of Political Economy* 70:80–93.

Svart, L. M. (1976) "Environmental Preference Migration: A Review," *Geographical Review* 66:314–330.

Tenhula, John. (1991) *Voices from Southeast Asia: The Refugee Experience in the United States.* New York: Holmes and Meier.

Thomlinson, Ralph. (1976) *Population Dynamics: Causes and Consequences of World Demographic Change.* 2d ed. New York: Random House.

Trewartha, Glenn T. (1969) *A Geography of Population.* New York: John Wiley and Sons, Inc.

Tyler, Charles. (1991) "The World's Manacled Millions," *Geographical Magazine* 58(1):30–35.

United States Agency for International Development (1973) Office of Population. *Population Program Assistance: Annual Report for Fiscal Year 1973.* Washington, D.C.: United States Agency for International Development.

United States Department of Labor (1977) Employment and Training Administration. *Why Families Move: A Model of the Geographic Mobility of Married Couples.* R and D Monograph 48. Washington, D.C.: United States Government Printing Office.

Vernez, Georges and Ronfeldt, David. (1991) "The Current Situation in Mexican Immigration," *Science* 251(4998):1189–1193.

Walker, Robert and Hannan, Michael. (1989) "Dynamic Settlement Processes: The Case of US Immigration," *Professional Geographer* 41(2):172–183.

Warren, Robert and Passel, Jeffrey S. (1987) "A Count of the Uncountable: Estimates of Undocumented Aliens Counted in the 1980 Census," *Demography* 24:375–394.

White, Paul and Woods, Robert, eds. (1980) *The Geographical Impact of Migration.* London and New York: Longman.

Wolpert, Julian. (1965) "Behavioral Aspects of the Decision to Migrate," *Papers and Proceedings of the Regional Science Association* 15:159–169.

Wolpert, Julian. (1966) "Migration as an Adjustment to Environmental Stress," *Journal of Social Issues* 22:92–102.

Zelinsky, Wilbur. (1971) "The Hypothesis of the Mobility Transition," *The Geographical Review* 61:219–249.

Chapter 9
Patterns of Urbanization

Cities are exciting places. Nowhere else do people live in such dense concentrations, and nowhere else is there such a concentration of jobs, entertainment, and commerce. Of course, they also contain the densest accumulations of pollutants along with high crime rates, traffic gridlock, and noise.

Cities are enigmatic: people are both drawn to them and repelled by them; they love and hate them. Yet people continue to move to cities in ever-increasing numbers, especially since the beginning of the Industrial Revolution. As geographer Brian Berry (1973, 1) noted, "A new kind of city emerged during the nineteenth century, built on productive power, massed population, and industrial technology." Strong forces were set into motion by the Industrial Revolution, forces that led to an increasing concentration of population in urban areas. Only recently, and then, as we shall see, in only a few places, have population trends begun to shift away from increasing population concentration.

▨ URBANIZATION: A BRIEF HISTORICAL VIEW

According to Lowry (1991), the history of cities goes back to ancient times, perhaps as far back as 5,500 years ago, when cities were small and surrounded by large numbers of rural residents. The original impetus for the development of cities was the shift from nomadism to settled agriculture, but there were many other contributing factors as well. The needs for commercial, religious, and political centers; for defense; for processing and manufacturing; and for recreation were all instrumental in the establishment of cities. However, compared to modern, twentieth-century cities, most of these early urban agglomerations were relatively small. Only a few early cities ever became large. For example, ancient Rome had an estimated population of about one million. For the most part, ancient cities were restricted in size because their surrounding agricultural lands were unable to provide sufficient quantities of food and other necessities to support large populations.

Origin of Ancient Cities

The original settlement patterns of people in urban places, as well as the processes involved, are impossible to trace. Much of what we believe about ancient cities is based on speculation, and the archaeological evidence is fragmentary. Certainly an important early step in the urbanization process was the development of settled agriculture and the associated cultivation of cereal grains. Concomitant with the advent of settled agriculture was the development of early agricultural technology, which included the (1) wheeled cart, (2) ox-drawn plow, (3) art of metallurgy, (4) development of new crops, and (5) improved irrigation techniques.

In addition to such technological advances, various power structures were needed to exploit, channel, and organize these advances. According to Sjoberg (1960, 67), "a power group in the feudal society can sustain itself only if its members concentrate in the kinds of settlements we call urban." Urban places became focal points of communication and transportation, as well as fortresses for protecting the elite from invaders. The power structure was instrumental in the expansion of both the size and numbers of cities, as well as the diffusion of cities into new regions. Much of the development of cities in new areas was due to empire-building by the power structure; new cities came after areas were conquered. A good example of this was the development of cities in Northwestern Europe and England after the Roman conquest (Northam, 1979).

Medieval Cities

During the medieval period, existing towns began to expand rapidly, and thousands of new towns were formed. These medieval cities were located at points of greatest accessibility and differed from earlier cities in several respects. Although early cities were large, self-sufficient, agricultural settlements, the medieval city developed into an economically specialized enterprise dependent on other areas. Specialization in mercantile and industrial activities led to the development of guilds, which were, with the exception of the Church, the most widespread form of corporate life.

Another outgrowth of urbanization related to the development of the mercantile system was the birth of the middle-class, the "bourgeoisie." According to Thomlinson (1976, 405):

> The association of a growing middle class with city development is common throughout the world: traditional rural areas often exhibit a two-class system of a few aristocratic landholders and a huge lower class, but city life and urban occupations are not especially consonant with such a feudal class structure.

Though many cities grew during the medieval period, the larger cities did not reach the same levels that they had attained earlier. Average city populations were in the 10,000 to 40,000 range. In 1350, for example, London reached a population of 40,000, which was close to its population during Roman times. Other large cities in Europe during that time were Paris, Venice, Florence, and Milan.

A review of the archaeological and historical record by Grauman (1976) pointed out that the urban population fluctuated between 4 and 7 percent of the total population from the beginning of the Christian era to about 1850. In 1850 Paris, London, and Beijing were the only cities with populations over one million while only 110 cities had populations of over 100,000 inhabitants (Golden, 1981).

Modern Cities and the Rise of Industrialization

In its modern form, at least in Western countries, urbanization has gone hand in hand with the Industrial Revolution. Although some large cities existed prior to the Industrial Revolution, the complex economic and technological changes associated with industrialization during that period brought about a profound change in both the size of cities and the proportion of people who lived in them. The later a country became industrialized, the more rapid its urbanization. Davis (1965, 43) pointed out that "the change from a population with 10 percent of its members in cities of 100,000 or larger to one in which 30 percent lived in such cities took about 79 years in England and Wales, 66 in the United States, 48 in Germany, 36 in Japan, and 26 in Australia."

Several others factors have been instrumental in the growth of modern cities. Increasing employment in tertiary or service occupations, particularly in the technically advanced countries, has encouraged urban growth. The largest cities tend to have higher proportions of workers in tertiary activities, but smaller cities and towns also have been stimulated by an increase in tertiary occupations. Social factors often have been important in the growth of modern cities as well. Cultural attractions such as art galleries, libraries, and symphony orchestras are important in drawing tourists and supporting the economic base. The impact of the automobile has been a critical factor in urban dispersal in the developed countries. In the United States, as well as elsewhere, the automobile made it possible for the modern city to expand its boundaries, because people could live much farther away from their places of employment.

Urbanization can be defined in two quite different ways—one static and one dynamic. As a static measure, urbanization is simply defined as the proportion of a population living in urban areas at a given time, typically at some census date. As a dynamic process, however, urbanization is defined as an increase in the percentage of a population living in urban areas. Though these two definitions are obviously related, it is the latter definition of urbanization as an ongoing process that is especially important. We should note that urban growth and urbanization are not synonymous; if rural and urban populations grow at the same rate, then cities will become larger without changing the proportion of the population living in the urban areas.

As a spatial process of population redistribution, urbanization has been closely related to modernization. For urbanization to occur, cities must grow faster than do rural populations. Because we argued earlier that fertility declines are likely to occur earlier and faster in cities than in rural areas, the major mechanisms for maintaining urban/rural population growth rate differentials during the modernization process must be rural-urban migration. During the nineteenth century some cities were so unhealthy that they had negative rates of natural increase; their growth was entirely dependent on the attraction of migrants.

Why, we must ask, are people drawn to cities in ever-increasing numbers? With modernization, urban areas grow as a reflection of a variety of forces, especially economic forces. As jobs are increasingly shifted from agriculture to the economy's manufacturing and service sectors, population concentration becomes necessary. If, as has been typical in the United States and Canada, the productivity of labor in agriculture rises also, then people who are no longer needed in rural areas will head for the cities where new, nonagricultural jobs are being created. Of course, such processes do not occur so neatly in reality; considerable variations on the theme may even be played out within a single country as regional populations change at different rates.

In our previous discussion of migration, we mentioned the "push" and "pull" factors driving the movements of people from one area to another. Rural overcrowding, increasing productivity in agriculture, high birth rates in rural areas, and low prices for agricultural products are among the factors that "push" rural populations toward the cities. To absorb rural-urban migrants, however, powerful attractive forces must be operating in the cities; otherwise they would ultimately "choke" on the influx of new residents. Haggett (1979, 326) noted:

> . . . the major benefits gained from high-density crowding are the so-called agglomeration economies. *Agglomeration economies* are the savings that can be made by serving an increasingly large market distributed over a small, compact geographic area. Economies of scale make production costs for each unit low, while the short distance separating buyer and seller in cities cuts back the costs of transporting goods.

The division of labor and specialization are essential ingredients in economic development, and their realization is most easily attained in the urban setting. However, in economically advanced societies, the largest cities may lose some of their advantages as diseconomies of scale become more apparent. Phillips (1978, 209) has noted that "Large cities, once viewed as centers of action and success, have acquired a negative image as being crime-ridden, dirty, confining, and expensive places to live." This view is evident in some developed countries, especially in the United States; but it is far less apparent in the underdeveloped countries where the majority of people still view cities as better places to live than are rural areas with respect to job opportunities, wages, social mobility, and the many benefits of modernization.

Lowry (1991, 158) commented that "the facts seem clear enough: cities are more attractive to rural folk than rural places are to city folk, so that the net flow of voluntary migration in developing countries is invariably from rural to urban places. Furthermore, objective indexes of welfare seem to confirm the judgment of those who have

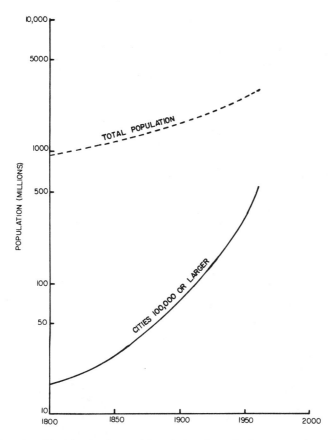

▩ **FIGURE 9–1** World Urbanization and Population Growth. SOURCE: Adapted from THE URBANIZATION OF THE HUMAN POPULATION by Kingsley Davis, September 1965. Illustration by Hatti Sauer Prentiss. Copyright © 1965 by Scientific American, Inc. All rights reserved.

voted with their feet; real wages are higher in cities, urban schools and health care are better than their rural counterparts, and those who seek upward mobility will find the best opportunities in cities."

▨ RECENT URBANIZATION: REGIONAL COMPARISONS AND CONTRASTS

Although the population of the world as a whole has been increasing rapidly, the increase of the urban population has risen even more rapidly, as shown in Figure 9–1. An analysis of urbanization by Northam suggested that it may be viewed as a three-stage process as shown in Figure 9–2.

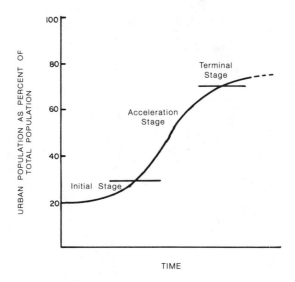

▦ **FIGURE 9–2** The Urbanization Curve and Stages of Urbanization. SOURCE: By Ray M. Northam. From *Urban Geography,* copyright © 1975 by John Wiley & Sons, Inc. Reprinted by permission of John Wiley & Sons, Inc.

In the Initial Stage the population is primarily rural, engaged in agricultural pursuits, and of a dispersed nature. The second stage, referred to by Northam as the Acceleration Stage, is a period in which an increasingly large share of the population lives in urban centers. During this stage there is a marked redistribution of the population, with the urban component rising from less than 25 percent to over 70 percent of the total population. The Acceleration Stage also involves a basic restructuring of the economy, with a concentration of economic activity in the city. Large numbers of people are employed in manufacturing industries as well as in service and trade activities.

The final stage in the urbanization process is referred to by Northam as the Terminal Stage. During this stage the urban population represents approximately 60 to 70 percent of the total population. Once the urbanization curve goes above 70 percent, it tends to flatten out. For example, the urbanization curve for England and Wales since 1900 has tended to level off after it reached the 80 percent level.

Today we might add another stage to Northam's model; a stage in which deconcentration begins in highly advanced "post-industrial" economies. Berry (1980, 13) noted that, "Urbanization, the process of population concentration, has been succeeded in the United States by counterurbanization, a process of population deconcentration characterized by smaller sizes, decreasing densities, and increasing local homogeneity, set within widening radii of national interdependence."

A worldwide regional analysis of urbanization shows that the world's nations are in various stages of urbanization. As a general rule, the developed nations might be considered as being in the Terminal Stage of urbanization. On the other hand, the developing nations are primarily in the Acceleration Stage although some nations, largely agrarian, could still be considered in the Initial Stage. Figure 9–3 shows the world pattern of urbanization.

The Primate City

A common observation of city systems in various countries is that usually one city is much larger and more powerful than the others in a country. Jefferson (1939, 226) called that city the Primate City, and he stated:

> . . . all over the world . . . the largest city shall be supereminent, and not merely in size, but in national influence. . . . A country's leading city is always disproportionately large and exceptionally expressive of national capacity and feeling. The primate city is commonly at least twice as large as the next largest city and more than twice as significant.

One city, according to Lowry (1991, 164), "usually the seat of government, becomes very large relative to other urban places in that nation. In 1980, at least a fifth of the total populations of Argentina, Iraq, Peru, Chile, Egypt, South Korea, Mexico, and Venezuela lived in such a 'primate city.' These places accumulate a large share both of the population and of economic and cultural activity."

The relationship between the rank and size of cities was formalized by Zipf (1949) in the rank-size rule, which can be stated by the equation

$$P_r = P_1/r,$$

where P_r is the population of a city of rank r,

    P_1 is the population of the largest city, and

    r   is the rank of a given city.

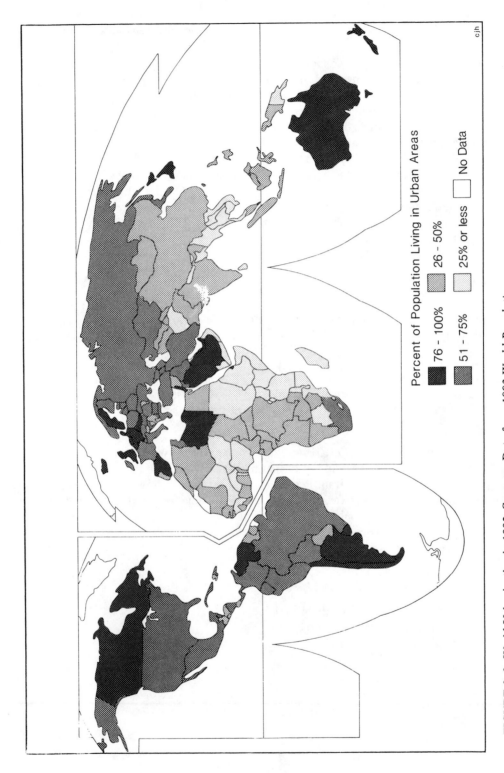

■ **FIGURE 9–3** World Urbanization in 1992. SOURCE: Data from *1992 World Population Data Sheet*. (Washington, D.C.: Population Reference Bureau, Inc.).

Percent of Population Living in Urban Areas

76 - 100%   26 - 50%

51 - 75%   25% or less   No Data

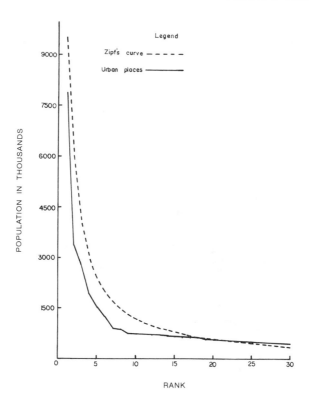

■ **FIGURE 9–4** City Size and Rank, United States, 1970, Compared with Zipf's Theoretical Curve. SOURCE: United States Bureau of the Census. *1970 Census of Population,* "Number of Inhabitants: United States Summary," PC(1)-A1 (Washington, D.C.: U.S. Government Printing Office).

Figure 9–4 shows a comparison of Zipf's ideal curve with the distribution of cities in the United States. According to Zipf, deviations from the curve indicate improper balance in the pattern of urbanization. However, others have noted that deviations are to be expected and that distributions should be viewed in terms of probability.

The rank-size rule and the primate city concept have been used in international comparison of the primacy rate—the population of the largest city compared with that of the second-largest city. For example, Thomlinson (1976, 422) noted:

> Countries with high primacy rates tend to be characterized by a low percent urban, low income, and recent political or economic dependency on another country; almost always the primate city is the national capital. . . . Most industrial countries have moderate or low primacy rates, generally traceable to strong pressures toward regionalism.

Furthermore, Berry (1961) found that the rank-size rule applied mainly to the larger and more complex countries with long histories of urbanization while Potter (1985, 62) argued that "primacy is frequently associated with a history of foreign dependence and low levels of internal interdependence."

▨ URBANIZATION IN DEVELOPING COUNTRIES

The growth of large cities is a well-recognized characteristic of developed nations, but urbanization is equally evident in developing countries. The twentieth century is the century of the urban transition; by the end of this century, nearly 3 billion people, almost half of the world's projected population at that time, will live in cities. Two thirds of those people will live in the less developed countries of Africa, Asia, and Latin America (United Nations, 1991).

The movement of people from farms to cities has had enormous consequences. Because of overcrowding and unemployment in rural areas, families leave the poverty-stricken countryside with the hope of making a livelihood in the city. Unfortunately, jobs are often equally difficult to find in the cities, resulting in unemployment and the growth of urban slums. Robert S. McNamara, when he was president of the World Bank, commented as follows on the problems of the developing countries with regard to urbanization:

> To understand urban poverty in the developed world, one must first understand what is happening to the cities themselves. They are growing at a rate unprecedented in history. Twenty-five years ago there were 16 cities in the developing countries with populations of one million or more. Today there are over 60. Twenty-five years from now there will be more than 200. (Population Reference Bureau, 1976, 17).

Of course, rapid urbanization is partly a function of rapid population growth in the developing countries, but it is more than that. An analysis of population growth shows that although the total population in these countries is growing at about 2.5 percent, the population of urban areas is growing at nearly twice that rate. Approximately half of that urban growth is due to migration from rural areas, and the remainder is due to natural increase.

These figures imply that cities in the developing countries are going to find it increasingly difficult to provide decent living conditions and employment for the hundreds of millions of new urbanites. According to Gugler (1988, 1), "Rapidly growing urban populations have to find employment in urban labour markets characterized by widespread unemployment and underemployment, increase demands for urban housing and services already considered inadequate, and, for better or worse, exacerbate popular pressures on political systems."

Current Patterns

Prior to 1975 the majority of the world's urban population was located in what the United Nations calls the "more developed" nations. However, since 1975, according to United Nations estimates, there has been a shift; at the present time the majority of urban residents live in the developing countries. If current trends continue, this pattern will become more pronounced. It has been estimated that between 1950 and 2000 the urban population in the developing countries will have increased 8 times, whereas the urban population of the developed countries will have increased only 2.4 times.

These statistics mean that by the end of our century approximately two thirds of the world's 3.1 billion urban residents will live in the less developed countries, compared with the 1950 population in which only one third of the urban population resided in the developing countries. According to Beier (1976, 3):

> From 1950 to 1975 the cities of the developing world absorbed just over a third (35.3 percent) of global population increase. Between 1975 and 2000 they will have to absorb over half (53.4 percent) of the increase—1.2 billion people. At the end of the century, the urban population of less developed countries will be close to 41 percent of the total population, compared to less than 16 percent in 1950.

A graphic illustration of these changes appears in Figure 9–5.

In the countries that are now highly urbanized—mainly the leading industrial countries of the developed regions— urbanization proceeded slowly at the beginning of the development process, then rose sharply in the beginning stages of industrialization, and finally tapered off when a saturation point was reached. Because of the relatively low rate of urbanization in Europe, the emergence of new political, social, and economic institutions kept pace with the urban influx. Urban growth in the developing countries is taking place under much more difficult conditions. Several important factors that have distinguished the rapid and dramatic urban growth in the developing countries were discussed by Beier (1976) and are summarized below.

First, the increase in population growth during the present century is the single most important factor distinguishing present from past urbanization. Population growth rates in Europe during its period of urbanization were around 0.5 percent a year, whereas in the developing countries today annual population growth rates are sometimes as high as 3.0 percent or more. In 1992 Kenya had a population growth rate of 3.7 percent. Significantly higher growth rates mean that the developing countries have both larger natural increases within their cities and larger population movements to their cities. This combination is straining the very fibre of many Third World cities.

Second, because of widespread communication facilities, populations in the developing countries are provided with more information about urban amenities and opportunities, thus increasing the "pull" of the city on rural populations. At the same time the cost of migration is lower because of better transportation facilities.

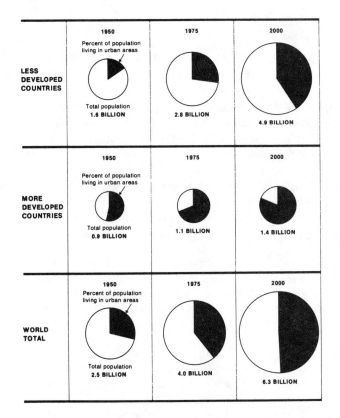

■ **FIGURE 9–5** World Urbanization: 1950, 1975, 2000. Source: George J. Beier. (1976) "Can Third World Cities Cope?" *Population Bulletin* 31(4):2. Courtesy of the Population Reference Bureau, Inc., Washington, D.C.

Third, unlike the urbanization experience of most of the developed countries, urbanization in the developing countries is generally confined within fixed territorial boundaries. Little opportunity exists for free migration of the surplus population to other countries.

It appears that the developing countries will find it more difficult to urbanize than did the developed countries, and that they will have to accomplish that task in a shorter period of time. Though there will be country-by-country differences, approximately one half of the new residents of cities will be native born while the remainder will be newcomers. These new urbanites most likely will be unskilled laborers and be relatively poor, undereducated, and probably illiterate. Only if they benefit materially from their urban experiences can we expect significant declines in their fertility. Such declines are essential in most Third World countries if those countries are to avoid having death rates control their population balances.

India is a good example for comparing urbanization in the developing countries with the earlier European experience. In 1951 India was only 11 percent urbanized, a level reached by many European countries between 1850 and 1900. At this level of urbanization, slightly over 50 percent of the population of European countries derived their livelihood from agriculture, whereas 65 to 70 percent of India's population were agriculturalists. Approximately 10 percent of India's population was employed in manufacturing, whereas about 25 percent of Europe's labor force had been so employed.

Although a common thread of rapid urban growth runs through the developing countries, widespread differences exist among them in terms of long-range urban growth prospects and in the necessary resources to support such prospects. Beier (1976) identified four patterns of urbanization that were likely to occur over the next 25 years. Each of his four types is summarized in the following discussion.

Type 1—Countries in which urbanization is well under way are included here. There are few pressures on natural resources and arable land, relatively high per capita incomes exist, and 50 percent or more of their people reside in urban areas. Most people will live in urban areas by the end of this century, and the rate of urbanization will decline. This description fits most of the countries of Latin America, for example.

Type 2—The urbanization process is more recent in these countries. Incomes are relatively low, and there is often a shortage of arable land. Over 50 percent of the population resides in rural areas. If resource restraints can be overcome and population pressures eased, then these countries may be as urbanized by the year 2000 as Type 1 countries are today. Included in this category are the semi-industrialized nations of North Africa and East Asia. Because of limited natural resources in most areas, continued successful development of these nations will depend largely upon slowing the population growth.

Type 3—This urbanization pattern is typical of the nations of sub-Saharan Africa. Recent urban growth there has resulted from large differences in the income levels of the rural and urban areas, differences that exist because of the development of manufacturing and other productive activities in cities. Agriculture probably will continue to absorb growing numbers of people in the rural areas because of the relative abundance of land. By the year 2000 these countries will remain predominantly rural. Urbanization in these countries will be more manageable than in other developing countries because of the relatively small size of the urban population.

Type 4—The final type of urbanization pattern is found in the large countries of Asia: Indonesia, India, Bangladesh, Pakistan, and the People's Republic of China. By the year 2000, if present trends continue, these countries will be dominated by large and growing rural populations living in absolute poverty. However, urban populations also will continue to increase. For example, estimates are that India's urban population will increase by 210 million people between 1975 and 2000.

TABLE 9–1 ■ Largest Urbanized Areas: 1950 and 2000

Urbanized Area	Year 2000 Rank	Country	Population in Thousands 1950	Population in Thousands 2000
Mexico City	1	Mexico	3,050	25,820
Tokyo–Yokohama	2	Japan	6,736	24,172
São Paolo	3	Brazil	2,760	23,970
Calcutta	4	India	4,520	16,530
Bombay	5	India	2,950	16,000
New York–NE New Jersey	6	U.S.	12,410	15,780
Seoul	7	S. Korea	1,113	13,770
Rio De Janeiro	8	Brazil	3,480	13,260
Shanghai	9	China	10,420	13,260
Jakarta	10	Indonesia	1,820	13,250
Delhi	11	India	1,410	13,240
Buenos Aires	12	Argentina	5,251	13,180
Karachi	13	Pakistan	1,040	12,000
Teheran	14	Iran	1,126	11,329
Dhaka	15	Bangladesh	430	11,160
Cairo–Ginza–Imbaba	16	Egypt	3,500	11,130
Baghdad	17	Iraq	579	11,125
Osaka–Kobe	18	Japan	3,828	11,109
Manila	19	Philippines	1,570	11,070
Los Angeles–Long Beach	20	U.S.	4,070	10,990

SOURCE: United Nations, Department of International Economic and Social Affairs. (1987) *The Prospects of World Urbanization Revised as of 1984–85.* Population Studies No. 101, and United Nations, Center for Human Settlements. *Global Report on Human Settlements 1986,* (New York: United Nations).

Cities in Developing Countries

More than a billion people live in the cities and towns of the developing countries. Their numbers are rapidly growing in almost every Third World country. By the end of the century, 17 of the 23 largest metropolitan areas, with populations over 10 million, will be in the Third World (United Nations, 1991).

Individual cities in the developing countries are already as large or larger than the major cities of the developed regions; and in a few years some may be considerably larger, as we see in Table 9–1. Some interesting contrasts also are evident. For example, Mexico City, the world's largest urban area, will have over 25 million inhabitants by the year 2000. In contrast, in 1950, the city had a population of only 3 million and was one fourth the size of the New York City urbanized area. The second largest city in the year 2000 will be Tokyo-Yokohama with 24.1 million people, followed closely by Sao Paulo with 23.9 million inhabitants.

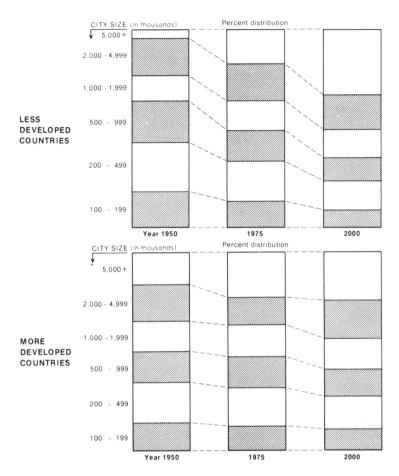

▨ **FIGURE 9–6** Distribution of Population in Cities Over 100,000 in 1970: 1950, 1975, 2000. SOURCE: George J. Beier. (1976) "Can Third World Cities Cope?" *Population Bulletin* 31(4):10. Courtesy of the Population Reference Bureau, Inc., Washington, D.C.

There will be a continued concentration of people in the larger cities of both the developed and the developing countries, as shown in Figure 9–6. Cities with more than 5 million inhabitants will undergo the most rapid increases, particularly in the developing countries.

Most of the increase in urban populations will occur through the expansion of existing cities. There will be few new cities, except where new resources are discovered. Because most of the choice urban locations are already usurped by urban centers, and because it is less costly to expand these areas than to develop new cities, it is unlikely that many new urban centers will appear.

Migration Impact

As we noted previously, rural-urban migration is a major aspect of urban growth. Its significance varies over time and from country to country. In Latin America and other areas that already have a significant proportion of their populations living in urban areas, there will most likely be a decline in rural-to-urban migration by the year 2000. However, in nations that are largely rural, like many in sub-Saharan Africa, migration will continue to play a key role in urban growth and distribution patterns for a long time.

The reasons why people migrate are many and varied; but the economic motive, the desire to better one's self and family, still seems to predominate. In most cases the migrants' expectations of economic improvement are met, as was suggested in the following comment by Yap (1975, 3):

> Not surprisingly, we find that migrants who stay in cities do seem to be better off, on average. Not everyone is employed immediately, but a large fraction of migrants find jobs in a reasonably short period. Incomes are higher, even for the unskilled; and many who start out in relatively undesirable jobs manage to find better ones in time.

Migrants come from varying cultural and socioeconomic environments. According to Berry (1973, 82), they "comprise a large and disparate array of social types both before and after migration."

Migration flows are important in explaining why large cities in the developing countries are growing relatively faster than the medium-sized and smaller cities. Migration has often occurred in steps—from rural areas to small local cities and then to the larger urban areas—especially during the early stages of urbanization (Shaw, 1975, 45–46). The evidence suggests that migrants are increasingly bypassing the smaller cities and moving directly to the larger urban areas. There are several reasons for this changing pattern, including the concentration of important economic opportunities in the larger cities and improved communication and transportation facilities.

Latin America

In Latin America, and throughout most of the developing world, there is an increasing concern with rapid urbanization and its consequences. Planning for population growth and economic growth at the urban, regional, and national scales is appealing to many Third World countries. Berry (1973, 99–100) commented:

> The feeling is that continued change within the framework of present economic systems will produce only more and worse problems, and that changes in the nature of urban systems must be produced to overcome the continuing constraints of low rates of economic growth, export orientation, and colonial inheritance that conspire

to confine modernizing influences to primate cities with little foreseeable hope for filtering to take place. The increasing feeling is that experiences of developed nations are irrelevant in the Third World today, and so radical new approaches to planning are being tried.

The importance of urban planning in the developing countries was also stressed by Potter (1985, 5), who stated that there is a "pressing need for the identification of soundly based and appropriate systems of urban and regional planning in Third World countries."

In 1979 Latin America was home to approximately 352 million people, of whom around 61 percent were living in urban areas. In 1992 the total population was 453 million inhabitants, with 70 percent of them living in cities. Within the Latin American realm, the Caribbean region was least urbanized; the highest levels of urbanization—above 75 percent—were found in Venezuela, Argentina, Chile, and Uruguay.

In Peru we find the cityward movement of people and rapid urban growth typical of Latin America. Three decades ago about 10 percent of the Peruvian population lived in Lima, whereas by 1980 that percentage had risen to around 25 percent. More than half of Lima's residents now live in slums, or *pueblos jovenes* (young towns); and rats, filth, poverty, and unemployment are their constant companions.

In Colombia further urbanization seems unavoidable. Modernization and industrialization most likely will continue to be concentrated in major cities, thus such cities will continue to act as magnets for migrants from small towns and rural areas. Colombia should be approaching a population of 50 million by the year 2000, about 75 percent of whom will be living in urban centers, if projections are correct.

Throughout Latin America the million-plus city will continue to play a major role in urbanization and in urban growth. In 1950 there were only six cities of this size, but by 2000 the number is expected to be forty or more.

Asia

Among Asia's developing countries, two urbanization types are found. Countries such as Korea and Malaysia display the Type 2 pattern, whereas the larger countries follow the Type 4 pattern. We will look in some detail at one country of each type, Malaysia and India.

In Malaysia, as in many Asian countries, urban growth has been rapid in recent years, giving rise to many problems. At the same time, urbanization has been related to a major social transformation, one that will undoubtedly continue throughout the remainder of this century. As elsewhere, part of the modernization process in Malaysia has been the migration of rural poor into the burgeoning urban centers. Absorbing these people, most of whom were traditionally agriculturalists, has placed a considerable burden on urban administrations. The Malays have grown increasingly aware of the importance of urban areas as centers of political and economic power. Their awareness of such significant rural-urban differences poses numerous political problems and conflicts. Differences in demographic characteristics and employment opportunities among major ethnic groups, primarily the Malays and Chinese, are among the greatest potential sources of conflict. Such problems have been intensified by urbanization and rural-urban migration while solutions have been slow to emerge.

Of course, urbanization has increased employment opportunities in the modern sector of the economy, especially in construction. Urban employment in other sectors has grown less rapidly; for instance, manufacturing has not been able to make a major contribution. However, in the decades ahead modernization and urbanization are likely to continue, as is the growth of most larger urban centers.

In India, urbanization levels increased gradually during the twentieth century from a level of about 10 percent in 1900 to almost 20 percent by 1970. In 1979, India had a population of approximately 660 million, 21 percent of whom lived in urban areas. By 1992 the population was nearly 890 million, with 26 percent living in urban areas.

Despite the slow change in the level of urbanization, characteristic of Beier's Type 4 urbanization pattern, India has a number of very large cities. Two decades ago, for example, India had eight cities in the over-one-million category: Calcutta, Bombay, Delhi, Madras, Hyderbad, Bangalore, Ahmedabad, and Kanpur. The Calcutta urban agglomeration alone in 1971 included more than 7 million people, and it had exceeded 11 million by 1990 just in the city. Since the 1960s, industrial cities, port cities, and capital cities have all grown at substantial rates.

Projections of India's urban and rural populations leave little room for optimism. At the projected level of urbanization, a major mobilization of resources will be required to provide the necessary housing, sanitation facilities and jobs for such massive population concentrations. India's large cities are expected to grow even larger through the remainder of this century; growth is likely to be accompanied by ever-increasing disparities between rural and urban populations with respect to incomes, education levels, and modernization.

Population growth and urbanization in India over the next two decades may impede rapid economic growth and modernization. High unemployment rates in urban centers will make absorption of rural workers increasingly difficult, resulting in rural stagnation and, quite possibly, in lower rates of urbanization. Throughout the Type 4 countries, similar problems are likely to occur. However, some differences among Type 4 countries and their likely future urbanization patterns do exist. Most notable among these differences may be the events that take place in the People's Republic of China. That China may end up as an exception among Type 4 countries was clearly suggested by Blecher (1988, 110):

> China's leaders have appreciated this problem with high imagination and broad vision. They have met with success: data indicate that townward migration has probably been lower in China than in any other developing country, despite the tremendous pressures for migration.

Africa

The most common urbanization pattern in Africa, south of the Sahara, is Beier's Type 3. Four decades ago Africa was the Third World's least urbanized region, with an urbanization level of around 14 percent. Between 1950 and 1992, however, African cities grew rapidly, and the level of urbanization more than doubled to 30 percent. Among the major regions of Sub-Saharan Africa, Eastern Africa is today the least urbanized while Middle Africa is the most urbanized. Although countries such as Ethiopia and Rwanda have urbanization levels below 10 percent, some, such as Zambia and Cameroon, are currently more than 40 percent urban. Thus, national variations in urbanization levels are considerable. Overall, by the year 2000 Africa is expected to be over 40 percent urban although regional variations in urbanization levels will remain.

Urbanization is expected to continue most rapidly in Middle Africa. Although urbanization elsewhere will be rapid as well, it will be slower in the other subregions than in Middle Africa mainly because of the more rapid growth rate expected for rural populations in those subregions.

In 1950 Africa contained only two cities with populations in excess of one million, both in North Africa. By 1970 there were 8 million-plus cities in Africa, and by 1985 there were as many as 18, accounting for 30 percent or more of Africa's entire urban population. West Africa alone had five cities with over one million residents by 1985. The future of African urbanization is unpredictable. Although sustained urbanization in Africa over the remainder of this century may be manageable, problems could lie ahead.

Urbanization has been a characteristic feature of population redistribution during the twentieth century in countries of the Third World. For the most part, urbanization is considered to be a healthy concomitant of economic development, as well as an almost unavoidable result of rapid overall population growth rates. However, the study of urbanization in a cross-cultural context has not been richly productive of useful generalizations. Spatial and temporal variations in modernization and urbanization are considerable, and social and cultural conditions in each country affect both processes in varying ways.

▓ URBANIZATION IN THE UNITED STATES

Urbanization in the developed countries has already reached Northam's Terminal Stage and, as we have suggested, has even begun to go beyond that stage in some places to a new counter-urbanization stage. Because the latter is best recognized in the United States and because the pattern of urbanization is quite typical of the developed countries, we consider it in some detail rather than providing a more general overview of urbanization in the developed countries.

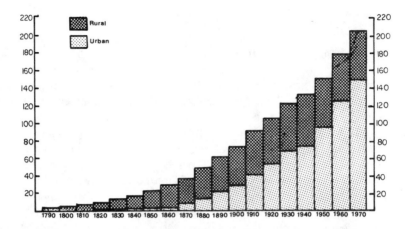

▨ **FIGURE 9–7** Urban and Rural Population: 1790–1970, United States. SOURCE: By Ray M. Northam. From *Urban Geography,* copyright © 1975 by John Wiley & Sons, Inc. Reprinted by permission of John Wiley & Sons, Inc.

Since the first census was taken in the United States in 1790, there has been an increasing concentration of Americans in urban areas. According to Berry and Dahmann (1977, 433), "In 1800, the United States was 6 percent urbanized; today, more than 75 percent of the population reside in urban areas." Many of the original urban centers in the United States were forerunners of present-day urban agglomerations. They were located on the eastern seaboard and in peripheral areas and included such cities as Boston, New York, and Philadelphia. During the eighteenth century more cities were formed on the eastern seaboard; but a large number of cities were founded in the Mississippi and Ohio River valleys as well as other riverene sites, as seen in Figure 9–7. This was also the time when the first major western seaboard cities were founded.

All sections of the country had some sort of urban agglomeration by the end of the nineteenth century, and most of the previously founded cities continued to grow. Cities formed during the nineteenth century were concentrated in the Midwest, primarily on navigable rivers and the Great Lakes. Approximately 40 percent of the United States population lived in urban centers by the end of the nineteenth century.

Rural-to-urban migration was a major component of urban growth in the United States in years past, but this pattern ended in the 1980s. According to Berry (1990, 99), "We are a completely urbanized society, with very few true rural residents left amidst large-scale factory style agriculture. Urban growth now is a product of natural increase and of foreign immigration."

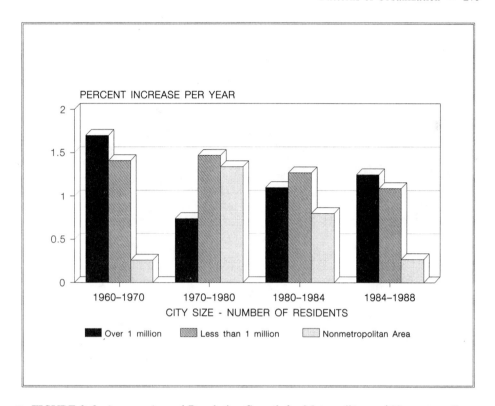

PERCENT INCREASE PER YEAR

CITY SIZE - NUMBER OF RESIDENTS

■ Over 1 million   ▨ Less than 1 million   ▢ Nonmetropolitan Area

■ **FIGURE 9–8** Average Annual Population Growth for Metropolitan and Nonmetropolitan Areas, 1960–1988. SOURCE: William H. Frey. (1990) "Metropolitan America: Beyond Transition," *Population Bulletin* 45(2):12. Courtesy of the Population Reference Bureau, Inc.

The nation's largest cities, and the suburban areas around them, have grown continuously since the nation's inception. Between 1910 and 1988 the national population grew by 167 percent, whereas the metropolitan population grew by 449 percent. Metropolitan areas with at least one million residents grew by 630 percent. In contrast, throughout this 78-year period, the nonmetropolitan population stayed within a narrow range between 56 million and 67 million (Frey, 1990, 5).

Recent changes in metropolitan and nonmetropolitan growth (Figure 9–8) show that during the 1960s there were large increases in the populations of cities with over one million inhabitants. In the 1970s, however, the large areas grew at about half the rate of the smaller metropolitan areas (less than one million inhabitants). Large metropolitan areas were especially hard hit by the recession in 1973–1975 and lost employment opportunities. In the 1980s, another shift took place. Statistics for the 1980–1984 and 1984–1988 periods show population gains once again for the nations

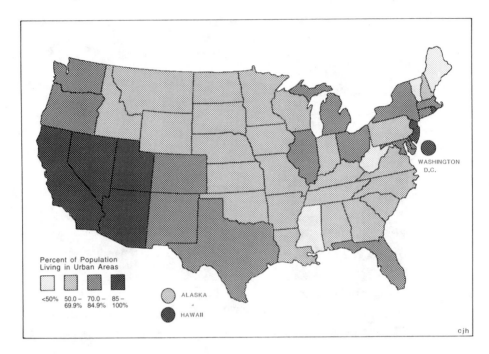

▨ **FIGURE 9–9** Percentage of Urban Population, 1990. SOURCE: United States Bureau of the Census.

"million-plus" metropolitan areas (Frey, 1990, 11). Metropolitan areas with less than one million inhabitants grew more slowly during the 1980s than they did during the 1960s or 1970s.

The "look" of American cities is also changing. According to a recent book by Joel Garreau (1991), the majority of metropolitan Americans live and work in areas that look nothing like our old downtowns. Garreau calls these new multiple urban cores "Edge Cities" and argues, quite convincingly, that they represent an important change in metropolitan development in this half century.

Figure 9–9 shows the pattern of urbanization in the United States by state. The states with the highest proportion of people living in urban places are found in the Middle Atlantic and New England regions, which generally have over 80 percent of their populations urbanized. High levels of urbanization are also found in the Southwest and in California. The states with the lowest levels of urbanization are found in the northern Great Plains and in parts of the Deep South. The states with the smallest proportions of urban populations are West Virginia, Louisiana, and North Dakota.

REFERENCES

Bala, Raj. (1986) *Trends in Urbanisation in India, 1901–1981*. Jaipur, India: Rawat Publication.

Beier, George J. (1976) "Can Third World Cities Cope?" *Population Bulletin* 31(4):1–36.

Berry, Brian J. L. (1961) "City Size Distributions and Economic Development," *Economic Development and Cultural Change* 9:573–588.

Berry, Brian J. L. (1973) *The Human Consequences of Urbanization*. New York: St. Martin's Press.

Berry, Brian J. L. (1980) "Urbanization and Counterurbanization in the United States," *Annals of the American Academy of Political and Social Sciences* 451:13–20.

Berry, Brian J. L. (1990) "Urban Systems by the Third Millennium: A Second Look," *Journal of Geography* 81(3):98–101.

Berry, Brian J. L. and Dahmann, Donald C. (1977) "Population Redistribution in the United States in the 1970s," *Population and Development Review* 3:443–471.

Blecher, Marc. (1988) "Rural Contract Labour in Urban Chinese Industry," in Josef Gugler, ed. *The Urbanization of the Third World*. Oxford: Oxford University Press.

Breese, Gerald. (1966) *Urbanization in Newly Developing Countries*. Englewood Cliffs, N.J.: Prentice Hall, Inc.

Davis, Kingsley. (1965) "The Urbanization of the Human Population," *Scientific American* 213(3):40–53.

Davis, Kingsley and Bernstam, Mikhail S., eds. (1991) *Resources, Environment, and Population*. New York: Oxford University Press.

Exline, Christopher H., Peters, Gary L., and Larkin, Robert P. (1982) *The City: Patterns and Processes in the Urban Ecosystem*. Boulder, Colorado: Westview Press.

Frey, William H. (1990) "Metropolitan America: Beyond the Transition," *Population Bulletin* 45(2):1–51.

Garreau, Joel. (1991) *Edge City: Life on the New Frontier*. New York: Doubleday.

Golden, Hilda H. (1981) *Urbanization and Cities: Historical and Comparative Perspectives on Our Urbanizing World*. Lexington, Mass.: D. C. Heath.

Grauman, John V. (1976) "Orders of Magnitude of the World's Urban Population in History," *Population Bulletin of the United Nations* 8:16–33.

Gugler, Josef, ed. (1988) *The Urbanization of the Third World*. Oxford: Oxford University Press.

Haggett, Peter. (1979) *Geography: A Modern Synthesis*. 3d ed. New York: Harper and Row, Publishers.

Hall, Peter. (1980) "New Trends in European Urbanization," *Annals of the American Academy of Political and Social Science* 451:45–51.

Jefferson, Mark. (1939) "The Law of the Primate City," *The Geographical Review* 29:226–232.

Lowry, Ira S. (1991) "World Urbanization in Perspective," in Kingsley Davis and Mikhail S. Bernstam, eds. *Resources, Environment, and Population*. New York: Oxford University Press, pp. 148–179.

Morrill, Richard L. (1979) "Stages in Patterns of Population Concentration and Dispersion," *Professional Geographer* 31:55–65.

Northam, Ray M. (1979) *Urban Geography*. 2d ed. New York: John Wiley and Sons, Inc.

Paul, Bimal K. (1986) "Urban Concentration in Asian Countries: A Temporal Study," *Area* 18:299–306.

Phillips, Phillip D. (1978) "New Patterns of American Metropolitan Population Growth in the 1970s," *Journal of Geography* 77:204–213.

Population Reference Bureau. (1976) *World Population Growth and Response 1965–1975*. Washington, D.C.: Population Reference Bureau, Inc.

Potter, Robert B. (1985) *Urbanisation and Planning in the 3rd World*. New York: St. Martin's Press.

Shaw, R. Paul. (1975) *Migration Theory and Fact*. Philadelphia: Regional Science Research Institute.

Sjoberg, Gideon. (1960) *The Preindustrial City*. New York: The Free Press.

Stockwell, Edward G. (1968) *Population and People*. Chicago: Quadrangle Books.

Thomlinson, Ralph. (1976) *Population Dynamics: Causes and Consequences of World Demographic Change*. 2d ed. New York: Random House.

United Nations Population Division. (1975) *Trends and Prospects in Urban and Rural Population, 1950–2000, as Assessed in 1973–74*. ESA/P/WP.54 New York: United Nations.

United Nations. (1991) *World Urbanization Prospects*. New York: United Nations.

United States Commission on Population Growth and the American Future. (1972) *Population Distribution and Policy*. Sara Mills Mazie, ed. Volume V of Commission Research Reports. Washington, D.C.: United States Government Printing Office.

Yap, Loren. (1975) *Internal Migration in Less Developed Countries: A Survey of the Literature*. World Bank Staff Working Paper No. 215. New York: The World Books.

Yaukey, David. (1985) *Demography: The Study of Human Population*. New York: St. Martin's Press.

Zipf, George K. (1949) *Human Behavior and the Principle of Least Effort*. New York: Addison-Wesley Press.

Chapter 10

Population and the Environment

The interrelationships among population growth, resource depletion, and the environment have been topics of concern for many scholars. As with many issues dealing with the relationship between population and other variables, there is considerable disagreement among the so-called experts. As Repetto (1987, 3) noted, "Both with regard to the past and outlook for the future, the connections between population growth, resource use, and environmental quality are too complex to permit straightforward generalizations about direct causal relationships. Further, many of these connections are manifested only at the local level and may be missed when the perspective is regional or global, where much of the debate has focused."

On the one hand there are those who feel that the root cause of most of our ecological problems is population growth, which they view as a major threat to the integrity of the environment. Others believe that many variables beside population are the critical elements in environmental deterioration, including the use or abuse of technology, which plays a significant role in environmental degradation. People's impact on the environment can be traced far back into history, and their attitudes toward the natural environment have varied considerably during different times and in various locations.

IMPACT OF EARLY CIVILIZATIONS

To understand the relationship of people to their physical environment in the modern world, it is helpful to trace the evolution of the people-environment interface. Several questions concerning this interface may be asked. What was the impact of early people on their environment? Have humans ever been part of an ecological community subject to control by ecological factors in the same way as other animals, or have humans always been able to influence their environment to a greater degree than any other animal?

Archaeological evidence strongly supports the thesis that early humans had at their disposal potent ecological devices with which they could alter their environment. For instance, humans have used fire for at least half a million years; it is a significant tool for modifying the environment, particularly in dry areas. Early humans also were able to modify natural vegetation and capture or kill animals with the aid of implements they had made. Perhaps more significant was the development of farming techniques, which provided humans with the ability to alter the natural environment considerably.

The relationship between population and land was discussed by Chinese writers at the time of Confucius, and Plato estimated that the ideal population for a Greek state would be 5,040 landholding households (Keyfitz, 1972, 12). As Eckholm (1976, 17) noted:

> Over the course of ten thousand years humans have successfully learned to exploit ecological systems for sustenance. Nature has been shaped and contorted to channel a higher than usual share of its energies into manufacturing the few products humans find useful. But while ecological systems are supple, they can snap viciously when bent too far. The land's ability to serve human ends can be markedly, and sometimes permanently, sapped.

Population growth was one response to improved agriculture; it further increased the need for food and made it impossible for agricultural people to avoid altering the ecosystem. For example, the development of agriculture in the wooded or parkland environment of the Near East and its eventual spread across Europe brought about the decimation of forests to open up more land for food production. Deforestation, in turn, frequently led to ecological disasters of one form or another.

The collapse of numerous ancient agricultural systems has been traced to ecological imbalances. For example, in the semiarid regions of North Africa and the Near East, this imbalance took the form of increased desiccation. It was not climatically induced; rather, it was a result of continued overgrazing and misuse of the land. Some of these areas remain unusable today. Another example of ecological imbalance brought about by population pressure can be seen in Mesopotamia, where efforts to extend agriculture into drier areas with the use of irrigation brought about disastrous results, including salinization and wind erosion of the land.

The pollution of air and water is not just a product of modern society; there is evidence that early cultures also experienced its effects. When Juan Cabrillo visited California in 1542 he noted that while anchored in San Pedro Bay he could see the mountain peaks in the distance but not their bases. A thermal inversion in the area trapped the smoke from Amerindian fires, bringing about air pollution and other hazards to human health.

The increased concentration of people in urban areas is also associated with water pollution problems. At least some urban cultures had to find ways to avoid water pollution problems to insure safe drinking water. The contamination of surface waters was sometimes recognized as a problem and led to the development of wells and water storage tanks. Canals were built in many areas in an effort to bring safe drinking water into urban areas. For example, the Aztecs under King Ahuitzotl brought in spring water through a stone pipeline.

▓ ENVIRONMENTAL DEGRADATION AND POPULATION GROWTH

There is abundant evidence that population growth and increased pollution went hand in hand in early civilizations. As the human population has grown and become more concentrated, there has been an increased potential for disrupting the earth's ecosystem.

Some Dimensions of the Problem

The problem of environmental degradation can be broken down into several key factors: pollution, climatic change, deforestation, and overgrazing. As discussed in this section, these factors have been some of the consequences of human activity for several thousand years.

Pollution. One important natural function of the earth's ecosystem is the absorption of waste material. Although the waste from one organism can be an important input to other organisms, when waste increases to the point that it can no longer be accommodated by the ecosystem, it becomes pollution.

We humans are currently polluting our planet at an unprecedented rate. The reasons for this are many and complex but, as Boulding neatly summarized it, "Our desire to conquer nature often means simply that we diminish the probability of small inconveniences at the cost of increasing the probability of very large disasters" (Boulding, 1966, 14).

Pollution can be either biological or chemical. Human population density often leads to increased biological pollution, as evidence from early civilizations has revealed. However, even today the crowding of large numbers of people into small places has brought about increased pollution. As a population grows, so does the accumulation of human organic waste. City water supplies may be contaminated when disposing of large volumes of waste becomes increasingly difficult. According to a study by Hardoy and Satterthwaite (1984, 49) for the International Institute for Environment and Development, only 209 of India's 3,119 towns and cities have even partial sewage systems and treatment facilities while 114 towns and cities dump raw sewage into the Ganges, the holy river of India. In the Bogota River, downstream from the city of Bogota, the average fecal bacteria coliform count of 7.3 million stands in sharp contrast to the safe drinking water limit of 100 and the safe swimming count of 200. Heavy metal contamination of water supplies is also common around many Third World cities.

Chemical pollution is another byproduct of a rapidly growing population and modern technology. Many streams and lakes have been polluted by the addition of toxic chemicals. Perhaps the most notable case was in Minamata Bay, Japan, where industrial waste containing mercury was dumped into the fishing waters. The result was several thousand cases of a debilitating disease now referred to as Minamata disease.

Pollution problems that usually were only local in scope during prior civilizations are now becoming global concerns. Chemical wastes that break down slowly may eventually reach the oceans, which are used by many as dumping grounds. As the population increases on the continental margins, the oceans become common sinks for industrial wastes and garbage. Compounds such as DDT have been carried to virtually all parts of the oceans.

Air pollution is also affected by population growth and concentration. Climatic changes are being induced by concentrations of people in urban areas and the concomitant increase in airborne pollutants. As Repetto (1987, 28) pointed out, "Estimated global emissions of carbon dioxide from the use of fossil fuels and burning of biomass have nearly tripled since 1950. Emissions of the most active chloroflourocarbons have increased from negligible amounts to almost 700,000 metric tons per year in 1985. . . . Samples of air trapped in ice cores suggest that the methane concentration has doubled."

In addition to lead, the urban atmosphere also contains high counts of microorganisms; gases, such as carbon monoxide and oxides of nitrogen; and a variety of other chemical compounds, including sulfur dioxide. Particulates and smog in the atmosphere cut down on visibility and produce a number of effects on people, from eye irritations to much more serious conditions.

The United States Office of Technology Assessment (1984) estimated that the effects of air pollution may cause 50,000 premature deaths in the United States each year—about 2 percent of annual mortality. Especially vulnerable are the more than 16 million people who are already suffering from asthma, emphysema, and other chronic respiratory disorders (National Research Council, 1985). The Environmental Protection Agency (EPA) and the American Lung Association estimate that approximately 150 million Americans live in areas whose air is considered unhealthy. This may lead to as many as 120,000 deaths each year (French, 1991, 97). Although the Clean Air Act of 1970 has been successful in reducing air pollution, Ehrlich and Ehrlich (1990, 138) estimated that if population had not grown, air pollution would now be only a little more than half the 1970 level.

With the increases in the human population and in industrial output over the past century, persistent contamination of the biosphere has become a serious global problem. Continued population growth and the concomitant new demand for food, shelter, and other goods and services will make it difficult to bring pollution under control.

Crowding. The pioneering work of Hall, who examined how different cultures perceive and evaluate personal space, has been of great interest to geographers and other social scientists (Hall, 1969). Obviously, as the population of an area grows there will be more people per square mile; nothing can change this. Similarly, personal space becomes smaller and smaller. Evidence suggests that individuals and cultures can tolerate different levels of crowding. What then is the effect of crowding on specific populations?

Studies with animal populations (including rats, mice, and deer) suggest what happens when overcrowding occurs in the various populations. In a series of rat studies, Calhoun pointed out the disastrous consequences of overcrowding (Calhoun, 1962). He found that high density resulted in the disruption of the rats' nesting patterns because of changes in their normal social behavior. Crowding intensified social interaction and the competition for resources. Infant mortality increased with the disturbance of nesting patterns, and some of the young were even consumed by other rats. Aggressive attacks became more frequent.

The relevance of these animal studies to the human situation has been debated. Freedman (1975) pointed out:

> . . . it is both difficult and risky to generalize directly from the behavior of one animal to that of another. It would be a mistake to conclude that dogs act a particular way just because cats do or that monkeys act the same way as lions; and it is of course much more difficult to conclude anything about humans from other animals. Humans are more intelligent, have language, and have an extremely complex social structure, are much more flexible and innovative than other animals . . . there is enough difference between humans and the rest of the animal world to make it difficult to conclude anything about humans from what other animals do.

Of course, as Freedman also noted, "work on animals is not only extremely interesting but can also be a source of ideas and suggestions about how humans behave" (Freedman, 1975, 41). A knowledge of animal behavior may suggest hypotheses about human behavior, but before accepting them we must test them by observing people. Even though some of the animal studies may not be directly transferable to people, we can not help but wonder about the quality of life that can be maintained as ever more people are crowded into cities.

Attempts have been made to correlate high crime rates with population density, partly because researchers have suggested that aggression increases with crowding and partly because it has been shown that urban crime rates are higher than rural crime rates. For example, in the United States the crime rate per 100,000 residents is over five times greater in the largest cities than it is in rural areas, whereas intermediate crime rates prevail in suburbs and small towns. Still, large populations do not necessarily mean high population densities, at least in a relative sense.

To date there have been few well-designed studies of the effect of population density on crime. After reviewing the results of several of those studies, Freedman concluded that "there are a great many reasons why people commit crimes, [and there are] many factors in modern, complex society that cause crime, but there is no evidence that crowding is one of them" (Freedman, 1975, 69). Part of the problem with most of the studies is the difficulty of isolating the effect of crowding from other variables such as poverty, ethnic composition, and education.

In an attempt to analyze the effects of concentrating more and more people into cities, the organization, Zero Population Growth devised an "urban stress test" and applied it to all 192 United States cities with populations over 100,000 people. The test looked at eleven criteria associated with urban blight and found that the 22 cities with the best scores averaged 116,000 people, with about 3,700 people per square mile while the 20 worst cities averaged 1,154,000 people with 8,200 people per square mile. According to Ehrlich and Ehrlich (1990, 156), "The message seems clear: measured either by social and environmental indicators together or by environmental indicators alone, more people mean more problems in American cities."

Regardless of the exact nature of the effect of crowding on human behavior, there is growing evidence that the quality of people's lives in many places is being diminished by population growth and the increased densities that often accompany it. For example, consider this statement by Brown, McGrath, and Stokes (1976, 42):

> Aerial photographs of Java reveal that people are actually moving into the craters of occasionally active volcanoes in their search for land and living space. Periodic evacuations and loss of life result. In Bangladesh, people are driven by population pressure into floodprone lowlands and onto low coastal islands previously uninhabited because of the danger of tidal waves and typhoons. *The New York Times* of November 15, 1970, reported more than 168,000 people killed by a tidal wave that swept the coastal area. Described as one of the worst natural disasters of the century, this loss of life is more accurately attributed to overcrowding than to any "natural" phenomenon.

Climatic Change.   There is increasing evidence that people have changed the climate of large areas of the world. Climatic changes induced by human occupance are far-reaching and have affected food production, human health, and living patterns.

At the local level, temperature and rainfall patterns are affected by human occupance. Agricultural and urban-induced dust pollution and increased carbon dioxide in the atmosphere due to the burning of fossil fuels have led to changes in local rainfall and temperature regimes. Dust particles in the atmosphere act as condensation nuclei and thereby increase rainfall. It has also been hypothesized that increasing quantities of airborne dust act as insulation by reflecting the sun's rays away from the earth and thus lowering temperatures (National Academy of Sciences, 1975).

On one hand, atmospheric dust has a cooling effect while on the other hand, another atmospheric pollutant, carbon dioxide, seems to have a warming influence because it traps the earth's heat. At the local level the results of increased population, coupled with the increased burning of fossil fuels, will maintain urban areas as heat islands (Bryson and Ross, 1972, 61).

One environmental issue that has received a great deal of attention in recent years is the idea of "global warming." According to this theory, an increase in atmospheric carbon dioxide, in conjunction with increases in other heat-holding gases (methane, nitrous oxide, etc.), has led or will lead to an overall temperature increase for the planet. There is still considerable debate among scientists about the precise nature and extent of this warming, but most scientists agree with the United States National Academy of Sciences that the warming over the next century will be from 1.5 degrees C to 4.5 degrees C. According to Stephen H. Schneider (1990, 30), head of Interdisciplinary Climate Systems at the National Center for Atmospheric Research, "The earth has not been more than 1 to 2 degrees C warmer during the 10,000-year era of human civilization. The previous ice age, in which mile-high ice sheets stretched from New York to Chicago, was only 5 degrees C colder than now."

The result of global warming at such an unprecedented scale could be catastrophic. Two of the most significant changes would be a rise in sea level, which could flood low-lying river deltas throughout the world, and changes in agricultural productivity that might be associated with shifting climate patterns. Christopher Flavin (1991, 82) believes that if global warming is permitted to continue, it may "soon affect economies and societies worldwide. Indeed, it can be compared to nuclear war for its potential to disrupt a wide range of human and natural systems."

The National Academy of Sciences (NAS), in response to a request from the United States Congress, released a study in 1991 on greenhouse warming. That study (National Academy of Sciences, 1991) linked population growth with global climatic change. Although the linkages between population growth and greenhouse warming were called "complex and not well understood," the NAS panel concluded that:

> More people create greater demand for food, energy, clothing, and shelter. Producing such products emits greenhouse gases. . . . Global population growth, which will largely take place in developing countries, is a fundamental contributor to increasing emissions of greenhouse gases. . . . Even with rapid technological progress, slowing global population growth is a necessary component for the long-term control of greenhouse gas emissions.

Control of population growth has the potential to make a major contribution to raising living standards and to easing environmental problems like greenhouse warming. The United States should resume full participation in international programs to slow population growth and should contribute its share to their financial and other support.

Deforestation. The increase in the world's population over the centuries has brought about a concomitant decrease in forested areas, as we suggested earlier. Trees have been cut down for a variety of purposes such as home building and firewood. The primary causes of deforestation, clearing land for agriculture and the gathering of wood for fires, are directly related to population growth. In some areas of the world, such as Algeria, Tunisia, and Morocco, forests at one time covered over 30 percent of the total land area, whereas today they cover only about 10 percent.

At the present time, forests are being cut down at a faster rate than they are being replanted. It has been known for centuries that deforestation results in floods, local changes in climate, and heavy soil erosion, but little has been done to stop or slow down the process. Certain areas that were once densely settled, such as the Middle

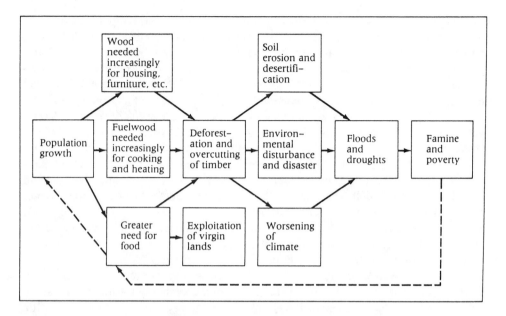

▪ **FIGURE 10–1** Population Growth and Deforestation. SOURCE: From *Resources, Environment, and Population: Present Knowledge, Future Options,* edited by Kingsley Davis and Mikhail S. Bernstam. Copyright © 1991 by The Population Council, Inc. Reprinted by permission of Oxford University Press, Inc.

East, were long ago deforested. At the present time many poor countries in other areas of the world are passing through the same stages of forest destruction but at a much more rapid pace. Hines, in discussing China (1973, 2), stated that:

> The Yellow River, which flows through an area of great population, rides high on silt from the surrounding lands and periodically floods the region through which it travels. Through the ages, overcutting of forests and exploitative farming practices have reduced China's cultivable land so severely that today the despoiled areas, together with those climatically and physically unsuited to agriculture, constitute 80 percent of its total land—all now useless for farming.

The continuous growth of China's population and the clearing and burning of forest tracts to enlarge land for cultivation have placed considerable stress on China's forest resources. According to Jing-Neng Li (1991, 256), a vicious circle (Figure 10–1) appears to characterize the relationship between deforestation and population growth, "in the final analysis the most important thing the Chinese government can do to break the vicious circle of overpopulation and deforestation is to promote the practice of family planning and to strictly control population growth."

Throughout many tropical regions shifting cultivation takes its toll of forest lands. The impact of agriculture, along with logging and ranching, seriously threatens to destroy the tropical forest ecosystem (Richards, 1973, 67).

There has been a clear downward trend in per capita forest production. Almost a billion hectares of forests and woodlands have been cleared since 1850. Although much of this deforestation took place in temperate forests, there has been a shift since World War II to other regions, with the current locus of deforestation in tropical areas. According to FAO estimates, more than 11 million hectares, an area the size of the State of Pennsylvania, was deforested each year in tropical regions during the 1980s.

Population growth and energy price increases have intensified the need for fuelwood and timber supplies in developing countries. The open savannahs of the Sahel region of northern Africa are also being rapidly stripped of their remaining trees. Annual fuelwood consumption alone exceeds annual tree growth by an estimated 30 percent (Repetto,1987,17). The worldwide estimate by the FAO is that 1.5 billion of the 2 billion people who rely mostly on fuelwood are cutting wood faster than it is growing back (World Resources Institute [WRI] and International Institute for Environment and Development [IIED], 1987, 272). Table 10–1 shows world land use by region from 1850–1980 and points out the vast decreases in forests that have taken place.

Tropical rainforests are being cut down at an alarming rate throughout the world. Although these forests only cover around 7 percent of the earth's land area, they play a disproportionate role in the biosphere. Rainforests are home to one half of all the species found on earth and are a gigantic storehouse for carbon. Although exact figures are hard to find, tropical deforestation and burning probably contributed between 7 and 31 percent of the carbon dioxide released into the atmosphere each year (Durning, 1991, 169).

Current estimates are that somewhere between one third and one half of the world's original tropical rainforests are now gone (Muul, 1989, 29). The remaining area is slightly larger than the United States. In many instances population pressure has forced people to move to marginal lands where they clear and burn the forests to provide agricultural land. Unfortunately, this provides only a temporary solution as land stripped of forests erodes rapidly and soils are quickly depleted of their nutrients. Saving the rainforests will involve efforts at both the national and international level (Table 10–2).

Overgrazing. The overgrazing impact of a growing population is similar to that of deforestation. As the human population increases, particularly in the poorer countries, there is a growing demand for livestock. The animals serve as food, security, repository of family wealth, and power to pull agricultural implements. Increasing numbers of livestock, like cattle or goats, can quickly denude a landscape of its natural grass cover. Denudation in turn will increase runoff, accelerate erosion, and increase siltation.

TABLE 10–1 ▓ World Land Use, by Region: 1850–1980

Region and Land Type	Area (million hectares)				Percent Change 1850–1980
	1850	1900	1950	1980	
Ten regions, total					
Forests and woodlands	5,919	5,749	5,345	5,007	−15
Grassland and pasture	6,350	6,284	6,293	6,299	−1
Cropland	538	773	1,169	1,501	179
Tropical Africa					
Forests and woodlands	1,336	1,306	1,188	1,074	−20
Grassland and pasture	1,061	1,075	1,130	1,158	9
Cropland	57	73	136	222	288
North Africa and Middle East					
Forests and woodlands	34	30	18	14	−60
Grassland and pasture	1,119	1,115	1,097	1,060	−5
Cropland	27	37	66	107	294
North America					
Forests and woodlands	971	954	939	942	−3
Grassland and pasture	571	504	446	447	−22
Cropland	50	133	206	203	309
Latin America					
Forests and woodlands	1,420	1,394	1,273	1,151	−19
Grassland and pasture	621	634	700	767	23
Cropland	18	33	87	142	677
China					
Forests and woodlands	96	84	69	58	−39
Grassland and pasture	799	797	793	778	−3
Cropland	75	89	108	134	79
South Asia					
Forests and woodlands	317	299	251	180	−43
Grassland and pasture	189	189	190	187	−1
Cropland	71	89	136	210	196
Southeast Asia					
Forests and woodlands	252	249	242	235	−7
Grassland and pasture	123	118	105	92	−25
Cropland	7	15	35	55	670
Europe					
Forests and woodlands	160	156	154	167	4
Grassland and pasture	150	142	136	138	8
Cropland	132	145	152	137	−4

TABLE 10–1 (Cont.) ⬛ World Land Use, by Region: 1850–1980

Region and Land Type	Area (million hectares)				Percent Change 1850–1980
	1850	1900	1950	1980	
USSR					
Forests and woodlands	1,067	1,014	952	941	−12
Grassland and pasture	1,078	1,078	1,070	1,065	−1
Cropland	94	147	216	233	147
Pacific developed countries					
Forests and woodlands	267	263	258	246	−8
Grassland and pasture	638	634	625	608	−5
Cropland	6	14	28	58	841

SOURCE: Table from WORLD RESOURCES 1987. Copyright © 1987 by the Institute for Environment and Development and the World Resources Institute. Reprinted by permission of Basic Books, a division of HarperCollins Publishers.

TABLE 10–2 ⬛ Saving Rainforests: Priorities for Action

At the international level

*Support sustainable development programs that attack root causes of poverty, including maldistribution of farmland.

*Support family-planning programs in poor nations.

*Reduce international debt in exchange for forest protection policies.

At the national level

*Recognize and defend indigenous people's rights, including the right to exercise effective control over traditional lands and natural resources.

*Launch aggressive family-planning and land reform programs; step up participatory poverty alleviation programs.

*Reform land tenure, credit, subsidy, and tax policies to eliminate antiforest bias.

*Carry out through landuse planning based on ecological capacities of soils and biological diversity to demarcate and enforce biological reserves, extractive reserves, sustainable forestry areas, and agricultural land.

*Develop and disseminate tree-garden techniques based on indigenous models.

SOURCE: Reprinted from THE WORLD WATCH READER ON GLOBAL ENVIRONMENTAL ISSUES, Editor: Lester R. Brown. By permission of W. W. Norton & Company, Inc. Copyright © 1991 by Worldwatch Institute.

There are many historic examples of overgrazing. At present, North Africa is largely unproductive and barren although at one time it was considered the granary of the Roman Empire. The Tigris-Euphrates Valley, known as the Fertile Crescent, probably supports fewer people today than it did during the pre-Christian era. According to Brown, McGrath, and Stokes (1976, 41), while overgrazing is not new, the current scale and rate of acceleration are. Damage that formerly took place over centuries is now being compressed into years by the fateful arithmetic of population growth. Populations are, in effect, outgrowing the biological systems that sustain them.

The expansion of arid areas, known as desertification, is at least partly due to overgrazing (Goudie, 1986, 46–50). As the size of the world's livestock herds increases, degradation of rangeland occurs. When the size of the livestock herds surpass the carrying capacity of perennial grasses on the range, the plant cover starts to diminish leaving the land exposed to the ravages of both water and wind. According to Postel (1991, 27), "In the most severe stages, animal hooves trample nearly bare ground into a crusty layer no roots can penetrate, causing erosion to accelerate. The appearance of large gullies or sand dunes signals that desertification can claim another victory."

The Ehrlich-Commoner Debate

One of the most widely discussed topics among ecologists and other scientists concerned with population growth is the exact nature of the relationship between the size of a human population and its effect on the ecology of an area. Foremost among advocates of two different views on this question are Paul Ehrlich of Stanford University and Barry Commoner of Queens College in New York City.

Ehrlich proposes that environmental deterioration is a direct consequence of population growth. Commoner, on the other hand, believes that although population plays a role in environmental deterioration, it is not the major determinant of the environmental crisis. He believes that other variables, primarily technology, play a much more significant role in the ecological crisis. Thus, those concerned with the relationship between environmental problems and population growth are served well by the confrontation of viewpoints held by Ehrlich and Commoner.

The Ehrlich Viewpoint

Ehrlich's basic argument is centered around five theorems that he believes provide a realistic framework for analysis. These five theorems originally were published in *Science* (Ehrlich and Holdren, 1971, 1212):

1. Population growth causes a *disproportionate* negative impact on the environment.
2. Problems of population size and growth, resource utilization and depletion, and environmental deterioration must be considered jointly and on a global basis.
3. Population density is a poor measure of population pressure, and redistributing population would be a dangerous pseudosolution to the population problem.

4. Environment must be broadly construed to include such things as the physical environment of urban ghettos, the human behavioral environment, and the epidemiological environment.
5. Theoretical solutions to our problems are often not operational and sometimes are not solutions. Ehrlich believes that each person has a negative impact on the immediate environment. In order to meet individual needs, each person simplifies ecological systems through the establishment of agriculture and is involved in the use of nonrenewable and renewable resources.

In a recent restatement of these ideas, Ehrlich and Ehrlich (1990, 39), note that the "population connection" is the key to understanding the root causes of our environmental problems. The numbers of people in an area relative to the carrying capacity of that area are used to determine if an area is overpopulated. If the long-term carrying capacity of an area is clearly being degraded by its current human occupants, then that area is overpopulated. By this standard the Ehrlichs believe virtually every nation today is overpopulated. According to Ehrlich and Ehrlich (1990, 58):

> The impact of any human group on the environment can be usefully viewed as the product of three different factors. The first is the number of people. The second is some measure of the average person's consumption of resources (which is also an index of affluence). Finally, the product of those two factors—population and its per capita consumption—is multiplied by an index of environmental disruptiveness of the technologies that provide the goods consumed . . . In short,

$$\text{Impact} = \text{Population} \times \text{Affluence} \times \text{Technology, or } I = PAT.$$

The Ehrlichs believe that this $I = PAT$ equation is the key part of the population connection and useful in understanding our environmental crisis. Under this formulation, environmental problems are found throughout the world because rich nations with relatively small populations and poor nations with large populations have a significant environmental impact (Espenshade, 1991, 332).

The Commoner Viewpoint

Commoner, Corr, and Stamler (1971) suggested two ways to test the validity of Ehrlich's assumption that population growth is the crucial variable. The first way is to quantify the variables in the equation. The second is to analyze a specific environmental problem and determine the exact nature of the impact of population growth.

The time period between 1946 and 1968 was chosen for analysis because many of the present-day environmental problems—for example, pollution from detergents, photochemical smog, and pollution from synthetic pesticides—began after World War II. In addition, many new production techniques were introduced during this period. Pollution levels in the United States between 1946 and 1968 increased 200 to 1000 percent, while the increase in the U.S. population for the same time period was approximately 43 percent. Commoner, Corr, and Stamler argued that population growth alone could not account for such large increases in pollution levels and that the population component was not large enough to balance Ehrlich's equation.

Their next step was to see whether economic growth and increased per capita consumption could account for the increases in pollution levels. They found that the data for that period show that income alone did not account for the increased pollution levels.

After analyzing changes in per capita consumption of a variety of selected products, Commoner concluded that increases in the consumption of some products were counterbalanced by decreases in consumption of others. This led him to his conclusion that the most important factor was the nature of technologies used to produce various goods and the impact of those technologies on the environment.

The largest increases in per capita consumption were related to products that turned out to be important causes of pollution. New technologies were the major culprit in rising pollution levels not an increase in population.

In a recent restatement of his position, Commoner (1990, 14) develops his own equation to measure total pollution as follows:

> The total amount of pollution generated can . . . be expressed by multiplying the pollution per unit good (technology factor) by the total amount of good produced. Finally, the latter figure can be broken down into the product of two factors: good produced per capita (the affluence factor) multiplied by the size of the population. In this way, the total amount of pollution can be expressed numerically in the form of an equation:

Total Pollution = Pollution per good × good per capita × population.

With this equation the total amount of pollution can increase when any of the factors increase. Thus, total pollution can be increased because of population increases (Ehrlich) or because of high-pollution technologies (Commoner).

Commoner goes on to look at these three factors relative to post-1950 production technologies and concludes (1990, 151) that, "the data both from an industrial country like the United States and from developing countries show that the largest influence on pollution levels is the pollution-generating tendency of the system of industrial and agricultural production and of the transportation and power systems. In all countries, the environmental impact of the technology factor is significantly greater than the influence of population size or of affluence."

This debate between Ehrlich and Commoner outlines two of the major viewpoints regarding the role of population in environmental degradation. Probably the truth, as often is the case in such complex areas, incorporates elements from both sides.

In another study of the importance of population growth and its role in environmental degradation, Ridker concluded that three generalizations can be made about this relationship (Ridker, 1980, 116): (1) most of the environmental effects of changes in assumptions about population growth are relatively small; (2) the resource and environmental impacts of changes in per capita income are significantly larger than those of an equal-percentage change in population in early years, but the latter impacts grow over time, so that by the year 2025 they are roughly equal in magnitude; and (3) other determinants, such as the extent of recycling, technological changes, changes in availability of resources, and specific policies directly aimed at reducing the emission of a particular pollutant, generally have larger impacts than either population or economic growth rates.

▓ POPULATION AND RESOURCES

The interrelationship between population and resources has been the subject of study for many natural and social scientists. With population growth and the concomitant increase in demand for goods and services, the pressure on resources also increases. In a recent evaluation of the need to balance population and resources, Hinrichsen (1991, 27) concluded that, "It is increasingly evident that many developing countries, struggling with rapidly growing populations and dwindling stocks of natural resources, must evolve strategic development plans that incorporate population and resource concerns." There are different opinions, however, about the impact of population growth on resource depletion.

Population-Resource Region

Geographers have always been concerned with regions and have spent a considerable amount of time and energy examining the problems of resource adequacy and population growth. If we try to define a population-resource region, then the concept of technology must be examined. Thus, the state of a country's technology is an important measure of the availability of its resources. In general, the greater a country's level of technology the greater its ability to exploit its resources.

A useful regional classification, based on population-resource relationships and technology, was developed by Ackerman (Ackerman, 1967). He divided the world into five categories: (1) European Type—technology-source areas of high population-potential resource ratios; (2) United States Type—technology-source areas of low population-potential resource ratio; (3) Brazil Type—technology-deficient areas of low population-resource ratios; (4) India-China Type—technology-deficient areas of high population-resource ratio; and (5) Arctic-Desert Type—technology-deficient with few potential food-producing resources.

Ackerman's discussion of population-resource regions points out some interesting observations. More than half of the world's population live in areas that could be considered technologically deficient and have high ratios of population to potential resources. The remaining population is rather evenly divide among three of the other population-resource types. The technology-deficient countries of low population-potential resource ratios, including much of Latin American and Africa, have about one sixth of the world's population. The Western European countries and Japan, which have another sixth of the world's population, are examples of regions where "industrial organization and technology permit them to extend their resource base through world trade, thus effectively meeting the deficiency of their low domestic per capita resource production" (Ackerman, 1967, 87). The remaining portion of the world's population live in technically advanced societies with low ratios of population to potential resources. These countries include the United States, Canada, Australia, and the Commonwealth of Independent States.

The Limits to Growth

One of the most ambitious attempts to bring together forecasts of resource depletion and its relationship to population growth was the publication of *The Limits to Growth* (Meadows et al., 1972). Through the use of System Dynamics, the authors developed a model with which they could examine the following five factors: population, agricultural production, industrial production, natural resources, and pollution.

One of the principal objectives of *The Limits to Growth* study was to examine the long-term outlook for the world. The various levels of human concern are depicted in Figure 10–2. All human concerns can be found somewhere on the graph depending on how far in time we wish to go forward and the amount of geographical space we are interested in. The concern of the majority of humankind would be concentrated in the lower left-hand corner of the graph. That is, most people are concerned with their immediate family on a day-by-day basis. However, the concern of the authors is depicted in the upper right-hand corner of the graph. They examined the long-range future, of the children's lifetime, of the entire world.

To examine this long-range future, a formal mathematical model was developed. The advantages of such a model are twofold: (1) all of the assumptions of the model are written out in a precise form and are thus open for inspection and criticism and (2) after all of the assumptions have been analyzed and revised to agree with the most current ideas, a computer can be used to determine the nature of the complex interactions. The construction of the model followed four principal steps (Meadows et al., 1972, 98):

1. Professionals in many fields (economics, demography, geology, and nutrition) were contacted and the literature was searched in order to identify the important causal relationships among the five levels of the model.
2. Using global data where they were available, each relationship was quantified as accurately as possible. If global data were not available local data were used.

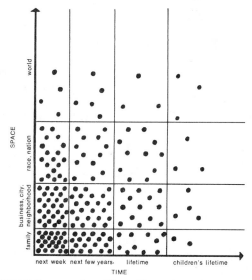

Although the perspectives of the world's people vary in space and in time, every human concern falls somewhere on the space-time graph. The majority of the world's people are concerned with matters that affect only family or friends over a short period of time. Others look farther ahead in time or over a larger area—a city or a nation. Only a very few people have a global perspective that extends far into the future.

▧ **FIGURE 10–2** Human Perspectives. Source: THE LIMITS TO GROWTH: *A report for The Club of Rome's Project on the Predicament of Mankind,* by Donella H. Meadows, Dennis L. Meadows, Jφrgen Randers, and William W. Behrens, III. A Potomac Associates book published by Universe Books, N.Y., 1972. Graphics by Potomac Associates.

3. The computer was used to calculate the simultaneous operation of all the relationships over time. The effects of the numerical changes were then tested in the basic assumptions in order to determine the principle and critical determinants of the system's behavior.
4. The fourth and final step was to test the effect of various policies currently being proposed on the global system. To apply the model to a single nation, or even a smaller areal unit, each relationship in the structure had to be quantified with numbers characteristic of that nation. For the model to represent the world, data on world characteristics had to be used.

After quantifying all of the above variables and their relationships, Meadows et al. used the computer to make graphs of the changes that would occur in each of the five factors from 1900 to 2100. The standard world model assumed that there were no major changes in the economic, physical, and social relationships that have historically determined the development of the world system. The mode of behavior for the world system in the standard run is that of overshoot and collapse. According to the authors of *The Limits to Growth* (Meadows et al., 1972, 129):

> Food, industrial output, and population grow exponentially until the rapidly diminishing resource base forces a slowdown in industrial growth. Because of natural delays in the system, both population and pollution continue to increase for some time after the peak of industrialization. Population growth is finally halted by a rise in the death rate due to decreased food and medical services.

In addition to the standard model, several other assumptions about the world system were also developed, and models of the system under those assumptions were run through the computer. Included were the following assumptions: (1) doubling of natural resources; (2) unlimited resources; (3) unlimited resources and pollution controls; (4) unlimited resources, pollution controls, and increased agricultural productivity; (5) unlimited resources, pollution controls, and perfect birth control; and (6) unlimited resources, pollution controls, increased agricultural productivity, and perfect birth control.

Based on their analysis of the world model under varying assumptions, the authors of *The Limits to Growth* arrived at the following conclusions (Meadows et al., 1972, 29):

1. If the present growth trends in world population, industrialization, pollution, food production, and resource depletion continue unchanged, then the limits to growth on this planet will be reached sometime within the next one hundred years. The most probable result will be a rather sudden and uncontrollable decline in both population and industrial capacity.
2. It is possible to alter these growth trends and to establish a condition of ecological and economic stability that is sustainable far into the future. A state of global equilibrium could be designed so that the basic material needs of each person on earth would be satisfied and each person would have an equal opportunity to realize his or her individual human potential.
3. If the world's people decide to strive for this second outcome rather than for the first, the sooner they begin working to attain it, the greater will be their chances of success.

The Limits to Growth model has received considerable attention and criticism throughout the academic world. For example, a group of thirteen scientists set out to critically examine *The Limits to Growth* model and published the results of their analysis in a book entitled *Models of Doom: A Critique of the Limits to Growth*. Their criticism of *The Limits to Growth* model was centered around the following three essential differences (Cole et al., 1973, 10):

1. *The Limits to Growth* emphasized purely physical limits, whereas the critics felt that a greater emphasis should be placed on the social and political limits to growth.

2. *The Limits to Growth* was criticized because it is said to have underestimated the possibilities of continuous technological progress, which is by its very nature difficult to predict. For example, the critics pointed out that a forecast made in 1870 would have omitted the principal source of energy in 1970: oil. It would have excluded not only all the synthetic materials, fibers, and rubbers but probably aluminum and sundry other metals as well.

3. The third essential difference is skepticism that world models developed from System Dynamics are useful tools for forecasting and making policy decisions. Golub forcefully argued that the world model approach is inherently dangerous and encourages self-delusion in five ways (Cole et al., 1973, 12):

> By giving the spurious appearance of precise knowledge of quantities and relationships which are unknown and in many cases unknowable.
>
> By encouraging the neglect of factors which are difficult to quantify, such as policy changes or value changes.
>
> By stimulating gross oversimplification, because of the problem of aggregation and the comparative simplicity of our computers and mathematical techniques.
>
> By encouraging the tendency to treat some features of the model as rigid and immutable.
>
> By making it extremely difficult for the nonnumerate or those who do not have access to computers to rebut what are essentially tendentious and rather naive political assumptions.

In a response to *Models of Doom,* the authors of *The Limits to Growth* expanded on the disagreements between the two views. A basic difference turns out to be different concepts of people, and they conclude (Cole et al., 1973, 240) that they see no objective way of resolving these very different views of humanity and our role in the world. It seems to be possible for either side to look at the same world and find support for their view. Technological optimists see only rising life expectancies, more comfortable lives, the advance of human knowledge, and improved wheat strains. Malthusians see only rising populations, destruction of the land, extinct species, urban deterioration, and increasing gaps between the rich and the poor.

Computer models provide a way to look at the dynamics of an ecological system. By altering variables and equations it is possible to observe the consequences of user's assumptions or proposed policies (Muir, 1991, 113). In a recent evaluation of the *The Limits to Growth* model, demographer Kingsley Davis (1991, 12) concluded:

> It is now two decades since *The Limits to Growth* was published. This is too brief a period to test the accuracy of even the short-term theoretical predictions, much less the long-term ones that were the main focus of interest in the project. Nevertheless, one cannot ignore developments in the last two decades that tend to support the study's findings. . . . Thus the grizzly truth may turn out to be that *Limits* was more prophetic than its detractors and even some of its defenders thought possible.

Again, the truth probably lies somewhere between the Technologists and the Malthusians. The relationships among population growth, environmental degradation, and resource depletion are difficult to define and understand, as evidenced by the considerable disagreement among social and physical scientists.

The Global 2000 Study

Another attempt to look at population, resource, and environmental problems was the *Global 2000 Study*. This study, prepared at the request of President Carter, used a variety of analytical techniques and computer models to focus on trends and changes that would take place "in the world's population, natural resources, and environment through the end of the century" (Barney, 1980, 6).

The conclusions of the *Global 2000 Study* were similar to those of *The Limits to Growth* study. If present trends continue, according to the study:

> . . . the world in 2000 will be more crowded, more polluted, less stable ecologically, and more vulnerable to disruption than the world we live in now. Serious stresses involving population, resources, and environment are clearly visible ahead. Despite greater material output, the world's people will be poorer in many ways than they are today.
>
> For hundreds of millions of the desperately poor, the outlook for food and other necessities of life will be no better. For many it will be worse. Barring revolutionary advances in technology, life for most people on earth will be more precarious in 2000 than it is now—unless the nations of the world act decisively to alter current trends (Barney, 1980, 1).

Unfortunately, this plea for decisive action has not been acted upon, and the Reagan and Bush administrations virtually ignored the recommendations of the *Global 2000 Study*. Whether population and environmental policies under a new Clinton-Gore administration will change significantly we don't yet know, though changes seem likely.

REFERENCES

Ackerman, Edward A. (1967) "Population, Natural Resources, and Technology," *Annals of the American Academy of Political and Social Science* 369:84–97.

Barney, Gerald O., ed. (1980) *The Global 2000 Report to the President of the U.S.* Vol. 1, New York: Pergamon Press.

Boulding, Kenneth E. (1966) *Human Values on the Spaceship Earth.* New York: National Council of Churches.

Brown, Lester R., McGrath, Patricia L., and Stokes, Bruce. (1976) *Twenty-Two Dimensions of the Population Problem.* Worldwatch Paper No. 5, New York: Worldwatch Institute.

Bryson, Reid A. and Ross, John E. (1972) "The Climate of the City," in Thomas R. Detwyler and Melvin G. Marcus, eds. *Urbanization and Environment.* Belmont, California: Duxbury Press, pp. 1–68.

Calhoun, John B. (1962) "Population Density and Social Pathology," *Scientific American* 206:139–146.

Cole, H. S. D., Freeman, Christopher, Jahoda, Marie, and Pavitt, K. L. R., eds. (1973) *Models of Doom: A Critique of the Limits to Growth*. New York: Universe Books.

Commoner, Barry, Corr, Michael, and Stamler, Paul J. (1971) "The Causes of Pollution," *Environment* 13:2–19.

Commoner, Barry. (1990) *Making Peace With The Planet*. New York: Pantheon Books.

Dasmann, Raymond F., Milton, John P., and Freeman, Peter H. (1973) *Ecological Principles for Economic Development*. New York: John Wiley and Sons, Inc.

Davis, Kingsley. (1991) "Population and Resources: Fact and Interpretation," in Kingsley Davis and Mikhail S. Bernstam, eds. *Resources, Environment, and Population*. New York: Oxford University Press, pp. 1–25.

Durning, Alan. (1991) "Cradles of Life," in Lester R. Brown, ed. *The Worldwatch Reader on Global Environmental Issues*. New York: W. W. Norton, pp. 167–188.

Eckholm, Erik P. (1976) *Losing Ground: Environmental Stress and World Food Prospects*. New York: W. W. Norton and Co.

Ehrlich, Paul R., and Ehrlich, Anne H. (1972) *Population, Resources, Environment*. 2d ed. San Francisco: W. H. Freeman and Co.

Ehrlich, Paul R. and Ehrlich, Anne H. (1990) *The Population Explosion*. New York: Simon and Schuster.

Ehrlich, Paul R. and Holdren, John P. (1971) "Impact of Population Growth," *Science* 171: 1212–1217.

Espenshade, Thomas J. (1991) "Book Review of *The Population Explosion*," in *Population and Development Review* 17(2):331–339.

Flavin, Christopher. (1991) "The Heat is On," in Lester R. Brown (ed) *The Worldwatch Reader on Global Environmental Issues*. New York: W. W. Norton, pp. 75–96.

Freedman, Jonathan L. (1975) *Crowding and Behavior*. San Francisco: W. H. Freeman and Co.

French, Hilary F. (1991) "You Are What You Breathe," in Lester R. Brown, ed. *The Worldwatch Reader on Global Environmental Issues*. New York: W. W. Norton, pp. 97–111.

Goudie, Andrew. (1986) *The Human Impact on the Natural Environment*. 2d ed. Cambridge, Mass.: The MIT Press.

Hall, Edward T. (1969) *The Hidden Dimension*. Garden City, N.J.: Anchor Books.

Hardoy, Jorge E. and Satterthwaite, David. (1984) "Third World Cities and the Environment of Poverty," *Geoforum* 15(3):42–56.

Hines, Lawrence G. (1973) *Environmental Issues; Population, Pollution and Economics*. New York: W. W. Norton and Co.

Hinrichsen, Don. (1991) "The Need to Balance Population with Resources," *Populi* 18(3): 27–38.

Keyfitz, Nathan. (1972) "Population Theory and Doctrine: A Historical Survey," in William Petersen, ed. *Readings in Population*. New York: Macmillan.

Li, Jing-Neng. (1991) "Population Effects on Deforestation and Soil Erosion in China," in Kingsley Davis and Mikhail S. Bernstam, eds. *Resources, Environment, and Population*. New York: Oxford University Press, pp. 254–258.

Meadows, Donella H., Meadows, Dennis L., Randers, Jorgen, and Behrens, William W., III. (1972) *The Limits to Growth.* New York: Universe Books.

Muir, Donald E. (1991) "Using Computers to Explore Ecological Issues: A Simple Limits-to Growth Educational Program," *Population and Environment* 13(2):113–117.

Muul, Illar. (1989) "Use Them or Lose Them: A Recipe for Sustainable Use of Tropical Forests," *The UNESCO Courier* January 1989, pp. 29–33.

National Academy of Sciences. (1975) *Understanding Climatic Change.* Washington, D.C.: National Academy of Sciences.

National Academy of Sciences. (1991) *Policy Implications of Greenhouse Warming.* Washington, D.C.: National Academy Press.

National Research Council. (1985) *Epidemiology and Air Pollution.* Washington, D.C.: National Academy Press.

Postel, Sandra. (1991) "Restoring Degraded Land," in Lester R. Brown, ed. *The Worldwatch Reader on Global Environmental Issues.* New York: W. W. Norton, pp. 25–42.

Repetto, Robert. (1987) "Population, Resources, Environment: An Uncertain Future," *Population Bulletin* 42(2):1–44.

Richards, Paul W. (1973) "The Tropical Rain Forest," *Scientific American* 232(6):58–67.

Ridker, Ronald G. (1980) *Resource and Environmental Consequences of Population and Economic Growth.* Reprint 172, Washington, D.C.: Resources for the Future, Inc.

Schneider, Stephen H. (1990) "Cooling It," *World Monitor* July 1990, pp. 30–38.

United States Office of Technology Assessment. (1984) *Acid Rain and Transported Air Pollutants: Implications for Public Policy.* Washington, D.C.: U.S. Government Printing Office.

World Resources Institute and International Institute for Environment and Development. (1987) *World Resources 1987.* New York: Basic Books.

Chapter 11

Population and Food Supply

Nowhere do we hear more echoes of early Malthusian arguments than in discussions of the relationship between population and the supply of food. Malthus believed that there would always be too many people and too little food. This idea was summarized in his famous Principle of Population: "The power of population is indefinitely greater than the power of the earth to produce subsistence for man."

Since Malthus first proposed this principle in 1798, many developments, unforeseen by Malthus, have occurred. For example, world cropland has more than doubled, new agricultural technologies have been developed to more than quadruple yields achieved by traditional farming methods, and international trade networks and communication links have led to a degree of global interdependence inconceivable in the eighteenth century (Hendry, 1988, 3).

As in the days of Malthus, the debate continues. Are there too many people? Can we eliminate hunger? Raw emotion often dominates such discussions, usually obscuring both the known facts and the complexity of people/food relationships.

In an earlier discussion of population growth, it was argued that throughout most of human history the number of people was limited by the supply of food, among other things. With the beginning of the Agricultural Revolution, perhaps 10,000 years ago, humans began to domesticate plants and animals. At the same time they also began a long process of diminishing the variation in their diets. Of the hundreds of different animals and thousands of different plants that were once consumed, only a selected few were domesticated. With the emergence of cities, variety in the diet was even further diminished, until finally, as Harlan (1976, 89) commented, "The supermarket and quick-food services have drastically restricted the human diet in the U.S., and their influence is beginning to be felt abroad." Golden Arches, Burger Kings, and Pizza Huts are strewn throughout the cityscapes of Europe and parts of Asia, for example. Harlan (1976, 89) also seriously questioned the revolutionary nature of early agricultural changes and went so far as to point out that "agriculture is not an invention or a discovery and is not as revolutionary as we had thought; furthermore, it was adopted slowly and with great reluctance."

One way or another, in response to an increasing ability to wrest a living from their environments, populations began to grow somewhat more rapidly although growth rates were far below those that we are experiencing in the world today. In turn, population growth created pressures for further increases in food production.

Today, even with signs of a decrease in the rate of world population growth, the number of new mouths to feed is rapidly increasing. Each year an additional 93 million or more people are added to a planet on which physical resources are obviously finite. The growing number of people, combined with the increasing affluence of many of the world's residents, is generating an enormous increase in the demand for food. The relationship between more people and increased food needs is obvious.

More subtle, however, is the effect of income increases that operate through changes in the nature of the diet. Mainly, increasing affluence leads to an increase in meat consumption, as is apparent in Table 11–1. Meat consumption per person ranges from 112 kilograms a year in the United States to a low of 2 kilograms in India (Durning and Brough, 1992, 68). In turn, then, producing the meat requires more cereals. We find that in the United States per capita consumption of cereals is nearly five times what it is in the developing countries although in the United States most of the cereal is consumed only indirectly, in the form of meat.

New challenges are at hand if world food production is to continue to meet the increasing demands for food. In the remainder of this chapter some of the major prospects for increasing food supplies are discussed, along with some of their associated problems.

▨ CURRENT TRENDS IN FOOD PRODUCTION

In recent years crops have been grown on perhaps 3 billion acres of land, or approximately 10% of the earth's entire land surface. About two thirds of this cultivated cropland is planted to cereals, which provide just over half of the entire human food-

TABLE 11–1 ◼ Meat Consumption Per Capita,
Selected Countries, 1990

Country	Meat[1]
	(kilograms)
United States	112
Hungary	108
Australia	104
Czechoslovakia	102
France	91
Germany	89
Argentina	82
Italy	77
United Kingdom	71
Soviet Union	70
Brazil	47
Japan	41
Mexico	40
China	24
South Korea	19
Turkey	16
Philippines	16
Egypt	14
Thailand	8
India	2

[1]Includes beef, pork, mutton, lamb, and poultry; based on carcass
weights. Poultry figures are for 1989.

SOURCE: Reprinted from STATE OF THE WORLD, 1992, A
Worldwatch Institute Report on Progress Toward a Sustainable
Society, Project Director: Lester R. Brown. By permission of W.
W. Norton & Company, Inc. Copyright © 1992 by Worldwatch
Institute.

energy intake. Wheat and rice are at the top of the list, as shown in Table 11–2. Typically, for any country, as income rises cereals make up an increasingly smaller proportion of total calories in the diet, and the share provided by livestock increases.

It is one thing to look at world agricultural output and talk about it in terms of
world per capita supplies of cereals and other foods. It is quite a different matter to
talk about geographic differences in the production and consumption of agricultural

TABLE 11–2 ▪ Sources of Humanity's Food Energy

Food	Percentage of Energy Supplied
Cereals	56
Rice	21
Wheat	20
Corn	5
Other cereals	10
Roots and tubers	7
Potatoes	5
Cassava	2
Fruits, nuts, and vegetables	10
Sugar	7
Fats and oils	9
Livestock products and fish	11
Total	100

SOURCE: Lester R. Brown with Erik P. Eckholm. (1974) *By Bread Alone.* The Overseas Development Council. Reprinted by permission of Praeger Publishers, A. Division of Holt, Rinehart and Winston.

commodities. As we would expect, and as Figure 11–1 illustrates, there are considerable variations in the average daily calorie supply from one place to the next. The relative abundance of food in the affluent countries is not necessarily a solution to the problems of food shortages or famines in the developing world.

That food distribution is in turn related to the distribution of wealth is hardly a new idea. The venerable Chinese poet Tu Fu (A.D. 712–770), writing twelve centuries ago, remarked that, "Behind those vermilion gates meat and wine go to waste/While out on the road lie the bones of men frozen to death. . . ."

Global food production between 1950 and 1990, usually measured by cereal grain production, increased approximately 2.6 times, exceeding the 2.1 times increase in the population during the same period (2.5 billion to 5.3 billion). More food is produced per person today, on the average, than was the case 40 years ago (Figure 11–2).

These average figures, however, are misleading. Since 1984, grain production per capita has actually fallen, and production increases have failed to keep up with population growth. In the late 1980s, global grain production received several setbacks (Ehrlich, 1991, 223), and per capita production has not returned to the 1984–1985 level. Also, the apparent progress in increasing food supplies in developing countries can be attributed primarily to significant production increases in one country, China, which accounts for 35 percent of the Third World's food output and 30 percent of its population. If China is removed from this calculation, food production increases in the other developing countries is barely matched by population growth, and in some areas it was significantly less than population growth (Hendry, 1988, 7).

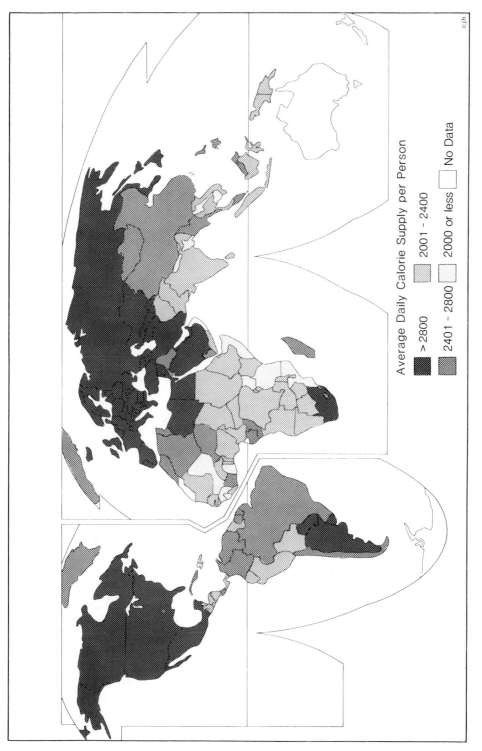

Average Daily Calorie Supply per Person

> 2800
2401 - 2800
2001 - 2400
2000 or less
No Data

■ **FIGURE 11–1** Average Daily Calorie Per Person. SOURCE: Peter Hendry. (1988) "Food and Population: Beyond Five Billion," *Population Bulletin* 43(2):6. Courtesy of the Population Reference Bureau, Inc.

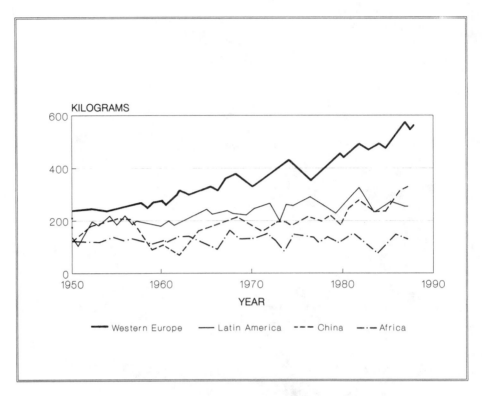

▪ **FIGURE 11–2** Per Capita Grain Production: 1950–1985. SOURCE: Peter Hendry. (1988) "Food and Population: Beyond Five Billion," *Population Bulletin* 43(2):20. Courtesy of the Population Reference Bureau, Inc.

A deterioration in diet and an increase in hunger is now a chronic reality in sub-Saharan Africa. Both the absolute number and the proportion of hungry people are increasing (Brown and Young, 1990, 77). More than any other world region (Figure 11–3), Africa has seen a significant decline in per capita food production. As Lester Brown (1989,32) said, "With more hungry people in the world today than when this decade began, there's little to celebrate on the food front as we enter the nineties."

Although some writers, like Simon (1983), have been led by ideology and "demographic quackery" to believe there is little relationship between population growth and food availability, many demographic scholars believe the real battle to feed the expanding human population may be just beginning. As Hinrichsen and Marshall (1991, 26) observed, "There are genuine fears that the world may be reaching a watershed in food production. There is not much more good land available for agricultural expansion; water suitable for irrigation is shrinking as demand grows; in many cases cur-

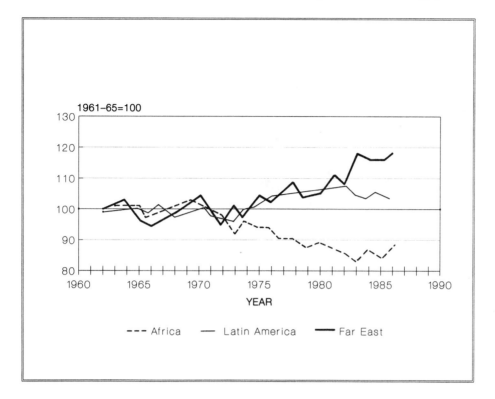

1961–65=100

Africa · Latin America · Far East

■ **FIGURE 11–3** Food Production Per Capita: 1962–1986. Source: John R. Tarrant, "World Food Prospects for the 1990s," *Journal of Geography,* Nov.–Dec. 1990: 235. Reprinted with permission.

rent cropland has been pushed to its productive limits; and additional inputs of fertilizers and pesticides are proving counterproductive."

A survey of 93 developing countries by the Food and Agricultural Organization (FAO) determined that to meet food production requirements at the end of this century, another 83 million hectares will have to be added to the present 770-million-hectare area of arable land (FAO, 1987). Although such expansion may seem modest, the FAO study cautions that most of these new arable lands contain only marginal soils (Figure 11–4), and some are located in areas of unreliable rainfall. According to Tarrant (1990, 235), "Pressure to conserve rainforests, difficulties and the expense of developing further agricultural areas, and the loss of agricultural land to other uses, erosion, desertification, and salinization, are together likely to mean that an expansion of the area of cultivation will continue to make only a small contribution to extra food production over the next decade."

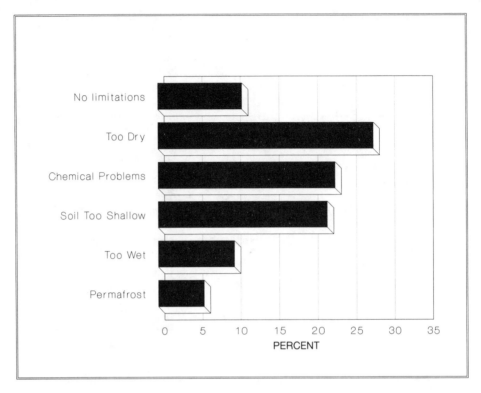

▦ **FIGURE 11–4** World Soil Suitable for Agriculture. Source: United Nations, Food and Agricultural Organization, New York.

Although a few countries, like Brazil, will be able to add more arable land, most will not; therefore, food for the 921 million people to be added to the world's population during the 1990s will come primarily from increasing land productivity. Most developing countries will have to improve yields from the same land to increase food production substantially (Figure 11–5).

An analysis of nutrition in developing countries by the World Bank (Reutlinger, 1985) provides some useful information for determining food security trends. This study was based on Food and Agriculture Organization/World Health Organization (FAO/WHO) calculations on the amount of food a person would need to function at full capacity in all daily activities. The FAO/WHO looked at people whose food consumption was 80 percent and 90 percent of this established level. The World Bank estimated that 340 million people fell short of the 80 percent consumption level. Falling below the 80 percent consumption level results in stunted growth and serious health risks. Half of these 340 million people were in the Indian subcontinent and one fourth in sub-Saharan Africa. The great majority, nearly four fifths, lived in poor countries with average incomes less than $400 per capita.

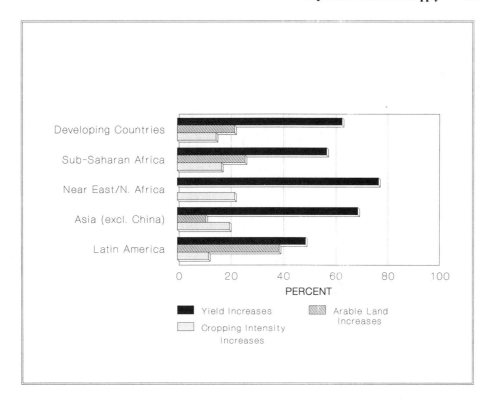

▨ **FIGURE 11–5** Possibilities of Increased Food Production: 1982/84–2000. SOURCE: Peter Hendry. (1988) "Food and Population: Beyond Five Billion," *Population Bulletin* 43(2):9. Courtesy of the Population Reference Bureau, Inc.

When looking at the 90 percent consumption level, a level where growth is not severely stunted but where people do not receive enough calories for a fully productive working life, the World Bank found approximately 730 million people in that category. Of this total, 150 million were in sub-Saharan Africa, 470 million in the Indian sub-continent, and the remaining 110 million in North Africa, the Middle East, and Latin America.

Another important measure of the current world food situation is the food security associated with *carry-over stocks* (Table 11–3). Carry-over stocks refer to grain in storage when the new crop begins to come in and would be readily available if transportation facilities were provided to ship the grain to needed areas.

Everyone is in favor of having large carry-over stocks of food; unfortunately, few are willing to pay for them. Such stocks are expensive both to acquire and to maintain. Although the most recent data indicate adequate supplies of carry-over stocks, great fluctuations can occur from year to year, and reserves can be rapidly depleted. A discussion of strategies for increasing food security is included in Table 11–4.

TABLE 11–3 ■ World Grain Production, Utilization and Carry-over Stocks

Year	Production	Utilization	Carry-over	Stocks as % Utilization
1960–61	447.9	437.2	109.7	25.1
1966–67	520.4	579.5	76.1	14.7
1971–71	629.1	615.4	87.0	14.1
1976–77	704.8	685.1	85.1	12.4
1978–79	755.1	746.8	103.6	13.9
1979–80	744.4	743.8	104.1	14.0
1980–81	732.0	743.9	92.4	12.4
1981–82	766.3	738.2	120.4	16.3
1982–83	784.2	752.9	151.9	20.2
1983–84	686.8	761.7	77.0	10.1
1984–85	814.0	783.1	107.8	13.8
1985–86	845.7	770.6	182.9	23.7
1986–87	839.1	800.4	221.6	27.7
1987–88	810.4	821.5	210.5	25.6

SOURCE: United States Department of Agriculture Foreign Agriculture Service

TABLE 11–4 ■ Strategies for Increasing Food Security

To stem falling per capita food production and resource degradation and to improve agricultural production, hard-pressed developing countries should undertake the following:

- Establish comprehensive national population programes;
- Provide integrated planning for future food needs that takes account of population growth, distribution, and rural-urban migration patterns;
- Implement sustainable development strategies that combat soil erosion and impoverishment, deforestation, falling agricultural output, and water mismanagement;
- Establish rural agricultural extension schemes that provide credit, seeds, fertilizers and advice to poorer farmers, whether men or women;
- Provide special agricultural and environmental extension services for and available to women, who do most of the land and water management in poorer areas of the developing world;
- Ensure that women can inherit, buy, and have full legal title to land and that they have access to credit and marketing facilities;
- Emphasize education for women and girls in rural areas. Better educated women are more effective as farmers and environmental managers, and have smaller families;
- Encourage community development strategies, including the setting up of agricultural cooperatives, where essential services such as purchasing, marketing, soil and water conservation, water supply, health care and family planning, sanitation, housing and education can be integrated;
- Establish comprehensive and accessible programes of maternal and child health care and family planning to reduce the size of families and to improve the health and well-being of the entire community;
- Support research on the integration of traditional and emerging technologies for food production.

SOURCE: Don Hinrichsen and Alex Marshall. (1991) "Population and the Food Crisis," *Populi* 16(2):32.

▨ INCREASING YIELDS ON LAND ALREADY UNDER CULTIVATION

There are four major means of raising crop yields: (1) chemical fertilizers, (2) pesticides and herbicides, (3) irrigation, and (4) genetic improvement of plants. These are not new developments; but their use in many places, especially in the developing countries, has come about only recently.

Fertilizer and Crop Yields

The use of fertilizers for improving yields is hardly new. For centuries farmers have added manure to fields to increase productivity. Even human wastes have been used by some farmers. In parts of East Asia it is referred to as "night soil." In 1847, Justus von Liebig, a German agricultural chemist, established the technological foundation for the use of chemical fertilizers when he demonstrated that all the nutrients could be added in chemical form. However, the escalating use of chemical fertilizers has mainly occurred in the last 35 years (Figure 11–6).

Chemical fertilizers can improve yields rather dramatically under favorable circumstances although there are decreasing returns as the amount of fertilizer is increased (see Figure 11–7). Between 1950 and 1989 world fertilizer use rose from 14 million tons to an estimated 146 million tons (Brown, 1989, 35). Since 1980, however, there has been a reduction in the rate of growth of fertilizer use. In addition, in the 1970s many Third World governments encouraged fertilizer use through subsidies, but these subsidies have recently either been eliminated entirely or significantly reduced.

Obviously, given the nature of the fertilizer response curve shown in Figure 11–7, farmers in the developing countries could benefit considerably from the increased use of chemical fertilizer. Yet, these are the very farmers least able to afford such fertilizers in many cases. A major redistribution of world fertilizer supplies would probably increase world agricultural output, but it is unlikely to occur for both political and economic reasons. Golf courses and lawns in the rich countries will remain lush and green while Indian farmers harvest their meager yields of wheat and rice!

Table 11–5 shows data for fertilizer use and world grain production. In 1950, when 14 million tons of fertilizer were used, grain production was 624 million tons, with a response ratio of 46. With the increasing use of fertilizer between 1950 and 1980, the response ratio fell from 46 to 13. During the next six years the ratio was constant, an indication of stability in the grain/fertilizer price relationship. According to Brown (1987, 130), "Growth in world fertilizer use is likely to remain slow in the absence of either a substantial improvement in the grain/fertilizer price ratio or technological advances that boost the fertilizer responsiveness of grain." Developing countries are also starting to experience diminishing returns in fertilizer use. Presently, both India and China have grain-fertilizer response ratios very similar to that of the United States (Brown and Young, 1990, 68).

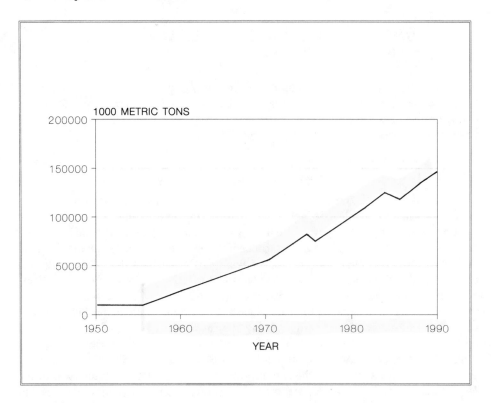

▒ **FIGURE 11–6** World Fertilizer Use, 1950–1989. SOURCE: Lester Brown, "Feeding Six Billion," *Worldwatch,* Sept.–Oct. 1989: 37. Reprinted with permission.

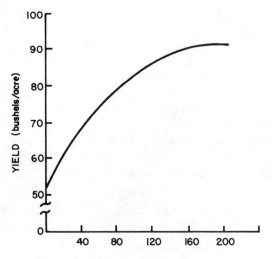

▒ **FIGURE 11–7** Typical Fertilizer Response Curve (Corn Yield in Iowa, 1964). SOURCE: United States Department of Agriculture.

TABLE 11–5 ▨ Ratio of World Grain Production
to Fertilizer Use, 1950–1988

Year	Grain Production	Fertilizer Use	Response Ratio
	(million metric tons)		
1950	624	14	46
1955	790	18	43
1960	812	27	30
1965	1,002	40	25
1970	1,197	63	19
1975	1,354	82	16
1980	1,509	112	13
1981	1,505	116	13
1982	1,551	115	14
1983	1,474	114	13
1984	1,628	125	13
1985	1,674	130	13
1986	1,661	131	13

SOURCE: Lester R. Brown. (1987) *State of the World 1987*. (New York: W. W. Norton) Table 7–3, p. 130.

This reliance on chemical fertilizers also will have an environmental impact in both the near and longer term. Hendry (1988, 25) noted that, "Beginning with Rachel Carson's seminal 'Silent Spring' in 1962, a growing body of literature documented the environmental and health hazards likely to arise from agricultural systems that depended too heavily on chemical inputs."

Herbicides and Pesticides

Some estimates suggest that as much as half of the world's food production is lost mainly to hungry animals and insects. Chemical control of pests would certainly help prevent some of this tragic loss, as would more adequate storage facilities. Yet, pesticides raise an environmental dilemma. Many such chemicals remain in the environment, and some become more concentrated as they move up through the food chain. DDT is one example.

Weeds are another menace to better crop production. Weeds compete with crops for sunlight and nutrients; hence, their control is another way to improve yields. Again the major means of control is the use of chemicals with their potential to create serious environmental problems.

In the developing countries, tradeoffs between increasing food production and preserving the environment often are unavoidable. Because food supplies must be increased, some risks are regarded as acceptable.

Irrigation

Although many large areas of the world receive sufficient rainfall to meet their agricultural requirements, many of the most densely populated countries are located in the drier climatic regions. Many of these countries are poor and do not have the resources to purchase food from other areas. Therefore, for many of these countries to produce enough food to feed their populations, it is imperative that they develop irrigation facilities. In the several thousand years since irrigation was first developed in the Middle East, it has diffused gradually throughout the world. Much of the increase in irrigated lands, however, has taken place in the past four decades. Between 1950 and 1985 the amount of irrigated land nearly tripled, a major factor in the explosive growth of world food production.

Irrigated agricultural land plays an important role in feeding the world's growing population and in providing an adequate living for rural populations. For example, in Pakistan 65 percent of its farmland is under irrigation, producing 80 percent of the country's food supply. In India 30 percent of cultivated land is under irrigation, and this area produces 55 percent of the food output. Similarly, 50 percent of China's croplands are irrigated, accounting for 70 percent of all the food produced (Hinrichsen and Marshall, 1991, 30).

The irrigated area grew most rapidly between 1950 and 1980, with an annual rate of almost 4 percent (Figure 11–8). However, the first half of the 1980s has seen irrigated land expand at a rate of less than 1 percent per year. After an initial rapid expansion of irrigated land, the amount of land being taken out of production has been rising while the amount of new land being put under irrigation has been declining. Also, there has been a decrease in the irrigated acreage per person on a worldwide basis (Ehrlich, 1991, 225). The reason for taking irrigated land out of production is primarily associated with what the FAO calls the three "silent enemies"—alkalization, salinization, and waterlogging.

In some countries we find that the amount of irrigated land is actually declining. In Africa, for example, a review of irrigation projects by Biswas (1985, 35) pointed out that "the development of new irrigation areas has barely surpassed the surface of older ones which had to be abandoned."

Only about 12 percent of the earth's cultivated land is currently being irrigated, although approximately one half of the world's food comes from these areas. Thus, on the surface it appears that there is a significant potential for expanding irrigation. However, the expansion of irrigation is limited both by the uneven distribution of water and the high capital costs of major irrigation projects.

Water will, however, be a key factor in raising agricultural output. Many scholars have attributed at least part of the failure of the so-called Green Revolution to inadequate water supplies.

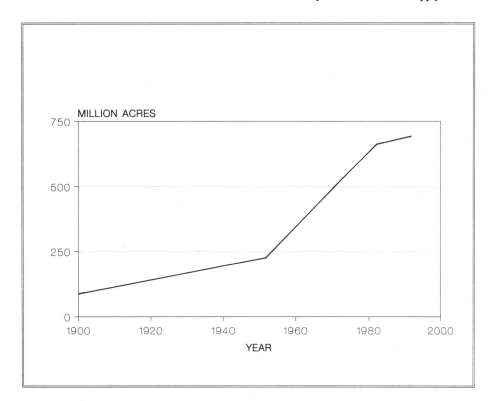

▪ **FIGURE 11–8** World Irrigated Cropland, 1900–1989. SOURCE: Lester Brown, "Feeding Six Billion," *Worldwatch,* Sept.–Oct. 1989: 35. Reprinted with permission.

New Strains of Plants and the Green Revolution

Since the beginning of the Agricultural Revolution, improvements in crops and livestock have made notable contributions to increasing the quantity and improving the quality of the human diet. Revolutions of varying dimensions have occurred many times over the past 10,000 years. Farmers have gradually kept and improved a few major plant species, while myriads of others have long since disappeared from the diets of most of the world's people.

Among such "revolutions" would be found the exchange of crops between the Old and New World, an exchange that began perhaps 500 years ago and continues even today, an exchange that certainly increased the world's food-producing capacity. (Consider Ireland before the potato, for instance.)

More recently a number of "revolutions" have resulted from discoveries in plant genetics which have led to the development of higher-yielding cereals. Hybrid plants also may be developed to better tolerate environmental conditions such as cold or drought, to be more resistant to problematic diseases, or to be more responsive to fertilizers. Improved strains of corn have been grown in the United States for several decades with good results. The breeding of short-season corn has extended the range of corn production in northern latitudes as much as 500 miles.

But the "Green Revolution" that has attracted the world's attention refers primarily to the so-called "miracle strains" of wheat and rice developed in the mid-1960s. These new strains are shorter and stiffer-strawed than traditional varieties. They are highly responsive to chemical fertilizers, mature earlier than traditional varieties, and have a reduced sensitivity to variations in the length of days. This latter property creates increased opportunities for multiple cropping.

The spread of the high-yielding varieties of wheat and rice occurred quite rapidly. Among the major countries to benefit from these new strains are India, Pakistan, the Philippines, and Indonesia. Countries sometimes went rapidly from being net grain importers to being net grain exporters.

Throughout the 1970s food production at least kept pace with population growth, thanks mainly to the new seeds. Some countries, such as India, Pakistan, the Philippines, and Thailand, proved that yields could be substantially increased by peasant farmers when conditions were favorable. By the end of the 1970s new varieties of corn, sorghum, and soybeans were available along with the new strains of rice and wheat. However, other crops still await significant improvement.

The Green Revolution was a major advance in international agricultural development, yet the agricultural progress made possible was not evenly distributed. The aggregate statistics hide a significant group of farmers who have not benefitted from the new technologies. Most of these farmers bypassed by the Green Revolution were subsistence farmers who were raising food for their families on rain-fed, marginal land. According to Dalrymple (1986) only about one third of the land planted to cereal grains in the Third World uses the high-yielding varieties. The rates of adoption also vary widely by region, with Africa having the lowest adoption rate, at only 1 percent of the grain area, Latin America with 22 percent, and Asia and the Middle East with the highest percentage of adoption with 36 percent of the grain area.

As Brown (1981, 34) noted, "Traditional farmers must also be trained and encouraged to use new techniques: how and when to plant the new seeds; how to control weeds, insects, and disease; and how to conserve and manage water." However, training programs are too often inefficient and poorly financed. Also, many countries still fail to provide sufficient incentives to encourage small farmers to adopt new seeds and more efficient farming techniques.

Although the Green Revolution undoubtedly helped in the battle against hunger, it has not been a panacea for food problems in the developing countries. In fact, rapid advances in agricultural production sometimes produced a complacency about population growth in these countries.

Young (1992, 97) believes that although the biotechnology industry could be an important weapon in the future fight to eradicate hunger, the industry is controlled largely by corporations who have little interest in plant research related to Third World food crops. "Firmer tomatoes and herbicide-tolerant corn, not hardier rice or cassava, are their objectives. These companies are not sinking money into less-profitable plant research that might help close the widening gap between the growth in world food supplies and that in human numbers."

World food production varies from year to year in response to climate, among other factors. Each swing upward or downward in production tends to generate a new wave of optimism or pessimism. The world currently produces enough food to provide everyone with a nearly adequate diet, yet hundreds of millions, mainly in the developing countries, are undernourished. Even when diets are adequate in terms of calories, they are often inadequate in terms of nutrients, especially protein. Such inadequacies lead to nutrient deficiency diseases such as kwashiorkor, which is caused by severe protein deficiency.

The specter of Malthus is regularly called upon in discussions of population growth versus food supplies in the developing countries. Although not always for the same reasons, experts generally agree that slowing the rate of world population growth is, if not an absolute necessity, at least a way of easing other problems. It is tempting at this point to agree with the following statement by Abercrombie and McCormack (1976, 489):

> It is becoming abundantly clear that the last quarter of this century is likely to be one of the most crucial periods in the history of mankind's efforts to feed a growing population. On the one hand, there is general agreement that if the right action is taken, population growth can be reduced, the increase in food production accelerated, and the purchasing power of the poorest people raised sufficiently for the virtual elimination of hunger and malnutrition by the end of the century. This could lay the foundations for a widely shared prosperity in the more distant future. On the other hand, the alternative is not hard to visualize. If sufficient political will cannot be found for the massive action that is necessary, there will not only be widespread starvation but also a gradual drift downward in the nutritional levels of the poorest people. This too might lead to eventual prosperity for a stabilized population, but the reduction in population growth would have resulted from higher infant mortality rather than deliberate fertility limitation.

▨ FOOD AND PEOPLE

Despite the impressive gains in agriculture brought about by better technology, irrigation, genetic engineering, and chemical fertilizers, there still appears, often among knowledgeable and competent scientists, the growing fear of creeping Malthusianism. On the other hand, there are scientists who feel that continued advances will keep the growth in food supplies somewhat ahead of population growth for awhile longer. Most would agree that a decline in the rate of population growth would ease the strain on resources and possibly allow adequate diets for an increasing proportion of the world's people. Some of these differing views are discussed in the following section.

The Paddocks and Triage

William and Paul Paddock, in a revised edition of an earlier book, made the following statement (1976, 8–9):

> A locomotive is roaring full-throttle down the track. Just around the bend an impenetrable mudslide has oozed across the track. There it lies, inert, static, deadly. Nothing can stop the locomotive in time. Catastrophe is foredoomed. Miles back up the track the locomotive could have been warned and stopped. Years ago the mud-soaked hill could have been shored up to forestall the landslide. Now it is too late.

The locomotive roaring straight at us is the population explosion. The unmovable landslide across the tracks is the stagnant production of food in the undeveloped nations, the nations where the population increases are greatest.

The collision is inevitable. The famines are inevitable. After accepting the veracity of the above statement, the Paddocks suggest that the most reasonable solution to the situation is to employ the concept of triage as a means of allocating America's food surplus to the "hungry nations."

The term *triage* has been used mainly in military medicine. It is a method of assigning treatment priorities to the wounded by classifying them into three categories: (1) those so seriously wounded that they will die regardless of the treatment they receive, (2) those who will survive without treatment, and (3) those who will live providing they receive prompt medical attention. Scarce medical resources, including doctors, may then be best allocated by treating those in the third category, thus allowing doctors to save the maximum number of lives. The Paddocks suggest that such a system should be used to classify the hungry nations of the world into the following three categories: (1) those who cannot be saved because of population growth and the lack of agricultural potential and leadership ability; (2) those who have sufficient resources, in agriculture and/or foreign exchange, to adequately deal with their population growth; and (3) those in which there is an imbalance between population growth and food supply which would be manageable if aid were received. Thus, the Paddocks suggest that America's scarce foreign aid resources can be best allocated if they are directed toward the countries in the third category.

As an approach to the solution of the world food crisis, triage seems attractive to a significant number of people. Too often, however, those same people have an inadequate understanding of the relationship between population growth and food supplies. Furthermore, the argument is morally questionable. *The New York Times* referred to this use of triage as "one of the most pessimistic and threadbare intellectual positions to be advanced since the demise of the Third Reich." (Cited in Simon, 1975, 36)

Hardin and the Lifeboat Ethic

Hardin, an eminent scientist, has popularized a view of the rich and the poor countries in an analogy using lifeboats. The rich countries are viewed as lifeboats filled almost to capacity. The addition of more people threatens to sink them, hence drowning everyone. The poor, of course, are struggling to enter the lifeboats and, hence, must be pushed away if the rich countries are to survive. In other words, in Hardin's view, feeding those in the hungry nations threatens those in the lifeboats, so it is not the thing to do. Like triage, the moral nature of this argument is extremely weak. Simon (1975, 36) challenged:

> Behind the lifeboat and triage theories lie some frightening, unspoken assumptions about the value of life. Is a hungry, impoverished Asian child less human, with less reason to live and less right to live, than our own children? Playing God in this regard is especially dangerous because we are easily seduced by answers that protect our own advantages, even if they cost lives. Furthermore, as many have already pointed out, the analogy itself is questionable. Why, for instance, are the rich countries portrayed as lifeboats rather than, as some have suggested, luxury liners?

▓ IS THERE HOPE?

Without question millions of people in today's world are hungry and malnourished, nor is there any doubt that everywhere the poor suffer the most. But do we take such a dim view of this large proportion of humanity that we simply turn our heads and disregard their existence? Fortunately, many think not.

No serious view of the future suggests that solving food and population problems will be easy or automatic. However, in his essay on raising agricultural productivity, Wolf (1987, 156) concluded that: "The world is far from having solved the problems of agricultural productivity. The conventional approach to raising productivity—combining new crop varieties with fertilizers, pesticides, and heavy use of energy—succeeded dramatically in increasing food production in industrial countries and in parts of the Third World. But new approaches are needed to reach farmers who could not afford to follow this path, as well as to correct inequities in the distribution of environmental problems.

Complementing the use of conventional resources with innovative biological technologies that maximize agriculture's internal resources can begin to achieve affordable and sustainable gains in agricultural productivity."

Although mass starvation appears unlikely in the near future, the 1990s promise to be a decade in which hunger and malnutrition remain widespread, especially in Third World countries. The specter of Malthusianism is unlikely to disappear in the decades ahead. More *people* implies a need for more *food*. Food supplies can be increased though possibly not without threatening the environment. Raising yields on land already under cultivation remains the best alternative for expanding food supplies in the years ahead.

Although it is scientifically possible to feed a growing population, given today's technology, the *major* determinants of success are political, social, and economic. Moral, rather than scientific, questions must be answered. For example, should the developed countries help feed the less fortunate ones? How can an equitable distribution of food be assured? Such questions cannot be answered by science alone.

REFERENCES

Abercrombie, Keith and McCormack, Arthur. (1976) "Population Growth and Food Supplies in Different Time Perspectives," *Population and Development Review* 2:479–498.

Biswas, Asit K. (1985) "Evaluating Irrigation's Impact: Guidelines for Project Monitoring," *Ceres* July/August 1985.

Brown, Lester R. (1976) *World Population Trends: Signs of Hope, Signs of Stress.* Worldwatch Paper No. 8, Washington, D.C.: Worldwatch Institute.

Brown, Lester R. (1981) "World Food Resources and Population: The Narrowing Margin," *Population Bulletin* 36(3):1–43.

Brown, Lester R. (1987) *State of the World—1987.* New York: W.W. Norton and Company.

Brown, Lester R. (1989) "Feeding Six Billion," *Worldwatch* September/October:32–40.

Brown, Lester R. and Young, John E. (1990) "Feeding the World in the Nineties," in Lester R. Brown, *State of the World 1990.* NY: W. W. Norton and Company, pp. 59–78.

Dalrymple, Dana G. (1986) *Development and Spread of High-yielding Rice Varieties in Developing Countries.* Washington, D.C.: U. S. Agency for International Development.

Durning, Alan and Brough, Holly. (1992) "Reforming the Livestock Industry," in Lester R. Brown, ed. *State of the World 1992.* New York: W. W. Norton and Company, pp. 66–83.

Ehrlich, Anne H. (1991) "People and Food," *Population and Environment* 12(3):221–231.

FAO (Food and Agricultural Organization). (1987) *Agriculture: Toward 2000.* Rome, Italy: FAO.

Grigg, D. B. (1980) *Population Growth and Agrarian Change: An Historical Perspective.* Cambridge: Cambridge University Press.

Harlan, Jack R. (1976) "The Plants and Animals that Nourish Man," *Scientific American* 235(3):88–97.

Hendry, Peter. (1988) "Food and Population: Beyond Five Billion," *Population Bulletin* 43(2): 1–40.

Hinrichsen, Don and Marshall, Alex. (1991) "Population and the Food Crisis," *Populi* 16(2): 24–34.

Knight, C. Gregory and Wilcox, R. Paul. (1976) *Triumph or Triage: The World Food Problem in Geographical Perspective.* Resource Paper No. 75–3. Washington, D.C.: Association of American Geographers.

Paddock, William and Paddock, Paul. (1976) *Time of Famines: America and the World Food Crisis*. Boston: Little, Brown and Company.

Reutlinger, Shlomo. (1985) "Food Security and Poverty in LDC's," *Finance and Development* December 1985.

Sanderson, Fred H. (1975) "The Great Food Fumble," *Science* 188:503–509.

Scrimshaw, Nevin S. and Taylor, Lance. (1980) "Food," *Scientific American* 243(3):78–88.

Simon, Arthur. (1975) *Bread for the World*. New York: Paulist Press.

Simon, Julian R. (1983) "Life on Earth is Getting Better, Not Worse," *The Futurist* August: 7–12.

Tarrant, John R. (1990) "World Food Prospects for the 1990's," *Journal of Geography* 89(6): 234–238.

United States Department of Agriculture. (1974) Economic Research Service. *The World Food Situation and Prospects to 1985*. Foreign Agricultural Economic Report No. 98, Washington, D.C.: United States Government Printing Office.

Wolf, Edward C. (1987) "Raising Agricultural Productivity," in Lester Brown, ed. *State of the World—1987*. New York: W.W. Norton.

Woods, Richard G., ed. (1981) *Future Dimensions of World Food and Population*. A Winrock International Study, Boulder, Colorado: Westview Press.

Wortman, Sterling. (1976) "Food and Agriculture," *Scientific American* 235(3):30–39.

Young, John E. (1992) "Bred for the Hungry," in Robert M. Jackson, ed. *Global Issues: 1992/1993*. Guilford, CT: Dushkin Publishing Company, pp. 97–104.

Chapter 12

Population Issues: Practical Applications and Case Studies

Population factors are important variables to consider in many aspects of everyday life. Almost every week the media—television, radio, magazines, and newspapers—refer to population issues and their impact on United States society. Population changes associated with birth, death, and migration are the bases for many social, political, and economic problems troubling today's world. Understanding these changes and their critical implications for the future must be a top priority of business, education, and government leaders, as well as of the ordinary citizen.

Demographic data and analyses provide important information for a variety of planning purposes. The Federal Government spends millions of dollars for demographic studies, and demographic expertise is essential to help state governments compete for the billions of dollars in federal funds allocated on the basis of population. The Defense Department relies on population information to plan its recruitment for the volunteer army. Demographic projections form the basis of education decisions by local school districts, particularly when decisions are made about school openings and closings.

The political process is also impacted by demographic variables. The 1990 Census of the United States was the basis for changes in the House of Representatives where some states, like Florida and Texas, gained seats while others, like New York State, lost seats. These new congressional members joined their colleagues in discussions about a host of population-related issues such as teenage pregnancy, abortion, illegal immigration, Social Security taxes, foreign aid, the Sunbelt-Frostbelt migration, and others.

In this chapter we consider a variety of population issues. The first part of the chapter analyzes the role of population dynamics in the world of business and discusses population variables that have a significant impact on the business community. The second part of the chapter discusses the importance of population analysis in educational decisions. The final section presents case studies of three countries, Cuba, China, and Sweden, to illustrate a variety of population issues. Because the spatial or geographic aspect of population is the primary focus of the book, the importance of population geography is highlighted and illustrated in the analysis of these population issues and case studies.

▨ POPULATION DYNAMICS AND THE WORLD OF BUSINESS

Demographic considerations and their spatial or geographic components play an important role in today's business world. Understanding these issues is of vital importance to business executives, who are increasingly turning to demographic experts for answers to a variety of problems. Business executives need to "understand population changes and their impact on basic corporate decisions such as labor supply, location of facilities, the changing nature of markets, and the age makeup of consumer groups" (Hyatt, 1979, 1).

Marketing relies heavily on demographic statistics and their spatial or geographic aspects. Market segmentation and differentiation now play a key role in marketing strategies. According to Francese and Renaghan (1991, 50), "many markets have become too complicated and too unforgiving to rely on just one or two demographic variables." A variety of variables, such as income, education, and age, have a symbiotic relationship and together form the basis of "database marketing." For marketers to succeed in the future, they will have to understand the multi-dimensional demographic profiles of their market segment.

The formation of households is an important variable to consider by planners for such utility firms as Pacific Gas and Electric and Chesapeake and Potomac Telephone. Changing fertility rates and divorce rates, as well as the increase in the number of late marriages, have a tremendous impact on household formation and thus are important variables when predicting consumer demand for utilities. The design of equal opportunity employment policies by the General Motors Corporation involved considerable input of geographic population data. The company needed to know where to find female and minority workers. The American Medical Association employs a population analyst who studies the mobility of doctors and the reasons that prompt doctors to move. These are just a few examples of the usefulness of population geography in the business world. Some population changes are obvious, whereas others are hidden. Some present important business opportunities, while others cause setbacks. All population changes are important, however.

Business Forecasting

Business people are always interested in the future. They are concerned about next week's sales, next year's profits, future changes in interest rates, and five-year capital investment schemes. Their natural tendency, however, has been to focus on the next fiscal quarter instead of the next quarter century. Short-term symptoms always seem to overshadow long-run causes. Worries about short-term problems tend to obscure the longer run; and, equally important, they obscure changes in population variables. For example, a home builder is usually concerned with changes in interest rates, but a shift in the divorce rate or a shift in migration patterns could be equally as important to that industry. Builders have only recently begun to appreciate the impact of the "Baby Boom" on various types of construction.

The impact of population change on business forecasting has recently taken on added importance. In a study on changing demographics and the future of business, James Hyatt observed that "while only a few years ago the attention was on worldwide population growth rates, analysts are beginning to understand that for the United States a much more complex set of population shifts are at work. Fast, slow, and no growth are all occurring at the same time in different parts of the country" (Hyatt, 1979, 5). This important geographic dimension of population change is now receiving more attention from business forecasters.

Many of the present and future problems and opportunities to be faced by business have their roots in the most striking demographic phenomenon of twentieth-century America: the unique high fertility period that followed World War II, the so-called "baby boom." During the baby boom period, between 1946 and 1964, there were nearly 60 million births in the United States, 50 percent more than during the preceding 15 years. The baby boom or "bulge" has far-reaching effects in housing, employment, retail sales, education, and many other areas of concern to the business community. According to Hyatt, "Business managers would be well advised to keep in mind the location of that bulge from year to year, just as they pay attention to other economic indicators" (Hyatt, 1979, 5).

In 1991 the first baby boomers, those born in 1946, reached their 45th birthday. According to Waldrop (1991, 24), "It will begin a population explosion among affluent, maturing householders. And it will turn the 1990s into peak years for consumer spending." These baby boomers entering midlife will bring about changes in a variety of business services. For example, the 1990s will see a rise in consumer demand for bifocal eyeglasses as those midlife boomers undergo inevitable changes due to the aging process. Visual and hearing impairments increase significantly after age 45.

Increasing attention will be paid to health concerns and boomers, in order to stay fit, will have to become more selective about food choices. Talk of ice cream and twinkies gradually gives way to conversations about cholesterol, monounsaturated fats, and triglycerides. This will most likely bring about a rise in consumption of food items like fish, poultry, low-fat milk, whole grain cereals, and fresh fruits and vegetables.

Although much of the attention of the business community has been focused on the young, there has been an increasing awareness of the aged and the aging of America (Soldo and Agree, 1988). Indeed, adults over age 65 now outnumber teenagers and have become one of the fastest-growing population groups in the country. In 1900, only 3.1 million people in the United States were 65 years of age and older; but by 1985 that figure reached 28.5 million, and projections for the year 2030 are that there will be 64.6 million. In 1985, one in nine Americans or 11.7 percent of the population was at least 65 years old; but by 2010, because of the maturation of the baby boomers, one in seven Americans will be at least 65 years old (Hooyman and Kiyak, 1988, 22).

As baby boomers become "senior" boomers, important "public policy questions regarding how we will support the needs of a growing older population and how we will structure policies to assure a fair and equitable distribution of resources for all age groups" must be addressed (Bouvier and DeVita, 1991, 27). Government bureaucracies, charged with planning the provision of services for the elderly, will be faced with a variety of decisions with both political and social consequences (Laws, 1991, 32). Some of these problems will be further complicated by the changing ethnic and racial composition of the United States.

Not only will there be more older Americans but because of their relatively high disposable incomes, they will present a growing market for the business community. England (1987, 8) points out that "Americans over age 65 are the second-richest age group in U.S. society. Only those Americans in the next-oldest age bracket, from 55 to 64, are better off." The aged have assets nearly twice that of the median for the nation. "The spending power of the mature market may be one of the best-kept secrets left in the age of demographic scrutiny (Lazer, 1985, 23)."

Zero Population Growth and Business

To most entrepreneurs the word "growth" is a magic trigger word, because they are naturally attracted to growth—be it in profits, sales, or incomes. Investors usually look for firms with solid growth records. Also, to most business managers a growing gross national product (GNP) means a stronger economy with more consumer spending, more employment, and more sales and services. There is, therefore, understandable trepidation by businesses when they contemplate the prospects of a slowing, or even cessation, of population growth. They fear reduced demand, which in turn means less profit, smaller dividends, more unemployment, and general economic uncertainty.

The impact of population growth on the economy of the United States is assumed to be positive because it has continued for so long. Economic theorists have, however, found it difficult to find a direct correlation between population growth and economic well-being in highly industrialized nations. During parts of the nineteenth century, population growth was high yet per capita income growth was modest. On the other hand, in the twentieth century, population growth slowed down while the GNP remained high.

Labor Force

The composition and quality of the labor force are important variables for human resource managers to consider. During the next few decades, the composition of the labor force will be considerably different from what it has been in the past. There will be more workers, and they will be better educated. There will be more minorities, and more will be female and the mothers of young children. The number of older workers over age 55 will be fewer in the next decade. Paradoxically, the average age of the labor force will be increasing. Many of these changes in the United States will be direct results of the baby boom. Millions of baby boom youths have been absorbed into the labor force.

The supply of workers available for businesses will be the result of two separate trends in the labor force. First is the size of the working age population, and second is the labor force participation rate. Among the most important demographic variables in determining the size of the work force is the age structure of the population. The bulge in the young working force cohort is now progressing through the population, so the number of young people entering the work force will be declining.

At the other end of the work force age spectrum, among those over 55 years of age, important changes also will take place. Changing attitudes about retirement could have far-reaching impacts on the corporate world. Can business easily absorb those older workers who decide to continue their careers? Will companies find it harder to promote young workers if retirement ages advance? Will older workers continue to be productive? These are all important questions to personnel managers and are underlain by demographic changes in society.

▨ EDUCATION ROLLER COASTER

The nation's education system, perhaps more than any other social institution, has been greatly affected by fertility variations. The impact of the postwar baby boom children on the schools was dramatic, costly, and painful. In the late 1950s and 1960s school enrollments soared. The elementary-school-age population (5 to 13 years) grew from 23 million in 1950 to 37 million in 1970. Secondary schools faced similar problems by the early 1960s, and the high school population doubled in size between 1950 and 1975 (Bouvier, 1980, 21). High school enrollments rose 14 percent in 1957 alone, and a critical shortage in classrooms was evident. Administrators projected a need for an additional 750,000 teachers in three years. This demand caused a rapid increase in school budgets.

School planners were totally unprepared for this rapid increase in enrollments. By the time colleges had geared up to graduate enough teachers and massive building programs had produced enough elementary and secondary classrooms, the crest of the baby boom wave was about to leave the school ages.

The mid-1960s saw enrollments in colleges and universities skyrocket. This increase was a result of both the sheer numbers of baby boomers and the increased proportion of young people going to college. In the 1950s only about 10 percent of those between ages 25 to 29 had completed at least four years of college. That proportion increased to 16 percent by 1970 and 23 percent by 1980. Between 1957 and 1975 college enrollments increased from 3 million to 11 million. The baby boom generation thus became the most highly educated generation in American history (Bouvier and DeVita, 1991, 14).

The major change in school enrollment in the past two decades has been a significant increase in nursery and preschool attendance. The percentage enrolled in nursery schools, pre-kindergarten or kindergarten programs, or child-care centers with an "educational" curriculum, increased from 11 percent in 1965 to 38 percent in 1988 (Bianchi, 1990, 30).

Today, another school turnaround is underway. After years of stable or declining enrollments, the school-age population is projected to increase by about 8 percent during the decade of the 1990s. This increase will be the result of the baby boomers' children filling the elementary and secondary schools across the country (Bouvier and DeVita, 1991, 15).

Geographic Differences

To understand these educational trends and their demographic causes, it is necessary to look beyond national statistics and to understand regional or more local circumstances. The geographic distribution of the population, as well as spatial differences in vital rates, presents a complicated picture. For example, the decline in births was not uniform across the United States in the 1960s and early 1970s. In some areas the peak in births was attained in 1957, whereas in other areas it was not reached until 1960 (Reinhardt, 1979, 10). Also, the decline in births within states was not uniform, and there were significant differences between metropolitan and nonmetropolitan areas.

These geographic differences, as well as other changes in population distribution, mean that some areas have had dramatic declines in the school-age population, whereas others have still been growing. Many rural areas and urban regions losing population have experienced dramatic declines; but many newly developing suburbs have enrollment increases, as do some inner-city areas. Nursery school attendance is more common in the Northeast than in other U. S. regions, and among children who live outside the central cities of metropolitan areas (Bianchi, 1990, 30).

Migration has also had a significant impact on school-age populations. Increases can be seen throughout much of the Sunbelt and the West, with declines in the Midwest and the Northeast. An analysis of college-age students also points out significant spatial differences, with many Sunbelt and Western states being net importers of college students. Changes in demographic factors can have a significant impact on school planning policy decisions and should be incorporated into the decision-making process at all levels.

▨ REVOLUTIONARY CHANGE: THE CASE OF CUBA

Cuba has probably received more attention from policymakers, the mass media, and scholars than most developing countries. Although it only ranks eighth in size among Latin American nations, it is the most populous nation in the Caribbean. Cuba is about the size of Pennsylvania, and its 1991 population of 10.7 million compares closely with the 12 million inhabitants of that state.

TABLE 12–1 ▥ Population Growth in Cuba: 1899–1992

Census Year	Enumerated Population	Growth Between Censuses (Percent)	Net International Migration
1899	1,572,797[a]		
1907	2,048,980	33.9	127,357(1900–1909)
1919	2,889,004	29.1	233,535(1910–1919)
1931	3,962,344	26.6	268,062(1920–1929)
1943	4,778,583	15.9	−147,963(1930–1944)
1953	5,829,029	21.1	−21,920(1945/49–1953)
1970	8,569,121	22.1	
1979[b]	9,772,855		−582,742(1959–1978)
1986	10,221,000		
1992	10,800,000		

SOURCE: Sergio Diaz-Briquets and Lisandro Perez. (1981) "Cuba: The Demography of Revolution," *Population Bulletin*, 36(1):5 and World Population Data Sheet 1992.

The importance of Cuba, and the reason for its attention, is clearly not because of its size but rather its unique history of social and economic change. It was one of the last American nations to sever ties with Spain, and it had a long and close relationship with the United States. When the revolutionary movement led by Fidel Castro overthrew the government of Fulgencio Batista in 1959, it became the first socialist nation in the Western Hemisphere, only 83 miles from Florida.

The social and economic revolution has had a profound impact on the socioeconomic fabric of the nation. Along with, and partly because of, this change in the social and economic order, the past few decades have brought about significant demographic changes. Among today's developing countries, Cuba probably has one of the lowest fertility rates (below replacement level) and one of the highest life expectancies.

Demographic Changes

Demographic changes in Cuba have been significantly different from those in most developing countries. It underwent its demographic transition before World War II, a time when most other developing countries had not started their transitions (Collver, 1965). The death rate started to decline in the early part of the twentieth century and birth rates started to fall in the 1920s. Migration also played an important role in Cuba's demographic development, with a large influx of African slaves and Chinese indentured servants in the nineteenth century, along with hundreds of thousands of Spaniards and other Europeans. As illustrated in Table 12–1, and quite unlike other developing countries, Cuba experienced a decline in its population growth rate from the beginning of the century to the immediate post-World War II period, and then, as with other developing countries, growth accelerated because of a decline in mortality.

Mortality Changes

Demographic trends in mortality prior to the revolution were primarily shaped by economic circumstances. The introduction of sanitary reforms during the United States' occupation of 1899–1902 and a vigorous economy fueled by large-scale foreign investments in the sugar industry during the first quarter of the twentieth century brought about a significant decline in mortality (Diaz-Briquets, 1977). With the depression of the 1920s and 1930s and its disastrous consequences for the Cuban economy, mortality rates stabilized. With the advent of modern drugs and insecticides following World War II, Cuba's mortality rates, like those of most other developing countries, experienced an accelerated decline.

On the eve of the communist revolution in 1958 Cuba was one of the most demographically advanced developing nations, with a life expectancy of over 60 years. Among developing countries of the Western Hemisphere, this life expectancy was surpassed only by those of Jamaica, Puerto Rico, Argentina, and Uruguay. Since the revolution, an enormous effort has been put into the development of medical facilities. Currently, virtually free or very low-cost medical coverage is available across Cuba through a system of polyclinics and rural, regional, provincial, and national hospitals (Danielson, 1979).

As the result of the development of medical programs, Cuba has now achieved excellent health standards with life expectancy of 76 years (1991), higher than that of the United States. Infant mortality was down to 10.7 per thousand live births by 1991, compared to 9.1 per thousand in the United States. Cuba's crude death rate in 1991 was 6.0, far below that of the United States, which was 9.0. This figure for Cuba reflects both the young age of the population and significant health improvements. As in developed countries, the leading causes of death have shifted from infectious to degenerative diseases.

Fertility Changes

Information about pre-revolution fertility is scarce, but the limited data suggest a decline in births during the depression years of the 1920s and the 1930s. This was the result of delayed marriages and more widespread adoption of abortion as a fertility limitation method (Gonzalez et al., 1978). Following World War II the crude birth rate stabilized in the low 30s, and by the eve of the revolution it had dropped to the mid to upper 20s.

Although fertility has fluctuated since the revolution, the general trend has been significantly downward (Figure 12–1). A few years before the revolution, the birth rate was around 26 per 1000. With the advent of the revolution in 1959, the birth rate rose from 26.1 in 1958 to 35.1 in 1963. This was the highest birth rate in the post-revolutionary period and similar to the level of the 1920s. After 1963 the birth rate fell, with only a brief rise in 1971, attributed to the disruption of normal activities in 1970 in an all-out effort to produce 10 million tons of sugar cane. Thousands of workers were moved from the city to rural areas to help with the harvesting, and the rise in

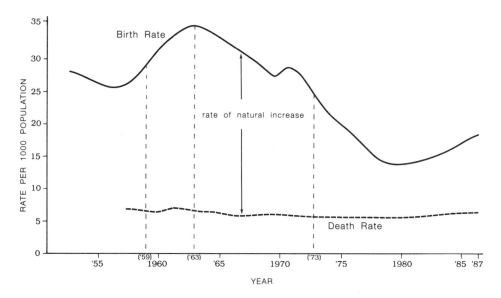

▨ **FIGURE 12–1** Cuba—Birth and Death Rates, 1953–1992. SOURCE: Sergio Diaz-Briquets and Lisandro Perez. (1981) "Cuba: The Demography of Revolution," *Population Bulletin* 36(1):13 and *1992 World Population Data Sheet.*

1971 might have been a reflection of the births averted in 1970 during the harvest. Also, the late 1960s and early 1970s saw a marked increase in marriages.

A dramatic decline occurred in the birth rate from 1973 to 1979, a decline of 40 percent. Overall, there was a 58 percent decline, 20.3 points in the birth rate, between 1963 and 1979. Since 1980, there has been a slight increase in the birth rate. Cuba's 1991 rate of natural increase of 1.1 percent compares with 0.7 for the United States and makes Cuba's rate among the lowest in the developing countries.

Though the age structure of the Cuban population tends to exaggerate this fertility decline, as depicted in the crude birth rate, other fertility measures also point toward a significant decline. Between 1970 and 1978 the total fertility rate dropped by nearly half, from 3.7 to an estimated 1.9 births per woman. The increase in births in the early 1960s can be directly attributed to the social, political, and economic changes brought about by the revolution. The primary factor behind the rise was probably the rise in real income among the poorer groups, who then felt that the future was more promising and that they could afford more children. At the same time marriage rates went up and the average age at marriage declined. There was also a shortage of fertility limitation and contraception materials—the result of the economic blockade of Cuba by the United States—and the disruption of contraceptive supplies as well as governmental restrictions on abortion.

An analysis of this birth rate surge shows distinct geographical differences (Figure 12–2). Birth rates increased most in the more urbanized provinces like Havanna, where

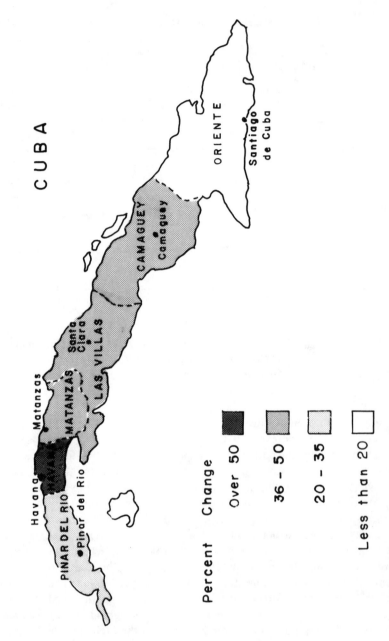

■ **FIGURE 12–2** Change in Crude Birth Rate by Province: 1958 and 1963. SOURCE: Compiled by authors from statistical data published by the Republic of Cuba.

the rate went up almost 60 percent between 1958 and 1963. In the least urbanized or modernized provinces, like Oriente, the rate rose only 17 percent.

The causes of fertility decline since 1963 are many and varied. The proximate determinants of the decline—changes in trends of abortion, marriage, divorce, and contraception use—are relatively easy to trace. Restrictions on abortion were eased in 1964 as part of changes in health laws. Since that time free hospital abortions have become available on request to women aged 18 and over during the first ten weeks of pregnancy. Later abortions are also available with a physician's permission. There has been a drop in abortion rates since Cuba's high in 1974 of 69.5 abortions per 1000 women aged 15 to 44. The drop suggests an increase in the use of contraceptives (Hollerbach, 1980). Though national statistics on contraceptive use are not available, evidence reviewed by Hollerbach (1980) suggests that contraceptive use is widespread. The IUD is the most prevalent form of contraception, with the pill second in usage.

The marriage rate has fluctuated since the revolution, the rate of 6.2 per 1000 population in 1978 was considerably less than the 10.8 per 1000 marriage rate in the United States. This decline could have contributed to the fertility decline, as could the fivefold increase in divorce rates since the revolution. Many socioeconomic changes since the revolution have also played a key role in fertility decline. One thing is certain: the decline was not the result of official antinatalist policies. The government's ideological position is that overpopulation is not one of the causes of poverty. The prevailing view is that changes brought about by the revolution have eroded societal norms favoring childbearing. A good summary of this viewpoint is presented in Hollerbach (1980, 100):

> The decline in fertility, especially rapid since 1973, has not been achieved through antinatalist policies (such as those of China), nor through the creation of demographic targets, which are characteristics of policies in some developing nations. Rather a variety of economic and political factors are responsible, the most significant of which have been increased educational levels . . . adult education programs and expanded enrollment in higher education; the urbanization of rural areas through the concentration of social services and development projects there; construction of small urban communities, and reduction of disparities between urban and rural income levels; and more recently, the incorporation of women into the labor force.

Hollerbach's main emphasis, as with those of other demographic analyses of Cuba, is that modernization has been primarily responsible for these demographic changes. Cuba's experience, therefore, has valuable lessons to be exported to other developing nations throughout the world (Harrison, 1980).

There are other demographic analysts, however, who believe that the view that Cuba's population has been affected uniformly and almost exclusively by modernization sparked by the revolution needs to be complemented by looking at other factors.

They believe that modernization explains the demographic changes for the most dis-advantaged groups in Cuba but that economic setbacks, particularly in recent years, also have had an impact. Their central argument is that different sectors of Cuban society have limited their fertility for different, though overlapping, reasons. According to a study by Diaz-Briquets and Perez (1981, 22):

> Cuba's fertility decline since the mid-1960s has been a response to difficult eco-nomic conditions as well as to the undoubted progress made in many social areas. This more comprehensive explanation makes it questionable that poor, high-fertility countries around the world might draw a lesson from Cuba's experience, as has often been asserted. The political, historical, and social context that produced the Cuban revolution is unique in many ways, and the fertility response appears to be just as unique.

Consequences of Fertility Changes

Unlike other developing countries, Cuba experienced a baby boom and bust sim-ilar to those in many developed nations like Canada and the United States. The large bulge in Cuba's population pyramid (Figure 12–3) illustrates the large number of people in the 10 to 24 year age group. The 10 to 19 age group bulge is a result of the baby boom in the 1960s and the marked decline in infant mortality rates at that time. The narrow base of the pyramid reflects the more recent fertility decline.

Like other countries that have experienced large changes in fertility rates, Cuba has had, and will continue to have, problems trying to adjust to the varying sizes in age cohorts. Cuba has had population-related problems similar to those in the United States. Perez (1977) has pointed out the problems of suddenly needing to accommo-date large numbers of children in the school system and of having large numbers of people attempting to enter the labor force at a time when job prospects are dim. Re-ports of increases in Cuba's crime rate can be associated with age structure. An in-crease in people 15 to 24 years of age is probably part of the reason for the rise in crime because, as in many other countries, crime rates are highest in this age group (Salas, 1979, 195).

Further evidence of pressures from the changing age structure and its effect on Cuba's economy was apparent in the 1980 Mariel sealift. Although there is no con-clusive evidence of government orchestration, emigration from the port of El Mariel to the United States certainly was of benefit to the Cuban economy: "As if by magic, thousands of housing units became available, unemployment pressures were somewhat reduced, and many young people, among whom the crime rates were highest, left the country" (Diaz-Briquets and Perez, 1981, 24).

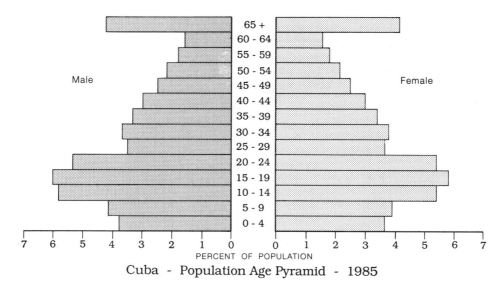

Cuba - Population Age Pyramid - 1985

▓ **FIGURE 12–3** Cuba—Population Age Pyramid: 1985. SOURCE: Compiled by authors from statistical data published by the Republic of Cuba.

Emigration

Migration has always played an important role in Cuba's population dynamics. During the nineteenth century large influxes of African slaves, Chinese indentured servants, Spaniards, and other Europeans migrated to Cuba. For the first three decades of the twentieth century migrants from Spain predominated although there were also significant numbers of migrants from Haiti, Jamaica, and other Latin American countries. Migration dwindled as an important factor by the early 1930s, then took on added importance again in the early 1960s. Between 1959 and 1980, approximately 800,000 people left Cuba for the United States (Table 12–2).

The most recent and largest wave of migrants came to the United States in the so-called Mariel sealift of April-September 1980. This emigration since 1960 from socialist Cuba is a reversal of the immigration pattern established in the nineteenth and early twentieth centuries. This most recent migration of Cubans to the United States has had a considerable impact on both Cuba and specific areas of the United States (Bach, 1980, 40), especially Florida. Continued migration to the United States is certainly possible and will depend on conditions in both Cuba and the United States.

TABLE 12–2 ▨ Cuban Migration to the
United States, 1959–1990

Year	Number
1959 (Jan. 1–June 30)	26,527
Year Ending June 30	
1960	60,224
1961	49,961
1962	78,611
1963	42,929
1964	15,616
1965	16,447
1966	46,688
1967	51,147
1968	55,945
1969	52,625
1970	49,545
1971	50,001
1972	23,977
1973	12,579
1974	13,670
1975	8,488
1976	4,515
Year Ending September 30	
1977	4,548
1978	4,108
1979	2,644
1980	122,061
Total, January 1, 1959– September 30, 1980	793,856
Total April 1–December 31, 1980	125,118
1981–1984	38,600
1985	20,300
1990	9,400

SOURCE: United States Department of Justice, Immigration and Naturalization Service (INS). (1980) "Cubans Arrived in the United States, by Class of Admission: January 1, 1959–September 30, 1980," October 1980, mimeo; and INS, Statistics Branch and *Statistical Abstract of the U.S., 1991.*

▧ CHINA: THE WORLD'S FIRST DEMOGRAPHIC BILLIONAIRE

At the end of the thirteenth century, before the exploration of the New World, the population of all of Europe was estimated at 75 million people. At the same time, the population of the Sung Dynasty already numbered 100 million. In the next six centuries the population increased to about 540 million in 1949.

Soon after this half-billion milestone was reached, China scholar John King Fairbank observed that, "the Chinese people's basic problem of livelihood is readily visible from the air: the brown eroded hills, the flood plains of muddy rivers, the crowded green fields . . . all the overcrowding of too many people upon too little land, and the attendant exhaustion of the land resources and of human ingenuity and fortitude in the effort to maintain life (Jacobson, 1991, 265)."

At about the same time Fairbank observed this overcrowding, the revolutionary leader of China, Mao Zedong, had other thoughts. In the early years following the Revolution, official policy more or less followed Marxist ideology. Marx argued that in the socialist state there would be no unemployment and no overpopulation. He felt that overpopulation was a function of the type of social and economic organization. Thus, overpopulation was a relative, rather than an absolute, situation.

However, following the 1953 census, which recorded a population of 583 million, there was an attempt to limit population growth. This early campaign was slow to get underway and was disrupted in 1958 by the Great Leap Forward. Following the Great Leap Forward, in 1962, the Chinese Government again began to promote family planning, but it lapsed into unpopularity again during the Cultural Revolution from 1966 to 1969. Since 1971 China has become what the demographer Tien (1983, 3) calls "a born-again advocate of population control."

In the early 1970s the Chinese government recognized the implications of population growth. The state family planning agency established a policy known as *wan-xi-shao,* which means "later-longer-fewer." This policy encouraged Chinese couples to marry later—preferably later than the average age of 20; to increase the time between births; and to have fewer children overall. Another slogan associated with this family planning program was, "One is not too few, two is good, and three is too many." Targets were set by the government for both family size and age at marriage. Recognizing the economic and cultural differences between the rural and urban areas, rural targets were to have no more than three children after delaying marriage until age 25 for men and 23 for women. For urban dwellers only two children were encouraged after delaying marriage until age 28 for men and 25 for women.

In 1977 the government, after realizing that population growth would not fall as quickly as desired, began to promote the two-child family throughout the country. In 1979 a new slogan was adopted. It said, "One is best, at most two, never a third."

The One-Child Family

In 1980 China launched a crash program to stabilize population growth by limiting families to only one child. Then Communist Party Chairman, Hua Guofeng emphasized that coercion was not permissible but that the country would rely on publicity and persuasion. Hua spoke out at the same time against overpopulation and bureaucratic obstacles to modernization.

Though some variation exists from place to place, a few specific family-planning regulations were well established early in the 1980s. Students and apprentices were not allowed to marry. Incentives were offered to couples that have only one child, whereas disincentives were used to discourage larger families. Incentives were also provided for sterilization after the birth of the first child. A monthly allowance was paid to couples that had only one child, and the child's medical and educational fees were waived. However, if a second child was born, a couple gave up all privileges accorded the one-child family and had to repay all cash awards that were received. The third child is denied free education, subsidized food, and housing privileges. That child's parents were penalized by a 10 percent reduction in wages.

China's family planning program, sometimes called its Strategic Demographic Initiative (SDI), has a stated goal of keeping the total population "within 1.2 billion." This was established in the late 1970s when China had a total fertility rate of around 2.3. To meet the plan's objective, the one-child policy would require full implementation. In 1981 China's Family Planning Commission was given cabinet status; a variety of scholars, including statisticians, system analysts, economists, and others, were called on to develop and set population policies (Song, et al., 1985). The impact of China's SDI has been substantial. According to Tien (1988, 7), "At the time of the program's start China's birth rate was nearly 34 and its total fertility rate exceeded 6 (the current total fertility rate is about 2.4) . . . the successes of China's initiative have been, and continue to be, impressive."

This one-child family initiative was an unprecedented attempt to change the reproductive behavior of an entire nation. The success of this program in lowering the rate, according to Jacobson (1991, 282), can be attributed to a variety of aspects of Chinese society. "The population is nearly homogeneous with a 93 percent Han majority. The closed nature of the political system, the Confucian tradition and the strong sense of family it fostered, and a 3,000-year history of allegiance to authority made the one-child family program succeed where it might otherwise have failed." Another important variable, according to Greenhalgh (1990, 80), was that the transition to socialism in the 1950s made a fundamental change in the relations between the state and society, thus state-dominated institutions could influence even the most private of decisions.

The one-child family policy has been criticized in a variety of ways. First, the compulsory nature of the program, at least in some areas, has been criticized and may, as some believe, produce a backlash like that which took place in India. Second, with fewer children, the next generation of elderly will have fewer laborers to support it; and third, most of the immediate economic benefits will not be realized in rural areas.

TABLE 12–3 ■ China Population Size: Birth, Death, and Natural Increase Rates; and Total Fertility Rates, 1970–1988

Year	Year-End Population (10,000)	Crude Birth Rate	Crude Death Rate	Natural-Increase Rate	Total Fertility Rate		
					Country	Urban	Rural
1970	82,992	33.43	7.60	25.83	5.81	3.27	6.38
1971	85,229	30.65	7.32	23.33	5.44	2.88	6.01
1972	87,177	29.77	7.61	22.16	4.98	2.64	5.50
1973	89,211	27.93	7.04	20.89	4.54	2.39	5.01
1974	90,859	24.82	7.34	17.48	4.17	1.98	4.64
1975	92,420	23.01	7.32	15.69	3.57	1.78	3.95
1976	93,717	19.91	7.25	12.66	3.24	1.61	3.58
1977	94,974	18.93	6.87	12.06	2.84	1.57	3.12
1978	96,259	18.25	6.25	12.00	2.72	1.55	2.97
1979	97,542	17.82	6.21	11.61	2.75	1.37	3.05
1980	98,705	18.21	6.34	11.87	2.24	1.15	2.48
1981	100,072	20.91	6.36	14.55	2.63	1.39	2.91
1982	101,590	21.09	6.60	14.49	2.65†	1.73*	n.a.‡
1983	102,764	18.62	7.08	11.54	2.08†	1.61*	n.a.‡
1984	103,876	17.50	6.69	10.81	2.03†	1.46*	n.a.‡
1985	105,044	17.80	6.57	11.23	2.04†	1.23*	n.a.‡
1986	106,529	20.77	6.69	14.08	2.44†	1.43*	n.a.‡
1987	108,073	21.04	6.65	14.39	2.84†	1.38*	n.a.‡
1988	109,660	20.78	6.58	14.20	n.a.‡	n.a.‡	n.a.‡

SOURCE: From Susan Greenhalgh, "Socialism and Fertility in China," *Annals, American Academy of Political and Social Science* 510, July 1990. Reprinted by permission of Sage Publications, Inc.

Rural-Urban Differences

China's family planning policies were most successful in urban areas. Although the total fertility rate (Table 12–3) declined precipitously in both urban and rural areas between 1970 and 1988, urban fertility fell a decade earlier and reached a lower level, measuring 1.1 to 1.4 in the early 1980s, well below the level of 2.5 to 3.0 in the rural areas at the same time. In 1985 the "In-Depth Fertility Survey" showed that "Whereas the vast majority of both urban and rural couples wanted two children, 80 to 90 percent of urban couples pledged not to have a second child, while fewer than 20 percent of rural couples signed the one-child pledge (Feng, 1989)."

There are several reasons for this disparity. Rural reforms in the early 1980s, which dismantled the collective farms, also reestablished the family as the principal unit of rural life and freed many farmers from the enforcement of the one-child policy by rural political cadres. In 1984 physical coercion was prohibited and could no longer be used by rural birth-planning cadres. With decollectivization, labor benefits of children also increased. Most rural dwellers are not included in a state-funded pension system and therefore have to rely on their children, especially their sons, to take care of them in old age. This preference for sons among a large sector of the Chinese population is a major problem in the acceptance of one-child families in rural areas. Sons are perceived as more important because they can do heavy farm work and are providers of social security. Boys get preferential treatment in health care, food rations, and schooling. Some scholars have suggested that higher than normal sex ratios among reported live births in China is due to female infanticide or sex selective abortions. However, a recent study by Johansson and Nygren (1991, 50) concluded that "large numbers of adopted children are females and the statistical evidence cannot determine the extent of female infanticide."

Recent Birth Rate Changes

Recent figures have indicated that the crude birth rate has risen in the past few years. After declining in the early 1980s and reaching a low in 1984, China's crude birth rate has increased. According to the State Statistical Bureau (1988), China's crude birth rate increased by 20 percent between 1984 and 1987. Sixteen of the 30 provinces, municipalities, and autonomous regions experienced an increase exceeding 10 percent between 1981 and 1987, while 26 experienced an increase of over 10 percent between 1984 and 1987. A variety of explanations have been offered for this increase, including relaxation of the one-child policy in rural areas, the weakening of local administrator's authority relative to family-planning concerns and economic incentives to have more children (Feeney, et al., 1989 and Zeng, 1989).

The crude birth rate is a joint function of three variables, the population age distribution, marriage patterns, and age-specific marital fertility. In a recent study, Zeng, et al. (1991) decomposed the recent changes in China's crude birth rate into these three components to assess and compare their contributions to China's recent increase in its crude birth rate. This decomposition of the crude birth rate into its three components was done for the country as a whole and for each province. Zeng, et al. (1991, 441) concluded that "the effect of the much larger cohorts born in China's second baby boom of the 1960's reaching childbearing ages was to increase the crude birth rate by 1.59 births per thousand between 1981 and 1987. The effect of the declining age at marriage was to increase the crude birth rate by 2.59 births per thousand. Marital fertility in 1987 was significantly lower than in 1981 and its impact reduced the 1987 crude birth rate by 3.01 births per thousand."

The decrease in age at marriage and the changing age structure were the primary factors associated with the rise in the crude birth rate. China's population growth is not "out of control" as some have suggested nor does the recent increase in the crude birth rate imply a significant change in marital fertility.

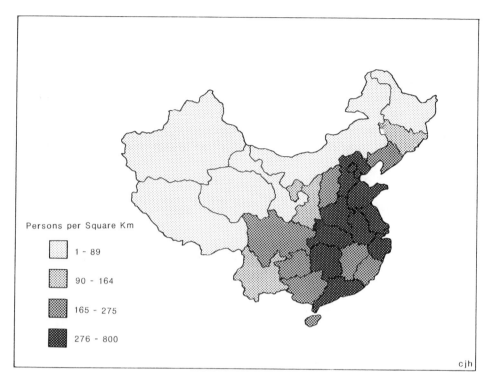

Persons per Square Km

■ 1 - 89

▨ 90 - 164

▨ 165 - 275

■ 276 - 800

cjh

▨ **FIGURE 12–4** China—Population Density, 1990. SOURCE: C. W. Pannell and J. S. Torguson, "Interpreting Spatial Patterns from the 1990 China Census," *The Geographical Review,* Vol. 81, No. 3, July 1991. Used by permission of the American Geographical Society.

The 1990 Census

On July 1, 1990, the Chinese government conducted a nationwide census. According to the State Statistical Bureau (1990), the total population for the People's Republic of China was 1,133,782,501 people. This figure did not include Hong Kong, Macao, or Taiwan. This was the fourth census the communist government has taken since coming to power in 1949, and most experts believe it was their most accurate census. Future plans are to conduct a census every ten years. This total population figure was larger than had been estimated, probably because of previous underreporting, particularly in rural areas where increasing numbers of couples with one female child were allowed to have a second child (Tien, 1990).

A number of interesting spatial patterns and variations were revealed by the census. Most of the Chinese people live in the eastern half of the country, where more intensive agriculture is practiced due to more favorable climatic conditions and better land resources (Figure 12–4). Although there has been migration to the interior and far west regions, they remain relatively sparsely populated. A doubling of the population since the 1950s has significantly increased the density in the eastern part of the country.

Ethnic diversity is also found in China, although the vast majority of people (92 percent) are of the Han nationality. There are 55 recognized minority nationalities that accounted for approximately 8.0 percent of the population in 1990. This figure is up from 6.7 percent in 1982. A more liberal government policy on family size for these minority groups is probably responsible for this increase. Most of these minority peoples are found in the sparsely populated interior regions that border foreign countries. Conflicts with the Han majority have taken place, with tensions the highest in Tibet due to the ruthless repression and occupation of that country by the Chinese in the 1950s.

As part of the 1990 census, Chinese officials developed a realistic definition and index of the urban population. The urban population in 1990 was 26.2 percent of the total population, an increase of almost 6 percent from the 20.6 percent level in 1982.

Dynamic changes have occurred in Chinese cities in the past decade. China has three of the world's largest cities; Shanghai, with a population of over 13 million; Beijing, with more than 10 million; and Tianjin, with approximately 9 million residents. Internal migration of redundant rural workers to neighboring urban centers has dramatically increased. This migrant population has increased the total urban population in several of China's largest cities by more than 10 percent (Goldstein and Goldstein, 1991). As a result of this migration, the cities of China are now beginning to have urban problems similar to that of other Third World countries.

The regional pattern of urbanization (Figure 12–5) indicates that the highest levels of urbanization are concentrated in the coastal and northeastern regions. According to Pannell and Torguson (1991, 315), "This pattern reflects the high degree of industrial activity and the comparatively well-established transportation networks in the regions in the aftermath of twentieth-century development."

▨ HEADING TOWARD ZERO POPULATION GROWTH: THE CASE OF SWEDEN

Sweden is one of the few nations in the world that has almost stabilized its population growth, and in the near future it may face zero population growth (ZPG). Its land area is approximately the same as California's, and its low density of 52 persons per square mile is similar to that of the United States with 72 persons per square mile. Of course, Sweden's population is not evenly distributed across the country. Rather, it is primarily concentrated in the southern half. Most of the population, 83 percent, live in "densely populated areas" of at least 200 persons. The population of 8.4 million (1987) is quite homogeneous in its ethnic and social character, with only a small number in ethnic minority populations (Gendell, 1980).

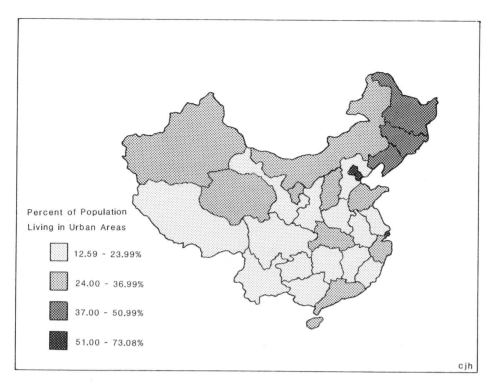

Percent of Population Living in Urban Areas

12.59 - 23.99%

24.00 - 36.99%

37.00 - 50.99%

51.00 - 73.08%

cjh

▒ **FIGURE 12–5** China—Levels of Urbanization, 1990. SOURCE: C. W. Pannell and J. S. Torguson, "Interpreting Spatial Patterns from the 1990 China Census," *The Geographical Review,* Vol. 81, No. 3, July 1991. Used by permission of the American Geographical Society.

Sweden is the envy of many countries because of its high standard of living; few slums and little poverty are in evidence. It provides a wide range of social, educational, and health services and has one of the lowest infant mortality rates in the world, surpassed only by that of Iceland and Finland. Sweden is one of a handful of countries, primarily located in Europe, where the number of births is almost equal to the number of deaths. It was a pioneer in the worldwide family-planning movement and the first developed country to provide family planning aid to the developing nations of the world.

Demographic Changes

Sweden and Finland were the first countries to collect national statistics on population, and they have been doing so continuously since 1749. In the middle of the eighteenth century Sweden's population was slightly under 1.8 million. For the next two hundred years it grew at an average rate of 7 per 1000 or 0.7 percent per year. In

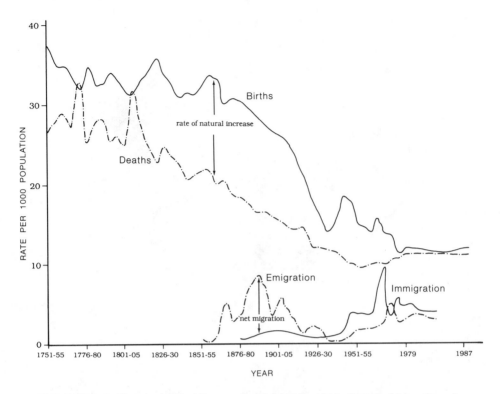

▩ **FIGURE 12–6** Changes in Vital Rates—Sweden, 1751–1992. Compiled by authors from various statistical sources including selected United Nations *Demographic Yearbooks* and *World Population Data Sheets* published by the Population Reference Bureau. Reprinted by permission.

1850 the population was 3.5 million, and it doubled again to 7.0 million by 1950. Since then the growth rate has varied; in 1987 the total estimated population was 8.4 million.

Trends in the birth, death, and migration rates are illustrated in Figure 12–6. Reliable figures are available for birth and death rates since the middle of the eighteenth century; information on migration rates, however, has only been available since the middle of the nineteenth century. During the second half of the eighteenth century, Sweden's crude birth rate was relatively high. It averaged 34 during that time, a rate similar to that found in many of today's developing countries. The death rate during this time was only 6 points lower.

The first half of the nineteenth century saw the start of Sweden's long-term demographic transition from high birth and death rates to low birth and death rates. The death rate declined steadily throughout the nineteenth century, with only periodic increases because of epidemics. The gap between births and deaths began to widen during this period and accelerated to its peak in the latter half of the nineteenth century. Like many other European countries, large numbers of people left Sweden for America, particularly during the 1880s and 1890s, thus relieving population pressures at home. The latter half of the nineteenth century also saw the start of Sweden's sustained decline in fertility (Hofsten and Lundstrom, 1976).

Since the start of the twentieth century, the principal features of Sweden's demographic character have been a continuing decline in both birth and death rates and a marked shift since World War II from a nation of emigration to a nation of immigration. During the first three decades of the twentieth century, Sweden's birth rate dropped to a low of about 14 in 1933 and 1934, during the economic depression. The birth rate climbed during the 1940s and again in the early 1960s. But since the 1965 level of almost 16, the birth rate has fallen almost uninterruptedly to an all-time low of 11.0 in 1992.

The death rate also has declined throughout the twentieth century to a low of around 10 in the 1950s and 1960s. There has been a slight increase in the death rate during the 1970s because there has been an increasing proportion of elderly in the population. Age-specific death rates, however, continued to decline during the 1970s, with concomitant increases in life expectancy (Table 12–4). Much of this gain in life expectancy was due to very low infant and child mortality rates. Sweden has a long history of concern for infants and children, and the American demographer Tomasson noted:

> . . . medical care, like education, has been regarded as both a communal responsibility and an individual right in Sweden [since] long before the advent of the modern welfare state. . . . Prenatal care, delivery, and postnatal care have been free and readily available throughout Sweden for many decades. Sustained professional care of pregnant women and later of their babies is universal (Tomasson, 1970, 970).

Sweden's low rate of natural increase, 0.59 per thousand, or less than 0.1 percent, puts it very close to zero population growth. The reason that Sweden's growth has not reached zero or turned negative is immigration. Immigration began to outweigh emigration during the 1930s; but substantial differences appeared after World War II, as Sweden's economy expanded and brought about a need for more workers. From 1943 through 1978, nearly 50 percent of Sweden's population growth resulted either directly or indirectly from net immigration (Gendell, 1980, 8).

The Swedish National Central Bureau of Statistics has developed several population projections using several alternative assumptions about fertility, mortality, and migration (NCBS, 1978). They concluded that Sweden's population will probably reach its maximum 8.36 million by 1986 and then decline to around 8 million by the turn of the century, with an accelerated decline in the first quarter of the next century, reaching somewhere between 7.0 million and 7.8 million by 2025. These numbers are obviously quite speculative, and demographic changes could easily make then invalid; however, most analysts agree that Sweden will probably be facing ZPG in the near future.

TABLE 12–4 ▥ Life Expectancy at Birth 1851–1992 Sweden

Year	Life Expectancy at Birth (Years)		Sex Differential
	Male	Female	(Female Minus Male)
Sweden			
1851–60	40.5	44.4	3.9
1901–10	54.5	57.0	2.5
1941–50	68.1	70.7	2.6
1951–60	70.9	74.1	3.2
1961–70	71.7	76.1	4.4
1971–75	72.1	77.7	5.6
1976	72.1	77.9	5.8
1977	72.4	78.5	6.1
1978	72.4	78.6	6.2
1984	73.8	79.9	6.1
1992	75.0	80.0	

SOURCE: Sweden: National Central Bureau of Statistics. (1980) *Population Changes 1978,* Part 3 (Stockholm), Table 4.17, p. 120; International: Population Division, United Nations, United States: National Center for Health Statistics, *Vital Statistics of the United States,* Vol. II, Section 5, *Life Tables* (Hyattsville, MD: 1980), and U.N. Demographic Yearbook 1985.

Coping with an Aging Population and ZPG

An analysis of a series of population pyramids (Figure 12–7) graphically shows the changes that have occurred in the Swedish population in the twentieth century. The pyramid for 1900 has the characteristic shape of a nation with a youthful population and a moderately high birth rate. The slightly smaller number of people in the 30 to 40 age group is a reflection of the mass emigration of young people from Sweden during the 1880s and 1890s. The late 1950 pyramid shows the many changes that occurred in the first half of the twentieth century. The indentation in the 10 to 24 age groups is an indication of the drop in the birth rate during the depression years, while the bulge at the base reflects the rising birth rates in the post-World War II period. The relatively long period of low fertility can be seen in the rectangular shape of the 1977 pyramid.

The pyramids for the years 2000 and 2025 are based on population projections that assume a total fertility rate of 1.85 by 1985, which would remain constant thereafter with no net immigration. These projections could change slightly, but it is almost certain that there will be a continued equalization of age cohorts and an increase in the average age of the population.

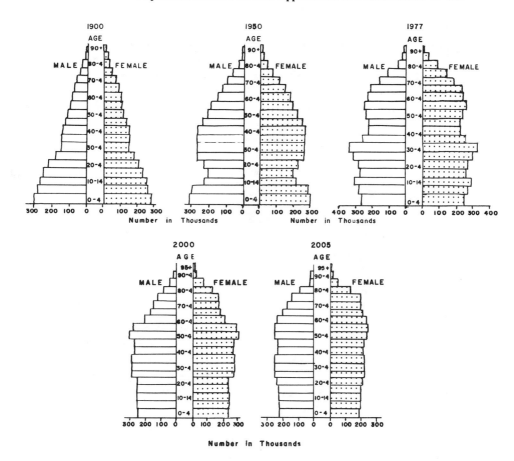

▨ **FIGURE 12–7** Sweden's Population Age Structure: 1900, 1950, 1977, and as Projected for 2000 and 2025.

The rising average age in Sweden means that there will be an increasing proportion of the population that will be elderly. The proportion of people 65 and over nearly doubled between 1900 and 1981, from 8.4 percent to 16.0 percent, compared with 11.0 percent for the United States. At the same time the proportion of children under 15 declined by 12.0 percent.

These large numbers of elderly people are causing what the Swedish demographer Holmberg calls a "crisis" in finding enough medical staff and facilities to provide the long-term care needed by the very old (Holmberg, 1977). The share of Sweden's national budget that is devoted to the elderly is escalating rapidly and has much to do with its growing budget deficit (Downie, 1980). As Sweden approaches ZPG, discussions of population issues and their impact on Swedish society are becoming more numerous. Some people contend that population decline must be stopped, because the decline and associated aging of the population bring about economic stagnation and increasing inequalities in income distribution.

This argument is countered by those who believe that Sweden's economic difficulties, as well as the crisis in that society's ability to take care of the old and sick, has nothing to do with fertility decline. They feel these problems can be solved by organizational changes, because "a sharp increase in the birth rate would lead to difficulties for the educational system and for new entries to the labor market when the large number of children born grow up" (Holmberg, 1980, 4).

Sweden faces several problems as a result of demographic changes; fortunately, the importance of these problems has been recognized by much of the population and by many decision makers. How Sweden responds to the challenges ahead will make it a test case worth watching.

▨ CONCLUSION

Today's world is beset by many problems, primarily social, economic, and political. A small proportion of people have vast amounts of wealth, while large numbers of people barely eke out an existence. Modern transportation and communications have brought about a time-space convergence that brings together people of many social and cultural traditions. In order to attempt to solve the world's problems, a knowledge of population dynamics and population geography is essential. In this book we have tried to present the basic concepts of population geography in the hope that a greater understanding of population issues will help to alleviate some of the world's pressing problems.

REFERENCES

Bach, Robert L. (1980) "The New Cuban Immigrants: Their Background and Prospects," *Monthly Labor Review* 103(10):39–46.

Bianchi, Suzanne. (1990) "America's Children: Mixed Prospects," *Population Bulletin* 45(1): 1–43.

Bouvier, Leon F. (1980) "America's Baby Boom Generation: The Fateful Bulge," *Population Bulletin* 35(1):1–36.

Bouvier, Leon F. and DeVita, Carol J. (1991) "The Baby Boom-Entering Midlife," *Population Bulletin* 46(3):1–33.

Collver, O. Andrew. (1965) *Birth Rates in Latin America: New Estimates of Historical Trends and Fluctuations.* Berkeley, California: Institute of International Studies, University of California.

Danielson, Ross. (1979) *Cuban Medicine.* New Brunswick, N.J.: Transaction.

Diaz-Briquets, Sergio. (1977) "Mortality in Cuba: Trends and Determinants, 1880–1971," Unpublished Ph.D. dissertation. Philadelphia: University of Pennsylvania.

Diaz-Briquets, Sergio and Perez, Lisandro. (1981) "Cuba: The Demography of Revolution," *Population Bulletin* 36(1):1–43.

Downie, Leonard, Jr. (1980) "Scandinavian Inflation Imperils Welfare States," *The Washington Post* May 10, 1980.

England, Robert (1987) "The Senior Citizen Secret," *Insight* (March 2):8–11.

Farnos Morejn, Alfonso. (1980) "Results of Population Projections," *Revista Cubana de Administracion de Salud* 6:134.

Feeney, G. F., Wang, F., Zhou, M. K., and Xiao, B. Y. (1989) "Recent Fertility Dynamics in China: Results from the 1987 One Percent Survey," *Population and Development Review* 15:297–322.

Feng, Wang. (1989) "China's One-Child Policy: Who Complies and Why?" (Paper delivered at the Annual Meeting of the Association for Asian Studies, Washington, DC, March 17–19.)

Francese, Paula A. and Renaghan, Leo M. (1991) "Finding the Customer," *American Demographics* 13(1):48–51.

Gendell, Murray. (1980) "Sweden Faces Zero Population Growth," *Population Bulletin* 35(2): 1–44.

Goldstein, S. and Goldstein, A. (1991) *Permanent and Temporary Migration Differentials in China.* Papers, East-West Population Institute 117, Honolulu: East-West Center.

Gonzalez, Gerardo, Correa, German, Errazuriz, Margarita M., and Tapia, Raul. (1978) *Development Strategy and Demographic Transition: The Case of Cuba.* Santiago, Chile: Centro Latinoamericano de Demografia.

Greenhalgh, Susan. (1990) "Socialism and Fertility in China," *Annals of the American Academy of Political and Social Science* 510:73–86.

Harrison, Paul. (1980) "Lessons for the Third World," *People* 7:2–20.

Hofsten, Erland and Lundstrom, Hans. (1976) *Swedish Population History: Main Trends from 1750 to 1970.* Stockholm, Sweden: National Central Bureau of Statistics.

Hollerbach, Paula E. (1980) "Recent Trends in Fertility, Abortion, and Contraception in Cuba," *International Family Planning Perspectives* 6:97–106.

Holmberg, Ingvar. (1977) "The Population Debate in Sweden in Recent Years," *Current Sweden* 169, Stockholm: The Swedish Institute.

Hooyman, Nancy R. and Kiyak, H. Asuman. (1988) *Social Gerontology: A Multidisciplinary Perspective.* Boston: Allyn and Bacon, Inc.

Hyatt, James. (1979) *Changing Demographics and How They Affect the Future of Business.* FOB Series No. 9, Washington, D.C.: Center for Strategic and International Studies.

Jacobson, Jodi L. (1991) "China's Baby Budget," in Lester R. Brown, ed. *The World Watch Reader on Global Environmental Issues*. New York: W. W. Norton and Company.

Johansson, Sten and Nygren, Ola. (1991) "The Missing Girls of China: A New Demographic Account," *Population and Development Review* 17:35–53.

Laws, Glenda. (1991) "Aging Population: A Planning Dilemma," *Earth and Mineral Sciences* 60(2):32–36.

Lazer, William. (1985) "Inside the Mature Market," *American Demographics* 7(3):3–25.

National Central Bureau of Statistics. (1978) *Population Projection for Sweden, 1978–2025*. Stockholm, Sweden: Information Prognosfragor.

Pannell, Clifton W. and Torguson, Jeffrey S. (1991) "Interpreting Spatial Patterns from the 1990 China Census," *The Geographical Review* 81(3):304–317.

Perez, Lisandro. (1977) "The Demographic Dimensions of the Educational Problem in Socialist Cuba," *Cuban Studies* 7:33–57.

Population Reference Bureau. (1981) *1981 World Population Data Sheet*. Washington, D.C.: Population Reference Bureau.

Reinhardt, Hazel H. (1979) "The Ups and Downs of Education," *American Demographics* 1(6): 9–11.

Salas, Luis. (1979) *Social Control and Deviance in Cuba*. New York: Praeger.

Soldo, Beth J. and Agree, Emily M. (1988) "America's Elderly," *Population Bulletin* 43(3): 1–53.

Song, Jian, et al. (1985) *Population Control in China*. New York: Praeger Publishing Co.

State Statistical Bureau. (1988) *Tabulations of China One Percent Population Survey*. National Volume. Beijing: China Statistical Press.

State Statistical Bureau. (1990) "Geographical Distribution, Density and Natural Growth Rate of China's Population," *Beijing Review* 33(51):25–27.

Tien, H. Yuan. (1983) "China: Demographic Billionaire," *Population Bulletin* 38(2):1–43.

Tien, H. Yuan. (1988) "A Talk with China's Wang Wei," *Population Today* 16(1):6–8.

Tien, H. Yuan. (1990) "China's Population Planning After Tiananmen," *Population Today* 18(9):6–8.

Tomasson, Richard T. (1970) *Sweden: Prototype of Modern Society*. New York: Random House.

Waldrop, Judith. (1991) "The Baby Boom Turns 45," *American Demographics* 13(1):22–27.

Zeng, Y. (1989) "Population Policy in China: New Challenge and Strategies," in J. M. Eekelaar and D. Pearl, eds. *An Aging World*. Oxford: Oxford University Press, pp. 61–73.

Zeng, Yi, et al. (1991) "A Demographic Decomposition of the Recent Increase in Crude Birth Rates in China," *Population and Development Review* 17(3):435–459.

Glossary

Abortion rate—The estimated number of abortions in a given year per 1000 women aged 15–44.

Age-sex structure—The composition of a population as determined by the number or portion of males and females in each age category. This information is an essential prerequisite for the description and analysis of many other types of demographic data. See also *population pyramid.*

Age-specific rate—Rate of population change obtained for a specific age group (for example, age-specific fertility rate, death rate, marriage rate, illiteracy rate, etc.)

Age structure—The percentage of people in various age groups in a population. It is best described by a population pyramid.

Antinatalist policy—The policy of a society, social group, or government to slow population growth by attempting to limit the number of births.

Baby boom—The period following World War II from 1946–1964 characterized by a rapid increase in fertility rates and in the absolute number of births in the United States, Canada, Australia, and New Zealand.

Baby bust—The period immediately after the "baby boom," characterized by a rapid decline in U.S. fertility rates to record low levels.

Basic demographic equation—An equation that ties together population change through the major demographic variables: deaths, births, and migration. The equation views the population of a place at some future date as a function of its present population plus births over the time interval, minus deaths over the time interval, plus in-migrants and minus out-migrants over the time interval.

Birth control—Practices adopted by couples that permit sexual intercourse with reduced likelihood of conception. The term is frequently used synonymously with such terms as contraception, family planning, and fertility control.

Brain drain—The emigration of a significant proportion of a country's highly educated, highly skilled professional population, usually to other countries offering better social and economic opportunities.

Carrying capacity—The number of people who can be sustained by a particular land area at a given technological level.

Child-woman ratio—The number of children under 5 years old per 1000 women aged 15–49 years in a population.

Cohort—A group of people sharing a common temporal demographic experience who are observed through time. For example, the birth cohort of 1950 would be the people born in that year. There are also marriage cohorts, school class cohorts, etc.

Communist-socialist theory—The idea, originally expounded by Karl Marx, that economic problems are not associated with population growth but are the result of the maldistribution of resources.

Completed fertility rate—The number of children born per woman to a cohort of women by the end of their childbearing years.

Crude birth rate—The annual number of births per 1000 people in a given population.

Crude death rate—The annual number of deaths per 1000 people in a given population.

Crude divorce rate—The number of divorces per 1000 population in a given year.

Demographic transition—The transition from a demographic regime characterized by high birth and death rates to one characterized by low birth and death rates.

Demography—The scientific study of the human population, focusing on population composition, change, and distribution.

Dependency ratio—The ratio of persons in the dependent ages (under 20 and over 64 years) to those in the economically productive years (20 to 64 years) in a population.

Developed countries—Countries that have industrialized and have relatively high levels of per capita income and per capita productivity.

Developing countries—Countries that have not industrialized and have relatively low rates of per capita income and per capita productivity.

Doubling time—The number of years required for a population of an area to double its present size, given the current rate of population growth. It is possible to closely approximate the doubling time for a population by dividing the annual rate of population growth into the number 70.

Emigration—The process of leaving one country to take up residence in another.

Emigration rate—The number of emigrants departing an area of origin per 1000 inhabitants at that area of origin in a given year.

Environmental population theory—Attempts to explain demographic behavior by a theory centered on cultural processes.

Epidemiologic transition—The transition a society goes through in which death rates decline and the major causes of death shift from communicative diseases to degenerative diseases.

Family planning—Policies and programs designed to help families achieve their desired family size.

Fecundity—The physiological capacity of a woman, man, or couple to produce a live child.

Fertility—The actual reproductive performance of an individual, a couple, a group, or a population.

Fertility trend—Any observed or predicted course of fertility over a specified period of time.

Forced migration—A movement of individuals or groups of people in which they participated without choice. The slave trade is a major example.

General fertility rate—The annual number of live births per 1000 women in the child-bearing age group (ages 15–44).

Green revolution—A rapid increase in agricultural output resulting from the application of new agricultural practices and the use of "miracle strains" of wheat and rice.

Gross migration—The total sum of all the people who enter and leave an area.

Gross reproduction rate—The average number of daughters a woman (or a group of women) would bear if she passed through her entire reproductive life at the prevailing age-specific fertility rates.

Growth rate—The rate at which a population is increasing (or decreasing) in a given year due to natural increase and net migration, expressed as a percentage of the base population.

Growth syndrome—It involves three primary characteristics: continuing growth of the human population in both developed and developing countries, rapid increase in the production and consumption of commodities, and misapplication of old and new technologies, leading to an increasing abuse and pillage of the human habitat.

Immigration—The movement of people into one country from another.

Infant mortality rate—The number of deaths among infants under one year of age in a given year per 1000 live births in that year.

Laissez-faire solution—A solution to population issues based on individual choice. Laissez-faire population exponents feel that those best able to decide on the costs and benefits of children are those who are contemplating having them.

Lee's migration model—A model developed to explain migration as the result of four sets of factors: (1) factors associated with place of origin, (2) factors associated with place of destination, (3) intervening obstacles, and (4) personal factors.

Life expectancy—The average number of additional years a person would live if current mortality trends were to continue.

Life table—A table that gives life expectancy and the probability of dying at each age for a given population, according to the age-specific death rates prevailing at that time.

Median age—The age that divides a population into two numerically equal groups with half the people younger and half older than this age.

Migration—The movement of people from place to place, usually across some political boundary, for the purpose of changing their permanent place of residence.

Migration differentials—Characteristics that make migrants different from the general population. Migrants are usually not random samples of the population from which they came but are "selected" by certain characteristics such as age or educational level.

Migration interval—The time interval over which migration is studied or observed.

Migration stream—An established movement of people between two places. For example, there is a migration stream between New York and Miami.

Morbidity—The frequency of disease and illness in a population.

Mortality—Deaths as a component of population change.

Multiple-round survey—A longitudinal sample survey whereby information about a specific group or problem is collected on a continuing basis.

Natality—Births as a component of population change.

Natural increase—The balance between births and deaths in a population in a given time period.

Neo-Malthusian—A current revival of interest in the ideas of Malthus. Neo-Malthusians believe that population growth will outrun the food supply and that the world cannot continue to support a growing population.

Neonatal mortality rate—The number of deaths to infants under 28 days of age in a given year per 1000 live births in that year.

Net migration—The difference between immigration and emigration for an area's population in a given time period, generally expressed as an increase or decrease.

Net reproduction rate—The average number of daughters that would be born alive to a woman (or group of women) during her lifetime if she passed through her childbearing years at the prevailing age-specific fertility and mortality rates.

Physiological density—The ratio of population to arable land.

Population—A group of objects or organisms of the same kind.

Population density—Generally refers to the number of people per unit of land.

Population distribution—The patterns of settlement and dispersal of a population.

Population equilibrium—The level at which the population is in balance with the natural resource base of an area. Because of the changing nature of technology and the resource base, it is difficult to translate population equilibrium into a precise number.

Population policy—An official government policy specifically designed to affect the size and growth rate of a population, the distribution of a population, or its composition. See *population program*.

Population program—The various means and measures that must be used to achieve the objectives of a population policy. See *population policy.*

Population projection—An estimate of the population of an area for some future date, usually based on a set of assumptions about the future course of births, deaths, and migration.

Population pyramid—A type of graph showing the age and sex structure of a population. It may be constructed for nations, states, cities, or even smaller areas.

Primary population theory—A theory that explains demographic behavior patterns by focusing on specific factors directly related to fertility, migration, or mortality.

Primate city—A city that dominates the state in size and importance. It is commonly at least twice as large as the next largest city and serves as the educational, political, industrial, and commercial center.

Primitive migration—The type of migration associated with groups that migrate because they are unable to cope with natural forces related to their physical environment.

Sample survey—A canvass of selected persons or households in a population usually used to infer demographic characteristics or trends for a larger segment or all of the population.

Secondary population theory—A theory that explains demographic behavior patterns by analyzing a broad class of social and physical phenomena that have demographic implications.

Sex ratio—The number of males per 100 females in a population.

Total fertility rate—The average number of children that would be born alive to a woman (or group of women) during her lifetime if she were to pass through her childbearing years conforming to the age-specific fertility rates for each year.

Triage—The idea that the world's nations can be put into three categories relative to their food resources: (1) those nations that can not be saved regardless of food aid from other countries, (2) those nations that will survive without food aid from other countries, and (3) those nations that could feed their people with some aid from the developed countries.

Urbanism—The characteristics or conditions of the way of life of those who live in cities.

Urbanization—The percentage of a population that lives in urban areas and the process by which this number increases over time.

Vital registrations—The recording and compilation of vital statistics at or near their time of occurrence. They usually include such events as deaths, fetal deaths, births, marriages, divorces, and at times disease and illness.

Vital statistics—Demographic data on births, deaths, fetal deaths, marriages, and divorces.

Zero population growth (ZPG)—An equilibrium population with a growth rate of zero, achieved when births plus immigration equal deaths plus emigration.

Index